Praise for *Great Lake*

"Part travelogue and part fact-filled guidebook, Maureen Dunphy's *Great Lakes Island Escapes: Ferries and Bridges to Adventure* presents the reader with an insightful and engaging account of the history, natural wonders, recreational opportunities, and local flavor of more than two dozen Great Lakes Basin islands."
—Phil Porter, Director of Mackinac State Historic Parks

"As a kid growing up on Grosse Ile, I was considered an 'Islander.' In *Great Lakes Island Escapes*, Maureen Dunphy skillfully weaves the information you need in order to visit with tales of why adventures in the middle of the Great Lakes are always superior to those on the mainland."
—Jim DuFresne, author of *Isle Royale National Park: Foot Trails and Water Routes*

"In this informative and entertainingly written book, Maureen Dunphy portrays these very special places from all across the Great Lakes. In doing so, she is able to beautifully capture the essence of the phrase 'Island Time.' This book will be a fine addition to the travel literature of our Inland Seas."
—Arthur M. Woodford, author of *This Is Detroit: 1701–2001*
(Wayne State University Press, 2001) and *Michigan Companion*

"*Great Lakes Island Escapes* is a combination of the author's personal experiences and loving reminiscences woven in with history, photographs, cultural attractions, local color, and her recommendations for each island's most compelling sites and captivating activities. Whether you're a Great Lakes island aficionado or a curious adventurer, Maureen Dunphy's unique guidebook is an essential, intimate, traveling companion."
—Michael Steinberg, founding editor of *Fourth Genre: Explorations in Nonfiction*
and author of *Still Pitching*, winner of the 2003 *ForeWord Magazine*
Gold Medal for Memoir/Autobiography

"In *Great Lakes Island Escapes*, Maureen Dunphy presents the islands as a network of understanding. Called *minisan* in Anishinaabemowin (Ojibwe), these little bits of earth are the ears and eyes and bellybuttons of Gichigaming, the single system of five connected Great Lakes. These are the places where senses are heightened, where the connection between land, water, and life is more apparent. In each stopping place, Dunphy shares the necessary details for navigation and recounts the way spirits are lifted, moose are greeted, lives are remembered, and fires are kindled. She helps readers see the balance between silent ancient gardens and the hum of ferry motors, lighthouses and shipwrecks, the natural and the hand-hewn. Mostly she helps readers hear the call of the lakes and the little islands strung like stars around them. It would be hard to read this book without heading for one of the islands in real life or your next dream."
—Margaret Noodin, assistant professor in English and American Indian studies
at the University of Wisconsin–Milwaukee and author of *Weweni: Poems in Anishinaabemowin and English* (Wayne State University Press, 2015)

GREAT LAKES ISLAND ESCAPES

Great Lakes
Island Escapes

FERRIES AND BRIDGES TO ADVENTURE

MAUREEN DUNPHY

To Bernadine
With much Gratitude
for this Adventure!
Maureen Dunphy
2017

A Painted Turtle book

DETROIT, MICHIGAN

20 19 18 17 16   5 4 3 2 1

ISBN 978-0-8143-4040-0 (paperback) / ISBN 978-0-8143-4041-7 (e-book)
Library of Congress Control Number: 2015958997

Designed and typeset by Andrew Katz
Composed in Garamond Premier Pro

Painted Turtle is an imprint of Wayne State University Press

Wayne State University Press
Leonard N. Simons Building
4809 Woodward Avenue
Detroit, Michigan 48201-1309

Visit us online at wsupress.wayne.edu

In memory of my maternal grandparents,
Madaline and Howard Klotzbach,
who taught me the value of travel as adventure,
the joys of taking pictures,
and the pleasure of keeping a travel journal

Contents

Preface

The book you are holding in your hands was conceived during an impromptu happy hour on one of the best known of the Great Lakes Basin islands, Mackinac. After a day exploring the island on rented bikes, my husband and I were relaxing on the porch of the Harbour View Inn B&B, enjoying goat cheese on crackers with a good sauvignon blanc we'd purchased up the street at Doud's Market, the oldest family-owned grocery store in the United States. Having shown up for other reasons than for Michigan's Republican Convention on the island, which was well under way, we were indulging in some serious people watching as visitors to the island streamed by on Main Street. I was trying, unsuccessfully, to imagine such a scene taking place on "our island," Canada's Pelee Island, a rural island where we'd owned a cottage for 15 years. How could two islands in the same freshwater system be so completely different?

We poured another glass of wine and reminisced about the other islands in the Great Lakes Basin we'd visited over the years: Belle Isle, Bob-Lo Island, and Grosse Ile in the Detroit River; Beaver Island in Lake Michigan; Manitoulin Island and Flowerpot Island in Lake Huron; South Bass Island and Kelleys Island, in addition to Pelee Island, in Lake Erie. That night, looking out our third-floor window beyond the lights at the pier on Haldimand Bay to the Straits of Mackinac, I was remembering what very wonderful—and very *different*—adventures we'd had on the 10 Great Lakes islands we'd visited. Could there be more islands to explore, ones that we'd missed? Surely there must be a book that would give me more Great Lakes island-hopping ideas. I looked when we got back to the mainland, but I could find no such book.[1]

So instead I found myself ordering a 1953 National Geographic map of the Great Lakes region and spreading it out on my dining room table. I started fantasizing about freshwater island-hopping. But when I looked more closely I discovered, much to my astonishment, that the Great Lakes Basin actually has approximately 35,000 islands. Apparently, I was going to need some criteria to frame my adventure destinations. First, the island had to be in the Great Lakes Basin—in a lake or in a river (or strait) connecting two of the lakes. Then, given that I wasn't keen on traveling either by small boat or plane, the island had to be accessible by ferry or bridge (or causeway). In my mind, I began stringing islands in the Great Lakes and their rivers together like rosary beads on a cord of water. Somewhere along the way, my fantasy became a plan, and ultimately, I discovered 136 (124 individually named) islands in the Great Lakes Basin that met my qualifications.

When I decided to revisit Grosse Ile, to see what I might find when I looked at a particular island destination as one of the many Great Lakes Basin islands, I asked my good friend Val, who had grown up on the island, if she'd like to accompany me. We had such a good time on the Saturday we'd chosen for our adventure that we went back again the next Saturday.

It was on these two trips that I realized the value of having a traveling companion, another pair of eyes, another personality through which to filter the island experience, to say nothing of the enjoyment of sharing an adventure with a friend (and later sharing the memories.) I invited 23 women friends to be future traveling companions, and 19 brave souls accepted the challenge. A handful of family members agreed to accompany me on a trip as well.

Between May 25, 2013, and August 21, 2014, I made 27 trips, each with a friend or family member, to 136 Great Lakes Basin islands. Although I know from my own experience on Pelee Island that spring and fall can be the best times to visit a Great Lakes island (and I've talked to residents on a number of islands who love—at least during the first bit of the season—the isolation that winter brings), most of my trips were taken between Memorial Day weekend and Labor Day weekend so as to experience what most island adventurers would find during summer day trips or vacations to the islands.

Great Lakes Island Escapes: Ferries and Bridges to Adventure is broken into 11 sections, one for each body of water in the Great Lakes Basin (the five Great Lakes, five connecting rivers, and the Straits). Although a number of other islands are briefly mentioned in sidebars along the way, each of the 38 "island" chapters of the book primarily highlights one island, except in the cases of two of the rivers (the St. Marys and the Niagara) or of featured archipelagos (the Les Cheneaux Islands, Walpole Island, the Toronto Islands, the Long Sault Parkway islands), where I've discussed the nature of more than one island within each chapter.

In this book, I have provided the information I learned in planning and experiencing my island trips. For each chapter, I've featured how to get to the island, what to expect when you arrive, and a number of paths to adventure: natural sites to explore, history that has been preserved, and cultural attractions. I've listed special events, where to get more information, and how you can support the island. You'll read selections of entries from my island journal, see scenes from each island in a few of the hundreds of photos I snapped on each, and have access to some of the maps I used.

This book may be for you if you like islands or adventure in general. Or if you're interested in the natural sciences—particularly birds, fossils, unusual habitats, or endangered species— American and/or Canadian history, or how community works. Islands are particularly special places for family day trips or vacations; serve as great venues for celebrating weddings, honeymoons, or anniversaries; and are perfect places for solo, couple, or group retreats. Because I had already experienced the transformative experience of being on an island as a result of our cottage experience on one, I was not surprised when the trips that went into making this book transformed me (and my friendships), island by island. I wish for you similarly enjoyable—but different, uniquely your own—island adventures.

Island adventures come in all different flavors but to my mind tend to be more concentrated, more piquant, both sweeter and more savory than mainland forays. All that water surrounding an island. All that distance from the mainland. When my maternal grandparents made their road trips to each of the contiguous 48 U.S. states and the 10 Canadian provinces in the 1960s, they brought back photographs and stories of each state or province that made the places appear very distinct from one another. That's not been my mainland experience in more recent years. But an island? Islands, at least Great Lakes Basin islands, tend to retain their individuality despite the homogenizing effects of modern life—they tend to be very different from one another and certainly often tell a very distinct tale from that of the mainland. Perhaps you've thought of islands merely as settings, but they are quite often the characters in their own stories, complete with the imprints of interesting historical plots and marked for better and for worse by conflicts of ownership and development to this very day.

I hope you'll use this book as an impetus to undertake your own island adventures. The islands are an easy way to get an intense "Great Lakes fix"—"fix" as in a dose of mind alteration but also "fix" as in a solution. You may not understand, or even know, what's going on in your life. Spend a day—and if you're fortunate, a night or more—on a Great Lakes island, and you will come back to the mainland with a different perspective, I promise. I've come to believe there is an island magic capable of inspiring a needed cure in our lives. Let the islands work their magic on you.

> Oh! You won't know why and you can't say how
> Such a change upon you came,
> But once you have slept on an island,
> You'll never be quite the same.[2]

Enjoy this armchair travel to the Great Lakes Basin islands. And then fantasize about, plan a trip to, and visit an island—or two or 100—and ultimately revel in your own island adventures. *Bon voyage!*

Acknowledgments

I am grateful to my family, particularly my maternal grandparents, Madaline and Howard Klotzbach, who took me on my first overnight Great Lakes island trip—to Mackinac Island—in the 1960s; my dad, William Arthur Dunphy, himself a writer, who first taught me the love of words and the pleasure of books; and my mom, the artist Caroline Dunphy, who gave me the gift of vision, as well as this book's maps of the 11 major bodies of water that make up the Great Lakes Basin, highlighting the accessible islands I visited.

I am grateful to each of my 28 island traveling companions, for helping me see the islands we visited together through another pair of eyes and for contributing her—in three cases, his—time, heart and mind, and friendship to our island adventures (also sprinkled throughout are a handful of other people who contributed to this book in a variety of important ways):

Ron Tiessen (founder and first director of the Pelee Island Heritage Centre and tour guide extraordinaire): Kelleys Island and South Bass Island, September 2008 (a group visit on the occasion of a Pelee Island Heritage Weekend), the trip that may have first gotten me thinking about the different natures of Great Lakes islands.

Valerie Overholt: Grosse Ile, April 20 and 26, 2012, Beausoleil Island, and, also in the Honey Harbour area, Picnic Island, Brandy's Island, and Potato Island, May 31–June 3, 2013, who helped me realize the value of sharing an island trip with a friend.

Susan Eggly: Catawba Island and Johnson's Island, May 25–26, 2013.

Bronwen Gates: Presqu'ile, Ontario, Prince Edward County, Big Island, Baker Island, Amherst Island, Howe Island, Hill Island, and Wellesley Island, June 9–14, 2013.

Karen Klein: Door Peninsula, Washington Island, and Rock Island, June 20–24, 2013.

Kim Haas: Kelleys Island, June 28–30, 2013.

Jan Prater: Beaver Island, July 14–18, 2011, and July 3–7, 2013.

Barbara Osher: Bois Blanc Island, July 8–11, 2013.

Judy Coomes Wachler: the Toronto Islands of Centre Island (including the Ward's Island community and Hanlan's Point), Middle Island, Olympic Island, the "Duck Pond" Island, Algonquin Island, North and South Chippewa Islands, Snake Island, RCYC Island, and South Island, July 13–14, 2013.

Michelene Eberhard: downtown Sault Ste. Marie, Michigan (aka "The Island"), North St. Marys Island, South St. Marys Island, Whitefish Island, and Sugar Island, July 19–21, 2013.

Nanci Baldridge: Grand Island, Beaver Island, Buckhorn Island, Unity Island (known at the time of our visit as Squaw Island), Tonawanda Island, Green Island, Goat Island, the Three Sister Islands (Asenath Island, Angeline Island, and Celinda Eliza Island), Luna Island, Cuyaga Island, and the Dufferin Islands, August 15–18, 2013.

Vicki Brennan: Grand Island, Madeline Island, and Isle Royale, August 21–28, 2013.

Barbara Lelli: Hamilton Island, the 13 Long Sault Islands (McLaren Island; Woodlands Island, which is actually two islands; Fraser Island; Hoople Island; Dickinson Island; Heriot Island; VanKoughnet Island; Phillpotts Island; Macdonell Island; Mille Roches Island; Snetsinger Island; Moulinette Island), Morrison Island, Nairne Island, Ault Island, Cornwall Island, Barnhart Island, and Wilson Hill Island, September 13–16, 2013.

Jeanne Seymour: Flowerpot Island, Manitoulin Island, Barrie Island, Twilight Isle, Burnt Island, Goat Island, Great LaCloche Island, September 25–30, 2013. (Jeanne, who is also my walking partner, accompanied me with her husband, Rick Seymour, and my husband on my first trip to Russell Island in 2011.)

Tom and Mary Lou Raume, mainland neighborhood walkers and also our cottage hosts on Russell Island, who invited Jeanne and me, with our husbands, to the 2011 Russell Island Annual Picnic and who welcomed Craig and me back in 2014.

Lynn Tiessen: Mackinac Island, October 3–6, 2013, and my Pelee Island walking partner.

Caroline Dunphy, my mom: Belle Isle, October 9, 2013, and the creator of the Great Lakes Basin body-of-water maps in this book. She received her training in watercolor at Wayne State University, 1946–48.

Pamela Mitzelfeld: Pelee Island, October 18–20, 2013.

Noreen Daly-Seiler, my sister-in-law: Walpole Island, May 21, 2014.

Joyce Johnson, director, Walpole Island Heritage Centre: May 21, 2014–October 5, 2015, who entertained my questions.

Margaret Noodin, poet, teacher of Anishinaabemowin, assistant professor in English and American studies at the University of Wisconsin–Milwaukee, and author of *Weweni: Poems in Anishinaabemowin and English* (Detroit: Wayne State University Press, 2015): September–November 2015, to whom I say *Miigwech* for helping me understand what Ojibwe terms to use; any mistakes I have made in this respect, however, are mine alone.

Carol Boyd: Harsens Island, June 3–4, 2014.

Lucinda Garthwaite: Wolfe Island, Simcoe Island, and Heart Island, June 19–22, 2014.

Kathy Wildfong, my patient, kind, and generous editor, who in the course of producing this book project has become an even better friend and with whom I often share a lane of the YMCA pool: South Manitou Island and North Manitou Island, July 11–15, 2014.

Nancy Lockhart: the Les Cheneaux Islands of Hill Island and Island No. 8, Drummond Island, Neebish Island, Little Neebish Island (aka Rains Island), Pine Island, Brown's Island, Bamford Island, St. Joseph Island, Campment d'Ours Island, Munroe Islands, Twyning Islands, July 21–26, 2014.

Carol Breitmeyer: South Bass Island, Middle Bass Island, and Gibraltar Island, July 28–31, 2014.

Caitlin Skye Barr, my younger daughter: Wooded Island in Chicago's Jackson Lagoon, August 2, 2014.

Meagan Mná Dunphy-Daly, my elder daughter: Presque Isle, Pennsylvania, August 15–17, 2014.

David R. Maracle, musician, whose *Spirit World: Universal Meditations* (2012) CD served as the soundtrack for the writing of this book.

All of the talented folks at Wayne State University Press and especially, for their unique skills, professionalism, and support: Bryce Schimanski, Carrie Downes Teefey, Emily Nowak, Bonnie Russell, Kristina Stonehill, Jamie Jones, Andrew Katz, and Jane Henderson.

Robin DuBlanc, copyeditor *magnifique;* the book you now hold would not have been *this* book without her journey to *all* of the islands with me: *Great Lakes Island Escapes,* the book, July–November 2015.

Craig Daly, my husband and best friend: Mackinac Island, September 26, 2009, when this book was first conceived; Russell Island, July 31, 2011, and July 27, 2014; Bob-Lo Island (the last island I visited for this project), August 21, 2014; and Birch Island in August 1987, where, on Dreamer's Rock, with our daughters (the younger in utero), a vision of this book was given to me, although I didn't understand it then. I'm grateful that vision became this book with Craig's love and support.

TEN REASONS YOU SHOULD VISIT A GREAT LAKES BASIN ISLAND

Reasons to visit a Great Lakes Basin island abound! While some islands are known for the partying—South Bass Island's Put-in-Bay—and some for the hunting—Bois Blanc—you can find a myriad of other reasons to visit these or any other of the islands.

- For the scale—Many islands can be completely explored on bike or by hike.
- For the speed, or lack thereof—When what you're exploring is smaller, you tend to slow down, a benefit many of us are looking for wherever we go.
- For the nature—When you're moving slower, you tend to see more, including, in the case of islands, the possibility of endangered species.
- For the history—Because they represent smaller geographical units, islands often have a more accessible history. Many of the Great Lakes Basin islands played important roles in Native American / First Nation history; some were involved in the endgame of the American Revolution, played major roles in the War of 1812, or starred in the Canadian rebellions of 1837; and a number served as depots on the way to freedom as part of the Underground Railroad or as bootlegging stopovers during Prohibition.
- For getting physical—Islands are excellent places to enjoy getting physical out of doors. They are great places to stroll, hike, jog, ride bikes, swim, row—the list goes on. Should you plan to train for an Ironman Triathlon, you couldn't find a much better place than an island to be.
- For the photographic opportunities—Take a camera, take your cell phone, take lots of pictures. Sunrises and sunsets, flora and fauna, people and places, monuments to the living and gravestones of the dead, natural features and architectural features. Islands provide no end of good shots to capture.
- For the rocks and fossils—Some islands, those within state, provincial, or national parks in particular, may prohibit removing rocks and/or fossils, but those that do not are wonderful places to find everything from puddingstones (Drummond Island and St. Joseph Island) to horn coral (Manitoulin Island), not to mention the beach glass.
- For the water—Wade or swim, canoe or kayak, float on a raft, fish from a boat, dive to a shipwreck. You're surrounded by water!
- For the people and community—You may actually find people you've never met waving a greeting to you as they pass you on an island road; if you ask a question of an islander, you may find yourself invited to dinner. A different, closer sense of community exists on an island, in part because people living on an island have to find ways to get along, and they have.
- For the adventure—Take a camera, you'll come home with a lot of good photos; take a journal, you'll come home with a bunch of great stories; if you set out to explore an island, you'll certainly find adventure!

You should expect to leave a Great Lakes Basin island with fine memories—and perhaps with plans to return (or plans to explore another island or 10!).

TWO QUESTIONS TO ASK ISLANDERS

Generally, the very best—and most accessible—resources for information about an island are its people, the islanders, themselves. Remember to ask the islanders you meet the two "magic" questions. Some of the most enjoyable island conversations I've had and many of the best island adventures I experienced were the result of asking one or both of these two questions of an islander:

- What do you think is special about your island?
- What would you especially want a visitor to be sure to see or experience while on your island?

Lake Superior Islands

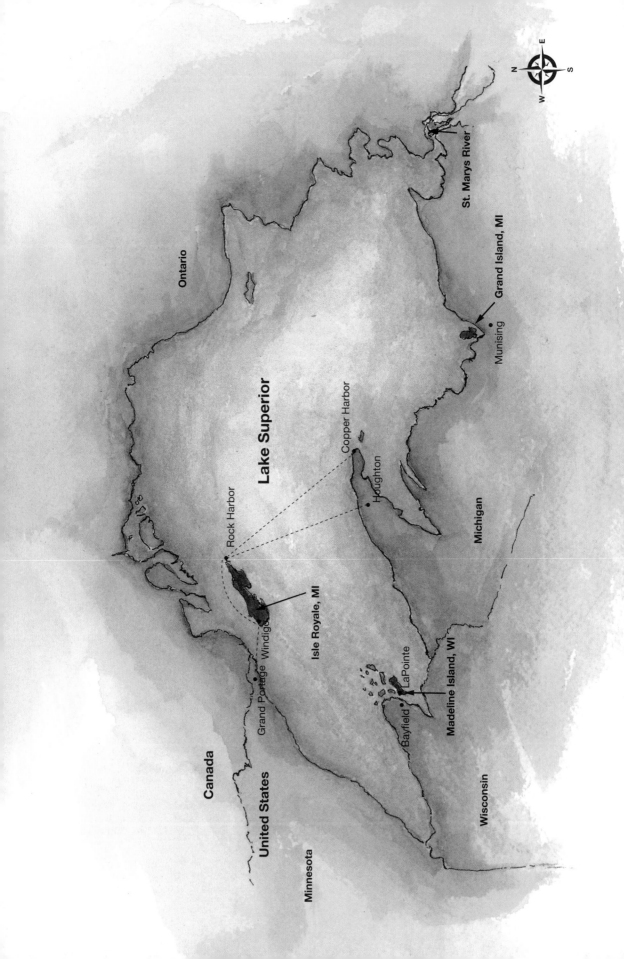

An Introduction to Lake Superior

It has been said that Lake Superior was created by fire and ice. In the beginning was the Canadian Shield, the 3.3-billion-year-old shell of the "Turtle Island" that is North America. Then came the drama of tectonic forces, which caused a rift and split this crust. Lava flowed out from the rift. It cooled and hardened into basalt, a dark, dense igneous rock. More lava flowed out, cooled, and hardened. More lava flowed—but you get the drift—which is the Midcontinent Rift, the source of a flowing, cooling, hardening process that went on for about 20 million years.

Eventually the crust began to sink along the rift, given what was now an almost 10-mile (16-kilometer) layer of basalt there. The sinking created a basin filled first with sediment, then with water, and then the glaciers formed. After the great Laurentide ice sheet, which covered most of Canada and a large part of the northern United States, began to melt, but before the glaciers were finished, there was Lake Duluth. This lake formed 11,000 years ago in the area that is now the southwestern lobe of Lake Superior.

As the glacier from the last of four glacial periods finally melted, it filled the basin that is now Lake Superior. Today, Lake Superior drains into Lake Huron through the St. Marys River. Lake Superior's shores are shared by Ontario, Minnesota, Wisconsin, and Michigan's Upper Peninsula.

If you've ever read the 1941 children's book *Paddle-to-the-Sea,* for which illustrator and author Holling Clancy Holling was awarded a Caldecott Honor, you may remember that the Nipigon River drains into Lake Superior. The river's source is Lake Nipigon, a secondary lake in the Great Lakes Basin—one of the bodies of water sometimes described as the sixth Great Lake—located northwest of Lake Superior and entirely in Ontario. Lake Nipigon drains into the Nipigon River, which drains into the Nipigon Bay of Lake Superior.

SUPERIOR IN SO MANY WAYS

Lake Superior is the *largest* lake in the world by surface area (31,700 square miles/82,103 square kilometers), holding as much water—about 3 quadrillion gallons—as all of the other Great Lakes combined, plus the amount of three extra Lake Eries, an amount equivalent to 10 percent of all the fresh water on Earth.

Of the Great Lakes, Lake Superior is the

- *highest* in elevation, averaging 602 feet above sea level;
- *coldest*, with an average temperature of 40 degrees Fahrenheit;
- *cleanest* and *clearest*, with underwater visibility of 27 to 75 feet;
- *deepest*, with an average depth of 483 feet and a deepest point of 1,333 feet.

Holling's *Paddle-to-the-Sea* is a great introduction to, or reminder of, how the fresh water flows through the Great Lakes Basin to St. Lawrence River and out to the Atlantic Ocean. The story's Native American character lives near Lake Nipigon. Speaking of the Nipigon River, he explains to Paddle-to-the-Sea, the little man with a paddle he has carved kneeling in a foot-long model canoe: "The river flows into the Great Lakes, the biggest lakes in the world. They are set like bowls on a gentle slope. The water from our river flows into the top one, drops into the next, and on to the others. Then it makes a river again, a river that flows to the Big Salt Water."[3] Then, after the geese have signaled the imminent start of spring, he sets Paddle-to-the-Sea down on a snowbank, positioning him facing south toward the Nipigon River. And so starts the Long Journey of Paddle-to-the-Sea.

We begin our Great Lakes island escapes in Lake Superior.

Three islands in Lake Superior are accessible by ferry (no Lake Superior islands are accessible by bridge):

- Isle Royale, with a ferry from Grand Portage, Minnesota, and from Copper Harbor or Houghton in Michigan's Upper Peninsula.
- Madeline Island, in the Apostle Island archipelago, with a ferry from Bayfield, Wisconsin.
- Grand Island, off of Michigan's Upper Peninsula, with a ferry from Munising, Michigan.

At least one contributing factor that makes all three of these islands compelling involves the approach to the island ferry's point of departure. Sixty-eight percent of the land near Lake Superior is forest. Take a look at a map of the mainland surrounding Lake Superior. You'll notice an abundance of green areas. Because neither Lake Superior's cool weather nor the poor soil of the region is amenable to farming, after the virgin forest was logged in the nineteenth and twentieth centuries, second-growth forest grew, and logging continues as an industry in the region today.

However, there are huge tracts of land where the heavy forest is now protected. Just some of the forests that touch Lake Superior are Grand Island National Recreation Area, Superior National Forest, Sleeping Giant Provincial Park, Pukaskwa National Park, Lake Superior Provincial Park, Sault Ste. Marie State Forest Area, Tahquamenon Falls State Park, Hiawatha National Forest, Porcupine Mountains State Park, Ottawa National Forest, Baraga State Forest Area, Crystal Falls Forest Management Unit, and Chequamegon National Forest.

Consider, too, that the relatively few people who live near Lake Superior are mostly residents of port cities that evolved from the original lakeshore settlements: Sault Ste. Marie, Ontario; Thunder Bay, Ontario; Grand Portage, Minnesota; Duluth, Minnesota; Superior, Wisconsin; Marquette, Michigan; and Sault Ste. Marie, Michigan. These cities are relatively few—and far between—given Lake Superior's approximately 1,826 miles (2,939 kilometers) of shoreline.

As is true of many Great Lakes Basin islands, what is striking about these islands has to do both with their natural wilderness and what humans over time have done with that original wildness. No matter from which direction you approach your launch to a Lake Superior island, you come to it through forest, encountering very few people and a lot of trees. Thus you experience the rare remove of forest wilderness before you experience the further remoteness of island.

For more information on Lake Superior, visit www.great-lakes.net/superior.html and consider looking for a used or library copy of the American Lake Series volume *Lake Superior*, by Grace Lee Nute, American Lake Series (1944; repr., Indianapolis: Bobbs-Merrill,

2000). Another interesting read is *Kitchi-Gami: Life among the Lake Superior Ojibway*, by Johann Georg Kohl, translated by Lascelles Wraxall (1860; repr., Saint Paul: Minnesota Historical Press, 1985).

Isle Royale, Michigan

THE WILDEST "ACCESSIBLE" ISLAND WILDERNESS IN THE GREAT LAKES

August 24, 2013, 8:38 a.m.
On MV Voyageur II
Grand Portage, Minnesota, to Isle Royale, Michigan

Our young captain, wearing a well-worn cap turned backwards, the brim against his neck, gives a speech, including instructions for "laughing at" the lake should the water get rough. He also mentions life preservers and rafts although, according to him, this boat has hit nothing in its 42 years "larger than a stack." (A stack of what? I wonder. A Lake Superior sea stack? The smokestack at the site of a Lake Superior shipwreck?)

But the lake could not be calmer, and for that I am grateful. I've spent the first half hour out on the deck at the stern, watching the mainland of Grand Portage recede. First, the immediate harbor gave way to the arms of a wider harbor. And now, we've been slipping into the reach of wider and wider arms, the evergreen ridges rising in profile behind us. One particular ridge I imagine to be the Canadian border, only seven miles from Grand Portage. A mist hovers over the green, and the smudge of a three-quarter cloud-moon hangs above it in blue sky. The air is chilly, the sun before us warm. I have added layers of clothing but, facing north, feel the chill on the side of my face and the backs of my hands. I find myself snapping a photo of a complete spiderweb on the window of the cabin and realize that the slowing-down mind-set of this island trip is already under way.

Inside, people are engrossed in their iPads and Kindles. I suspect some are listening to music. I am listening to the thrum of the motor, the crest and slice of the ripple of wake, the murmur of voices of the five other people sharing this small deck with me: two couples and a single man wearing a birding hat and drinking a cup of coffee. They all seem very matter-of-fact. Although I imagine that I, too, may outwardly appear to be taking this trip in stride.

Nothing could be further from the truth. Why has this trip become the biggest challenge of all of the island trips I've planned or can imagine? Not because of the possibility of a bout of seasickness (been there, survived that), nor because of the remoteness of the island, six and a half hours by passenger ferry. After all, much of that time, we'll be cruising along the shoreline of the island as we circumvent it.

I was happy to learn there are no bears on the island—the one bad experience I have had of bears (involving a rogue adolescent male) is more than enough. I consider bears much in the same light as did Christopher Robin: "of little brain." There are moose and wolf, neither of which I've yet seen in the wild, but I've read that wolves avoid humans, and I have no intention of coming between a moose and her calf.

What is it then? As the sun rises higher in the sky, I gradually allow my uneasiness to sink into the lake's rocking.

10:30—As we approach the island for the first time, at the end of Isle Royale's long Washington Harbor, just as we slip past Lake Superior's Beaver Island toward Windigo—a docking and refueling port on Isle Royale and a ranger station for Island Royale National Park—I spot something on the shoreline and blurt out the question in a uncertain voice: *moose?*

Suddenly, everyone's out on the deck. It is a moose in the water. And then we spy what the moose, apparently a female moose, is looking at in front of her: two calves! With the arrival of our boat, the three draw together, the twins falling into tight formation behind their mother, who picks up her pace, lifting her knees up heavily above the surface of the water, plodding parallel to the boat. What a welcome to Isle Royale!

During our 10-minute orientation to the park on the Windigo dock, the park ranger wipes her forehead with a bandana and explains, "In these record temperatures—moose don't sweat—they need to get in the lake to cool down."

Vicki and I hike past eight moose antlers lying on the ground next to the park's welcome sign, up a trail that just ahead appears to lead into a deep thick forest. We stretch our sea legs, getting used to the solidity of the ground again. When a blast from the boat summons us back, I am reluctant to return. Despite the boat having taken on additional passengers, our departure feels—I, myself feel—lighter.

My unexpected love affair with Isle Royale has begun.

GETTING THERE: Passenger-only ferry; seaplane; private boat (docking permit required)

GETTING AROUND: Limited options: foot traffic only on trails; paddling only on inland lakes and streams; canoe and kayak rentals available (personal watercraft prohibited); motor vehicles and wheeled devices (other than wheelchairs) prohibited

OVERNIGHT ACCOMMODATIONS: Rock Harbor Lodge and cottages; Windigo Camper Cabins; campgrounds

FOOD: Bring your own

DAY TRIP? Possible, but not recommended

STATE / PROVINCIAL / NATIONAL PARK? Isle Royale National Park

---

Isle Royale is simply where you go to return the wilderness to your soul. Here are loon and owl, moose and wolf, "the Lady," who is Lake Superior, and the island itself, which contains more than 45 inland lakes. What is not lake is the hush of magnificent boreal forest on bedrock where trails await your feet.

Native people came to Isle Royale to tap the maples, dig for copper, and fish for whitefish, all communal activities. Today, many visitors come to the island seeking solitude and the individual challenge found in submerging oneself in this rare wilderness.

In between these two ways of being on the island, a number of formalities took place. The island became part of the United States with the 1783 Treaty of Paris, and in 1843, the Ojibwe relinquished claim to the island. In 1931, President Hoover authorized Congress to find and conserve "a prime example of North Woods Wilderness," and on April 3, 1940, Franklin D. Roosevelt established Isle Royale National Park, containing the large island of Isle Royale and over 450 smaller islands. Isle Royale was designated as a National Wilderness Area in 1976 and as an International Biosphere Reserve in 1980. The park also houses the world's

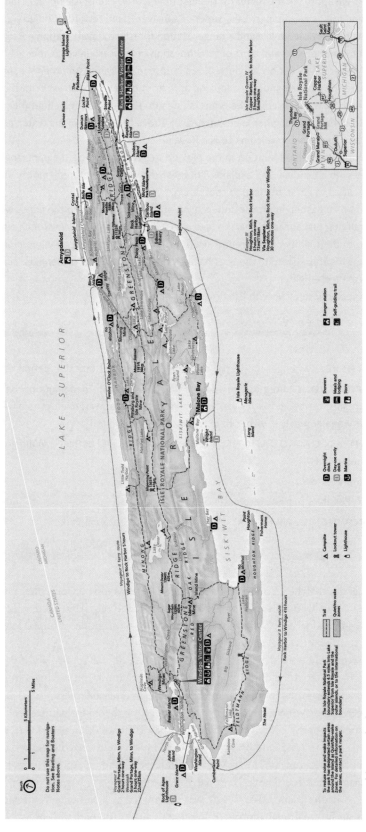

Courtesy of the National Park Service

Part of over 150 miles of Lake Superior's rocky shoreline along Isle Royale's boreal forest.

longest-running large-mammal predator-prey study on the planet; the island has been the site of a wolf- and moose-monitoring project since 1958.

For hikers and recreational boaters, the National Park Service provides 36 campgrounds, dotted throughout the main island's 45- by 9-mile (72- by 14-kilometer) sprawl. However, even if you are not a backpacker or a camper, even if you have young children or are a senior citizen, you can still enjoy the "wildest" wilderness accessible by bridge or ferry on a Great Lakes island by making reservations at the Rock Harbor Lodge, in one of 20 housekeeping cottages (duplexes with kitchenettes) in the woods between Rock Harbor Marina and Tobin Harbor, or at one of the one-room rustic Windigo Camper Cabins on the western end of the island.

How to Get There

Nowhere in the Great Lakes Basin do you have so many choices of how to get to an island: four different passenger ferries and three ferry departure points. Depending on which you select, you will have a different length of trip, destination point, and experience.

Isle Royale is the only Great Lakes Basin island you can get to by ferry from Minnesota (and there are no Great Lakes Basin islands connected to Minnesota by bridge). You can also depart from two locations in Michigan's Upper Peninsula, both located on the Keweenaw Peninsula. Ferries start running for the season in May and end in September; current schedules are available online. Advance ferry reservations are recommended for all ferries.

From Grand Portage, Minnesota, passenger ferries are operated by Grand Portage–Isle Royale Transportation Line, Inc. (www.isleroyaleboats.com):

Sea Hunter III—A 65-foot, 68-passenger vessel. This excursion is one of two opportunities for a day trip to the island. The journey to Windigo takes just one and a half hours, and you have four hours to spend on the island before your return.

MV *Voyageur II*—A 65-foot, 48-passenger vessel. This trip gets you to Windigo in two hours and then continues on to Rock Harbor, another five hours. The *Voyageur II* travels clockwise around the island, overnighting at Snug Harbor in the Rock Harbor area. The advantage of taking this ferry is that you have your choice of a number of different drop-off points on the boat's circuit of the island. Moreover, you have the opportunity to glean a better understanding of the size and wildness of the island from observing the approximately 100 miles (161 kilometers) of spectacular coastline you pass by over the course of the round trip.

From Copper Harbor, Michigan:

Isle Royale Queen IV—A 100-foot, 100-passenger vessel operated by the Isle Royale Line (www.isleroyale.com). The ferry departs in the morning for the three-hour trip to Rock Harbor, from which it departs in the afternoon, providing another opportunity for a day trip but with a layover of only about two and a half hours.

From Houghton, Michigan:

Ranger III—A 165-foot, 128-passenger vessel operated by the National Park Service (www .nps.gov/isro). It is five hours one way to Mott Island (park headquarters) and six hours one way to Rock Harbor.

Rock Harbor Lodge on Isle Royale as seen from the deck of MV *Voyageur II*, en route from Grand Portage, Minnesota.

Seaplane service is also available to Isle Royale from the Houghton County Airport from mid-May to mid-September. Thunder Bay International Airport and Duluth International Airport are the closest international airports in Canada and the United States, respectively.

What to Expect

Wilderness!

The Great Smoky Mountains National Park averages more visitors in one *day* than Isle Royale does in one *year*. Fewer than 20,000 people visit the island annually. That said, while this island will answer the call of the wild for many, at least two other facets of the island, besides the available lodging already mentioned, make this a doable destination, even for those not inclined to camp or backpack.

With respect to concerns regarding encounters with wildlife, while you may be fortunate enough to see a (not-too-near-in-proximity) moose, it is unlikely that you will see a wolf. Other wildlife includes red fox, beavers, red squirrels, snowshoe hares, and otters, but there are no deer, raccoons, or wildcats of any kind. You may see painted turtles and garter snakes, eagles, ospreys, ravens, loons, and merganser, as well as a variety of songbirds, woodpeckers, gulls, and ducks.

Another plus is that the Windigo Store (at the western end of the island) and the Rock Harbor Dockside Store (at the eastern end) both sell food and supplies. The prices are a bit higher than you would expect to pay on the mainland but reasonable nonetheless, given the cost of getting the items to the island.

A few things to keep in mind: Leave what natural or historic objects you find on Isle Royale where you find them, and when backpacking, abide by the "pack-it-in, pack-it-out" rule.

Be aware that there are no medical services available on the island. Be sure to pack a first-aid kit.

No public telephone or cell phone service exists on the island. All communication is via the rangers' radios.

Both the Windigo Visitor Center and the Rock Harbor Visitor Center, staffed by park rangers, are places to view displays, browse or purchase publications, receive your back-country permit, find out what interpretive programs are being offered, and have your questions answered.

Paths to Adventure

The National Park Service offers different types of interpretative programs in July and August at three locations: Windigo, Rock Harbor, and the Daisy Farm Area. Check at the park's visitor centers for more information.

MV *Sandy* offers a variety of guided tours from Rock Harbor. The Rock Harbor Visitor Center will provide details and a schedule.

NATURAL SITES

With Isle Royale's approximately 165 miles (266 kilometers) of groomed trails and approximately 50 inland lakes, you could spend a lifetime hiking and/or paddling there. Helpful resources for these activities are National Geographic's topographic map *Isle Royale National*

GREENSTONE

The Greenstone Ridge, considered the backbone of the island, as it is the highest and longest ridge, was named for the greenish color of the underlying basalt Greenstone Flow, which is up to 800 feet thick. The theory is that it is part of the largest lava flow on Earth, once covering an area from Kansas up into Canada. The pebble beaches and reefs of Isle Royale National Park contain Isle Royale greenstone, or chlorastrolite ("green star stone"), a greenish, legume-sized stone uncommon outside of Isle Royale. In 1973, Isle Royale greenstone was designated Michigan's official state gemstone. Collecting Isle Royale greenstone specimens is prohibited in the park.

Park, a publication of its *Trails Illustrated* series, and Jim DuFresne's *Isle Royale National Park: Foot Trails & Water Routes.*

Hike—There are several trails/common trail combinations that are more than 12 miles (19 kilometers) in length.

- Greenstone Ridge Trail—40 miles (64 kilometers) between Windigo and Rock Harbor.
- Minong Ridge Trail—28.3 miles (45.5 kilometers) between Windigo and McCargoe Cove.
- Feldtmann Ridge Trail plus Island Mine Trail—29.8 miles (48 kilometers).
- Rock Harbor Trail plus the Lake Richie Trail—13.2 miles (21.2 kilometers).
- For a list of shorter trails (11 miles/18 kilometers or less in length), consult Jim DuFresne's definitive *Isle Royale National Park: Foot Trails and Water Routes,* 4th ed. (Seattle: Mountaineers, 2011). The National Geographic *Isle Royale National Park Trails Illustrated* topographic map is also helpful (and waterproof for boots-on-the-ground use).

Canoe or kayak—Canoe and kayak rentals are available from the Windigo Store and the Rock Harbor Lodge. From Windigo, explore Washington Harbor and Washington Creek. From Rock Harbor, paddle Tobin Harbor, a good way to get to Lookout Louise Trail (two-mile/3.2-kilometer round trip), or paddle to Raspberry Island (two-mile/3.2-kilometer round trip). Whether you're paddling along the shore or hiking on the trails, look for the tangle of old man's beard draped over spruce and fir trees, and keep an eye out for the majestic black-and-white pattern of loon plumage in summer on the lake. If you're lucky, you may see one or two loon hatchlings hitching a ride on a parent's back. Listen for the four types of beautifully eerie calls of the common loon from anywhere on the island or lake: tremolo, yodel, wail, and hoot.

Fish—In Isle Royale's 50 inland lakes, where you do not need a fishing license, northern pike, trout, perch, and walleye abound. You do need a license to fish in Lake Superior. Boats can be rented from Rock Harbor Lodge.

Dive—Shipwrecks are littered throughout the Isle Royale National Park, which extends 4.5 miles (7.2 kilometers) out into Lake Superior from the above-water island. The cold water of Lake Superior has preserved a variety of shipwrecks. Divers must register at Rock Harbor or Windigo visitor centers before diving. Licensed dive charters are available in the park. For more information, or if you are considering diving on your own off Isle Royale, consult www.nps.gov/isro/planyourvisit/scuba-diving.htm.

View from Isle Royale's Mt. Franklin, looking north to some of the over 400 smaller Lake Superior islands that are included in Isle Royale National Park.

HISTORY PRESERVED

Smithwick Mine—In the Rock Harbor area on the Stoll Trail a sign points the way, and an information plaque, which includes a map of the major Isle Royale mine sites, explains what is not obvious from the remains of one of the oldest post–Ojibwe-era copper mines, in operation from 1847 to 1849.

Edisen Fishery—This preserved historic fishery is located across Rock Harbor from Daisy Farm and was owned and operated for almost 60 years by one of the last pair of commercial fishing partners on Isle Royale, Pete and Laura Edisen. At one time, there were as many as 40 similar small seasonal operations run by Scandinavian families on Isle Royale.

Rock Harbor Lighthouse—The oldest lighthouse on Isle Royale, completed in 1855, was active for only a few years before copper mining on the island came to a halt and it was no longer needed. Now the lighthouse contains museum displays on shipwrecks, lighthouses, and the mining activities of Isle Royale. The tower offers panoramic views of the island, Rock Harbor, the Middle Island Passage, and Lake Superior.

Daisy Farm—Seven miles (11.3 kilometers) southwest of Rock Harbor, this is one of the flatter areas on the island and the site of the former town of Ransom, a sizable (by Isle Royale standards) historic settlement of miners and loggers founded in 1846.

Ojibway Fire Tower—At the highest point of the eastern end of the island, just a short hike from Daisy Farm, you will find this tower, once a fire watch station. The tower room is now closed to visitors, as it is filled with scientific instrumentation that supports a nationwide atmospheric monitoring program, but you can climb partway up the stairs for excellent views of the island's inland lakes and bays.

Minong Mine—Located west of McCargoe Cove Campground, this site, listed on the National Register of Historic Places in 1977, contains evidence of prehistoric mining activity in pits up to 30 feet deep, dating to 4,500 years ago, as well as the remains of a nineteenth-century copper mine owned by the Minong Mining Company of Detroit from 1872 to 1885. At its height, the nearby settlement of Cove supported a community of about 150 miners as well as a railroad, a post office, a dam, a stamp mill, a dock, and a blacksmith's shop. During 10 years of operation, the company produced 249 tons of copper. "Minong" is related to an Ojibwe word for "island" specifically denoting what we now know as Isle Royale.

Passage Island—A rugged island, 3.25 miles (5.23 kilometers) northeast of Isle Royale, where moose have not left their mark on the vegetation and the site of the 1881 Passage Island Lighthouse.

Raspberry Island—At the southeast end of the park, across Rock Harbor from Snug Harbor, this island offers a boardwalk hike through a spruce bog.

Belle Isle—At the northeast end of the park, an island where, in 1837, the American Fur Company established a fishing camp. Later, in the resort era of the early twentieth century, this island was the site of a nine-hole golf course.

The SS _Monarch_ shipwreck site—One of at least 10 shipwrecks in the park, the _Monarch_ was a wooden passenger-package freighter built in Sarnia, Ontario, in 1890. It sank on a run from Thunder Bay to Sarnia in a snowstorm in 1906. Large pieces of wooden wreckage are scattered on the bottom of the lake at depths of between 10 and 80 feet. The shipwreck was placed on the National Register of Historic Places in 1984.

OTHER ISLAND THINGS TO DO

Besides hiking, paddling, diving, and sightseeing? Sketch or paint, write, take photographs, make music, meditate. "Keep close to Nature's heart, yourself; and break clear away, once in a while, and climb a mountain or spend a week in the woods. Wash your spirit clean."[4]

SPECIAL ISLAND EVENTS

Isle Royale is certainly the best place in Michigan—being the farthest north and certainly surrounded by the darkest sky—to catch the neon flickers and fireworks of the Aurora Borealis (the Northern Lights). All that's needed is a clear night and the solar flare of a storm on the sun.

COPPER

In 1874, the Minong Mine produced a 5,720-pound nugget of copper, displayed first on the courthouse lawn in Detroit and later at the 1876 Centennial Exhibition.

LARGEST ISLANDS TIMES TWO

Ryan Island on Isle Royale's Siskiwit Lake is the largest island in the largest lake on the largest island in the largest freshwater lake in the world.

For More Island Information

www.nps.gov/isro/—The website of the Isle Royale National Park (U.S. National Park Service).

Wolf's Eye—The Isle Royale & Keweenaw Parks Association newsletter, published three times a year and archived online at irkpa.org/get-involved/eye.

Isle Royale National Park: National Geographic Trails Illustrated Map (Evergreen, CO: National Geographic Maps, 2006).

Isle Royale National Park: Foot Trails & Water Routes, 4th ed., by Jim DuFresne (Seattle: Michigantrailmaps.com, 2011).

Island Life: An Isle Royale Nature Guide, by Ted Gostomski and Janet Marr (Houghton, MI: Isle Royale Natural History Association, 2007).

Mac's Pocket Guide: Isle Royale National Park, by Stephen R. Whitney and Elizabeth Briars Hart (Seattle, WA: Mountaineers Books, 2006)—A guide to animals and birds.

Minong—The Good Place: Ojibwe and Isle Royale, by Timothy Cochrane (East Lansing: Michigan State University Press, 2009).

Time by Moments Steals Away: *The 1848 Journal of Ruth Douglass,* by Robert L. Root Jr. (Detroit: Wayne State University Press, 1998).

Diaries of an Isle Royale Fisherman, by Elling Seglem, edited by Robert Root and Jill Burkland (Houghton, MI: Isle Royale Natural History Association, 2002)—Seglem's diary entries and other written accounts, 1919–32.

Becoming Wilderness: Nature, History, and the Making of Isle Royale National Park, by Amalia Tholen Baldwin (Houghton, MI: Isle Royale and Keweenaw Parks Association, 2011).

The Wolves of Isle Royale: A Broken Balance, by Rolf O. Peterson (Minocqua, WI: Willow Creek, 1995).

A View from the Wolf's Eye, by Carolyn C. Peterson (Houghton, MI: Isle Royale Natural History Association, DBA Isle Royale and Keweenaw Parks Association, 2008).

Isle Royale: Moods, Magic, and Mystique, by Jeff Rennicke (Houghton, MI: Isle Royale Natural History Association, 1989)—Includes a list of additional suggested readings.

Naked in the Stream: Isle Royale Stories, by Vic Foerster (Traverse City, MI: Arbutus, 2010).

The Island within Us: Isle Royale Artists in Residence, 1991–1998, edited and compiled by Robert Root and Jill Burkland (Houghton, MI: Isle Royale Natural History Association, 2000).

How You Can Support the Island

Isle Royale & Keweenaw Parks Association (www.irkpa.org)—Join to help "provide needed financial support of efforts to share the stories of these two very special parks with park visitors, schoolchildren, and people around the world."

Isle Royale Families and Friends Association (www.isleroyalefamilies.org)—Support to help "continue the over 100-year presence of family heritage, culture and rich human tradition on Isle Royale; to assure the preservation of historic family dwellings; to enhance the experience of NPS staff and Park visitors by serving as authentic links to Isle Royale's rich human history."

Parting Thoughts

August 27, 2013, 9:10 a.m.
On MV Voyageur II
Isle Royale, Michigan, to Grand Portage, Minnesota

As the *Voyageur II* departs from Rock Harbor, Vicki and I are aboard, still savoring the "Big Breakfast Burrito" we shared at the Greenstone Grill.

We are traveling in the very thickest of fogs. It had been clear at 3:30 when I got up to take Advil to ease the ache in my paddling arms (four hours in a canoe on the Tobin Harbor yesterday) and my left hiking foot (11 miles of anything but flat ground to and back from Mt. Franklin the day before). But now, the week's record temperatures in the 80s are mixing it up with the Lady's cool.

Our valiant vessel heads out of Rock Harbor, laboring through the waves of the Middle Island Passage to Chippewa Harbor. From where I sit, on a pine bench at the back of the cabin, I can look forward and see our captain, his feet planted firmly against the roll. I am grateful to be inside, reading and writing. At least for now. My stomach is happy, my brain engaged, my heart light. Who would have thought? What was so daunting became not only doable but desirable.

10:40—Leaving Chippewa Harbor, I slip back out through the wood door at the rear of *Voyageur II*'s passenger cabin and am surprised to find how thrilled I am by the gray rolling waters, the churning froth thrown up by our motor, the wake of our passage. The bright orb of sun is trying to burn through the thick walls of fog on either side and behind us.

On the deck of the stern, I sit on the slatted wood bench, its gray paint peeling, a metal-cleated floor under my feet. The foghorn sends out its reassuring warning every two minutes as we soldier on, the air mild despite the fog. Island-inspired questions rattle around pleasantly inside me, infused with the bit of wilderness I'm taking back home with me.

Two redheaded women, separated by a generation, are in earnest conversation, their backs against the deck rail. A man with crumbled paper like that covering a drinking straw stuffed in his ears, wearing well-worn hiking boots, sits ramrod straight directly under the foghorn speaker, cupping his ear periodically and drifting in and out of sleep.

The sun is making headway; I unzip my jacket. We are heading west along the south shore of the island, where the fog is grayer.

Before we stop in Malone Bay, where the fog is beginning to lift off the water, I have made the acquaintance of Bruce Moore, an environmental engineer from Bayfield, Wisconsin, who works with wetlands. This was not his first visit to the island. He stays in a housekeeping cottage above Tobin Harbor and hikes day trips. He says the view from Mt. Franklin rivals that from Mt. Ojibway. This long voyage back from the island is fine for going inward while one's body sways on an outdoor bench, for forging new acquaintanceships, and yes, for planning a return visit. I would like to able to compare the view from Mt. Ojibway myself.

Back out on the water, we are holding our ears against the blasts of the foghorn. The sun is hot on my blue-jeaned legs; I've slipped my jacket off. A comment from deckhand Benny interrupts my thoughts and sticks: "In a bad nor'easter, the water level raised at Windigo . . . the docks were chattering." Other than one nighttime thunderstorm that we'd welcomed, leaving open our lodge balcony door over the lake, we had not experienced the Lady's wrath.

After our last island stop at Windigo, we begin across "the Big Water." But surprisingly, after exiting the harbor in fog, the fog around us completely clears. And although the base of Isle Royale remains shrouded in fog to the southeast, the points of the balsam fir and white spruce show above the haze, following the island's backbone.

Three and a half miles west of Isle Royale, the Rock of Ages Lighthouse at first look appears to be missing its top in the fog, but now, as I watch, it materializes in its entirety, a single sentinel standing above the bits of island that have receded below the horizon line of the lake or, perhaps, into the cloud of mist. This last sight provides a most appropriate exclamation point at the end of our island adventure: Isle Royale!

"What is it you plan to do with your one wild and precious life?"[5]

Madeline Island, Wisconsin

THE END OF THE ANISHINAABE SEVEN-ISLAND MIGRATION

August 23, 2013, 1:35 p.m.
Outside the Madeline Island Museum

This page is rippled because I dropped my journal in Madeline Island's Big Bay after swimming yesterday. Beautiful beach, a warm bay, even with the day's lengthening shadows. The most comfortable swim I've ever had in Lake Superior, but it felt warmer than the Lady should ever feel. Vicki and I explored Big Bay at the Township Park yesterday afternoon, the town of La Pointe last night, and today, I'm discovering we could spend all day at the Madeline Island Museum.

The story I'm about to share is not mine to tell, but it is a history I didn't know before I visited Madeline Island, and I want to remember it. More than any other island story, it has made me aware of how very little I really knew about the Native history of the region where I have always lived, a place I am passionate about, especially when it comes to the area's Great Lakes.

So here is a cobbled-together history, working back through the years; first I must remind myself of what happened *after* this story-not-mine-to-tell. Before Madeline Island became involved in the conservation movement and the American Indian Movement of the 1970s it, like many other Great Lakes Basin islands, had experienced the rising influx of tourism from the 1890s forward and before that had boomed and subsequently suffered during the resource extraction period, resulting—in the case of the Apostle Islands—in the depletion of brownstone, timber, and fish.

Before that, of course, were the fur-trading years, when the beaver population of the Great Lakes was almost decimated and the Beaver Wars were fought, with the English and Dutch encouraging the Iroquois—encouragement that included supplying them with guns—to gain a competitive fur-trading advantage over the French and Algonquin-speaking peoples. Along the way several entire tribal confederacies were wiped out, and the territories of Native people were significantly realigned.

But before all of this history happened (which I suppose might have been at least touched on in my classrooms in the 1960s), there is another history. The Ojibwe are remarkable storytellers; Joseph Boyden and Louise Erdrich come most readily to mind. The Ojibwe storyteller who shares this story-not-mine-to-tell is Edward Benton-Banai in his *The Mishomis Book: The Voice of the Ojibway* (published by the University of Minnesota Press in 1988), which I first saw at the gift store at this wonderful Madeline Island Historical Museum.

Mishomis is the Ojibwe word for "grandfather." The contents of *The Mishomis Book* come from stories passed down by Ojibwe grandparents. Benton-Banai is "a full-blooded Wisconsin Ojibway of the Fish Clan," a spiritual teacher of the Lac Court Orielles Band of the Ojibway Tribe, one of the original founders of the American Indian Movement, and the founder and executive director of the Red School House in St. Paul, Minnesota.[6]

According to some, the final phase of this particular story ends two years before Christopher Columbus's arrival in what the Europeans came to call the New World. This history is an integral part of the Ojibwe oral tradition and is also recorded on birch-bark scrolls. In this story, 1490 marked the end of a seven-island, 500-year migration from the northeastern seaboard by the Anishinaabe, the Native "Original People" (also known as Anishinaabeg, Anishinaabek, Ojibway, Ojibwe, Ojibwa, Chippewa, and sometimes Algonquin, the language group of which they are members). The Anishinaabe had begun their journey to find a new home when it was prophesized that a light-skinned people would land on their shore, bringing death and destruction.

After a great council meeting, the Ojibwe started traveling westward, following the signs of a sacred vision along the way. The vision, clearly serving as an early navigational system, informed them that they would know they had reached their destination when they witnessed "food growing on the water."

The tribe moved inland, following the St. Lawrence River to the Ottawa River, through to Lake Nipissing, and on to the Great Lakes. Their approximate/actual seven-island/island-area stopping places were Mooniyaa, near Montreal, Quebec; near Niagara Falls; near Detroit; Manitoulin Island; Sault Ste. Marie; Spirit Island near Duluth; and Madeline Island.

When the Ojibwe reached Madeline Island, they found wild rice: food growing on the water. Consequently, Madeline Island became and is still, to this day, considered the Ojibwe's spiritual center.

How could it be that I had never heard of this migration story before?

GETTING THERE: Car ferry; private boat; private plane

GETTING AROUND: Many options: ferry your own car and/or bike; bicycle, moped, canoe, kayak, and motorboat rentals; water-taxi service

OVERNIGHT ACCOMMODATIONS: Inns and motels; cabin, home, and condo rentals; campgrounds

FOOD: Restaurants; groceries

DAY TRIP? Yes, but you could easily fill a week with island adventures!

STATE / PROVINCIAL / NATIONAL PARK? Big Bay State Park

Madeline Island is the largest of the 22 Apostle Islands, but it is not a part of the Apostle Island National Lakeshore, as are the other 21 islands and a 12-mile (19-kilometer) stretch of mainland shoreline. Unlike the other Apostle Islands, Madeline Island, 14 miles long by three miles wide (23 kilometers long by five kilometers wide), is a year-round community that has been commercially developed with an eye toward tourism. Most of that development is in the town of La Pointe, the only settlement on the island. Big Bay State Park and Big Bay Town Park make Madeline Island an ideal destination for both day-trippers looking for a beach experience and campers.

Like many other Great Lakes Basin islands, Madeline Island has had many names over the centuries. The evolution of its name provides a window into its history. The island was known as Mo-ning-wun'-a-kawn-ing by the Anishinaabe, whose migration story is traced above. *Moningwunakauning* means "Home of the Golden-Breasted Woodpecker." The bird referred to today by that name is not found in North America. Of the 20 woodpeckers that breed in North America, the only one bearing significant flashes of yellow and whose summer breeding ground range includes the island is the beautiful yellow-shafted common flicker. (Another translation of *moningwunakauning* is the "Place That Was Dug.") The French called the island Ile/Isle St. Michel in the seventeenth century, possibly as a tribute to the Archangel Michael, a patron and protector of the Catholic Church from the time of the apostles. The French Jesuits who were among the first Europeans to explore the islands were most likely also responsible for the name of the archipelago: the Apostle Islands. The entire island came to be known as La Pointe, or "The Point," named after the fortified French trading post located there from 1693–98 and 1718–59. The current city of La Pointe on the island developed as an American Fur Company outpost, beginning in the late eighteenth century under the leadership of the métis (of both Ojibwe and French Canadian descent) explorer and trader Michel Cadotte. The island became more widely known as Michael's Island, after Cadotte, but when Equaysayway, the daughter of Ojibwe Chief White Crane on the island, married Michel Cadotte, the chief renamed the island in honor of his daughter, who took the name Madeleine when she was baptized as a Christian.[7] It is unclear why or when the spelling changed to "Madeline."

How to Get There

Make your way to Bayfield on the east side of the Bayfield Peninsula on the southern shore of Lake Superior in Wisconsin. From when the ice breaks up until the water freezes again (typically March or April through mid-January), four vehicle ferries ply the Chequamegon Bay between Bayfield and the town of La Pointe on Madeline Island, a 2.6-mile (4.2-kilometer), 20-minute crossing. The ferry crosses hourly during tourist season (from the end of June to Labor Day).

Madeline Island Ferry Line
PO Box 66
La Pointe, WI 54850
715-747-2051
www.madferry.com

When the ferry is not operating during the winter, an ice road, a wind sled, or a passenger van may be available for transportation across the ice. Call 715-747-5400 for more information.

Year-round, Madeline Island Airport provides another way to and from the island.

Note: No public transportation or taxi service is available on the island.

BROWNSTONE

The beautiful old Bayfield County Courthouse, which now houses the Apostle Islands National Lakeshore Visitor Center, is a good example of brownstone, a reddish-brown sandstone once popular in building, particularly in the nineteenth century. Basswood Island, one of the Apostle Islands, was the site of a quarry run by the Bass Island Brownstone Company, which operated from 1868 into the 1890s. The brownstone from this and other Apostle Islands quarries was in great demand in the midwestern cities of Minneapolis and St. Paul, Milwaukee, Chicago, Detroit, and Cleveland, where it was used to build some of those cities' landmarks.

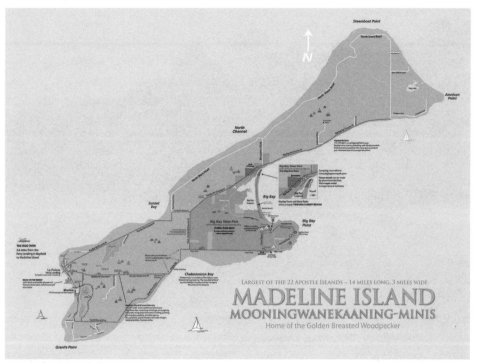

Courtesy of Madeline Island Ferry Line

What to Expect

You can expect to see white-tailed deer and the tracks of coyote, fox, and even black bear. You may see owls, woodpeckers, and blue jays in the winter and a host of other birds during migration seasons, particularly warblers. A list of the 240 bird species spotted in Big Bay State Park is available at the Park Office.

Paths to Adventure

NATURAL SITES

At Big Bay, on the east side of Madeline Island, opportunities abound to picnic or swim in the summer, to snowshoe or cross-country ski in the winter, and to hike or camp in the summer or winter.

Big Bay State Park—Six miles (9.65 kilometers) from La Pointe, this state park includes a 1.5-mile (2.4-kilometer) beach and more than nine miles (14.5 kilometers) of hiking and self-guided nature trails, including the .5-mile (.8-kilometer) Boardwalk Trail over the Big Bay Sand Spit and Bog (site no. 156), owned by the Wisconsin Department of Natural Resources (DNR) and designated a State Natural Area in 1980. Other trails include Bay View Trail, Lagoon Ridges Trail, and Point Trail. A wildlife observation deck is on the east side of the lagoon, and a beach wheelchair is available for adventurers with disabilities. In the summer there are interpretive programs for all and 60 campsites for campers. In the winter you can enjoy designated campsites and 5.2 miles (8.4 kilometers) of groomed cross-country ski trails. The park does not have a boat launch, but visitors may

Swimming in Lake Superior's Big Bay in Big Bay Town Park on Madeline Island.

bring their own canoes or kayaks and from the water explore the picturesque sandstone bluffs with caves where Lake Superior meets the shore. For more information, visiit http://dnr.wi.gov/topic/parks/name/bigbay/.

Big Bay Town Park—Seven miles (11 kilometers) from La Pointe, this park has a picnic shelter with a fireplace, woodlot, and 61 campsites plus six remote tent-only sites along the Lagoon Ridges Trail. A private organization rents canoes, paddles, and rowboats.

Joni's Beach—Two blocks from the ferry landing, this beach features a sheltered picnic area and a playground for younger children, a dock, a sandy beach, and public restrooms.

HISTORY PRESERVED

Ojibwe National Prayer Pole/Memorial Park—Sacred cedar and other trees surround a peaceful pond to honor the enduring relationship between the Ojibwe and Madeline Island.

St. Joseph Mission Cemetery (aka La Pointe Indian Cemetery and Old Indian Cemetery)— Ojibwe, French Canadian, American, and métis persons "of historical note" are buried here, including Chief Buffalo and Michel Cadotte. The cemetery is closed to the public, but the headstones may be viewed from outside the fence.

St. Joseph's Catholic Church—Founded by Bishop Frederic Baraga in 1838.

Madeline Island Museum—In downtown La Pointe and surrounded by a cedar picket stockade, this museum, a Wisconsin Historic Site, offers a good video introduction to the island and great interpretative displays in four historic buildings: the American Fur Company Building, the Old Jail, the Old Sailors' Home, and the Pioneer Barn.

Madeline Island Heritage Center—Features three 100-year-old buildings depicting island life in another time, restored and operated by the Madeline Island Historical Preservation Association.

Bad River Reservation—The Bad River Band of the Lake Superior Chippewa have a reservation of almost 2,000 acres at the northern end of the island (as well as four communities on the mainland).

CULTURAL ATTRACTIONS

Tom's Burned Down Café—At the site of an old tavern that burned in 1992, leaving only the outdoor decks, owner Tom Nelson parked a 40-foot trailer, built more decks, strung up a tarp for a roof, and added a bar and a number of entertaining signs (motto: "Out of the Ashes, Something More Terrible, More Strange and Beautiful"). The café is also home to the Middle Road Literary/Arts Society.

Woods Hall Studios & Gallery—Located next to St. John's United Church of Christ, which was instrumental in its start in 1955, this cooperative displays the work of over 40 island artists and craftspeople who have gallery and/or studio space here and sell woven items, pottery, and other gifts.

La Pointe Center Art Guild and Gallery—Showcases local and regional artists.

Bell Street Gallery—Housed in a turn-of-the-century former fishing shack, this gallery features work by more than 40 local and regional artists.

Island Carvers—Chainsaw- and hand-carved creatures.

Madeline Island School of the Arts—Supports local artisans and attracts instructors and artists from all over the country. May through October, the school offers five-day workshops for adults in writing, painting, quilting, photography, and yoga.

OTHER ISLAND THINGS TO DO

Madeline Island Bus Tour—Operated by the Madeline Island Ferry Line.

WHAT'S SO SPECIAL ABOUT WILD RICE?

Manoomin (the good berry) signaled to the Ojibwe that they had arrived at their new homeland, a fulfillment of the prophecy to resettle where "food grows on water."

Despite looking and cooking like rice, this "wild rice" is not really rice at all; it is an annual semiaquatic grass seed (*Zizania aquatic* and *Zizania palustris).* In the wild, in Minnesota's and Canada's cold shallow bays, wetlands, and slow rivers, in water two to four feet deep, manoomin grows abundantly. Manoomin grown in Minnesota state waters is regulated and may be reaped only by licensed harvesters in the traditional Native American way: from canoes powered only by long poles and using a beater stick to knock the ripe seeds into the bottom of the canoe.

In spite of decades of attempts, wild rice has proven challenging to domesticate successfully, primarily because the species has evolved to produce seeds that mature at different times, a strategy that prevents the plant from being entirely wiped out by an early frost or migrating waterfowl.

In recent years, concern by the Ojibwe has arisen over agricultural scientists mapping the wild rice genome and water issues related to the wild rice fields and harvest. A dietary staple for the Ojibwe, manoomin is also considered a sacred gift from the creator. Since 2009, the University of Minnesota and the Mille Lacs Band of Ojibwa have cohosted four biennial symposiums, "Nibi [Water] and Manoomin: Bridging Worldviews," the purpose of which is to promote discussion between Anishinaabe tribal elders and university researchers to explore their shared concerns and responsibilities in protecting wild rice and the waters in which it grows.

Perhaps manoomin will prove to be sacred in another way as it facilitates this exchange of teachings; perhaps there is more to the prophecy than we know.

Big Bay Lagoon, a Lake Superior freshwater estuary in Big Bay Town Park on Madeline Island.

Self-Guided Driving Tour CD—The CD is a good introduction to the island and is free to borrow from the Madeline Island Information Station, the ferry line office, and the Madeline Island Chamber of Commerce office.

Walking Tours—There are several to choose from.

- Historic Downtown Walking Tour—Features nine points of interest.
- Everyday La Pointe Art Junket Tour—Features 13 points of interest.
- Grant's Point Route—Features 10 points of interest, including the location of Michel Cadotte's fur-trading fort and a view of the New La Pointe Light Tower on Long Island from a private beach easement at Grant's Point.
- Capser Trail Route—Walk the interior of the island on a 1.1-mile (1.8-kilometer) (one-way) family-friendly gravel trail. The Nucy Meech Trail, an undeveloped path, branches off and then rejoins the Capser Trail.

Bike the island—Bicycles or mopeds can be rented at the dock. Madeline Island is one of seven islands with a chapter in *Biking the Great Lakes Islands,* by Kathleen Abrams and Lawrence Abrams (Wausau, WI: Entwood, 1985), 12–23.

Head for the lake—Kayaks, paddleboards, and snorkeling or scuba diving equipment can be rented on the island. Sailboat cruises, boat tours, and fishing excursions are also available.

Go fishing—Cast your hook and line for northern pike in the park's lagoon and several species of trout in Lake Superior.

Golf—Madeline Island Golf Club, located south of town on Old Fort Road, is a private Robert Trent Jones Golf Course on which public play is permitted by prior arrangement.

Take an Apostle Island Cruise (apostleisland.com)—See some notable Great Lakes sea caves and/or choose a glass-bottom boat tour.

SPECIAL ISLAND EVENTS

Madeline Island Summer Solstice Celebration (June).
Annual Apostle Island Inline Skating Marathon (June).
Big Bay's Annual Sand Castle Day (August).

The oldest structure on Madeline Island, an American Fur Company building, built in 1835 in La Pointe, and one of four adjoining historic log structures that, along with a modern expansion, make up the Madeline Island Museum, a Wisconsin Historic Site.

For More Island Information

Madeline Magic—A free annual vacation guide to Madeline Island that includes maps of attractions and businesses available on the island.

Madeline Island Information Station—Located across from the ferry landing in Bayfield, the Information Station provides visitor information, promotes island attractions and businesses, and highlights island artists, museums, parks, restaurants, shops, and lodging.

Big Bay State Park—http://dnr.wi.gov/topic/parks/name/bigbay/.

Madeline Island Chamber of Commerce—www.madelineisland.com.

Kakagon Bad River Sloughs—http://wisconsinwetlands.org/Gems/SU4_Kakagon-Bad_River_Sloughs.pdf.

Ojibwe.net—This site offers the opportunity to hear Anishinaabemowin, take Anishinaabemowin lessons, and discover language resources.

History of the Ojibway People, by Warren Wilson (1885; 2nd ed., Saint Paul: Minnesota Historical Society Press, 2009).

The Mishomis Book: The Voice of the Ojibway, by Edward Benton-Banai (Minneapolis: University of Minnesota Press, 1988)—This book includes a reconstruction of the migration of the Anishinaabe (aka Ojibwe).

Weweni: *Poems in Anishinaabemowin and English,* by Margaret Noodin (Detroit: Wayne State University Press, 2015)—This book provides the opportunity to see the Ojibwe language (Anishinaabemowin) on the page as well as enjoy the accompanying English (lyric) translations by Noodin, Ojibwe poet and Anishinaabemowin professor at the University of Wisconsin–Milwaukee.

Holding Our World Together: Ojibwe Women and the Survival of Community, by Brenda J. Child (New York: Penguin Books, 2012)—This book features the chapters "Women of the Great Lakes and Mississippi," "Madeline Island: Ojibwe Women in Fur Trade Society," "Reservations," and "Nett Lake: Wild Rice and the Great Depression," among others.

Books & Islands in Ojibwe Country: Traveling through the Land of My Ancestors, by Louise Erdrich (New York: HarperCollins, 2003).

The Birchbark House, by Louise Erdrich (New York: Hyperion Books for Children, 1999).

La Pointe: Village Outpost on Madeline Island, by Hamilton Nelson Ross and Thomas Vennum Jr. (Madison: Wisconsin Historical Society, 2000).

Women of Madeline Island, by Maureen D. Mack (Friendship, WI: New Past, 2006)—Ozhahguscodaywayquay and Jane Johnston Schoolcraft are two of the women featured in this book.

Madeline Island and the Chequamegon Region, by John O. Holzhueter (Madison: Wisconsin Historical Press, 1974).

"Madeline Island," in *Biking the Great Lakes Islands,* by Kathleen Abrams and Lawrence Abrams (Wausau, WI: Entwood, 1985), 12–23—The four Madeline Island biking routes detailed are Big Bay Island Park, South Shore Road, North Shore, and Extended North Shore.

For More Area Information

Around the Archipelago—The official annual newspaper of the Apostle Islands National Lakeshore, published by the National Park Service.

The Apostle Islands National Lakeshore Bayfield Visitor Center
415 Washington Ave.
Bayfield, WI 54814
715-779-3397
www/nps.gov/apis

At the visitor center, you can view audiovisual programs and study exhibits about the park's history, natural history, and recreation opportunities.

Northern Great Lakes Visitor Center
29270 County Hwy G
Ashland, WI 54806
www.nglvc.org

Located 20 miles (32 kilometers) south of Bayfield, Wisconsin, between Michigan and Minnesota, the Northern Great Lakes Visitor Center, which is partnered by the National Park Service and the Wisconsin Historical Society, provides information about the Lake Superior region and is open year-round, 9:00–5:00, seven days a week. Admission is free.

How You Can Support the Island

Madeline Island Wilderness Preserve (MIWP)
PO Box 28
La Pointe, WI 54850-0028
http://miwp.org

This nonprofit 2,500-acre land trust, which includes forest, wetlands and trails, was formed in 1987 and is dedicated "to the protection and preservation of natural areas on Madeline Island for everyone's enjoyment."

Friends of the Apostle Islands National Lakeshore
PO Box 1574
Bayfield, WI 54814
FriendsoftheApostleIslands.org

The organization's mission is "to promote an appreciation for, and preservation of, the natural environment and cultural heritage of the Apostle Islands National Lakeshore."

Apostle Islands Area Community Fund (AIACF)
300 Manypenny Ave., PO Box 332
Bayfield, WI 54814
www.apostleislandscommunityfund.com

AIACF supports area—Bayfield, Madeline Island, and Red Cliff—nonprofits through annual grant making.

Bad River Band of the Lake Superior Tribe of Chippewa
PO Box 39
Odanah, WI 54861
www.badriver-nsn.gov

Help prevent mining in the Bad River watershed, which threatens the only remaining extensive coastal wild rice bed in the Great Lakes region.

Parting Thoughts

Vicki and I drove along the boundaries of the Bad River Band of the Lake Superior Chippewa at the very northern tip of Madeline Island, but I didn't learn anything about the Kakagon and Bad River Sloughs, just east of Chequamegon Bay, on the mainland, until after leaving Madeline Island . . .

The Kakagon and Bad River Sloughs is designated as a Wetland of International Importance, the list of which is referred to as the Ramsar List, a part of the Ramsar Convention, an intergovernmental treaty adopted in the Iranian city of Ramsar in 1971, which the United States entered into in 1987.[8]

The sloughs, covering 10,760 acres, were also designated as a National Natural Landmark on February 2, 2012, and have been described as "a largely undeveloped wetland complex composed of sloughs, bogs, and coastal lagoons that harbor the largest natural wild rice bed on the Great Lakes." The area is protected as a conservation area by an integrated resource management plan under the jurisdiction of the Bad River Band of the Lake Superior Tribe of Chippewa. "The site . . . protects wild rice beds that are becoming increasingly fragmented on Lake Superior—as the only remaining extensive coastal wild rice bed in the Great Lakes region, it is critical to ensuring the genetic diversity of Lake Superior wild rice."[9]

The endangered gray wolf and threatened Canada lynx live here. The site provides necessary feeding, resting, and nesting habitat for both migrating and local populations of birds, and one of the two remaining sites for the endangered piping plover is located immediately north at Long Island.

"The largest ecological threat to the site is from invasive species and from controversial potential mining activity in the Penokee-Gogebic Range upriver."[10] Hopefully, the "food growing on the water"—this symbol that marked the end of a 500-year, seven-island migration— will be protected from destruction.

Grand Island, Michigan

A MICROCOSM OF HUMAN HISTORY PRESERVED

August 21, 2013, 3:00 p.m.
Williams Landing

Waiting on the Grand Island Transportation minibus, I've just realized that two years ago on the very same day of the year, I was happily here on this island, so close to the mainland but relatively wild—I remember because it is the day after my husband's birthday. I'm not, however, happy to realize that I'm doing the same thing this time as last time, just with a different companion: Vicki and I have come across on the passenger ferry just in time to take the 3:30 Altran Alger County Transit Interpretive Tour (the second of the two presented daily in summer) and plan to head back after the tour on the last of the boat's eight summer daily trips to the mainland.

The tour, however, is fascinating. As part of the Hiawatha National Forest, the island is classified as a National Recreation Area and falls under the jurisdiction of the U.S. Forest Service, which is a part of the Department of Agriculture. The department seems to have a different philosophy than the National Park Service when it comes to "wilderness" areas. The cultural artifacts of the place from before it was part of the national forest have been retained, and visiting them, in addition to stopping at the scenic overlooks, comprises much of this tour. Some of the places we stop at are different from those included on the other tour I'd taken.

Our tour guides (Eric today, Simone the first time) are knowledgeable about the interesting history of the island, right down to the details, like the first Euro-American settler Abraham Williams's stem and leaf design on the handle of the door of the Stone Quarry Cabin. As Eric is answering questions from fellow passengers, I begin to consider the layers of history on many of the Great Lakes Basin islands, how the trajectory of change within the last 400 years has been, in many cases, similar.

When we get out on Thunder Cove Trail at Waterfall Beach, I notice the side of the bus is painted with silhouettes of a mountain biker, the island's lighthouse, and a couple of back-packers, set amid a scene of forest and beach and the motto "Cross over to Adventure." The generous (almost three-hour) tour—which includes showing us campsites in some of the most beautiful spots on the island, perhaps in all the Great Lakes islands—only reinforces the idea that there is a lot of adventure to be had here. But probably not so much from the inside of an air-conditioned bus.

In conversation, I have discovered that two cabins are available for weekly rentals on the west, the sunset, side of the island, so even if one isn't a camping aficionado, one can comfort-ably take advantage of the amazing hiking opportunities here. I study the map of island trails as we bump along the sporadically lightning-lit dark forest tunnel on the one-way gravel road. We were surprised by a violent summer thunderstorm suddenly appearing over the lake at our last stop. I can see that if I had come over on the 9:00 a.m. boat, which would have given me nine hours on the island before the last boat left at 6:30, I could have taken advantage of a number of good hiking options. Being dry and safe doesn't quite make up for the missed opportunity, but it does give me a chance to figure out how to reclaim it.

GETTING THERE: Passenger-only ferry; personal boat or kayak (no docks)

GETTING AROUND: Altran tour vehicle (by Alger County Transit); bring your own bike; bike rentals on island; sea kayak rental on mainland in Munising

OVERNIGHT ACCOMMODATIONS: Camping sites; cabin rentals

FOOD: Bring your own

DAY TRIP? Yes

STATE / PROVINCIAL / NATIONAL PARK? Grand Island National Recreation Area

The history of Grand Island invokes the litany of one common Great Lakes Basin island development paradigm, with perhaps one variation: Native seasonal camp becomes fur-trading post becomes company investment becomes hunting camp becomes resort community becomes logging site becomes environmental and/or cultural preserve.

The Anishinaabe (Ojibwe/Chippewa) and earlier people used the island as a seasonal home for 5,000 years. In *An Account of Lake Superior, 1792–1807,* Irish fur trader John Johnston reported that Grand Island "is the summer residence of a small band of Indians, who cultivate maize, potatoes, and pumpkins" in the island's "excellent soil" and fish for trout and whitefish.[11]

The island participated in the fur trade via the establishment of a trading post by Anna and Abraham Williams, the first permanent white settlers, who arrived on Grand Island from Decatur, Illinois, in 1840 at the invitation of the Ojibwe Chief Omonomonee. Williams died in 1873.

The island was sold to the Cleveland-Cliffs Iron Company in 1901. (This company investment is the more unusual feature of island development.) The president of Cleveland-Cliffs, William Gwinn Mather, made the island his summer home, creating a deer camp and eventually a personal game preserve of animals exotic to Michigan, such as caribou and elk, fencing off the northern portion of the island to keep the animals in and poachers out of his "little Yellowstone." Mather invited his friends to build on lots leased from the company, and ultimately, he transformed the island into a resort community featuring the Hotel Williams.

A year after Mather's death in 1951, Cleveland-Cliffs began 20 years of logging, reportedly harvesting, incredible as it seems, four out of every five trees.

In 1989, Hiawatha National Forest purchased all but 40 acres of the island to be used as a National Recreation Area.

Today, the Grand Island National Recreation Area is overseen by the U.S. Department of Agriculture (USDA) Forest Service as part of the Hiawatha National Forest, also known as the "Great Lakes National Forest." The Forest Service promotes Grand Island as offering opportunities to "interpret natural and cultural history in diverse recreation settings." While there are many opportunities on and around the island to camp, canoe or kayak, fish, and hike or mountain bike, the cultural history of the island has also been well preserved in the landscape artifacts, in the interpretation available in the Grand Island Visitor

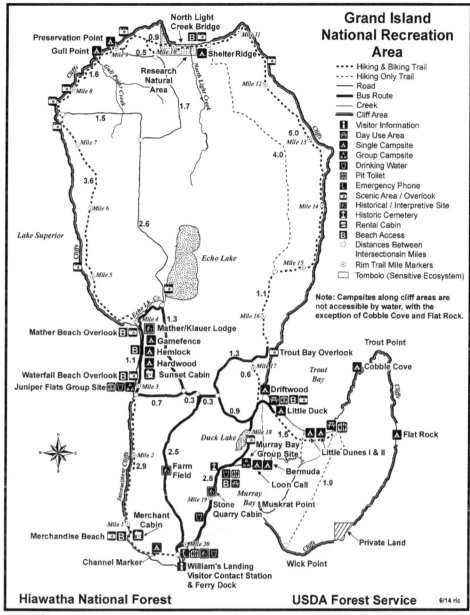

Courtesy of the USDA Forest Service

Contact Station at Williams Landing, and by the guides with the Altran Alger County Transit minibus tour.

How to Get There

Departure by passenger ferry to Grand Island is from Grand Island Landing in Munising, Michigan, which is located in the central Upper Peninsula of Michigan between the cities of Manistique and Marquette, on the south shore of Lake Superior.

The Grand Island Landing ferry dock is located off M-28, about 2.5 miles (four kilometers) west of Munising's one blinking light. The passenger ferry, after a .5-mile (.8 kilometer), ten-minute crossing of Munising Bay, docks at Williams Landing on the Grand Island and is operated by

Grand Island Ferry Service
N8016 Grand Island Landing Rd.
Munising, MI 49862
906-387-2600
www.grandislandup.com

The ferry operates from the beginning of June until the end of September. Note that traveling to and from the island in your own motorcraft may be hazardous.

What to Expect

A 10-minute passenger ferry ride will get you, and possibly your bike, if there's room (mountain biking is allowed on the trails; you can rent a bike from the Grand Island Ferry Service at Williams Landing), across the .5 mile (.8 kilometer) of the bay's West Channel, which is between Munising, "Place of the Great Island," and the island itself, to Grand Island. Williams Landing, where passengers disembark from the six-passenger pontoon boat, is the site of the Grand Island Visitor Contact Station as well as the place to embark on the Alger

Alger County Transit offers a two- to three-hour tour of both natural and historic island sites via the Grand Island Transportation minibus.

County Transit bus tour of the island. Visiting the small visitor center with its information boards and taking the two- to three-hour tour with 10 to 12 stops at points of interest are good ways to begin your island visit.

Rustic camping sites are available on the island. In addition, two Grand Island cabins are available to rent, both on the West Rim Trail: Merchant Cabin by Merchandise Beach and Sunset Cabin by Waterfall Beach.

Island wildlife includes some 12 to 20 black bears. Humans created problems in 2002 and 2014 when campers or tourists were apparently feeding some of the bears on the island, and the bears began seeking out campers looking for food. In response to the latest incidents, camping was suspended while eight black bears were trapped and removed from the island. If you camp, remember to follow good bear-country etiquette and make use of the food pole or box at your designated campsite and do *not* feed the bears. Other resident and visiting wildlife include white-tailed deer, sandhill cranes, bald eagles, American pine marten, mink, and fox.

Expect to feel much farther away from the mainland than .5 mile (.8 kilometer) and much farther away from your day-to-day than you may have expected.

Paths to Adventure

NATURAL SITES

Once you venture away from Williams Landing, you enter 13,500 acres of lush forest (only 40 of these acres are private property) with trails to hike or mountain bike. Grand Island has a 35-mile (56-kilometer) coastline featuring both pristine white sand beaches to enjoy and striking 300-foot wave-cut cliffs of Jacobsville and Munising sandstone and caves at which to marvel, whether you're backpacking or kayaking.

East Rim Trail and West Rim Trail—Two perimeter trails that run a total of 23 miles (37 kilometers) around the island. (The latter is the more scenic of the two.)

Murray Bay—A large open day-use area with picnic tables, grills, and a long stretch of beach as well as two campsites and a group site.

Duck Lake—A small, 20-acre lake, originally a Lake Superior lagoon, home to much of the island wildlife, especially waterfowl, is 2.5 miles (four kilometers) north of Williams Landing, just off the East Rim Trail, west of the tombolo in hemlock and pine forest.

The Tombolo—The sand ridge that connects the main body of Grand Island to its "thumb."

Trout Bay Overlook—An eastside overlook about 100 feet above Lake Superior provides a magnificent view of Pictured Rocks National Lakeshore. Four designated camping sites are located at the beach here.

Trout Bay Beach—This long stretch of arching sugar-sand beach connects the main body of Grand Island to its "thumb" and provides fantastic views of Trout Bay Cliffs.

North Beach—A beautiful secluded beach, 10 miles (16 kilometers) from Williams Landing, with white sand and cliffs.

Echo Lake—In the center of the main part of the island and in existence for many years, this lake was created from Echo Creek entirely by beavers' damming efforts and is, at about one mile (1.6 kilometers) long and just under .5 mile (.8 kilometer) wide, the largest such lake in the United States. The lake is known for bass and pike fishing.

Mather Beach Overlook—On the west side of the island, this beach provides some of the best views from Grand Island. Three campsites are here.

The beach at Trout Bay on Grand Island.

Waterfall Beach—South of Mather Beach, stairs lead down to a narrow cobbled beach below, much different from the sandy beaches found on the rest of the island. Nearby Williams Island and Wood Island are visible.

Thunder Cove Trail—This 800-foot trail runs along the hemlock- and pine-forested cliff's edge. The roar of the waves pounding in the rocky coves below gave this trail its name.

HISTORY PRESERVED

Grand Island has several historic buildings still standing, and artifacts dating back to 200 BC have been found on the island. Even if you just have an afternoon to spend on the island, it is worth taking the Altran Alger County Transit tour for a good overview of the island's history. Some stops on the tour may include:

Williams Landing—Named after the first European settler on Grand Island, Abraham Williams. The landing, situated as it is, makes the perfect place to land any sort of boat and surely has seen many sailors dock here over the different eras of the island.

Historic District—A few buildings remain from the resort era of the Williams Hotel, when Cleveland-Cliffs owned the island and Mather, the company president, was urging friends and business associates to build summer homes. These brown-painted buildings are sometimes referred to as the Brownies.

Farrell Cottage—One of the "Brownies," built in 1912 for Cleveland-Cliffs employee Austin Farrell by local contractor William Johnson. A large cottage, it has been renovated and is used by the Forest Service to house archaeologists and artists in residence. An artesian spring water faucet is located in front, and a small waterfall flows behind the cottage.

Stone Quarry Cabin—Built circa 1845 as a frontier cabin and named for the lakeside stone quarry near it, this is one of the oldest standing buildings anywhere on Lake Superior's shoreline. From 1900 to 1960, it was used as a part of Mather's resort. From the 1960s to the 1990s, its windows and flooring replaced, it served as a family cottage. In 1998, restoration began on the cabin by three organizations interested in preserving it. During the process of lifting the building to replace the foundation, a number of items from the past were found, and a team of archaeologists was called in to interpret the findings. The information board outside the cabin relating the archaeological examination of the site is a good start to imagining what history—outside the history books—this island has seen.

Grand Island Township Cemetery—The oldest non-Native cemetery in Alger County, located just west of Murray Bay. As well as non-Native island residents, shipwreck victims have been buried here, amid a number of unmarked graves. Today, only descendants of Abraham Williams and their spouses may be buried here.

Historic Mather Lodge—A six-bedroom cottage on the west shore built during the Mather era to house Mather and his hunting friends and purchased by the U.S. Forest Service in 2012. The Klauer Family and the Mather Foundation donate funds to support the restoration and preservation of the lodge, which currently serves as a museum and hosts summer archaeological field schools. In 2015, during restoration, the lodge became known as the Mather-Klauer Lodge.

Note: Both lighthouses on the island—the Grand Island East Channel Lighthouse and North Light—are on private property.

The historic Mather Lodge, built when much of Grand Island was William G. Mather's private game preserve.

OTHER ISLAND THINGS TO DO

View the island's flora—From late April through September. Grand Island is host to a number of Michigan native plant communities, from rich mesic northern hardwood forest and conifer swamps to Great Lakes shoreline with a unique dune-swale ecosystem and a tombolo to marshes. The island's diverse flora includes both boreal and southern species as well as western disjuncts. At an old five-acre farm field—where at one time, Williams employed Ojibwe in maple-sugaring and farming—native plant restoration is in progress. Since 2006, over 500,000 native wildflowers and grasses have been reintroduced to the island. For more information, see www.fs.fed.us/wildflowers/regions/eastern/GrandIslandNRA/index.shtml.

Dive the Alger Underwater Preserve—Located near Munising on Lake Superior's south shore, this preserve includes Pictured Rocks National Lakeshore, Grand Island, and Munising Bay and offers several unusual diving attractions including "sea caves," intact shipwrecks, and underwater interpretive trails.

Nearby: Mainland Munising offers Glass-Bottom Boat Shipwreck Tours. For more information, see www.shipwrecktours.com or call 906-387-4477.

SPECIAL ISLAND EVENTS

Michigan Ice Fest (February)—Sponsored by Munising, this event features instruction in ice-formation climbing on Grand Island and at Pictured Rocks National Lakeshore. For more information, see www.michiganicefest.com.

Free Fishing Weekends (two days, twice a year, in February and June)—For more information, see www.michigan.gov/freefishing.

Grand Island Trail Marathon & 10K (July)—For more information, see www.greatlakes endurance.com/michigan-races/grand-island-trail-marathon.html.

For More Island Information

USDA Forest Service
Hiawatha National Forest
Grand Island National Recreation Area (NRA)
Munising Ranger District
400 East Munising Ave.
Munising, MI 49862
906-387-3700
www.fs.fed.us (Enter "Grand Island" into search box for a listing of information sources for the island.)

Grand Island Ferry Service
N8016 Grand Island Landing Rd.
Munising, MI 49862
906-387-2600
www.grandislandup.com

U.P. Tourist Information Center
501 E. State
Hwy. M28
Munising, MI 49862
906-387-5710
www.exploremunising.com/tourist-center/

    The U.P. Tourist Information Center has area maps, brochures, and information on local attractions and businesses; an art gallery; and books, attire, and other gifts for sale.

The Grand Island Story, by Beatrice Hanscom Castle (Marquette, MI: Marquette County Historical Society, 1974).

A Face in the Rock: The Tale of a Grand Island Chippewa, by Loren R. Graham (Berkeley: University of California Press, 1999).

Death at the Lighthouse, by Loren R. Graham (Traverse City, MI: Arbutus, 2013).

How You Can Support the Island

Grand Island East Channel Lighthouse Rescue Project
c/o Alger County Historical Society
PO Box 201
Munising, MI 49862

Parting Thoughts

August 21, 2013, 6:00 p.m.
Williams Landing

On my next trip, I could hike the island's "thumb" on the other side of the tombolo, where the dunes are, certainly a doable day trip. But what I'd really like to hike is the West Rim Trail along the cliffs.

    When I ask him about it, Eric points out that the same bus Vicki and I have been riding on for the tour will provide special prearranged express service for hikers to the north end of the island. That would make the entire 10.5 to 12 miles or so of the West Rim Trail from the north end back to Williams Landing a day-trip possibility. I decide to believe that the second-best gift with which to leave an island—in lieu of actual island adventures, of course—could prove to be the ability to translate a newfound familiarity with the island into a return plan involving future adventures.

    Gray skies, bringing with them the threat of more lightning, help me quickly ascribe to this belief as the last boat of the day prepares to leave, ahead of schedule to avoid being prevented from doing so by the coming storm. The engine of the pontoon kicks to life, cutting short my fantasies of a return to this aptly named island. Instead, as we speed away, I focus on the island getting smaller and darker against the gathering storm

St. Marys River Islands

Ontario

North St. Marys Island, ON
South St. Marys Island, ON

Sault Ste.
Marie, ON

Island Number 1

Lake Superior

Whitefish
Island

"The Island"

Sault Ste.
Marie, MI

Sugar
Island

Barbeau

Neebish
Island

Little Neebish
(Rains) Island

Michigan

St.
Marys
River

N
W E
S

Lake Huron

An Introduction to the St. Marys River

Today, the St. Marys River serves as part of the boundary between Canada and the United States, the border that falls between the eastern shore of Michigan's Upper Peninsula and a western edge of southeastern Ontario. But what has probably *always* been the very big deal about the St. Marys River are the rapids, located between Sault Ste. Marie, Michigan, and Whitefish Island on the Canadian side of the river. In its length of 74.5 miles (120 kilometers), the St. Marys River drops 23 feet in elevation during its downstream flow between the basins of Lake Superior and Lake Huron. The river flows from Whitefish Bay in Lake Superior southeast under the Sault Ste. Marie International Bridge, which connects the twin cities of Sault Ste. Marie, Michigan, and Sault Ste. Marie, Ontario, two parts of one city until after the War of 1812. Then there is a 20-foot drop within just the one-mile (1.6-kilometer) stretch of the St. Marys Rapids. At the rate of 73,700 cubic feet per second, the St. Marys flows out to Lake Huron past a jumble of "puzzle-piece" islands.

Along its course, the river splits around the American Sugar Island, for a time becoming Lake Nicolet to the west and then emerging through the Detour Passage between the Upper Peninsula of Michigan and the American Drummond Island—where the Drummond Island vehicle ferry crosses regularly—to the main basin of Lake Huron. The 74-foot-tall DeTour Reef Light welcomes watercraft to Lake Huron or to the St. Marys River, depending on which way the boat is headed.

On the east side of Sugar Island, for a bit, the river is known as Lake Huron, and it is this side that carries the international border to Canada's St. Joseph Island, where the St. Marys River laps against the western shore, and on the eastern side, the St. Joseph Channel leads into North Channel of the Canadian Georgian Bay. (Georgian Bay might have been a sixth Great Lake—or seventh, if you're counting the basin's secondary Lake Nipigon—but for the expanse of open water between Manitoulin Island and the Bruce Peninsula that connects Georgian Bay to the main basin of Lake Huron.)

At the southern tip of the American Neebish Island, ship traffic on the St. Marys River splits. Vessels headed upstream (to Lake Superior) pass the easterly coast, between Neebish Island and St. Joseph Island. Ships headed downriver (to Lake Huron) take the westerly route, through an artificial cut 900 feet long and 300 feet wide, between Neebish Island and the mainland of Michigan's Upper Peninsula. The Neebish Island Ferry crosses this route at the northern end of the cut, which leads into the Munuscong Lake area of the river.

Before any such cut, the United States, or Canada existed, French explorer Étienne Brûlé and his companion Grenolle were the first known Europeans to travel up the St. Marys River, in a journey undertaken between 1621 and 1623. The earliest European name we know of the rapids—the Sault de Gaston (named for the French king's brother)—appears on Samuel de

Champlain's map of 1632. *Sault* is old French for "falls" or "rapids" that "tumble or roll" and is related to the verb "to jump" (*sauter*). Watching the rapids tumbling over the river's rocks, you can easily imagine the water is jumping.

In 1641, the Jesuit priests Isaac Jogues and Charles Raymbault, following Brûlé's route, named the river St. Marie. They found some 2,000 Ojibwe at the rapids, and the French referred to them as Saulteaux (people of the falls). In 1668, Father Jacques Marquette and Father Claude Dablon established the first mission in Michigan here, naming it Le Sault Sainte-Marie. The mission chapel and its residence may have been the first permanent buildings in what was to become Michigan. They were the first buildings of the fur-trading settlement that built up around them and, as such, became the first European-established city of the Midwest. Today, Michiganders refer to the area as the Soo.

The Ojibwe name for this place is Baawitigong (or Bawating), which means the "Place of the Rapids." The river's nature—both how the water flowed and the nature supported by the river—made the river important to Native people, most recently the migrating Ojibwe. Historically, according to the Lake Superior State University Aquatic Research Lab, the St. Marys Rapids provided one of the most productive habitats for fish on the entire continent. Baawitigong was known as a gathering place, primarily because of the plentiful whitefish that could be caught in these rapids. Once the trading post was established, other locally available resources in addition to the whitefish, such as furs and maple sugar, brought the Ojibwe and French together.

There were only two choices for navigating past these rapids: portage boats and cargo around the falls (the route on the Michigan shore where that transpired is now known as Portage Avenue) or make alterations to the shore. As early as 1797, the North West Company began building a small canal on the Canadian side for canoes, but this was destroyed by the Americans in 1814 during the War of 1812. In 1853, with the construction of the State Lock, an effort was begun on the U.S. side of the river. In 1881, the U.S. secretary of war took possession of the lock and a second lock, the Weitzel Lock, that opened that year. In 1896, the Poe Lock opened. In 1914, the Davis Lock, rarely used today, opened and in 1919 the Sabin Lock, which is no longer used, opened. The McArthur Lock opened at the site of the old Weitzel Lock in 1943. A new Poe Lock opened in 1969 on the site of the old Poe Lock.

In 1870, the infamous *Chicora* Incident led to the need for the Canadians to build their own lock, which was completed in 1895. This lock experienced a wall failure and was closed in 1987. It was reopened in 1998 with a new lock—now used exclusively for recreational and tour boats—built inside the old lock.

THE *CHICORA* INCIDENT

Anglo-Irish colonel Garnet Wolseley was on his way to suppress the Canadian Red River Rebellion led by métis leader Louis Riel in the area of Fort Garry (now known as Winnipeg). It was 1870, shortly after the end of the American Civil War, and Colonel Wolseley, in the service of the British Army, was traveling aboard the SS *Chicora*. Did I mention the SS *Chicora* had formerly been a blockade-runner during the Civil War? Wolseley was refused use of the American lock for his "foreign" military expedition by the American government, via Michigan governor H. P Baldwin. Wolseley emptied the steamer of soldiers, munitions, and supplies, which had to be transported overland in Ontario, between Lake Huron and Lake Superior, and then attempted to get the empty steamer through. However, the ship was still prevented from using the lock for two weeks until the issue was resolved between the two countries.

Today, the use of the locks on either side of the border is free of charge for any vessel, from Big Paul, the "thousand-footer" MV *Paul R. Tregurtha* lake freighter, to the smallest pleasure craft.

Geographically and/or historically, the locks are related to four of the eight St. Marys River islands: on the Canadian side of the river North St. Marys Island, South St. Marys Island, and Whitefish Island, and on the American side "The Island" (the downtown area of Sault Ste. Marie, Michigan). The other "puzzle pieces" of islands in the St. Marys River (which are American and accessible by bridge or ferry) are Island No. 1, Sugar Island, Neebish Island, and Little Neebish Island (also known—particularly in the past and on the Canadian side of the border—as Rains Island, after an early British settler).

Near the mouth of the St. Marys River are two very large islands: the Canadian St. Joseph Island, accessible by bridge, and the American Drummond Island, accessible by ferry. Both of these islands, along with two very small residential islands accessible by bridge—Pine Island and Brown's Island—are more often identified as Lake Huron islands.

Islands at Sault Ste. Marie, Michigan and Ontario

THERE'S MORE AT THE "SOO" THAN LOCKS

July 19, 2013, 4:00 p.m.
On Nokomis
St. Marys River

Michelene and I make it to the dock just in time for the two-and-a-half-hour, 10-mile, international Soo Locks Boat Tour. *Nokomis*, our 65-foot-long, 25-foot-wide vessel, licensed to carry 280 passengers but carrying nowhere near that many at the end of the day—a good time to take the trip, apparently—heads out onto the St. Marys River and into late afternoon sun glinting off the river in all directions.

What I plan to overcome in engaging with this area is my own unappreciative grade-school self. In fifth grade, we learned that Sault Ste. Marie is "the oldest city in the Midwest." Very cool now. But—yawn—sorry, Mr. Toth, boring then. Earlier, in third grade, from our first social studies book, we were supposed to be learning about these very American locks, the ones we're headed toward right now. But everything involved with the building and running of them were guy things: the designing, the excavating, the engineering, even the ships going through them. Girls couldn't do any of that stuff then, not even when they grew up. So none of it interested me then, and I didn't pay much attention. On this trip, I have more than a few things I want to catch up on . . .

We learn that the freighters waiting to go through the American locks are behind schedule by 45 minutes, so our captain, John Lowes, swings the *Nokomis* around to the single relatively small Canadian lock. When the original Canadian lock was completed in 1895, the historic Sault Ste. Marie Canal was the last link in an all-Canadian navigation route from Lake Superior to the St. Lawrence River. Then, it was the world's longest lock and the first lock to be operated with electric power. Now, under Parks Canada, the lock itself has been used solely for recreational and tour boats since 1998, when the current iteration was built within the older lock that failed in 1987.

As we approach the lock's open gate at the Lake Huron water level, we have a spectacular view of the Sault Ste. Marie International Bridge, a steel truss arch affair. A knot of towheaded siblings hangs over our boat's railing, the fifth-grade girl as eager as I am to see just how this works. In the *Nokomis* goes, as if she were entering a large concrete and roofless boathouse, full of late afternoon shadow, and heads directly for what appears to be a solid wall ahead of us in the water. Behind us, we watch the sides of the lock in one area transform themselves into large lock gates, as they appear from out of the sidewalls and begin to close. Heavy ropes are tossed, looped in figure eights, and tightened around posts, one end of the line up on the side of the canal, the other on the deck of the boat. Steep concrete walls are on either side of us. Then, as the captain explains the process, we begin to rise until eventually we are back in the sun, level with the concrete walkways and green grass beside us. The gates before us open and we sail out, past several beautiful red sandstone historic buildings trimmed in white limestone, and slip between two of the three Sault Ste. Marie, Ontario, islands I've come here to visit: North St. Marys and South St. Marys, which I suspect were—pre-lock—one and the same island. I'm particularly looking forward to visiting the third island, Whitefish Island, tomorrow.

GETTING THERE: All of these islands are accessible by bridges

GETTING AROUND: Bring your own car/bike
    Foot traffic only on South St. Marys Island and Whitefish Island
    Orient yourself with a boat tour through the Soo Locks

OVERNIGHT ACCOMMODATIONS: B&Bs, hotels, and motels are available in Sault Ste. Marie, MI, and Sault Ste. Marie, ON
    No camping on Whitefish Island, North or South St. Marys Islands, or "The Island"
    Camping is available in the areas surrounding the St. Marys River islands on both sides of the border

FOOD: Restaurants and groceries only in downtown Sault Ste. Marie, MI (or areas surrounding the islands on either side of the border, including Sault Ste. Marie, ON)
    Snack bar on North St. Marys Island at the Sault Ste. Marie Visitor Centre
    Sunday afternoon tea is occasionally served in the historic Superintendent's Residence on the Sault Ste. Marie Canal

DAY TRIP? Yes; only option for Canadian islands at the Soo

STATE / PROVINCIAL / NATIONAL PARK? Sault Ste. Marie Canal National Historic Site in Ontario is managed by Parks Canada

Many visitors to Sault Ste. Marie, Michigan, or Sault Ste. Marie, Ontario, the sister cities connected by the Sault Ste. Marie International Bridge, take the boat tour through the locks in order to experience them firsthand. Islands are not always what one thinks about in this area, but islands there are! Four of the islands in the Sault Ste. Marie area, on both sides of the border, offer different lock-related adventures accessible by foot.

North St. Marys Island—On the Canadian side of the river, this island once formed a single island with South St. Marys Island before it was divided by construction of the Sault Ste. Marie Canal. North St. Marys is accessible by vehicular bridge on Canal Drive and is home to a number of historic buildings related to the Sault Ste. Marie Canal and the Canadian lock, maintained by Parks Canada as the Sault Ste. Marie Canal National Historic Site.

South St. Marys Island—Accessible by a pedestrian bridge across the actual lock gates when they are closed, this island is in more of a natural state, with trails but no structures on it.

Whitefish Island—At one time separated from St. Marys Island by the Whitefish Channel, which, since 1855, has primarily dried up due to the construction of the American and Canadian locks and the use of compensating dams to control water levels, this island was once claimed by Canada, but its possession was restored to the Batchewana First Nation. The island is accessed by new pedestrian bridges.

"The Island"—The fast-running water of the St Marys proved more than just a hindrance to travelers on the river; to take advantage of its power, three hydroelectric power plants were built in the Soo area. One of these, the Saint Marys Falls Hydropower Plant south of the locks, begun in 1898, is at the eastern end of the Edison Sault Power Canal, a 2.25-mile (3.62-kilometer) canal that separates downtown Sault Ste. Marie from the mainland. In giving directions, locals refer to this area of Sault Ste. Marie as "the Island." This artificial island is accessible by seven vehicular bridges.

One interesting island story among many about this particular location on the river involves Whitefish Island, a 22-acre island over which the international bridge passes. This island today belongs to neither the United States nor Canada.

The Sault Ste. Marie Canal, completed in 1895, cut through the island originally known as St. Marys Island. When the railroad crossed the river, a portion of Whitefish Island, St. Marys Island's neighbor, was expropriated, between 1902 and 1913, as railroad territory, after which the remainder of Whitefish Island became a Parks Canada property. In 1981, the island was designated as a National Historic Site of Canada, based on it being at the location of the historic Sault Ste. Marie Canal.

However, the island no longer belongs to Canada; it never really did. Native people have used this 22-acre island for over 2,000 years. "Two treaties, the 1850 Robinson Huron and the 1859 Pennefather, specifically retained Whitefish Island and the small islands used as fishing stations for [the Batchewana First Nation of Ojibways'] benefit and use," according to the sign welcoming visitors on the island. However, at the beginning of the twentieth century, the federal government gave the land to railway companies. Whitefish Island residents and the Anishinaabe Burial Grounds were moved off the island by 1906 and the land was taken over.

The Batchewana First Nation's legal rights to Whitefish Island were restored—under the treaty with Britain in 1850—after an 18-year legal battle that began in 1980 with the legal process, leading to filing a land claim in 1982 and continuing with the occupation of the island by Chief Edward James Sayers Nebenaigoching, first with a group of family and friends and then alone, beginning in 1989. The occupation ended when the claim was settled in 1992. Damages of $3.5 million were paid and the island was returned to "Indian reserve" status as the Whitefish Island Reserve of the Batchewana First Nation in 1998.

Today, the Batchewana First Nation is in the process of building an educational, cultural, and interpretive center on the island. Phase 1 of the project, which included installing bridges, establishing wide trails, and building a traditional village of birch-bark wigwams, a smokehouse, and a longhouse, was achieved through a partnership with Parks Canada and Brookfield Power. The structures were created using the skills of the Anishinaabe people on both sides of the international border. Part of the project has included building a boardwalk that provides the very best view of the St. Marys Rapids, which, by the way, were much more impressive, according to historic accounts, before the river and its water level underwent the human-directed transformation involving canals, locks, and dams.

A second phase of the Batchewana First Nation project on Whitefish Island will be a second village that re-creates the setting experienced by the island residents around the 1900s before they were forced from the islands to allow for development.

Whitefish Island is not the only land—and there are no *occupied* structures on this island—that belongs to the Batchewana First Nation, nor is it the only First Nation land along or on islands in the St. Marys River. The Batchewana First Nation of Ojibways is located in the northeastern corner of Lake Superior and the St. Marys River area, adjacent to the city of Sault Ste. Marie, Ontario. This First Nation has a total population of 2,400, of which approximately 72 percent live off the reserve. Batchewana First Nation is comprised of four reserve communities: Rankin Reserve, Goulais Bay Reserve, Obadjiwan Reserve, and Whitefish Island Reserve. The administrative offices are located on Rankin Reserve, which is bordered on three sides by the city of Sault Ste. Marie, Ontario, and the St. Marys River on the fourth.

The Sault Ste. Marie Tribe of Chippewa Indians, commonly shortened to Sault Tribe of Chippewa Indians or the more colloquial Soo Tribe, is an indigenous community located in what is now Michigan's Upper Peninsula. The tribal headquarters are in the major city of the region, Sault Ste. Marie. The area was originally known as Baawitigong by Native residents of the region prior to Europeans arriving in the mid- to late 1500s. Baawitigong, sometimes written as Bawating or Bahweting, is an Ojibwe word meaning the "Place of the Rapids." Historically, these rapids became a gathering place for the five major clans of the Ojibwe nation.[12]

Known in Ojibwe as Gnoozhekaaning, or Place of the Pike, the Bay Mills Indian Community (BMIC) is an Indian reservation forming the land base of one of the many Sault Ste. Marie bands of Chippewa Indians (not to be confused with the Sault Ste. Marie Tribe of Chippewa Indians located in Sault Ste. Marie, Michigan). The largest section of the reservation is located in Chippewa County, Michigan, approximately 15 miles (24 kilometers) west-southwest of Sault Ste. Marie, in Bay Mills Township and Superior Township. A smaller section lies on the western side of Sugar Island, an island in the St. Marys River accessible by vehicle ferry.

How to Get There

On either side of the international border, head for the Soo! Either Sault Ste. Marie at the northeast edge of the Upper Peninsula of Michigan or Sault Ste. Marie, Ontario, right across the river from it.

In the United States, take I-75 north through Michigan until the interstate highway ends at the Sault Ste. Marie International Bridge at the northeastern tip of Michigan's Upper Peninsula. In Canada, take Ontario Highway 17 to Highway 550 to Carmen's Way and follow the approach to the Sault Ste. Marie International Bridge (Queen Street West to Huron Street).

To visit the community and its attractions across the river from your point of origin, merely drive across the Sault Ste. Marie International Bridge and go through U.S./Canadian Customs. Approaching the bridge from either country, be sure to follow the signage to get off the highway if you do not intend to cross the international border.

What to Expect

Besides the Soo Lock Boat Tour, there are a number of other things to see on the four islands at these twin cities straddling the U.S.-Canadian border. But, of course, the rapids are the reason for all that is here, the oldest European settlement in what was to become the Midwest as well as the locks. However, today, the St. Marys Rapids have been so significantly altered by canals, locks, and dams they are only about *a quarter of the size* they were when the Ojibwe gathered freely at this Place of the Rapids to fish and when the first Europeans portaged these jumping waters.

Looking north past the much-diminished rapids of the St. Marys River from Whitefish Island, a historic Ojibwe fishing station, to the Sault Ste. Marie International Bridge and historic International Sault Ste. Marie International Railway Bridge, with "The Island" of downtown Sault Ste. Marie, Michigan, on the opposite bank.

These same alterations caused the entire St. Marys River to be designated as an Area of Concern by the US-Canada Great Lakes Water Quality Agreement in 1985: "Centuries of channel modifications, and industrial and urban development have diminished the river's ability to support healthy fish and wildlife populations."[13] However, on the majority of the accessible islands on the St. Marys River, you can witness at least the appearance of a balance, perhaps the first indication of a return to a lost nature.

Paths to Adventure

NATURAL SITES

Whitefish Island (on the Canadian side)—The Attikamek Nature Trail, an easy 1.3-mile (2.1-kilometer) trail, affords the best spot from which to view the St. Marys Rapids. *Attikamek* is Ojibwe for "caribou of the waters," a reference to the onetime bountiful whitefish found here.

To access Whitefish Island, cross the walkway atop either of the gates of the Canadian lock from North St. Marys Island to South St. Marys, and then follow the trail to the bridge crossing over a channel from South St. Marys Island to Whitefish Island.

Winding through cranberry, chokecherry, hawthorn, and other fruit-bearing shrubs that support birds and small mammals (mink, muskrat, beaver) and leading you past numerous beaver dens, the nature trail on this piece of wildness—so close to an urban area—also extends under the Sault Ste. Marie International Bridge.

When you reach the island's south shoreline, you may find people fishing, knee-deep, in the rapids.

HISTORY PRESERVED

The John Johnston Family Home (405 E. Water St., Sault Ste. Marie, MI)—A 1941 plaque placed by the Sault Ste. Marie Chamber of Commerce on a large stone to the side of the building's front door commemorates the "Former Home and Trading Post of the John Johnston Family; second-oldest building in the Northwest, built in 1795–96. Here, in 1824, Henry Rowe Schoolcraft, Historian, married Jane, daughter of Johnston and his Ojibwe wife, descendant of Chief Waub-O Jeeg."

Wadjiwong (Brady Park, Sault Ste. Marie, MI)—An ancient Anishinaabe burial ground (*wadjiwong* means "hill" in Ojibwe) along the St. Marys River, just east of the Soo Locks, that was used for hundreds of years. In 1999, the Sault Ste. Marie Tribe of Chippewa Indians and the Bay Mills Indian Community were notified about a project proposed by the U.S. Army Corps of Engineers for Brady Park. The tribes did not want the site disturbed. Negotiations began in 2004 between the two tribes, the City of Sault Ste. Marie, and the Army Corps of Engineers. Ultimately in 2005, with the 150th anniversary of the Soo Locks approaching, 1,200 feet of steel picket fencing was installed to protect the burial ground, and the tribes hosted a memorial dedication. The burial ground has four spirit houses and traditional burial markers bearing the person's clan symbol. The upside-down crane on the arch above the gate marks the place as a burial ground. For more information, see http://indiancountrytodaymedianetwork.com/2009/07/16/cooperation-protect-84773.

Parks Canada Sault Ste. Marie Canal, National Historic Site of Canada (North St. Marys Island, ON)—Completed in 1895, the canal that formed the last link in an all-Canadian

The Soo Locks tour boat *Nokomis* emerging between the opening gates from the chamber of the Canadian lock, having circumvented the 23-foot drop of the St. Marys River between Lake Superior and Lake Huron at the St. Marys Rapids.

navigation system stretching from the St. Lawrence River to Lake Superior. At the time, it was the world's longest lock (274 meters long and 18 meters wide; that's 300 yards long and 20 feet wide) and the first to be operated by electric power. After a lock wall failure in 1987, it was rebuilt and reopened for recreational use in 1998.

Museum Ship Valley Camp (501 E. Water St., Sault Ste. Marie, MI)—A Great Lakes freighter containing a 20,000-square-foot museum with over 100 exhibits in its cargo hold.

River of History Museum (531 Ashmun St., Sault Ste. Marie, MI)—Opened by the Sault Ste. Foundation for Culture and History in 1992 to preserve and promote the history of the St. Marys River.

Canadian Bushplane Heritage Center (50 Pim St., Sault Ste. Marie, ON)—Dedicated to preserving the history of bush flying and forest protection in Canada.

CULTURAL ATTRACTIONS

Soo Locks Visitor Center (312 W. Portage Ave., Sault Ste. Marie, MI)—Alongside the American locks, you'll find a park and a visitor center with a three-story observation deck that puts you right next to the ships coming through the locks.

Soo Locks Boat Tours (1157 E. Portage Ave. or 515 E. Portage, Sault Ste. Marie, MI)—"Ride with the Freighters" is the company's motto, and its boats have been taking passengers on tours since 1934. Today the company has five tour boats, two docking facilities, and a website (www.soolocks.com) that describes available tours and cruises: sightseeing tours, lighthouse cruises, themed dinner cruises, fireworks cruises, dinner cruises, fireworks dinner cruises, luncheon cruises, special cruises, and charter cruises.

John Rowswell Hub Trail (Sault Ste. Marie, ON)—A 16-mile (25-kilometer) multiuse, non-motorized trial system that connects many points of interest, including the waterfront walkway, Bellevue Park, Algoma University, Sault College, and the Fort Creek Conservation area, linking together culture, historical, and natural areas of the community. The trail is named after a former mayor of Sault Ste. Marie, Ontario, who was elected for three terms (2000–2010) and under whose watch the Hub Trail was developed.

Clergue Park and the Waterfront Walkway (Sault Ste. Marie, ON)—Clergue Park is a riverfront park that serves as a venue for many special events in the city. The waterfront boardwalk runs from the Great Lakes Power Plant on Canal Drive to Roberta Bondar Park and ends at the Civic Centre on Foster Drive.

Tower of History (326 East Portage Ave., Sault Ste. Marie, MI)—A 210-foot tower provides impressive views of the locks and the world's busiest inland shipping channel.

SPECIAL ISLAND EVENTS

Annual International 500 Snowmobile Race (February)—"NASCAR on Ice" in the Upper Peninsula (www.i-500.com/the-race/more-than-a-race/).

Sault Ste. Marie: Soo Locks Engineers Weekend (June).

Rendezvous in the Sault (July)—A weekend of living history (1668–1840) event that takes place along historic Water Street and showcases the historic homes of John and Susan Johnston, Henry Rowe and Jane Johnson Schoolcraft, and Bishop Frederic Baraga. (www.historicwaterstreet.org/rendezvous/index.htm).

Sault International Marathon (September)—Full and half marathon distances across the Sault Ste. Marie International Bridge and along the St. Marys River.

For More Information

Sault Ste. Marie Canal Historic Site—www.pc.gc.ca/eng/lhn-nhs/on/ssmarie.

Whitefish Island—www.batchewana.ca/content/content.html?page=17.

Sault Ste. Marie, ON—www.city.sault-ste-marie.on.ca.

Sault Ste. Marie, MI Chamber of Commerce—www.saultstemarie.org.

Sault Ste. Marie Visitors Bureau, UP Northern Michigan—www.saultstemarie.com.

Sault Ste. Marie Ontario, Canada—www.saulttourism.com.

City of the Rapids: Sault Ste. Marie's Heritage, by Bernard Arbic (Allegan Forest, MI: Priscilla, 2003).

Upbound Downbound: The Story of the Soo Locks, by Bernard Arbic (Allegan Forest, MI: Priscilla, 2005).

Locks and Ships, vol. 5, by Soo Locks Boat Tours (Sault Ste. Marie, MI: Reed Books, 2010).

Sault Ste. Marie, City by the Rapids: An Illustrated History, by Frances M. Heath (Windsor: Windsor, 1988).

The Mighty Soo: Five Hundred Years at Sault Ste. Marie, by Clara Ingram Judson (Chicago: Follett, 1955)—Written for young people by a biographer, this book, according the author in her foreword, is a "biography of a place: of one square mile [2.6 square kilometers] of land and water at Sault Ste. Marie."

The Border at Sault Ste. Marie, by Graeme S. Mount, John Abbott, and Michael J. Mulloy (Toronto: Dundurn, 1995).

"Area 5: St. Mary's River," in *The North Channel and St. Mary's River: A Guide to the History,* by Andrea Gutsche, Barbar Chisholm, and Russel Floren (Toronto: Lynx Images, 1997).

How You Can Support St. Marys River Islands

St. Marys River Bi-national Public Advisory Council (BPAC)
www.lssu.edu/bpac/

The St. Marys River Bi-national Public Advisory Council is a stakeholders' and citizens' group with representatives from both Canada and the United States. The BPAC is dedicated to ensuring that the river quality and the ecosystem are improved and protected for all users of the river.

Parting Thoughts

July 20, 2013
Whitefish Island at the Rapids

Having spent last evening exploring "The Island"—the downtown area of Sault Ste. Marie, Michigan—this morning we crossed the Sault Ste. Marie International Bridge to Ontario by car, parked on a city street, and headed for the river and the Canadian Sault Ste. Marie islands on foot.

We walked along the river on the St. Marys River Boardwalk, the downtown waterfront section of the John Rowswell Hub Trail, from today's bustling Rotaryfest site at Roberta Bondar Park, where three tall ships were docked on their tour commemorating the military events of the War of 1812, to the Canadian lock our tour boat had gone through yesterday. On our way, we crossed the pretty white arching footbridge across a small offshoot of the river, where mallards congregate and Queen Anne's lace, purple-stemmed aster, and sweet white clover bloom in abundance above the bank's rubble, punctuated by the occasional patch of daisies and the yellow punch of common tansy. We passed the historic marker for the North West Company fur-trading post, which moved here in 1797 and became a Hudson's Bay Company post in 1821, and arrived at a sign for the Sault Ste. Marie Canal, a National Historic Site of Canada. From atop the canal wall, we watched *Nokomis*, our tour boat of yesterday, go through the lock, and we waved to the passengers.

Then we set off to take a look at the beautiful red sandstone historical buildings built in the late 1800s on North St. Marys Island: the administration building, the superintendent's residence, the canalmen's shelter, the powerhouse, and the stores/blacksmith workshop. The sandstone was dug up and cut into blocks in the course of the canal's construction. The visitor center, located in the powerhouse, presents the story of the design, construction, and operation of the canal in the context of the Great Lakes–St. Lawrence Seaway. It was worth stepping inside just to see the "Great Lakes-St. Lawrence Waterway Today" exhibit, which showed the different levels of the bodies of water that flow from Lake Superior to the Atlantic Ocean over 1,392 miles (2,240 kilometers).

We strolled back out and across the railed top of the gates of the lock to get from North St. Marys Island, the historical canal site, to South St. Mary on the other side of the canal and onto the Attikamek Trail leading to Whitefish Island of the Batchewana First Nation of Ojibways which, according to one of the posted signs, has been used by Natives for over 2,000 years. In 1641, when the Jesuits arrived, there were about 2,000 Natives at the rapids.

Here, we read the interpretive signs and take in what is around us from a number of observation areas. What we see: a series of beaver dams built across a channel that leads toward the best view of the international bridge in the distance, orange hawkweed in bloom, the graceful bones of several Native structures, the beautiful red-patterned sandstone—the same sandstone that was used to build the historical buildings, but here it is not cut, has moss growing on it— birch trees and a teepee covered in birch bark and, in the longhouse, a long black snake with a bright yellow stripe and a lump of lunch in the middle of its length. At the shore, clumps of water iris and out in the rapids men in waders are fishing. The blue sky is reflected in the river, the sun jumping in the rapids. Here, one can begin to imagine what this river might once have been. Now, one can imagine what this island must once have meant.

Islands of the Lower St. Marys River, Michigan

SWEET SPOTS OF REMOTENESS

July 21, 2013, 9:30 a.m.
Aboard Sugar Island II

We drive southeast along the river in Sault Ste. Marie toward the historic Clyde's Drive-in Restaurant. At Clyde's, always one of the Soo's highest-rated restaurants, you can watch the freighters go by up close while enjoying selections from a menu that includes a 3/4-pound cheeseburger, a buffalo burger, and six flavors of shakes and malts—and the ambiance of a dining experience from the 1950s. One diner claims that her parents had eaten there as teenagers over 64 years ago. Lunch is as good as the reviews.

Between Aune-Osborn Campground and Clyde's, we catch the vehicle ferry *Sugar Island II* to Sugar Island, a mostly undeveloped forested island. An easy ferry to catch, it makes the round trip twice an hour except during the wee hours, when it runs just once an hour for a few trips. Cash only; you pay for the round trip on your way over.

The ferry lets us off on Island No. 1, one of several islands in the St. Marys River that were named with numbers when government surveyors' creativity faltered (all those islands!). From Island No. 1, disembarking vehicles drive across the causeway, 1½ Mile Road (and another small island, unnamed *and* unnumbered, perhaps man-made) onto Sugar Island Road. Toward the east, the road rises up before us.

GETTING THERE: Sugar Island and Neebish Island by car ferry
Little Neebish by causeway from Neebish Island

GETTING AROUND: Bring your own car and bike
Fishing boats and outboard motors available on Neebish Island

OVERNIGHT ACCOMMODATIONS: Sugar Island: Vacation rentals
Neebish Island Resort: Cabins, balcony apartments, and campground

FOOD: Sugar Island: groceries at Ed & Esther's Bayview Store
Neebish Island: groceries at Neebish Country Store

DAY TRIP? Yes, or camping destination

STATE / PROVINCIAL / NATIONAL PARK? No

In addition to the four islands at the Soo, there are four other accessible islands that almost fill the St. Marys River, from bank to bank, like puzzle pieces. These islands farther downstream are accessible from the Michigan mainland in batches of two, by ferry: Island No. 1, at which the Sugar Island ferry lands, and Michigan's Sugar Island, Michigan's Neebish Island, and Little Neebish Island (also known as Rains Island), accessible from Neebish Island by bridge.

Because of the abundance of sugar maple trees on the island, the Native people call Sugar Island *Sisibakmatominis* (Maple Sugar Island). It must be beautiful in the fall, with dark evergreen punctuating all the orange. This island is big: 49 square miles (127 kilometers) with a population of under 700. In 1945, Sugar Island was nominated as a location for the United Nations. Both the Bay Mills Indian Community and the Sault Tribe of Chippewa Indians have reservations on the island.

How to Get There

The ferry *Sugar Islander II,* run by the Eastern Upper Peninsula Transportation Authority (EUPTA), plys the river, a very short distance, between Sault Ste. Marie, Michigan, and Sugar Island. The ferry dock is located about 2.5 miles (6.5 kilometers) south from the Soo Locks Park Visitor Center (site of the Locks Observation Platform) in downtown Sault Ste. Marie. Take W. Portage Avenue, which becomes Riverside Drive southeast of the downtown area. If you are coming from the south, taking I-75 to East Three Mile Road and then heading north on Riverside Drive when you come to the river may be the easiest route. For an up-to-date ferry schedule to Sugar Island, see http://eupta.net/userfiles/files/sugar.pdf.

The ferry *Neebish Islander II,* also run by EUPTA, makes the quick trip between Barbeau, Michigan, and Neebish Island. If you were to follow the river southeast from the Soo or northwest from De Tour Village on South Scenic Drive just south of 15 Mile Road, you'd come to East Neebish Ferry Road in Barbeau, Michigan (not to be confused with the actual East Neebish *Island*, across the St. Marys River—not accessible by ferry or bridge—located just east of Sugar Island and belonging to Ontario). For an up-to-date ferry schedule to Neebish Island, see http://eupta.net/userfiles/files/neebish.pdf.

Little Neebish Island (also known, particularly to Canadians, as Rains Island) is attached to the southeast end of Neebish Island on South Parr Road, just south of East 17½ Mile Road by bridge across what you may hear called the "dark hole" or the "black hole."

What to Expect

Expect deep forest, some (for the most part out-of-view) cottages, and very few people on each of the three inhabited islands (Island No. 1 is uninhabited; the ferry landing is at the northwest tip of it.)

Paths to Adventure: Sugar Island

NATURAL SITES

The University of Michigan Biological Station (UMBS) operates the Chase Osborn Preserve, a 3,200-acre site near the southern tip of the island and one of only 47 biosphere reserves in the United States. Founded in 1909, the UMBS has 150 buildings and a full-time staff of 15. The station is measuring climate change. The UMBS is home to Michigan's most endangered species and one of the most endangered worldwide: Hungerford's crawling water beetle, which lives in only five isolated locations in Michigan and Ontario.

Bailey Lagerstrom Nature Preserve—422 acres with over two miles (five kilometers) on the St. Marys River. Billed as one of Little Traverse Conservancy's "largest, wildest and most remote nature preserves," it is reportedly an excellent spot for viewing migratory great gray and snowy owls (http://arc2earth1954390720.s3.amazonaws.com/LTC_Preserves/preserve_pdf/Bailey_Lagerstrom.pdf).

Other preserves dot the island: Cook Island, Koren, and Pickering Hay Point.

HISTORY PRESERVED

Willwalk Native American Cemetery (also written "Will Walk" and "Wilwalk")—A beautiful setting filled with traditional, and some not-so-traditional, grave markers, including sculptures of Native chiefs, warriors, and bears; spirit houses; and fenced manicured gardens.

Holy Angels Catholic Church—"Built by Bishop Baraga circa 1856" reads a penciled addition to the church's sign.

1926 Finn Hall—Sugar Island Historical Preservation Society's Restoration Project (at the intersection of S. Homestead Road and E. 6½ Mile Road).

Mary Murray Culture Camp (Sugar Island)—The Sault Tribe considers Sugar Island a part of its ancestral homeland and facilitates the Mary Murray Culture Camp (also known as the Sugar Island Culture Camp), founded in 1975 to provide a place to maintain and preserve the tribe's traditional way of life.

CULTURAL ATTRACTIONS

Ed & Esther's Bayview Store—"Hunting & Fishing Licenses, Gas, Ice Cream, Souveniers [*sic*], Groceries, Beer-Wine." (The hand-lettered sign on the door reads, "Yes, We're Open, or Ed Forgot to Change the Sign.")

A spirit house in Willwalk Native American Cemetery on Sugar Island.

NEEBISH ISLAND AND LITTLE NEEBISH ISLAND (MICHIGAN)

Neebish Island is primarily a fishing-and-hunting sort of island. However, fishing and hunting licenses are *not* available on the island. When you disembark from the ferry, you find yourself in the lovely Neebish Botanical Park and Memorial Gardens, which is followed by a few roadside gardens. There is incline on Neebish Island, and one hill proved an excellent spot to watch sandhill cranes strutting between the rolls of hay in the mowed fields.

Home to fewer than 100 people year-round, the island boasts the Neebish Presbyterian Church, built in 1927; a Catholic cemetery; and a community center.

If you make it down to the Little Neebish (at the southeast tip of Neebish Island), you'll find a Michigan Historic Site Marker for the Johnston Homesite, homesteaded in 1864 by John McDougal Johnston; his wife, Justine; and their six children. Johnston's father was the successful British Sault Ste. Marie fur trader John Johnston (1762–1828), and his mother was Ozhaguscodaywayquay (also spelled Ozhahguscodaywayquay), "Woman of the Green Glade," the daughter of an Waubojeeg (White Fisher), an Ojibwe chief in what is now northern Wisconsin. John Johnston served as an interpreter for his brother-in-law, the Indian agent Henry R. Schoolcraft. One of the Johnston daughters, Miss Molly, called this spot, where she remained with a brother after the rest of the family moved to a farm near the Sault, O-non-egwud (Happy Place). The name suits it well. St. Joseph Island is very close, across the St. Marys, on the other side of the international border. (For more about why Little Neebish has also been known as Rains Island, see the St. Joseph Island chapter.)

Neebish Island Resort, which offers campsites and furnished cabins, is about the extent of the accommodations available on the island. The resort has a small store for campers, Neebish Country Store. The cash register is watched over by the wall-mounted head and shoulders of a growling black bear, shot by owner Bryce's grandfather at the age of 77 in 2001. Besides bear, deer, moose, Canada lynx, bobcat, and even, according to Bryce, mountain lion have been seen on the island. The occasional elk swims over from the elk farm on St. Joseph Island, Ontario, obviously not concerned with border control.

OTHER ISLAND THINGS TO DO

See if you can find the Sugar Island "Weather Station"—It's an "island thing." You'll know it when you see it.

SPECIAL ISLAND EVENTS

Sugar Island: Sault Tribe Annual Tribe Traditional Powwow and Summer Gathering (July)—https://www.facebook.com/sugarislandpowwow2.

Sugar Island: Music Fest (August)—This annual three-day festival raises funds for the Sugar Island Nature Walk and Beach Access (SINWABA) at Eight Mile Road. sugarislandfest.org.

For More Information

Sugar Island—www.sugarislandtownship.com/.

Sugar Island Sampler, by Bernard Arbic (Allegan Forest, MI: Priscilla, 1992).

Neebish Island—www.neebishislandresort.com/.

Neebish Island Memories, 1921–1927, by Irja Harju (self-published, out of print, but available at a number of Michigan libraries, and used copies can be found for sale online)—A fascinating memoir of growing up on Neebish Island almost 100 years ago.

Parting Thoughts

The weekend Michelene and I were on Sugar, the annual Sugar Island Pow Wow was being held. A hand-painted sign read, "No Drugs, No Alcohol"—and someone had added in Sharpie below, "No Politics!!!"

From atop its nest across the water, an osprey—not particularly concerned with politics, borders, or us—watched the ferry as, with us aboard, it headed back to the mainland.

Lake Michigan Islands

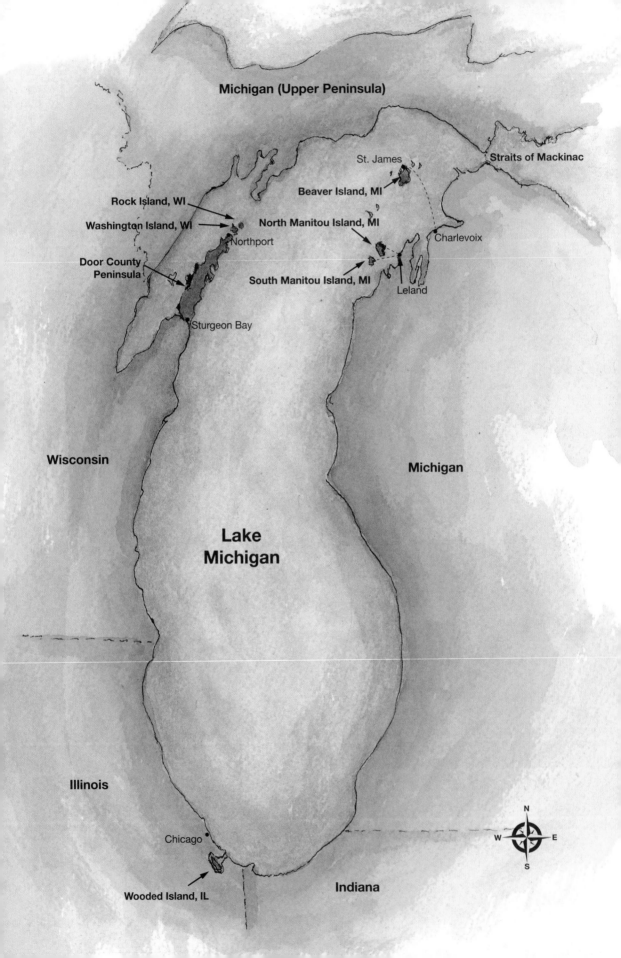

An Introduction to Lake Michigan

During the last ice age, the peninsulas we know as the Lower Peninsula and the Upper Peninsula of Michigan jutted out into an earlier proglacial lake, Lake Algonquin, a lake that was to become the three discrete bodies of water we now call Lake Michigan, the Straits of Mackinac, and Lake Huron. After it was part of Lake Algonquin and before it became Lake Michigan, the lake had another iteration. Prehistorically, the smaller Lake Chippewa formed as water levels decreased and filled only the deepest basin of what is now Lake Michigan, having a shoreline that ranged from 10 to 30 miles (16 to 48 kilometers) out into the current basin. At one point, Lake Chippewa had no outlet; its current outlet, the Straits of Mackinac, was a narrow dry canyon. Eventually, the water level rose again and water flowed into and through the canyon at the Straits, reattaching what is now Lake Michigan to the Great Lakes Basin through the Straits of Mackinac, which run between the northern ends of Lake Michigan and Lake Huron.

Lake Michigan is the only one of the Great Lakes that is entirely in the United States; the other four are shared with Canada. Lake Michigan is bordered by the states of Michigan—both the Lower and Upper Peninsulas—Indiana, Illinois, and Wisconsin.

By surface area, Lake Michigan is the third-largest Great Lake and the sixth-largest freshwater lake in the world. Lake Michigan stretches 307 miles (494 kilometers) from south to north and 118 miles (190 kilometers) from east to west. Its average depth is 279 feet; at its deepest, the lake is 925 feet. Since lake levels have been recorded at various gauge stations around Lake Michigan/Lake Huron (the two lakes are considered the same body of water, hydrologically, because they share the same elevation), between 1860 and 2004, average elevation varied only by a little over six feet and is currently at 577 feet.

There is a diversion from the lake into the Mississippi River basin through the Illinois Waterway at the Chicago River.

Historically, Lake Michigan in its current form has borne a number of different names. The French explorer Samuel de Champlain identified Lake Michigan as Grand Lac on his map of 1632. Later, on Nicolas Sanson's 1656 map, the lake was named Lake of the Stinking Water, the English translation of Lac de Puans, after the people (Puans or Puants were the tribe we know now as the Winnebagoes) who occupied its shores. This name referred to their place of origin, possibly the stagnant water of Green Bay or other waters where the tribe came from, not the condition of Lake Michigan at the time of European discovery and naming.

In 1676, Jean Claude Allouez, a Jesuit missionary and explorer, called the lake Lac St. Joseph, a name often used by early writers. In 1679, the lake became known as Lac des Illinois, as it is shown on the first printed map of western New France in 1688 by the Italian Franciscan monk and cartographer Vincenzo Coronelli, because it gave access to the country of the

Illiniwek tribe. Reportedly, explorers René-Robert Robert Cavelier, Sieur de La Salle, and Father Zenobius Membré called it Lac Dauphin.

Other names for the lake recorded in different historical accounts include, but are not limited to, Lake Machihiganing, Lac Mitchiganong ou des Illinois, Miesitgan, and Missigan.

Through the further explorations of Louis Jolliet and Father Jacques Marquette, who crossed it from St. Ignace to Green Bay in 1673 on their way to the Mississippi River, the lake received its final name of Lake Michigan. In Algonquin, the language spoken by the Ojibwe, Ottawa, and Potawatomi tribes, *michigami* means "great water."

The islands of Lake Michigan accessible by ferry (or in one case, bridge) are relatively few:

Washington Island—A 35-square-mile (91-square-kilometer) Wisconsin island accessible by a 25-minute ride on the Washington Island Ferry Line vehicular ferry from Northport Pier at the tip of the Door Peninsula.

Rock Island—Another one of the Door County Islands, the 912-acre Wisconsin Rock Island State Park is accessible by a 10-minute ride on the *Karfi* passenger ferry from Washington Island.

Wooded Island—A 16-acre Illinois island in the Jackson Lagoon in Chicago, created by landscape architect Frederick Law Olmsted for the 1893 Columbian Exhibition, accessible by pedestrian bridge from Jackson Park. The island is home to the Garden of the Phoenix (formerly the Osaka Japanese Garden) and the Paul H. Douglas Nature Sanctuary.

South Manitou Island—A Michigan island just over eight square miles (21 square kilometers), part of the Sleeping Bear Dunes National Lakeshore, accessible by an hour-and-a-half (16-mile/26-kilometer) passenger ferry ride from Leland, Michigan.

North Manitou Island—A 22-square-mile (57-square-kilometer) Michigan island, part of the Sleeping Bear Dunes National Lakeshore, accessible by a just under an hour (12-mile/19-kilometer) passenger ferry ride from South Manitou Island, or just over an hour from Leland, Michigan.

Beaver Island—A 53-square-mile (137-square-kilometer) Michigan island accessible by a ferry ride of just over two hours (32 miles/52 kilometers) on the Beaver Island Boat Company vehicular ferry from Charlevoix, Michigan.

For more information on Lake Michigan, visit www.great-lakes.net/michigan.html and consider looking for a used or library copy of the American Lake Series volume *Lake Michigan*, by Milo M. Quaife (Indianapolis: Bobbs-Merrill, 1944).

Washington Island, Wisconsin

"NORTH OF THE TENSION LINE"

June 21, 2013, 1:45 p.m.
Sturgeon Bay, Door County, Wisconsin

After spending the night at Karen's daughter and son-in-law's beautiful Arts and Crafts home in Milwaukee, we are on our way, heading up the Door Peninsula. In a downpour, we stop at the Sturgeon Bay Visitor Center and discover, looking at the map on the counter, that we've just unknowingly crossed onto a "mainland island." We're just an hour away from the ferry to Washington Island, the first of the true Door County islands we're off to explore.

GETTING THERE: Many options: car ferry; passenger ferry; private boat or plane

GETTING AROUND: Bring your car and/or bike; tour vehicles; bicycle, moped, and kayak rentals

OVERNIGHT ACCOMMODATIONS: Motels, hotels, inns, and B&Bs; rental cottages and vacation homes; campground

FOOD: Restaurants; groceries

DAY TRIP? Yes, but you could easily fill a week with island adventures!

STATE / PROVINCIAL / NATIONAL PARK? No

Where are you if six American white pelicans, with their massive black-edged wings, appear overhead as you cross Death's Door? Most likely, you are enjoying the 30-minute crossing from the Door Peninsula across "Death's Door" (Porte des Morts)—the strait between Lake Michigan and Green Bay and between the northern tip of the Door Peninsula and the archipelago known as the Potawatomi Islands—on your way to Washington Island.

Surprisingly, "death's door" does not refer to the danger inherent in crossing the narrow strait—although it *is* littered with shipwrecks—but instead came through the French, who kept the name already bestowed on this passage by earlier islanders, the name earned in an incident of treachery between Potawatomi and Winnebago that took place one dark and windy night.

Washington Island, the largest of over 30 Door County islands, is part of the Grand Traverse Islands chain of the Niagara Escarpment that runs from Door Peninsula to the Garden Peninsula in Michigan. The island was appreciated by the Potawatomi as an easily defensible home as early as 1600. French explorer Jean Nicolet may have visited it in 1635. The island

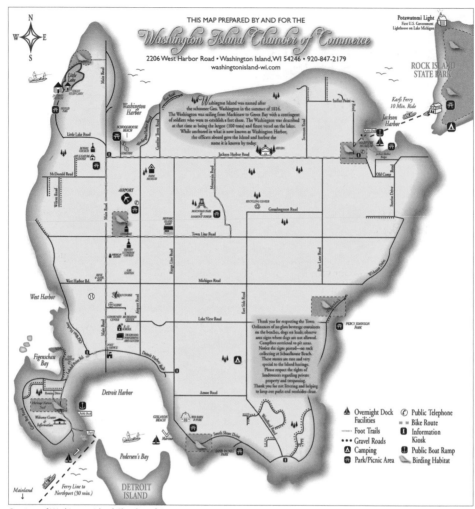

Courtesy of Washington Island Chamber of Commerce

was settled in the eighteenth and nineteenth centuries primarily by Scandinavians, most of whom were from Iceland, and also by some Irish.

In 1850, Washington Island was included as part of the new town of Washington, which today also encompasses five nearby islands (one of these, Rock Island, on which the town was founded, is also accessible by ferry).

In early times, the island was known for fish, lumber, stone, and maple syrup. Later, in the 1950s and 1960s, it produced dairy products, particularly cheese, and between 1948 and 1970 Washington Island potatoes were grown there.

How to Get There

Drive north to the tip of Door Peninsula, Wisconsin. Door County is considered a peninsula, but you may notice—when you cross the Sturgeon Bay on Wisconsin Highway 57—that the northern half of this finger of land became a "mainland island" with the creation of the Sturgeon Bay Ship Canal in 1880. Northport Pier, the mainland dock for the

Washington Island Ferry Line, is northeast of Ellison Bay, at the very end of Highway 42. You can view the ferry schedule at http://wisferry.com/.

Washington Island Airport (K2P2) has two public grass runways.

What to Expect

Washington Island is a relatively big island, covering 35 square miles (91 square kilometers) and serving as home to about 700 year-round residents, a number that swells to 1,600 when seasonal residents return.

The island has a number of interesting sites of natural beauty, unique attractions related to the history of the island and its people, and special island businesses. Many of these attractions are scattered across the island's over 100 miles (260 kilometers) of paved roads, so to "see it all," you need a motorized vehicle. The island ferry landing area hosts a welcome center; bike, moped, and boat rentals; the tour train departure point; and restaurants. However, the downtown area is located 3 miles (5 kilometers) from the ferry dock. Here you will find restaurants and taverns; gas stations; hardware, liquor, and general stores; a post office; and a medical clinic.

Paths to Adventure

NATURAL SITES

Jackson Harbor Ridges State of Wisconsin Natural Area—This area protects several Great Lakes coastal plan communities and a number of uncommon plants. The topography of

Jackson Harbor Ridges, a state natural area on Washington Island, with Rock Island in the background glimpsed through the mist.

the area is what is called "swell and swale," areas of dry, sandy ridges separated by low, wet, valley-like intersections between adjacent higher land. A trail allows for exploration.

Carlin's Point—This trail off Old Camp Road goes through a habitat of rare boreal forest plants; you can also reach the point by hiking the trail from the Maritime Museum over the Jackson Harbor Ridges.

Door County Land Trust Nature Preserves:

- Detroit Harbor Preserve
- Richter Community Forest Preserve
- Domer-Neff Nature Preserve and Bird Sanctuary
- Little Lake Nature Preserve
- Coffey Swamp State Natural Area
- Big and Little Marsh State Natural Area

Schoolhouse Beach—This limestone beach, purportedly one of only five such beaches in the world, lies on the edge of the deep Washington Harbor, with its clear water perfect for swimming, and consists of piles of smooth, rounded stones. (Note: A $250 fine is charged for removing any stones.)

Percy Johnson Memorial Park—The county purchased these five acres of wooded property on the island's east side, with 500 feet of sand beach and a grassy area for picnic tables, in 1947. The park has a view of Lake Michigan and Hog Island, a National Wildlife Refuge.

Sand Dunes Park—A sand beach on the island's south side.

People's Park—Near Little Lake, the park features picnic tables and a view of Green Bay.

Mountain Wayside Park and Lookout Tower—286 steps up to a remarkable view of other Grand Traverse Islands.

Note: The only place available to camp on Washington Island is Washington Island Campground, LLC (www.washingtonislandcampground.com/). More scenic, primitive camping is available a second short ferry ride away at the Rock Island State Park (see Rock Island below for more information).

HISTORY PRESERVED

Jacobsen Museum (at Little Lake)—In 1931, 64-year-old Danish-born Jen Jacobsen built this rustic log structure to display and share his collections of fossils, rocks, and artifacts from the Potawatomi village located in the area. A restoration of his summer residence, Camp Jacobsen, is at the site as well.

Jackson Harbor Maritime Museum (at Jackson Harbor)—Located in two former fishing sheds, this museum holds artifacts and photographs and features videos on local maritime history, including area shipwrecks and the Coast Guard, as well as commercial fishing, which continues in this harbor.

Washington Island Farm Museum (Jackson Harbor Rd.)—Farm buildings taken from different locations on the island have been assembled here with collections of farm tools representative of the island's farming history between 1870 and 1940.

Historic Island Dairy—Once the center of the island's dairy business, the property has been renovated for a number of public purposes, including a ballroom venue. It is also the site of Fragrant Isle Lavender Farm and Shop, an island history exhibit, and Type & Ink Gallery, an art and vintage poster gallery.

Cherry Train Tours—Two-hour open-air tram tour with selected stops and a tour guide who presents island history and folklore.

One of four museums on Washington Island, Jacobsen Museum, located at Little Lake, houses natural and historical artifacts of the island, including those of the Potawatomi.

CULTURAL ATTRACTIONS

The Art and Nature Center (ANC)—Housed in a 1904 schoolhouse, the ANC was founded in 1965 to preserve and promote the creative arts and the natural history of Washington Island. Local artists exhibit and sell their work, and interpretive displays crafted by local naturalists explain island features.

Sievers School of Fiber Arts—Since 1979, weekend and weeklong classes have been offered here by professional fiber artists, whose work is for sale in the gift shop.

The Stavkirke (Stave Church)—Often a venue for weddings, this is a 1990s replica of a church in Borgund, Norway, a type of church built in the eleventh through thirteenth centuries, so named because the walls were constructed of staves, upright planks. A Prayer Path winds through the nearby woods. Members of the Trinity Evangelical Lutheran Church, a 1948 stone church across the road, built the Stavkirke to honor the island's Scandinavian roots.

The Stavkirke, a ministry of the Trinity Evangelical Lutheran Church on Washington Island, is a replica of a stave church in Borgund, Norway.

Trueblood Performing Arts Center—A nonprofit, multipurpose performance venue that hosts many annual island events, including school and community performances.

Red Barn Park and Gislason Public Beach—The Red Barn offers summer events such as family story time and live musical and theatrical entertainment at an alcohol-free park, which includes a playground, a picnic area, grills, volleyball, and trails.

OTHER ISLAND THINGS TO DO

Go bird-watching—On one of the main north-south migration routes, Washington Island is known for its excellent bird-watching opportunities. The Art and Nature Center has more information. A downloadable "Washington Island Bird Guide" map and checklist is available at http://wisferry.com/birding/.

Fish—The island's protected harbors are known for panfish and "record-size" smallmouth bass. Waters around the Town of Washington islands are known for large northern pike, and trolling for salmon in the deeper waters off Washington and Rock islands is another option.

Golf—Deer Run Golf Course has both a nine-hole regulation course, with carts and clubs available to rent, and an 18-hole miniature golf course.

Join the club—You, too, can become a member of the historic Washington Island Bitters Club at Nelsen's Hall Bitters Pub & Restaurant by imbibing a shot of Angostura aromatic bitters. You will be issued a Bitter's Club certificate stating: "You are now considered a full-fledged Islander and entitled to mingle, dance, etc. with all the other Islanders."

SPECIAL ISLAND EVENTS

Door Islands Bird Festival (May).
Washington Island Canoe and Kayak Event (June).
Art in the Park (July).
Washington Island Music Festival (August).
Washington Island Literary Festival (September).

The Washington Island Chamber of Commerce posts a full listing of island events for the year on the Washington Island Events page: http://washingtonisland-wi.com/category/events/.

For More Island Information

www.washingtonisland.com.

Northport Pier Visitor Center (before you board the ferry).

Washington Island Welcome Center (a short drive from the ferry landing).

Washington Island Observer, the island newspaper, advertised as "owned and published by more than a dozen families who love the island and live [there] at least part of the year" (http://washingtonisland-wi.com/category/news/).

Washington Island Library, a Door County library branch.

The Naming: A Part of the History of Washington Township, by Conan Bryant Eaton (Washington Island, WI: Jackson Harbor, 1966)—The first of Eaton's four-book Island Series.

Death's Door: The Pursuit of a Legend; A Part of the History of Washington Township, by Conan Bryant Eaton (Washington Island, WI: Jackson Harbor, 1996)—Originally published in 1967, one of Eaton's four-book Island Series.

Washington Island, 1836–1876: A Part of the History of Washington Township, by Conan Bryant Eaton (Washington Island, WI: Jackson Harbor, 1997)—Originally published in 1972, one of Eaton's four-book Island Series.

Let's Talk about "Washington Island": The Washington Island Centennial Yearbook, 1850–1950, by Anne T. Whitney (n.p., 1950).

Islanders Speak: Profiles and Personalities, by members of the Washington Island Archives (Washington Island, WI: Jackson Harbor, 2000).

Over and Back: A Picture History of Transportation to Washington Island, by Richard Purinton (n.p., 1990).

Words on Water: A Ferryman's Journal, Washington Island, WI, by Richard Purinton (Ellison Bay, WI: Cross+Roads, 2009).

Bridges Are Still News: Island Essays, Poems and Photos, by Richard Purinton (Washington Island, WI: Island Bayou, 2010).

"Washington Island," in *Biking the Great Lakes Islands,* by Kathleen Abrams and Lawrence Abrams (Wausau, WI: Entwood, 1985), 24–35—The three Washington Island routes detailed are Circle Tour to Jackson Harbor, Circle Tour to Mountain Park Lookout, and Southern Shore Circle Tour.

For more on Door Country as a whole—which includes both Washington Island and Rock Island—as well as the Door Peninsula, peruse this compilation of the impressions and visions of writers and artists focused on the preservation of specific pieces of land: *The Nature of Door: Door County Writers and Artists on Preservation of Place,* edited by Norbert Blei and Karen Yancey for Door County Land Trust (Elison Bay, WI: Cross+Roads, 2006).

How You Can Support the Island

Door County Land Trust
PO Box 65
Sturgeon Bay, WI 54235
www.doorcountylandtrust.org

Jacobsen Museum Fund
c/o Town Clerk/Treasurer
PO Box 220
Washington Island, WI 54246
http://washingtonisland-wi.com/jacobsen-museum/

The Art and Nature Center
1799 Main Rd.
Washington Island, WI 54246
www.wianc.org/membership.html

Parting Thoughts

June 23, 2013, 4:05 p.m.
Detroit Harbor

One May morning, after snapping a shot of five white pelicans resting, along with two great blue herons and two great egrets, at the edge of Detroit Harbor on Washington Island, retired Washington Island ferryman and writer Richard Purinton blogged, "Old-timers would have choked on their Plow Boy chew if someone claimed to have seen a pelican or an egret on Washington Island, but these birds have been as regular as robins in recent years." Those white pelicans, with their nine-foot wingspan and graceful flight, their soaring high and wheeling in unison against a broad expanse of blue, may contribute to the magic that helps dispel the tension islanders and island visitors alike claim to feel slip away as they cross to Washington Island.

When Karen and I visited the shop at the island's lavender farm, Kathy, who was working there, claimed there is a "vortex" on the island. She did not explain how such a vortex might influence the way energy transports itself on the island or if it might somehow account for the presence of the white pelicans, but she appeared quite certain of its existence.

The question is where—not if—you will find magic swirling around you, too, on Washington Island.

Rock Island, Wisconsin

AN ICELANDIC LEGACY

June 23, 2013, 11:45 a.m.
Jackson Harbor, Washington Island

A raft of four white pelicans is adrift off the *Karfi* dock, where Karen and I are waiting to board the noon passenger ferry to Rock Island. We're eager to see what Chester Thordarson—the inventor with the Icelandic heritage—created on the island in the 1920s.

When we pass by the Jackson Harbor breakwater beacon light, while chatting with Syd and Nancy, two Rock Island lighthouse docents traveling to their annual work week on the island, four coal-black cormorants look down at us bemusedly. And then I notice what looks like the fluke of a whale tail in the water between the ferry and the bank of fog shrouding the island. As the *Karfi*'s angle changes, the sight we are now all straining to identify is transformed into a head and then a doe swimming, quite energetically, out in front of the ferry. But then we lose track of her as we try to decipher the limestone of Thordarson's Boathouse and Great Hall from the thick fog on the water.

Soon—the crossing is only a mile—the bright-colored clothing of the campers waiting for the ferry at the base of the boathouse is discernible. We step out among them and the fog onto the dock. Columbine is blooming against strewn stone; clumps of Asian jasmine sprout from limestone walls. Hundreds of nesting swallows fill the boathouse with swoop and dive.

A magic I'm not familiar with seems to inhabit this place, and it strikes me how little I know about Iceland, the land that apparently still held Thordarson in its spell on Rock Island.

GETTING THERE: Passenger-only ferry; private boat (limited and nonreservable dock space; nightly fee for overnight mooring)

GETTING AROUND: Limited options: foot traffic only; no wheels of any sort allowed!

OVERNIGHT ACCOMMODATIONS: Camping only

FOOD: Bring your own

DAY TRIP? Yes

STATE / PROVINCIAL / NATIONAL PARK? Rock Island State Park

Almost all of the mostly wooded 912 acres of Rock Island is owned and managed by the Wisconsin Department of Natural Resources as Rock Island State Park. The U.S. Coast Guard owns the other one-quarter acre, where a solar-powered navigational light is maintained next to the historic Pottawatomie Lighthouse (also known as the Rock Island Light). No permanent residents reside on the island. Friends of Rock Island docents stay at the lighthouse.

Rock Island was originally inhabited by Native Americans. A band of Ojibwe was living there when the first non-Native settlers arrived, but the island had been used by other Native American tribes earlier. By the mid-1970s, archaeologist Ronald Mason of Lawrence University, conducting fieldwork on Rock Island to determine the Native American history there, had excavated more than 80,000 artifacts from the south and southeastern shores. More

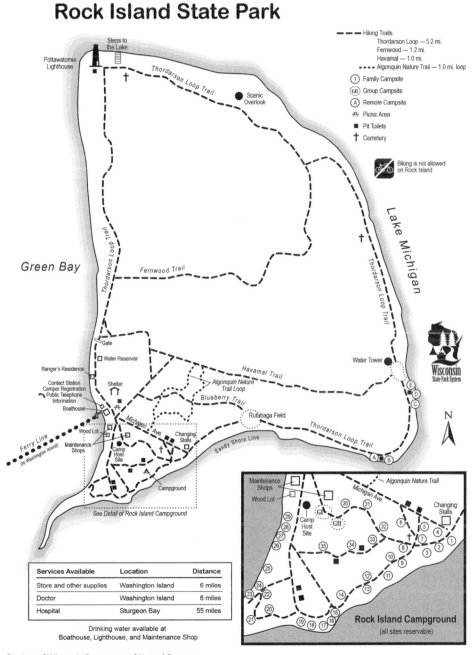

Rock Island State Park

Hiking Trails
Thordarson Loop — 5.2 mi.
Fernwood — 1.2 mi.
Havamal — 1.0 mi.
Algonquin Nature Trail — 1.0 mi. loop

1 Family Campsite
GII Group Campsite
A Remote Campsite
Picnic Area
Pit Toilets
Cemetery

Biking is not allowed on Rock Island

Pottawatomie Lighthouse
Steps to the Lake
Thordarson Loop Trail
Scenic Overlook

Green Bay
Fernwood Trail
Thordarson Loop Trail

Lake Michigan

Wisconsin State Park System

Gate
Water Reservoir
Water Tower
Ranger's Residence
Contact Station
Camper Registration
Public Telephone
Information
Boathouse
Shelter
Havamal Trail
Algonquin Nature Trail Loop
Blueberry Trail
Ferry Line
(to Washington Island)
Wood Lot
Maintenance Shops
Camp Host Site
Changing Stalls
Michigan Ave.
Rutabaga Field
Thordarson Loop Trail
Sandy Shore Line
Campground
A B
E
D
C

See Detail of Rock Island Campground

Services Available	Location	Distance
Store and other supplies	Washington Island	6 miles
Doctor	Washington Island	6 miles
Hospital	Sturgeon Bay	55 miles

Drinking water available at
Boathouse, Lighthouse, and Maintenance Shop

Maintenance Shops
Wood Lot
Algonquin Nature Trail
Michigan Ave.
Changing Stalls
Camp Host Site
GI
GII

Rock Island Campground
(all sites reservable)

Courtesy of Wisconsin Department of Natural Resources

recently, a DNR archaeologist has suggested that Rock Island is "the second most important archaeological site in the Midwest."

Jean Nicolet, the first European to discover Lake Michigan and what is now Wisconsin, visited the island in 1634. The site was chosen, around 1835, for the first settlement in Door County by non–Native Americans and European immigrants, who established a small fishing village on the east shore of Rock Island, which was abandoned during the 1850s and 1860s.

The island was uninhabited by the twentieth century, when two-thirds of the land was owned by Rasmus Hanson, a boatbuilder from Washington Island, who used Rock Island as a source of timber.

Beginning in 1910, and over the course of more than 35 years, Chester H. Thordarson, the island's new owner, made his distinctive imprint on Rock Island. The island provided him with both a retreat and the opportunity to create a monument to his Icelandic heritage. Thordarson's vision for the island remains one of the most notable features of Rock Island today.

The island was purchased by the State of Wisconsin, after several years of negotiations, from Thordarson's heirs in 1964 for $175,000. The Wisconsin Department of Natural Resources took over the property, and the island has been Rock Island State Park since 1965.

How to Get There

Rock Island, a part of the Grand Traverse Islands, is northeast of Washington Island, which itself is northeast of the tip of Wisconsin's Door Peninsula. The *Karfi*, a passenger ferry, makes the 10-minute crossing from Washington Island to Rock Island. To get to the *Karfi* ferry dock, take the Washington Island ferry from Northport Pier at the tip of Door Peninsula. Check the ferry schedule as you plan your trip: http://wisferry.com/. Depending on the season, there are four or eight daily round trips between the mainland and Washington Island.

Allow at least 20 minutes to drive the 8.2 miles (13.2 kilometers) across Washington Island, from Detroit Harbor in the southwest corner, where the ferry disembarks, to Jackson Harbor, where the *Karfi* docks, in the northeast corner of Washington Island. Park and leave your vehicle (or bike) there.

Take the *Karfi* passenger ferry across the mile-wide (1.6-kilometer-wide) strait from Jackson Harbor to Rock Island. Check the *Karfi* schedule in advance of your trip: http://wisferry.com/rock-island-ferry/. The *Karfi* typically has hourly departures from the end of June to the beginning of September and runs three round trips a day the rest of June and September and at the end of May and the beginning of October.

Private watercraft can dock for a small per-foot fee. In winter, when the ice is thick enough, snowmobiles can cross the passage between Washington and Rock islands.

What to Expect

About 25,000 visitors visit the park annually, and many of them enjoy some or all of the approximately 10 miles (16 kilometers) of trails that wrap around and across the island, but only on foot as no "wheeled vehicles," including bicycles, are allowed on the island. While hiking, you may see some of the island's wildlife, which is primarily deer, fox, red squirrel, birds, and nonvenemous snakes. Something else you may note that you see in few places these days: one pay phone is available for use at the Park's Contact Station. (Note: Cell phone service coverage may be weak, and no electricity is available to charge a cell phone.)

Paths to Adventure

NATURAL SITES

Sand dunes—.5 mile (.8 kilometer) of sandy shoreline on the island's south end.

Dolomite cliffs—On the east side of island, these are impressive from the water, too.

Rock Island Woods—A State Natural Area featuring a northern hardwood forest, northern wet-mesic forest, forested seeps, and shaded—by both trees in the island's interior and the dolomite face of the eastern shore—cliff community. The moist conditions resulting in this community are ideal for the propagation of mosses, fragile ferns, and wood ferns.

HISTORY PRESERVED

Thordarson's Viking Hall and Boathouse—Modeled after the Icelandic parliament building in Reykjavik and containing furniture with carvings of the Norse myths by Halldor Einarsson, an Icelandic wood carver, this building is on the National Register of Historic Places.

WHO WAS CHESTER H. THORDARSON?

Born in 1867 in Iceland, Thordarson immigrated to the United States with his family at a young age. He received little formal education but was significantly influenced by an Icelandic physics text, from which he learned much. Eventually, he realized his dream of getting a job in a Chicago electrical manufacturing shop.

In 1895, he began his own Chicago company, Thordarson Electrical Manufacturing (later Thordarson Transformer Company) and became an inventor of laboratory apparatus for universities, coils for the auto industry, radio amplifiers and transformers, neon signs, and X-ray devices. In 1904, he won a gold medal for his million-volt transformer at the World's Fair in St. Louis. Ultimately, he held patents on more than 350 electrical inventions and employed 1,500 people.

Thordarson started buying up Rock Island in 1910 and owned all of it, except for the federal lighthouse parcel, by 1912. In 1914, he renovated a fishing village settler's cabin on the east side of the island, but unable to maintain a dock in Lake Michigan's waves, he established a 30-acre estate on the southwestern part of Rock Island, across from Washington Island. Wood buildings, more typical of a nature preserve, preceded the six stone structures he later built to manifest his Icelandic vision.

Thordarson received an honorary master of arts degree from the University of Wisconsin for "his inventiveness, his interest in self-education, and his collection of rare books"; an honorary PhD from the University of Iceland in Reykjavik; and the Order of the Falcon from the king of Denmark, Christian X, in 1939 for "meritorious service and contributions to society."[14]

By the time Thordarson died in 1945, at the age of 78, he had collected over 11,000 books on subjects related to Iceland, scientific thought, technology, and nature. He is buried on the island, where much evidence of his personality and interests remains. The log buildings from his earlier vision of nature preserve are gone, but the six stone structures he built during the late 1920s endure.

Chester H. Thordarson's Boathouse and Viking Hall on Rock Island as seen from the *Karfi*, the ferry from Jackson Harbor on Washington Island.

Oriental Open-Air Pavilion—Also known as the Pagoda, this consists of six columns made of dolomitic limestone cobble suspending a red-tiled pagoda-style roof above a rectangular platform of stone with stone stairs leading up to it and low stone walls rising from its edges; used for picnics, now as then.

Small Cottage—This building, made entirely of dolomitic limestone placed in particularly pleasing patterns at the door and window lintels, has a red-tiled roof and forest-green trim. Originally it served as lodging for Thordarson's guests; today the Rock Island park ranger lives there.

Water Reservoir—What appears to be a much larger stone cottage houses a huge concrete water tank.

Greenhouse—Built of stone and glass, this building allowed Thordarson to propagate plants that then were moved to grace his garden, where they were enjoyed often, to his dismay, by the island's deer.

Stone Tower—Rising out of the woods on the island's east side, built by Thordarson out of dolomitic limestone collected on the island and topped by a red tile roof, this structure was built, but never used, as a water tower.

There are several other island structures of historic interest:

Japanese Garden Gate—A quirky driftwood gate is what remains of the fencing used to keep deer out of Thordarson's garden.

Pottawatomie Lighthouse—Built in 1836, making it Wisconsin's oldest, the lighthouse is located on the high bluff, Pottawatomie Point, at the northwest point of Rock Island. The third lighthouse on Lake Michigan, it was replaced in 1858, after the original one was washed away due to faulty mortar, some say. A free tour of the lighthouse is offered from Memorial Day to Columbus Day, seven days a week, 10:00 a.m.–4:00 p.m. A gift shop sells Friends of Rock Island items. A stairway leads down the dolomite cliffs to the Lake Michigan beach.

Former small fishing village site—Circa 1835, the remains of the village are located atop cliffs on the east side.

Three old cemeteries—Two containing marked graves.

OTHER ISLAND THINGS TO DO

Hike—Rock Island has six maintained hiking trails, including Thordarson's Loop, a 5.2-mile (8.4-kilometer) island circumference trail, and the self-guided Algonquin Nature Trail Loop.

Paddle—Rock Island received the 2010 Gold Seal award for the best kayaking/canoeing park in the state of Wisconsin.

Swim—Enjoy the cool, clear waters of Lake Michigan from the south shore's crescent of sand.

Ski—Cross-country ski in the winter hush of the island's deep woods.

Camp—The island has 35 family, two group, and five backpacking campsites that can be reserved online at http://wisconsinstateparks.reserveamerica.com/camping/rock-island -state-park/r/campgroundDetails.do?contractCode=WI&parkId=60039. Facilities include pit toilets, picnic tables, and fire rings in the campground; flush toilets and shelter in the picnic area. Garbage is collected at the dock; recycling is mandatory. No showers,

The great 80-year-old weathered gate, encountered on the hike from the Boathouse to the Pottawatomie Lighthouse, was built by Thordarson as a part of a 30-acre fence that was not successful in keeping deer from grazing on his rare plantings.

Pottawatomie (Rock Island) Lighthouse at the northern point of Rock
Island is Wisconsin's oldest lighthouse.

ice, or store. Rock Island State Park Backpack Campsite C was named the "Best Walk-in
Site" in the state of Wisconsin in 2012.

SPECIAL ISLAND EVENTS

The annual July 4th Rock Island State Park fund-raiser, featuring a cookout, free concert in
the Boathouse, and silent auction.

For More Island Information

http://dnr.wi.gov/topic/parks/name/rockisland/.
Rock Island State Park Guidebook, by Timothy Sweet, Douglas A. Rossman, Sharon C. Ross-
man, William H. Olson, Paul Dailey, and Charlotte Manning (Washington Island, WI:
Jackson Harbor, 2002).

Thordarson and Rock Island: Chester Hjörtur Thordarson, by Richard Purinton (Washington Island, WI: Island Bayou, 2013).

Rock Island: A Part of the History of Washington Township, by Conan Bryant Eaton (Washington Island, WI: Jackson Harbor, 2002)—Originally published in 1969, one of Eaton's four-book Island Series.

Valhalla in America: Norse Myths in Wood at Rock Island State Park, Wisconsin, by Douglas and Sharon C. Rossman (Washington Island, WI: Jackson Harbor, 1999).

"Chester Thordarson's Rock Island," by Tim Sweet (*Voyageur: Northeast Wisconsin's Historical Review* [Summer/Fall 2005]: 36–44).

"Rock Island: The Personification of Chester H. Thordarson," by Carol Lohry Cartwright (*Wisconsin Magazine of History.* 69, no. 3 [1986]: 211–27)—This publication includes a map of the Thordarson estate on p. 216.

A THIRD DOOR COUNTY "ISLAND"

This Door County island is accessible by bridge.

Door Peninsula is the westernmost part of the Niagara Escarpment and separates southern Green Bay from Lake Michigan. Just over halfway up the 78-mile (126- kilometer) finger, the Sturgeon Bay gouges into the land from Green Bay, a large nick on the little finger. In 1870, there was a proposal before Congress to connect Green Bay with Lake Michigan and open a new harbor on the west shore of the lake. By 1881, with the help of a group of private investors led by William B. Ogden, then president of Chicago and North Western Railway, that nick became the site of an "amputation," the top half of the finger severed from the lower half by the Sturgeon Bay Ship Canal. Dredging the Sturgeon Bay and cutting a 1.3-mile (2.14-kilometer) canal from the bay to Lake Michigan created this approximately seven-mile (11-kilometer) canal that completed a watery route across the peninsula.

Before this project, an average of eight ships a year were being lost in the channel at Death's Door, between the tip of the peninsula and Washington Island, where three other, smaller islands are located (Plum, Detroit, and Pilot). With the advent of the canal came a shortcut and a safer route. Instead of ships having to head north out the bay, traverse the dangers of Death's Door passage—at the risk of loss of vessel, cargo, and sailors—ships could cut through the middle of the peninsula from Green Bay to Lake Michigan, shortening the voyage from Green Bay to Chicago by one-fifth.

Another result of the shipping channel was to transform the northern half of the Door Peninsula into an "island," separated from the mainland on all sides by water. Two bridges stitch together the northern and southern parts of the peninsula: the historic Sturgeon Bay Bridge, built in 1929 and opened in 1931, also known as the Michigan Street Bridge, and the Bay View Bridge, which carries both Door County, Wisconsin, highways, 42 and 57, across the canal.

The population of Door Peninsula, in its entirety, swells from its 28,000 year-round figure to as many as 250,000 in the summer. Those "summer extras" are lured by the many activities as well as sights that Door County offers visitors, with an emphasis on both the natural and the gustatory. Wineries, breweries, and a distillery can be found here as well as a number of venues where you can experience a fish boil. Mild Lake Michigan whitefish steaks are added to a kettle of boiling potatoes and onions over an outdoor fire. Kerosene is thrown into the fire, causing a fierce blaze, the water to boil over, and the fish oil to exit the pot. What you get is the tasty mild fish dish that once fed Wisconsin lumberjacks and fishermen. If you're lucky, you'll have the opportunity to finish your meal with a slice of Door County cherry pie.

How You Can Support the Island

Friends of Rock Island State Park (FORI)
1924 Indian Point Rd.
Washington Island, WI 54246
www.fori.us

    FORI is a nonprofit organization that supports the Wisconsin Department of Natural Resources in operating and maintaining the Rock Island State Park. To raise money, FORI sells FORI merchandise and memberships. Members receive a quarterly newsletter, *Rock Island Beacon,* and priority of selection in being chosen for annual lighthouse docent duty.

Parting Thoughts

On our hike to the lighthouse, we stop to rest on the long bench at the base of the bizarre driftwood gate that Thordarson created to keep the deer out of his garden. Chester Thordarson has been gone from the island for over 70 years, but a different magic lives here still. Founding FORI member Tim Sweet described Thordarson's relationship with the island: "Rock Island's secluded location supplied the quiet, isolation, and inspiration that allowed an inventor the time and space needed to think, dream, and create. It also provided an ideal setting for [Thordarson] to pursue interests in nature, landscaping, and botany and offered solace from the hectic pace of Chicago."[15]

    Having to catch two ferries to get to Rock Island may make your trip to this island a little more hectic, a bit more challenging than other island adventures. Or not. But it is worth it. As a visitor to Rock Island, you witness how one remarkable man's vision transformed the island wilderness into a magical retreat: a retreat to not only another place but also another time. If you're lucky, you may also gather from the island retreat's quiet and isolation "the time and space needed to think, dream, and create" for yourself.

Wooded Island,
Jackson Lagoon, Illinois

A JAPANESE GARDEN RETREAT IN THE WINDY CITY

August 2, 2014, 1:53 p.m.
In the Japanese garden

Wooded Island is my favorite urban green space of all time. The surprise of stepping into the unfamiliar wildness of restored prairie habitat of the Paul H. Douglas Nature Sanctuary is reason enough to visit. But it is the island's Japanese garden that has brought me back again.

My first visit to the 16-acre Wooded Island—Chicago's one Great Lakes Basin island, accessible by pedestrian bridge—coincided with the last day of winter. Then, I saw my first robin of 2011 and came across a picture-perfect patch of snowdrops under a leafless tree. Today, spending a special afternoon exploring the island with my daughter Caitlin, we found something in the garden I'd never seen before, except in a photograph . . .

GETTING THERE: Pedestrian bridges

GETTING AROUND: No cars allowed

OVERNIGHT ACCOMMODATIONS: None

FOOD: Bring your own

DAY TRIP? Yes, the only option

STATE / PROVINCIAL / NATIONAL PARK? No, island is part of Jackson Park, a Chicago Park District park

Initially, I found it odd that the American Institute of Architects would consider Wooded Island, a place with only two small wooden structures, one of "150 great places in Illinois." It is a fascinating story in its entirety, as you can see in the bones of it below.

When Chicago won its bid to host the 1893 World Columbian Exposition, celebrating the 400 years of achievement since Columbus had "discovered" the continent, the island was a peninsula. Renowned landscape architect Frederick Law Olmsted transformed this peninsula of sand ridge and marshes into "Wooded Isle," creating an island now known as Wooded Island, to serve as a respite from the exposition's White City.

When the countries participating in the exhibition chose their display areas, Japan picked the centrally located Wooded Isle to demonstrate its "emergence from centuries of diplomatic isolation."[16] Its entry was the Ho-o-den (Phoenix Temple), three connected Japanese buildings filled with Japanese artifacts and art to symbolize the country's rich artistic heritage.

The Ho-o-den engaged the imagination of architect Frank Lloyd Wright, who was working on the exhibition's Transportation Building. According to critics, the Japanese exhibition became a major influence on his "destruction of the box" and his creation of the Prairie style of architecture. Japan donated the Ho-o-den to Chicago at the close of the 1893 fair.

Forty years later, for the 1933 Century of Progress World's Fair, Chicago and Japan constructed a traditional teahouse on Chicago's lakefront, created a garden on Wooded Island's northeast side, and refurbished the Ho-o-den. In 1935, after the close of the fair, a torii gate, the Nippon Tea House, and lanterns were moved to Wooded Island. More work was done on the Japanese garden, adding many of the elements we recognize today.

Between 1941 and 1946, wartime anti-Japanese sentiment sparked two incidents of arson in which the buildings were destroyed, and the site was vandalized and neglected.

In 1973, Chicago formalized a sister-city relationship with Osaka, Japan, Jackson Park was placed on the National Register of Historic Places, and the Park District began a number of improvement projects. "Birdman" Douglas Anderson began leading bird walks on Wooded Island in 1974: "Former 5th Ward Alderman Leon Despres called on him . . . to help clean up a crime wave on Hyde Park's Wooded Island, [and] the nature lover jumped at the chance. At the time Hyde Park's nature preserves were prime real estate for young criminals looking to mug bird watchers and afternoon strollers out alone. . . . So Anderson, a juvenile probation officer by trade, decided to bring those nature lovers together to make the park safe again by touring the preserves in packs."[17]

These bird walks, along with People in the Park events held by the Hyde Park–Kenwood Community Conference and Open Lands, led to the public rediscovering the Japanese garden and, ultimately, to its restoration. Beginning in 1981, a number of renovations to the Japanese garden were undertaken, and in 1995, the garden's name was changed to Osaka Garden to honor Chicago's sister city.

In 2013, 120 flowering cherry trees were planted in Jackson Park, including on Wooded Island, and the garden's name was changed again, to the Garden of the Phoenix, to commemorate its 120th year.

How to Get There

Wooded Island, part of Chicago's 500-acre Jackson Park, is situated in the Jackson Lagoon, just off Lake Michigan. The Museum of Science and Industry—the large limestone Beaux-Arts building capped by a green dome at 5700 Lake Shore Drive—is a good landmark; the island is just south of it.

To find the island, head for Jackson Park, bordered by South Lake Shore Drive on the east, 57th Street on the north, and 67th Street on the south, aiming for the vicinity of the 59th Street harbor.

From Lake Shore Drive, turn west on Science Drive, which intersects Columbia Drive. Heading south (left) will take you around the back of the museum, where you should see a sign posted for the Osaka Garden (or signs may reflect the more recent name, Garden of the Phoenix).

Following the garden signs will lead you behind the museum, where the wide, pedestrian Clarence Darrow Memorial Bridge spans the narrowest spot between the Columbia Basin and the East Lagoon (where Chicagoan Darrow's ashes were scattered by his friends at his

Waterfall in Wooded Island's Garden of the Phoenix.

request) and then a narrower curving footbridge, with East Lagoon on one side and West Lagoon on the other, brings you onto Wooded Island.

What to Expect

As Frederick Law Olmsted once remarked, "A park is a work of art, designed to produce certain effects upon the mind."[18] Stepping onto the island, you may feel like you've entered some alternative reality—certainly this can't be Chicago. And this alternative reality is being enhanced. At the end of 2014, the Chicago Park District, in collaboration with the Army Corps of Engineers, began a five-year, $12 million Great Lakes Associated Restoration Project of Jackson Park. The ecological project includes planting hundreds of species of native plants, stocking game fish in the Columbia Basin, and restoring the lagoons to support fish found in Lake Michigan dunal ponds. Eighteen fish species, four varieties of mussels, and

Wooded Island's moon bridge in the Garden of the Phoenix.

one amphibian—the eastern newt—will be introduced. Currently, in addition to the many resident and migratory birds, from the shoreline, you may see beaver and muskrat.

Paths to Adventure

NATURAL SITES AND HISTORY PRESERVED

The Garden of the Phoenix—This Japanese-style garden, the site of which embodies 120 years of history, contains, as it did from its inception, a double pond with islands, a cascading waterfall, a stone walkway, flowering cherry trees, rock formations, stone lanterns, and a moon bridge—the arched bridge, on a sunny day, with its reflection forming a circle, symbolic of the moon.

You will also find two other wooden structures at the garden. At the entrance to the garden, a traditional torii gate (said to symbolize the transition from the temporal world to a sacred place) and, in its interior, a pavilion styled like a Noh stage (Noh is a form of classical

Japanese musical drama that has been performed since the fourteenth century; the style of the stage is derived from that of the traditional theatrical dance stage of Shinto shrines).

Paul H. Douglas Nature Sanctuary—Native trees, shrubs, and perennials have been planted on the site of the old rose garden that had been established for the fair. The aim of the sanctuary is to restore the island's natural character while providing a greater food supply and enhanced shelter for both migrating and resident birds. Indigo buntings and eastern bluebirds, among other species, grace the area in spring.

The sanctuary is named for the Democratic U.S. senator from Illinois (who served from 1949 to 1967), known for his support of environmental protection in the 1960s, including leading the congressional effort to create the Indiana Dunes National Lakeshore.

OTHER ISLAND THINGS TO DO

Go birding—250 bird species have been spotted on the island, while over two dozen species of birds, including a well-studied population of feral monk parakeets, descendants of pet birds that escaped in the 1960s, call Jackson Park home. Recently a purple martin nesting site has been established near Wooded Island, alongside the Columbia Basin.

Take a bird walk—The Chicago Audubon Society offers Wooded Island bird walks on Wednesdays and Saturdays, year-round (www.chicagoaudubon.org/).

Join a walking tour—including Wooded Island—of the former grounds of the 1893 World's Columbian Exposition in Jackson Park. The free 90-minute tour is offered by the Jackson Park Advisory Council with Friends of the White City (www.friendsofthewhitecity.org/programs/white-city-tours).

Hike—The trails on the island connect to Jackson Park mainland trails that, in turn, connect to the Lakefront Trail.

Fish (nearby)—The Chicago Park District prohibits fishing from Wooded Island, but folks do fish in the East and West lagoons from the "mainland" as well as in the Columbia Basin. The Illinois Department of Natural Resources stocks these waters, and catches have included coho and chinook salmon; steelhead and brown trout; yellow perch; warmouth, smallmouth, largemouth, and rock bass; bluegill; crappie; carp (25+-pound class); and channel catfish.

Visit the Museum of Science and Industry (across the bridge over the East Lagoon)—Learn more about the White City and the 1893 World's Columbian Exposition, the impetus for the creation of Wooded Island (www.msichicago.org/).

SPECIAL ISLAND EVENTS

Wooded Island Restoration/Work Days are sponsored by a number of local organizations.

- Chicago Hyde Park Village on the fourth Saturday of every month—www.chpv.org.
- Openlands—www.openlands.org.
- Chicago Conservation Corps—http://chicagoconservationcorps.org.
- Accelerate77—www.accelerate77.net/.

White City Revisited, a two-hour tour led by the Chicago Architecture Foundation, explores the World Columbian Exposition footprint that includes the garden on Wooded Island—www.architecture.org/.

For More Island Information

The Garden of the Phoenix Foundation—www.gardenofthephoenix.org/.

Green heron fishing from Wooded Island in Chicago's Jackson Lagoon.

Friends of the White City—www.friendsofthewhitecity.org/.
Jackson Park Advisory Council—www.jacksonparkadvisorycouncil.org/.
Hyde Park–Kenwood Community Conference Parks Committee—www.hydepark.org/
    parks/osaka2.htm.
Project 120 Chicago—www.project120chicago.org/.
"U.S. Japanese Gardens"—http://us-japanesegardens.com/tag/wooded-island/.

How You Can Support the Island

The Garden of the Phoenix Foundation
203 N. LaSalle St., Suite 2500
Chicago, IL 60601
www.gardenofthephoenix.org/our-foundation

Parting Thoughts

August 2, 2014, 2:10 p.m.
In the Japanese garden

I've had a fondness for blue herons for some 30 years now, and ever since I saw a photo of a green heron, I've been on the lookout for one, curious about how a bird so much smaller could still look heron-like in real life.

But I haven't been looking for one today. Instead, I am reveling in being in my daughter Caitlin's company, only peripherally feeling the sun on my skin, hearing the waterfall's cascades behind us accompanied by a low murmur from the two martial arts practitioners training in the pavilion. Caitlin and I are seated on rocks at the path's edge, eating the sandwiches we brought with us.

Suddenly, just a few yards in front of us, our attention is snagged by the scurry of a dark shadow by one of the rocks at the lagoon's edge. The can be no doubt: a green heron! Fishing amid the lily pads at the edge of the garden, the bird is intent upon his task and not troubled by our presence. Caitlin and I admire his agile moves for some time.

Off in the distance, a blue heron wades out into the lagoon, the curve of neck disappearing into hunch of shoulder, profile of beak aiming the staring yellow eye. As is true of the nature of many other things on this particular day—an island retreat from the city, a prairie habitat splashed with sun and vibrating with butterflies, the fine-spun gauze of mother-daughter relationship, peace unfolding in a Japanese garden—there is no mistaking heron-ness.

The Pair of Michigan Manitous

July 12, 2014, 10:40 p.m.
Bay Campground
South Manitou Island

Rain ticking on the tent, foghorns on the lake. Kathy and I are enclosed in the womb of our backpacking tent like two peas in a pod, like the "twins" we are discovering ourselves to be on this trip to "twin" islands (will they be as dissimilar as I've heard?). Already, after our day, Kathy is breathing deep into sleep.

And what a day on South Manitou Island it was! We hiked from 10:00 to 7:30: Bay Campground to the village to Florence Lake to Valley of the Giants (white cedars, that is) to the SS *Francisco Morazan* shipwreck and all the way to the Perching Dunes and back, to the schoolhouse (where we stumbled on the opportunity for an impromptu tour of the interior, courtesy of two rangers) to the cemetery and finally to the old cemetery, which we'd tried unsuccessfully to find yesterday. Old farm roads, forest sand trails, vegetation on miles of widespread dunes.

No problem with any sort of flies, no poisonous snakes, just pretty ribbons of garter snakes, a red-and-black-striped millipede, and monster chipmunks apparently proficient in the art of zippers. One managed to extract a three-ounce bag of Traverse City dried cherries from my daypack, chew a hole in the bottom of the package, and devour all three ounces while we were, very briefly, otherwise occupied.

The 1871 marble gravestone of James A. Sheridan in the forest, surrounded by wooden pickets, and the carving of the mail boat on a school desk will be the stuff of tonight's dreams.

South Manitou Island and North Manitou Island are both a part of the Sleeping Bear Dunes National Lakeshore, the mainland portion of which lies on the northwest coast of Michigan's Lower Peninsula. Together, the mainland and two islands offer 69 miles (111 kilometers) of protected shoreline to explore and enjoy.

Long before the National Park Service united the three sites into the park, a legend of the Anishinaabe explained their connection. Long, long ago, a mother bear, Mishe Mokwa, and her two cubs attempted to cross Lake Michigan to escape a raging forest fire on the shore of what we now call Wisconsin. The mother bear survived the swim, but her twin cubs could not make it and drowned in Michigan ("Big Lake"). Manitou, the Great Spirit, covered the cubs with sand, transforming them into islands, and named the two after himself: South Manitou and North Manitou. The great mother bear, the Sleeping Bear Dunes, lies onshore, vigilant forever, awaiting her cubs' arrival.

For more information on Sleeping Bear Dunes:

The Legend of Sleeping Bear, by Kathy-jo Wargin, illustrated by Gijsbert van Frankenhuyzen (Ann Arbor, MI: Sleeping Bear, 2013).

Sleeping Bear: Its Lore, Legends and First People, by George Weeks (Glen Arbor, MI: Cottage Book Shop of Glen Arbor and the Historical Society of Michigan, 1988)—This book was written by a journalist appointed by the secretary of the interior to serve on the Sleeping Bear Dunes National Lakeshore Advisory Commission.

How to Get There

Manitou Island Transit has been making the 16-mile (26-kilometer) trip across the Manitou Passage to South and North Manitou islands since 1917. Today, the National Park Service of the Department of the Interior authorizes the ferry service to provide public transportation at Sleeping Bear Dunes National Lakeshore on Lake Michigan. The ferry, the *Mishe Mokwa,* departs to "her cubs"—South Manitou Island and North Manitou Island—from the historic Fishtown Dock at the mouth of the Leland River on Lake Michigan in Leland, Michigan. Leland is located just about where the first knuckle of the little finger would be on the mitten (that is, if the mitten were a glove) that is Michigan.

Make ferry reservations before you drive or fly to Leland. Cherry Capital Airport is located in Traverse City, Michigan. Rental cars are available, and it is about a 45-minute drive to Leland. Confirm off-season trips (May, September, and October) with the ferry service:

Manitou Island Transit
231-256-9061
www.manitoutransit.com

Although departure times can vary depending on weather conditions, the ferry is scheduled during the season, mid-June through Labor Day, to daily make the one-and-a-half-hour trip to South Manitou Island at 10:00 in the morning, allowing day-trippers four and a half hours to explore South Manitou Island and arrive back in Leland at 5:30. You can also camp at one of the three campgrounds on the island, the only places where camping is allowed (see below). No transportation is available to transport camping gear; you must "pack it in," carrying all of your gear from ferry to campsite.

You cannot take a day trip by ferry to North Manitou; you must spend the night. No wheeled vehicles of any kind are allowed on the island—this includes carts, wagons, strollers, and bicycles. The island offers backpackers 15,000 acres of wilderness in exchange for a backcountry permit fee. There is one campground in the village area with eight designated sites, two community fire rings, and one outhouse. This is the only place where fires are allowed on the island. Potable water is available only in the village; a water purification system is needed elsewhere on the island.

South Manitou Island, Michigan

DAY TRIP OR CAMPING, FARMS AND FOREST

GETTING THERE: Passenger-only ferry; private boat (docking is limited to 20 minutes)

GETTING AROUND: Limited options: foot traffic only except for open-air motorized tours to select sights

OVERNIGHT ACCOMMODATIONS: Limited options: camping at three established campgrounds only

FOOD: Bring your own

DAY TRIP? Yes, but a longer stay is recommended; ferry schedule permits less than five hours on the island

STATE / PROVINCIAL / NATIONAL PARK? Sleeping Bear Dunes National Lakeshore

South Manitou Island is a great destination for a family camping trip, with potable water, outhouses, and a beautifully rustic campground within hiking distance of the dock. Expect just over eight square miles (21 square kilometers) of trails through farm and forest with buildings, left from earlier island days, in various stages of decay. Expect sandy beach along much of the shoreline. More adventures await here than can be undertaken in one visit. This island is one to return to again and again if you like to camp or are interested in history.

You needn't be concerned about running into a skunk or porcupine. And while there are no red squirrels and only one species of mouse—the woodland deer mouse—this island is home to voracious chipmunks that understand the simple equation: "Campers equal food." Snowshoe hares and a variety of snakes, turtles, and frogs also call the island home. You may be fortunate enough to see an otter, beaver, salmon, or bald eagle in or by a water source in the interior of the island. As is true with the other member of this island pair, South Manitou is a wonderful place to look for birds, including the endangered piping plover. You may, as we did, meet one or more young scientists doing research related to the island's piping plover or pitcher's thistle populations.

Paths to Adventure

NATURAL SITES

Lake Florence—A sweet lake in the woods. Any boat, canoe, raft, tube, waders—anything that goes into the water—must first be decontaminated, free of charge, by the rangers to prevent the spread of zebra mussels and other nonnative species. Nothing with wheels can

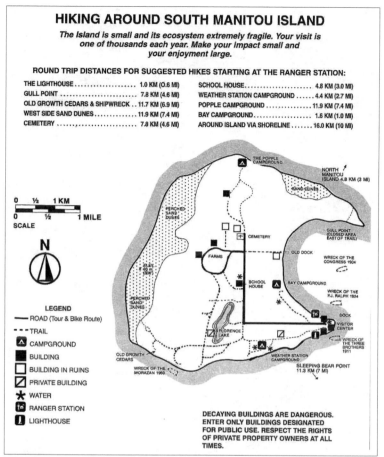

HIKING AROUND SOUTH MANITOU ISLAND

*The island is small and its ecosystem extremely fragile. Your visit is
one of thousands each year. Make your impact small and
your enjoyment large.*

ROUND TRIP DISTANCES FOR SUGGESTED HIKES STARTING AT THE RANGER STATION:

THE LIGHTHOUSE	1.0 KM (0.6 MI)	SCHOOL HOUSE	4.8 KM (3.0 MI)
GULL POINT	7.8 KM (4.6 MI)	WEATHER STATION CAMPGROUND	4.4 KM (2.7 MI)
OLD GROWTH CEDARS & SHIPWRECK	11.7 KM (6.9 MI)	POPPLE CAMPGROUND	11.9 KM (7.4 MI)
WEST SIDE SAND DUNES	11.9 KM (7.4 MI)	BAY CAMPGROUND	1.6 KM (1.0 MI)
CEMETERY	7.8 KM (4.6 MI)	AROUND ISLAND VIA SHORELINE	16.0 KM (10 MI)

LEGEND
- ROAD (Tour & Bike Route)
- TRAIL
- CAMPGROUND
- BUILDING
- BUILDING IN RUINS
- PRIVATE BUILDING
- WATER
- RANGER STATION
- LIGHTHOUSE

**DECAYING BUILDINGS ARE DANGEROUS.
ENTER ONLY BUILDINGS DESIGNATED
FOR PUBLIC USE. RESPECT THE RIGHTS
OF PRIVATE PROPERTY OWNERS AT ALL
TIMES.**

Courtesy of the National Park Service

be used to move boats, no boat motors are allowed, and only artificial lures are allowed
when fishing here.

Giant cedar trees—In the southwest corner of the island, a grove of virgin white cedar trees
still flourishes. One of the fallen cedars had 528 growth rings; it was alive before Columbus arrived on the continent!

Perched dunes—Located along the western side of the island, this is one of Michigan's
two major perched dune systems. Perched dunes are found atop a high bluff of glacial
moraine. Waves have eroded the bluff, leaving dunes exposed to the wind, which blows
the sand off the face of the bluff and onto the flat upland atop the bluff. South Manitou
Island's perched dunes rise more than 400 feet above Lake Michigan and are one of the
island's most impressive natural features.

HISTORY PRESERVED

South Manitou Visitors Center and Museum—This building was formerly the island's general store. Currently, it contains a fascinating collection of photos and a few artifacts that
show what the island was like in the years when logging, farming, and the U.S. Life-Saving Service were what this island was about. Be sure to drop in and guide yourself back
through some of the island's history.

The Old Dock (aka Burton's Wharf)—Take a stroll on the beach of Crescent Bay and about
midway, near where Chicago Road (aka Old Dock Road) dead-ends at the beach, you'll

Perched dunes, unusual dunes that are "perched" atop a cliff, exist on South Manitou Island, rising more than 400 feet above the Lake Michigan shoreline on high limestone bluffs.

come across dock pilings sticking up above the water. This was William Burton's dock, built in the mid-1830s when the island was first settled. He built the dock as a site from which to provide cordwood as fuel for Great Lakes steamships in this, the only natural deepwater harbor between Chicago and Buffalo. You can also reach it by hiking through Bay Campground until you come to Chicago Road (aka Old Dock Road), turning right, and heading for the water.

South Manitou Lighthouse—Active from 1871 to 1958, this 100-foot lighthouse marks the location of the only deepwater natural harbor between the Buffalo and Chicago, where steamers stopped to get more wood for their boilers and ships took refuge in storms. A keeper's house is connected by a covered passage. Tours, given by park rangers, are available, and the view from the top is amazing!

South Manitou Coast Guard Station—The former Coast Guard station was built in 1901 as a U.S. Life-Saving Service Station and currently is the South Manitou Island Ranger Station, not open to the public, serving as a private residence and office for the rangers. From 1915 to 1958, it served as a U.S. Coast Guard Station.

South Manitou Island One-Room Schoolhouse—Located on Ohio Road, this schoolhouse was built in 1899 for students in first through eighth grades (one had to go to the mainland to attend high school). The school was also used as a venue for community meetings and island social events.

SS *Francisco Morazan* Shipwreck—A Liberian freighter that ran aground on the southwest shore of the island in a storm on November 29, 1960. The 15 people on board were rescued. The remains of the ship, with its current healthy "crew" of cormorants, are visible from shore. The shipwreck and the old-growth cedar trees make two wonderful destinations on a seven-mile (11-kilometer) hike from the dock, a hike which can be extended to include the perched sand dunes as well. (I would not, however, recommend that one undertake the longer hike during a day trip to the island, given the time constraints imposed by the ferry schedule.)

Cemetery—Located about a mile (1.6 kilometers) north of the schoolhouse on Ohio Road, two miles (3.2 kilometers) from the village, this is the main marked cemetery and includes several descendants of early island settlers. Look for the names Beck, Burdick, Haas, Hutzler, and Peth. You can find the 2006 South Manitou Island Cemetery Survey at the website http://manitouislandsarchives.org/archives/genealogy/smimaincemetery/2006CemeterySurvey/index.html.

Old Cemetery—Islanders were buried in places on the island other than the main cemetery. One place that we couldn't find on our first try but did on our second is near the signpost that points to the Popple Campground and Farms in one direction and the Village Dock and Bay Campground in another. From there, into the forest we went, past the old site of the Burdick General Store, which had been located near the old dock, north of the Bay Campground. When you come upon a fenced-in area, inside this "crib" you'll find the

The *Francisco Morazan*, built in 1922, ran aground in 1960. Off the shore of South Manitou, it is one of 16 shipwrecks in the Manitou Passage Underwater Preserve. The *Morazan* is currently inhabited by double-crested cormorants.

The headstone of James Allen Sheridan, South Manitou farmer, who died in 1871. He is buried in a small cemetery now in the forest.

gravestone of James A. Sheridan, who died in 1871 at age 70 years and three months. This is one of two such graves in this area.

Wagon Tour—Offered by the Manitou Transit Company. Ride in (historic) style on the benches of a farm wagon pulled behind a tractor. Two tours have been offered in the past: one to the shipwreck and giant cedar trees and the other to historic farms.

Manitou Passage State Underwater Preserve—This is one of the best areas in Michigan for shipwreck diving. The Manitou Passage surrounds South and North Manitou and lies between the two islands and the mainland Sleeping Bear Dunes National Lakeshore. Two circumstances contributed to the large number of shipwrecks in this area. The first is the sheer volume of traffic; during the lumbering era in Michigan, this part of the state was booming, and ships were used to transport the lumber. Second, during storms, ships tended to seek shelter in the area of the islands, and some of them didn't make it. In addition to the *Francisco Morazan*, divers can explore 15 other shipwrecks as well as seven docks, offering a variety of experiences that cover two centuries of history.

TO REWILD OR PRESERVE?

An interesting conversation is taking place in the twenty-first century about how to make land-management decisions that integrate the natural landscape—the process of "rewilding"—with artifacts of the cultural landscape—"historic preservation." As you explore the island, you may want to keep this issue in mind. How would you decide what to preserve, what to remove, what to replace?

OTHER ISLAND THINGS TO DO

Hike—The island has trails of varying distances (measured from the Ranger Station near the dock) leading to 10 destinations, from a trail a little over .5 mile (.8 kilometer) to the lighthouse to 10 miles (16 kilometers) around the island via the shoreline.

Camp—The island had three distinctly different campgrounds, *the only places on the island where camping is allowed.*

- Bay Campground—Closest to the dock (.5 mile/.8 kilometer) and the village, this eastside campground has 25 individual sites, three group sites, and great access to the beach at Crescent Bay. Drinking water and community-share fire rings are available at the campground.
- Weather Station Campground—Located on bluffs overlooking Lake Michigan, this south-end campground is 1.33 miles (2.14 kilometers) from the dock and has 20 individual sites and three group sites, all in a forested area and relatively secluded from each other. Drinking water and community-share fire rings are available at the campground.
- Popple Campground—The most secluded of the three, this north-end campground has only seven individual sites. While it offers great beach access, you should note that it is a 3.5-mile (5.6-kilometers) hike from the Ranger Station, water filtration equipment is required, poison ivy is plentiful, and no fires are permitted.

Watch for birds—In the air: bald eagles, woodcocks, and snipes as well as many varieties of warblers; in the water, mergansers, scaups, goldeneyes, Canada geese, loons; and at the beach, piping plovers.

Watch for wildlife—There are 11 species of mammals on the island: fox, coyote, beaver, chipmunk, fox squirrel, snowshoe hare, deer mouse, and four bat species.

Dive—The Manitou islands are surrounded by some 50 shipwrecks, several of which are popular, and protected, sites for diving.

For More Island Information

Sleeping Bear Dunes National Lakeshore—www.nps.gov/slbe/planyourvisit/southmanitou island.htm.

www.manitouislandsarchives.org—This site provides background on many of the residents of both Manitou Islands. (Click on the "Archives" link on the left and then "History.")

Coming through with Rye: A Historic Agricultural Landscape Study of South Manitou at Sleeping Bears Dunes, by Brenda Wheeler Williams, Arnold R. Alanen, and William H. Tishler (Omaha: Midwest Field Area, National Park Service, 1996), available at https://archive.org/details/ComingThroughWithRye.

The Manitou Islands, the pdf of a booklet compiled by Kerry Kelly, is available at http://
friendsofsleepingbear.org/wp-content/uploads/2011/09/Manitou-Islands-20150107a
.pdf.

*Exploring North Manitou, South Manitou, High and Garden Islands of the Lake Mich-
igan Archipelago: A Hiking, Backpacking and Historical Guide, Including Individual
Histories and Trail Descriptions for These Eastern Lake Michigan Islands in the Sleeping
Bear National Lakeshore and the Island Group,* by Roberth H. Ruchhoft (Cincinnati:
Pucelle, 1991).

How You Can Support the Island

Friends of Sleeping Bear Dunes
PO Box 545
Empire, MI 49630
www.friendsofsleepingbear.org

Preserve Historic Sleeping Bear (PHSB)
PO Box 453
Empire, MI 49630
231-334-6103
www.phsb.org

The park's partner group mission, as described on its website, is "to preserve and interpret the rich heritage of historic structures and cultural landscapes of Sleeping Bear Dunes
National Lakeshore."

Manitou Islands Memorial Society (MIMS)
http://manitouislandsmemorialsociety.org

This nonprofit organization helps preserve the history and cultural traditions of Michigan's Manitou Islands by distributing educational and interpretive materials and programs,
keeping records of burials and gravesites of original settlers and others interred on the
islands, promoting the proper care of the islands' historic and cultural assets, and supporting
the National Park Service as volunteers on the islands.

North Manitou Island, Michigan

REWILDING VERSUS PRESERVATION

GETTING THERE: Passenger-only ferry; private boat (docking is limited to 20 minutes)

GETTING AROUND: Limited options: foot traffic only; no wheels of any sort allowed

OVERNIGHT ACCOMMODATIONS: Limited options: camping only

FOOD: Bring your own

DAY TRIP? No, a minimum one-night stay, per ferry schedule, is required

STATE / PROVINCIAL / NATIONAL PARK? Sleeping Bear Dunes National Lakeshore

All 7.75 by 4.25 miles (12.5 by 6.9 kilometers)—approximately 15,000 acres—of North Manitou Island, with its 20 miles (32.2 kilometers) of shoreline, is managed as "wilderness," all of it, that is, except for the 27 acres of the village. No wheels are allowed on the island, just feet on the ground. Pets are prohibited. Finding solitude on this island is not a problem. Although we visited the island in mid-July, during one full day of hiking we came across only a few other hikers. You may find you have the designated campground entirely to yourself! Except for raccoons. Despite having been killed off by disease by 2002, raccoons are back and represent the enemy for campers/backpackers here.

Although some of the same activities took place on North Manitou Island as on its partner to the south—farming, logging, fishing—the island's unique history, of which vestiges still remain, includes the story of possession by big landowners. Unlike the community on South Manitou Island, North Manitou, when settled, was primarily owned by one or only a few landowners. Two such, Roger Sherman and George McConnell, owned much of the island in the early 1920s. Their ownership led to the establishment of the Manitou Island Syndicate, which became the Manitou Island Association (MIA), the party responsible for hatching the plan to develop the island into a hunting preserve.

In 1925, the MIA introduced a small herd of nine deer, which eventually grew to 2,000, altering the island landscape significantly. In 1926, William R. Angell bought up most of the island. You can read a fascinating account of this island period written by Rita Hadra Rusco, who lived on the island for almost 50 years, in *North Manitou Island: Between Sunrise and Sunset.*

Paths to Adventure

NATURAL SITES

The description of the island's topography provided by the National Park Service is rather poetic: "The highest point on the island is in the northwest corner, 1,001 feet above sea

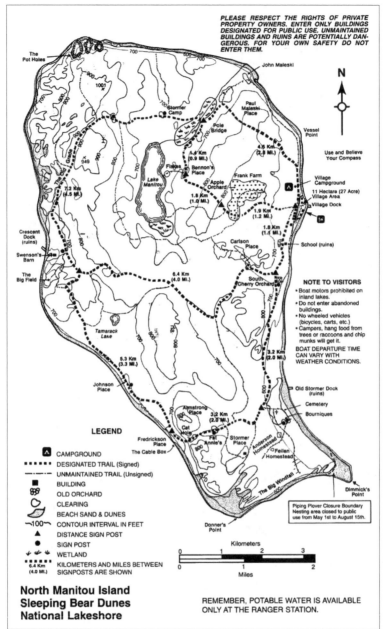

PLEASE RESPECT THE RIGHTS OF PRIVATE PROPERTY OWNERS. ENTER ONLY BUILDINGS DESIGNATED FOR PUBLIC USE. UNMAINTAINED BUILDINGS AND RUINS ARE POTENTIALLY DANGEROUS. FOR YOUR OWN SAFETY DO NOT ENTER THEM.

N

Use and Believe Your Compass

NOTE TO VISITORS
• Boat motors prohibited on inland lakes.
• Do not enter abandoned buildings.
• No wheeled vehicles (bicycles, carts, etc.)
• Campers, hang food from trees or raccoons and chipmunks will get it.

BOAT DEPARTURE TIME CAN VARY WITH WEATHER CONDITIONS.

Piping Plover Closure Boundary Nesting area closed to public use from May 1st to August 15th.

LEGEND

🏕 CAMPGROUND
▪▪▪▪ DESIGNATED TRAIL (Signed)
—— UNMAINTAINED TRAIL (Unsigned)
■ BUILDING
🌳 OLD ORCHARD
☘ CLEARING
〜 BEACH SAND & DUNES
〜100〜 CONTOUR INTERVAL IN FEET
▲ DISTANCE SIGN POST
● SIGN POST
🌿 WETLAND
▪▪▪▪ KILOMETERS AND MILES BETWEEN
6.4 Km SIGNPOSTS ARE SHOWN
(4.0 MI.)

**North Manitou Island
Sleeping Bear Dunes
National Lakeshore**

Kilometers
0 1 2 3
0 1 2
Miles

REMEMBER, POTABLE WATER IS AVAILABLE ONLY AT THE RANGER STATION.

Courtesy of the National Park Service

level or 421 feet above Lake Michigan. . . . Low, sandy, open dune country on the southeast side grades into interfingering high sand hills and blowout dunes on the southwest side of the island."

Bluffs—On the northwest side of the island.

Dunes—On the southwest side of the island.

Lake Manitou—In the north-central part of the island, with an elevation of 675 feet, this lake is suitable for fishing.

Tamarack Lake—A cedar swamp.

North Manitou Island provides habitat for several rare and endangered species, both flora and fauna: pitcher's thistle (a federally listed endangered species), pumpelly's brome grass (a Michigan threatened species), American chestnut (a Michigan threatened species), piping plover (a federally listed endangered species), and bald eagle (a federally listed endangered species).

HISTORY PRESERVED

The village is where you will find the only historical preservation efforts on the island.

Blossom Cottage (aka Monte Carlo Cottage)—Built in 1893 and rumored to have been designed by Frank Lloyd Wright at 26 years of age, before he was renowned as an architect.

Cottage Row—A development of 10 lots, many containing cottages built between 1893 and 1924 by Chicago residents, that remained an active resort until 1950. As well as a park between the shoreline and the buildings, it includes:

- Katie Shepard Hotel—The residence on Cottage Row lot 1 was built by Mr. and Mrs. William Shepard in 1895 for their daughter Katherine, "Miss Katie." Shepard turned the house into a hotel known as the Beeches around 1908, during the lumbering era, when the dining hall at the end of Cottage Row stopped serving meals. She ran the hotel and a dining room into the 1930s. Recently, over a six-year period, the Preserve Historic Sleeping Bear organization restored this structure to serve as a boardinghouse for overnight rustic accommodations in the future.

U.S. Life-Saving Service Complex—Designated as a National Historic Landmark and placed on the National Register of Historic Places in 1998, the complex is located at the beach near the dock in the village and includes the Surfman's Residence, the Hans Halseth House (1890s), the Volunteer Rescue Station (1854), the U.S. Life Boat Station and Capstan

The eastside beach on North Manitou Island.

Monte Carlo Cottage, built in 1893, was likely designed by the young, then-unknown Frank Lloyd Wright. Note the braces on the building; Preserve Historic Sleeping Bear volunteers are working to save this structure.

(1877), the U.S. Life-Saving Service Dwelling (1887), the Crew Ready Room (1895), the Root Cellar (1899), and two smaller 20th-century structures.

What began as a volunteer operation in 1854 was taken over by the new U.S. Life-Saving Service 20 years later and then became a part of the U.S. Coast Guard from 1915 until 1938, when it was sold to the Manitou Island Association. In 1984, the National Park Service acquired the buildings. "The North Manitou Island Station is the only remaining station [out of a network of nearly 200] that represents the entire lifesaving service history from [the] volunteer era through the Coast Guard."[19]

Manitou Island Association (MIA) Office—The small, simple fieldstone building in the village. The Manitou Island Association maintained an extensive farming operation, including beef cattle and orchards. The MIA, eventually under William Angell, bought up most of the island during the 1920s and 1930s and ran a large-scale hunting camp and resort. The small herd of white-tailed deer established on the island in the 1920s was supplemented in the 1930s by raccoon, pheasant, ruffed grouse, and wild turkey, making the island a desirable retreat for sportsmen. The former Cottage Row Dining Hall was transformed into the MIA Lodge for hunters. A final deer hunt was held in 1977–78, in preparation for the National Park Service takeover of the island. Annual hunts, by permit only, have occurred since 1985.

Elsewhere on the island, outside the village area, you can see reminders of the time the island supported a small community:

Cemetery—Located in the southeast corner of the island is a cemetery where a number of the island's former inhabitants are buried.

Old buildings—Scattered across the island are homes, barns, sheds, and in some cases the ruins of buildings—from the island's logging and farming eras.

CULTURAL ATTRACTIONS

Photovoltaic Power Array—Providing all of the power on the island, the array is located in the village.

You will be asked by the National Park Service to engage in two efforts, one to prevent a "culture" and one to protect another:

- Exotic species prevention—To help prevent nonnative, invasive species from taking root on the island, make use of the boot brush on the Leland docks and at the island ferry dock to scrape off "hitchhiking dirt and seed sources from your footwear." You are advised to check your clothing and equipment for seeds and burrs as well.
- Piping plover protection—To help this endangered rare shorebird survive—one of the few nesting areas in the Great Lakes region is at the island's Dimmick's Point—respect the area's annual closure from May 1 through August 15.

Hiking is what one does on North (and South) Manitou Island(s).

OTHER ISLAND THINGS TO DO

Backpack, camp, and hike—These are the three most popular activities on the island. The island has a trail system, the remnants of an unpaved road as well as the roadbed of the Smith & Hull logging railroad track. For nighttime accommodations, you can choose a site in a very rustic campground or take your choice of backcountry sites in the 15,000 acres of wilderness.

Watch for birds—In the air, bald eagles, woodcocks, and snipes, as well many varieties of warblers; in the water, mergansers, scaups, goldeneyes, Canada geese, loons; and at the beach, piping plovers.

Watch for wildlife—Coyote, beaver, white-tailed deer, white-footed mice, eastern chipmunk, raccoon, and garter snakes.

Dive—The Manitou islands are surrounded by 50-some shipwrecks, several of which are popular, and protected, sites for diving.

SPECIAL ISLAND EVENTS

White-tailed Deer Hunt—From the four male and five female deer originally introduced onto the island in the 1920s, there grew an estimated population of 2,000 by 1981. Two problems resulted: (1) the island's vegetation took a hit when the deer ate all of the yew and young maple trees, and (2) deer starved when the vegetation could not sustain the herd.

A special deer hunt is conducted on North Manitou Island in October and November to control the herd and preserve the natural vegetation. Participation in this special hunt requires the hunter to submit a current North Manitou Island Deer Hunt application, attend a ranger orientation, obtain a backcountry permit, and check in with rangers upon arrival on the island. For more information, see www.nps.gov/slbe/planyourvisit/nmihunting.htm.

For More Island Information

Sleeping Bear Dunes National Lakeshore—www.nps.gov/slbe/planyourvisit/northmanitouisland.htm.

www.manitouislandsarchives.org—This site provides background on many of the residents of both Manitou Islands. (Click on the "Archives" link on the left and then "History").

For North Manitou Shoal, see www.lighthousefriends.com/light.asp?ID=714.

Tending a Comfortable Wilderness, by Eric MacDonald with Arnold R. Alanenn (Omaha: U.S. Department of the Interior, National Park Service, Midwest Field Office, 2000), available at https://archive.org/details/TendingAComfortableWilderness.

North Manitou Island: Between Sunrise and Sunset, 2nd ed., by Rita Hadra Rusco (n.p., CreateSpace, 2014).

The Manitou Islands, the pdf of a booklet compiled by Kerry Kelly, is available at http://friendsofsleepingbear.org/wp-content/uploads/2011/09/Manitou-Islands-20150107a.pdf.

Exploring North Manitou, South Manitou, High and Garden Islands of the Lake Michigan Archipelago: A Hiking, Backpacking and Historical Guide, Including Individual Histories and Trail Descriptions for These Eastern Lake Michigan Islands in the Sleeping Bear National Lakeshore and the Beaver Island Group, by Roberth H. Ruchhoft (Cincinnati: Pucelle, 1991).

How You Can Support the Islands

Friends of Sleeping Bear Dunes
PO Box 545
Empire, MI 49630
www.friendsofsleepingbear.org

Preserve Historic Sleeping Bear (PHSB)
PO Box 453
Empire, MI 49630
231-334-6103
www.phsb.org

The park's partner group mission, as described on its website, is "to preserve and interpret the rich heritage of historic structures and cultural landscapes of Sleeping Bear Dunes National Lakeshore."

In 2014, PHSB volunteers made their sixth trip to the North Manitou Island to spend 10 days working on the Katie Shepard Hotel on Cottage Row. The organization has been working to determine the next steps to take in the preservation of the Monte Carlo, thought to have been designed by Frank Lloyd Wright. After review, the National Park will determine the scope of work.

Manitou Islands Memorial Society (MIMS)
http://manitouislandsmemorialsociety.org

This nonprofit organization helps preserve the history and cultural traditions of Michigan's Manitou Islands by distributing educational and interpretive materials and programs, keeping records of burials and gravesites of original settlers and others interred on the islands, promoting the proper care of the islands' historic and cultural assets, and supporting the National Park Service as volunteers on the islands.

Parting Thoughts

July 14, 2014, after dark
Village Campground
North Manitou Island

On the boat to South Manitou, one of the crew had suggested I look up Dave Hooper, park ranger on North Manitou Island in the 1990s and, in his retirement, longtime volunteer historian. Before meeting with him, I compiled a list of 10 questions, the last of which was "What would you recommend visitors to North Manitou see and do?"

Dave's answer was simply, "Just walk around and enjoy the experience." A man after my own heart.

So walk we did; we walked for many miles. And yes, it certainly would be difficult for us not to have enjoyed the experience!

Beaver Island, Michigan

AMERICA'S EMERALD ISLE

July 4, 2013, 4:45 p.m.
Beaver Island

On the Fourth of July, late in the afternoon, I'm sitting on the weather-silvered deck of my friend Janet's year-round house. The house, the aluminum rowboat with her fragrant herb garden planted in it, and I are perched atop a dune on the sunset side of the island, overlooking Lake Michigan.

Suddenly, above the rowboat, a rapid motion catches my eye. I follow it up against a backdrop of tall cedars and then, just as I realize what it is, the hummingbird pauses and perches on the electrical wire.

This is the only time I've ever witnessed a hummingbird pause to perch. Perhaps the "island time" that adventure seekers claim to experience on this island in particular affects even these most high-strung members of the avian community. Probably less accessible to hummingbirds are the waves of history, stories, and magic available to human travelers on Beaver Island as we shift into island time.

GETTING THERE: Car ferry; daily air service; private boat or plane

GETTING AROUND: Bring your car and/or bike; bicycle and kayak rentals; tours available

OVERNIGHT ACCOMMODATIONS: Motels, lodges, and B&Bs; cottage and house rentals; campgrounds

FOOD: Restaurants; groceries

DAY TRIP? Possible, but not recommended

STATE / PROVINCIAL / NATIONAL PARK? No, but one-third of the island is Michigan State Forest, including Beaver Island State Forest Campground

Beaver Beacon, Beaver Island's news magazine since 1955, in "A Brief History of Beaver Island," states that the island's history "can be roughly divided into three time periods: Indian, Mormon, and Irish."[20] Beaver Island is the only place in the United States that once had a ruling king. When Joseph Smith, the founder of the Church of Jesus Christ of Latter-day Saints, died, most Mormons considered Brigham Young to be Smith's successor. Those who didn't followed James J. Strang. The Strangites originally settled in Wisconsin, but to avoid persecution, Strang moved his followers to Beaver Island in 1848.

Courtesy of the Beaver Island Chamber of Commerce

There, Strang founded the first newspaper in northern Michigan, the *Northern Islander*. He was elected to the Michigan House of Representatives in both 1853 and 1855. In between his arrival on Beaver Island and his political wins, he made several major declarations: he declared himself a polygamist (1849), his expression of which led to five wives, with whom he fathered 14 children; he declared himself king of the 2,600 Strangites on the island (1850); and he declared that female Strangites were to be attired in bloomers. The last of these edicts perhaps led to the trouble that ultimately resulted in Strang's assassination in 1856, after which his followers were driven off the island.

Many of the original non-Native settlers, fishermen who had been driven off the island by the Mormons, returned in 1856 when the Mormons were expelled. Many of those fishermen were Irish. They sent word of the cheap land and good fishing home, and home for many happened to be the island of Arranmore, off the coast of Donegal. "The Irish community prospered and grew in the 1860s, 70s, and 80s. In the 1890s over 100 fishing boats docked at St. James. . . . When the century changed there were about 2000 Beaver Islanders, many of them second-generation Irish immigrants."[21] In the first decade of the twenty-first century, a full seven generations later, visitors from Arranmore visited Beaver Island on October 7, 2000, and a contingent of Beaver Islanders "returned the favor by taking a trip to Arranmore in 2003 for the Árainn Mhór and Beaver Island Twinning." One Beaver Islander posted an update from Ireland: "The memorial at the lake on Arranmore is a tremendous structure which has a Beaver and an Otter facing each other with a [fish] between them symbolizing the unity we both share."[22]

To find out more about the island's Irish community and Strang's reign as well as other interesting historical facets of Beaver Island—including the island's Native American inhabitants, the island's musicians, and the island's much beloved doctor, Feodor Protar—visit the Beaver Island Historical Society Museum in the Old Mormon Print Shop (where Strang published the *Northern Islander*), the only building left on the island from the time of the Mormon king's rule, in St. James (yes, named after Strang).

How to Get There

Before we address the fruits of shifting to island time, understand that it does take a bit of time just to get to this island—but it is well worth it. While the distance to Beaver Island does not involve *the* longest ferry ride in the Great Lakes Basin, you may experience a stress-provoking departure unless you know what to expect and plan accordingly. The ferries of the Beaver Island Boat Company pull up anchor from the tony vacation destination of Charlevoix:

Beaver Island Boat Company
103 Bridge Park Dr.
Charlevoix, MI 49720
www.beaverislandboatcompany.com

Once you get through the backed-up traffic on two-lane Bridge Street, jammed with sightseers, shoppers, and all the cars held up by the drawbridge between Lake Charlevoix and Lake Michigan, it may be a bit closer to departure time than you had hoped—only to find out that if you're not taking your motor vehicle on the ferry with you, it needs to be parked about a mile (1.6 kilometers) away (note, your ferry ticket must be bought *first*), and after parking your vehicle, you then must wait to be shuttled back, arriving back at the dock feeling, perhaps, just a tad frantic.

So plan ahead. Plan to get to Charlevoix *at least* two hours before the ferry departs; allow even more time if you can, and consider that your navigation system most likely knows nothing about the "Charlevoix Choke." Arriving in town early will give you time to buy your ticket, park your car, and be shuttled back to the dock in time to get a ice cream cone or sandwich from one of the many establishments catering to tourists on Bridge Street.

Also, arriving on the early side will give you the opportunity to think about how "mainland time" feels while you're experiencing it before you board the ferry and begin the shift to "island time" and all of the history, nature, art, stories, and magic this shift brings with it.

St James Harbor, Beaver Island, at sunset with the Beaver Island Harbor Light and CMU Biological Station at the point of Gull Harbor Natural Area.

An alternative to riding the ferry is taking one of the multiple daily flights offered from two flight services:

Fresh Air Aviation, flights from Beaver Island/Charlevoix (www.freshairaviation.net).
Island Airways, flights from Beaver Island/Charlevoix (www.islandairways.com).

What to Expect

Expect a little Irish on this 58-square-mile (150-square-kilometer) island, the largest island in Lake Michigan. *Céad Míle Fáilte*, Gaelic for "A Hundred Thousand Welcomes," appears on the Beaver Island Boat Company tickets and above the door of the Stony Acre Grill. This island reminds me of Ireland more than any Great Lakes Basin Island I've visited, and history shows the Irish felt very at home here, too.

While you can expect to find motel lodging, restaurants, a full grocery store plus two convenience stores, gas stations, a hardware and building supply store, a spa, and car and bike rentals in St. James Township on the island, rustic camping is also available, April through November, at the north-end 12-site St. James Township Campground and the island's eastside 22-site Bill Wagner Peaine Township Campground (www.beaverisland.org/camping/). The latter is the state forest campground, managed by the township.

Scattered across the island are seven lakes—Font Lake, Barney's Lake, Round Lake, Egg Lake, Fox Lake, Greene's Lake, and Lake Geneserath—and more than a few ponds (some count Miller's Marsh as an eighth lake).

Paths to Adventure

You can order a detailed map of Beaver Island featuring roads and trails, topography, and nature preserves. The map has a detailed legend and visitor information, including points of interest, an enlarged map of the town of St. James, phone numbers, and a brief summary of the island's history. Pick one up at the museum or send $7.00 in advance of your visit to the island to:

Beaver Island Chamber of Commerce
PO Box 5
Beaver Island, MI 49782

NATURAL SITES

Before planning a hiking adventure, download a Beaver Island Trail Map: www.beaverisland .org/wp-content/uploads/2013/06/BI-Trails-R.pdf.

Barney's Lake Nature Preserve—120 acres in the north-central part of the island, with 2,200 feet on Barney's Lake; habitats include open meadows with apple trees, hardwood forest, peatlands, sedge meadows, and cedar swamp. The old O'Donnell homestead site is east of the lake across from the boat-launching site. Once cleared fields are now a study in plant succession. Stones are piled along boundaries of what were once fields and pastures. A total of 1.75 miles (2.82 kilometers) of trails, including a two-track road, allow for walking. Wildlife includes loons, great blue herons, white-tailed deer, beavers, and snowshoe hares.

Little Sand Bay Nature Preserve—118 acres includes much of Little Sand Bay, mixed conifer forest, thick cedar swamp, and sand dune habitats as well as 1,300 feet of sandy shoreline. A .4-mile (.6-kilometer) trail and footbridges allow exploration without damage to the sensitive habitat. There is public access to the lake and to a shallow marsh beach. Threatened/endangered species include Lake Huron tansy and Michigan monkey flower, the latter known to be found in only about 20 other places in the world.

Miller's Marsh—230 acres of the largest and most diverse marsh on the island, which includes a combination of open shallow water, extensive sedge, and sphagnum mats surrounded by a vast mature second-growth beech-maple forest, home to frogs, waterfowl, and migratory birds.

Petritz Family Nature Preserve—27 acres, including 500 feet on Lake Michigan, serves as natural habitat for deer, wild turkey, and other animals as well as the state-threatened pitcher's thistle and Lake Huron tansy. The preserve also provides significant waterfowl and migratory bird habitat.

Conn's Cove Nature Reserve—A 20-acre preserve on the east side of the island with 700 feet on Lake Michigan.

Carl E. Erber Nature Preserve—.5 acre with 450 feet of Lake Michigan shoreline.

Gull Harbor Natural Area—This habitat is shoreline, cedar shrub, and marshy ponds, with a few wooded areas behind the open ones at the water. It is an excellent area to observe waterfowl, wading birds, shorebirds, and raptors. The area is used extensively by migrating songbirds in the spring and fall. During the summer months, the nonvenomous northern watersnakes are active in and around the ponds.

Central Michigan University Biological Station on Beaver Island (33850 East Side Dr.)—This station supports research and learning about the island's freshwater ecosystems, natural

Beaver Island Historical Museum and Mormon Print Shop. Northern Michigan's first newspaper was published here by followers of "King" James Jesse Strang, who reigned as monarch of America's only kingdom for eight years until he was assassinated in 1856.

habitats, and seven biologically unique inland lakes, providing, according to its website, "an unmatched learning and research environment" for researchers and students alike (www.cmich.edu/colleges/cst/cmubs/about/Pages/default.aspx).

Beaver Island's Birding Trail—Encompasses more than 12,000 acres of state and township lands and four Little Traverse Conservancy preserves.

Beaver Island State Forest Area—Rustic campground with 22 tent sites, vault toilets, and potable water from a hand pump. No reservations are taken; sites available on a first come, first served basis. See www.michigandnr.com/parksandtrails/details.aspx?id=608&type =SFCG.

HISTORY PRESERVED

Beaver Island Historical Museum at the Old Mormon Print Shop (26275 Main St.)—Built by followers of King James Jesse Strang, the museum was first used as a print shop and today is on the National Register of Historic Places.

Beaver Island Historical Society Marine Museum—An authentic net shed, built in 1906, houses memorabilia from when St. James Harbor was a fishing center.

The Protar Home—On the National Register of Historic Places, this cabin was the home of Dr. Feodor Protar from 1893 to 1925. The building is open during Museum Week in July and by special appointment. Protar's tomb is .25 mile (.4 kilometer) west of the cabin.

Heritage Park—On Donegal Bay Road, this park features outdoor exhibits of a portion of the narrow gauge track used during the island's lumbering days and mechanical

The Protar Home: Beaver Island's much-beloved unofficial doctor, Feodor Protar, lived here from 1893 until he died in 1925.

equipment such as Beaver Island's first generator, the island's first road grader (brought to the island for a development in 1970), and the island's first thresher (purchased in the late 1940s and used cooperatively until the mid-1950s, when farming on the island was no longer profitable). Also on display is a side-dispensing harvester, a plow, a seeder, and a mower. All of the equipment was donated by island residents. During summer Museum Weeks, Heritage Park is a place where children have the opportunity to try their hand at butter churning, goat milking, crosscut sawing, starting a fire with flint, and walking on stilts.

Beaver Island Head Light and Keeper's House—At the southernmost end of the island, this lighthouse was requested in 1838 to help ship traffic between the Straits of Mackinac and Green Bay. Funds were finally appropriated in 1850, and it was built by the end of 1851. The first keeper was arrested, and the next two were Strangites. The position was then briefly taken by an original settler returning to the island, after which another Strangite became keeper. The tower of the original lighthouse fell in 1957, and a new one, still standing, was built in 1958. The light was automated in 1938, and the lighthouse was decommissioned in 1962. In 1975, the property was purchased for $1 and deeded to the Charlevoix Public Schools. Today, the Beaver Island Lighthouse School serves as a residential school for students, 16 to 19, in northwest Michigan who have dropped out of school or are at risk of doing so.[23]

"Whiskey Point" Lighthouse—Located at the entrance to St. James Harbor—you'll pass it on the ferry—this is Beaver Island's Harbor Light (aka St. James Light), built in 1856 and referred to as the Whiskey Point Lighthouse because it is on the former site of a trading post that apparently traded much in the way of whiskey.[24] An interesting historical note is that one of the keepers of this lighthouse was Elizabeth Whitney (Van Riper) Williams, who came to the island when she was four years old and as an adult staffed this lighthouse, first with her husband, until he drowned during a rescue, and then solo for 12 years, until her request to transfer to the mainland to serve as the first keeper of the Little Traverse Lighthouse was granted. It was here that she wrote her book *A Child of the Sea and Life among the Mormons,* first published in 1905, describing her early Beaver Island experiences.[25]

The Stone Circle—This large-scale landscape artifact, consisting of a group of stones, some quite large and some bearing carvings, located on the island's west side, has been investigated by archaeologists. The current thought is that this stone circle was, and may still be, used as a site for Native American ceremonies.[26]

CULTURAL ATTRACTIONS

St. James Boat Shop (38230 Michigan Ave.)—A shop specializing in rustic handcrafted cherrywood canoes and dinghies, longboards, paddleboards, paddles, push sticks, treasure boxes, buckets, and bowls, all made on the island using the craftsmanship of another era. www.stjamesboatshopcom.

Beaver Island Toy Museum (37970 Michigan Ave.)—Artist Mary Stewart Rose (Scholl) has built a toy store and museum on the island that has to be experienced to be believed (www.youtube.com/watch?v=Z3_oOxtvug8).

Livingstone Studio—Artists who live on the island year-round or seasonally display works of clay, fiberglass, metal, and wood, photography, and paintings for sale. www.livingstone studio.com.

Visit one of the Island's "Irish" bars:

- Stony Acres Grill and Donegal Danny's Pub (26420 Carlisle Rd.)
- Shamrock Bar and Restaurant (26245 Main St.)

OTHER ISLAND THINGS TO DO

Golf on the Beaver Island par-35 public golf course.

Paddle (kayak, canoe or paddleboard) or bike (Happy Paddle and Bikes has rentals).

Take a nature walk with the Historical Society and CMU professors from the CMU Biological Station.

Fly in a biplane or a floatplane.

SPECIAL ISLAND EVENTS

St. Patrick's Day on "America's Emerald Isle" (March).

Warblers on the Water (May).

Beaver Island Bike Festival (June).

Fourth of July Parade on Main Street (July 4).

Beaver Island Music Festival—Music in the Woods (July).

Beaver Island Historical Society Museum Week (July).

Baroque on Beaver—A Festival of Classical Music (July–August).

Homecoming (August).

Beaver Island Half-Marathon and Paradise Bay 5K (September).

Bite of Beaver Island Food Fest (October).

The Island Boodle 5K Run (October).

For More Island Information

Beaver Island Historical Society
231-448-2254
www.beaverislandhistory.org/

Beaver Island Chamber of Commerce
231-448-2505
www.beaverisland.org

Beaver Island State Forest Campground—www.michigandnr.com/parksandtrails/Details
.aspx?id=608&type=SFCG.
Beaver Island: A Brief History (Beaver Island, MI: Beaver Island Historical Society, 2007).
Queen of the Island: The Birth of a Kingdom: Beaver Island, Michigan, 1850, by Jo Ann
Mazoué (Davisburg, MI: Wilderness Adventure Books, 1993).
A Child of the Sea and Life among the Mormons, by Elizabeth Whitney Williams (Beaver
Island, MI: Beaver Island Historical Society, 2004)—This book (two books, actually)
was originally published in Harbor Springs, Michigan, on July 10, 1905, by Whitney Wil-
liams, who spent 50 years in lighthouse service at Harbor Point and on Beaver Island.
Protar: A Different Life, by Antje Price (Beaver Island, MI: Beaver Island Historical Society,
2006).
"Beaver Island," in *Biking the Great Lakes Islands,* by Kathleen Abrams and Lawrence
Abrams (Wasau, WI: Entwood, 1985), 36–49—The three Beaver Island biking routes
detailed are Around Beaver Harbor, Historical Tour, and Lighthouse Circle Tour.

How You Can Support the Island

Beaver Island Historical Society
231-448-2254
www.beaverislandhistory.org

Friends of Beaver Island
PO Box 5
Beaver Island, MI 49782
www.facebook.com/beaverisland

Beaver Island Association
"Supporting Environmental and Economic Sustainability"
PO Box 390
Beaver Island, MI 49782
www.beaverislandassociation.org

Institute for Great Lakes Research
Central Michigan University
Carlin Alumni House
c/o Gift Processing
Mt. Pleasant, MI 48859
800-358-6903

Parting Thoughts

July 6, 2013, 9:55 p.m.
Beaver Island

Wonderfully entertaining concert at the beautiful Beaver Island Community Center auditorium tonight by the remarkable Chenille Sisters, whom we ran into this afternoon coming up from the beach while we were walking the dog. We came out of the concert to twilight, cool air, and a quiet street. We were getting into the truck when Janet suggested we stop for a glass of wine.

We ended up back at Stony Acres. In between dart games, we ran into the almost mythic Robert Cole, whom, it has seemed, everyone has been telling me I must meet for a wide variety of reasons since before I'd even gotten off the ferry. Cole, a fifth-generation Beaver Islander and local historian, began an oral history project on the island in 1990 by interviewing 10 "island notables" and then revived the project in 2000, even traveling off "The Rock" and ultimately collecting over three years' worth of interviews with islanders and then former islanders in Chicago, Grand Rapids, and St. Clair Shores.

But by our second glasses of wine, we'd traveled back past these relatively recent island histories, and Robert was serving up more island stone circle stories, stories in which Beaver Island was connected to far more than the old sod of Arranmore.

Straits of Mackinac Islands

Michigan
(Upper Peninsula)

Lake
Michigan

Lake
Huron

Mackinac Island

Bois Blanc Island

St. Ignace

Straits of Mackinac

Mackinaw City

Pointe aux Pins

Michigan

Cheboygan

An Introduction to the Straits of Mackinac

The Straits of Mackinac connect Lake Michigan to Lake Huron, flowing between the pointed tips of Michigan's two peninsulas. The Mackinac Bridge (the Mighty Mac), with a shoreline-to-shoreline span of five miles (eight kilometers), crosses over the Straits of Mackinac, connecting the Lower and Upper Peninsulas of Michigan—Mackinaw City and St. Ignace—between which the Straits run.

To the west of the bridge, there is one tiny (266-acre) uninhabited island: St. Helena Island. Other than the St. Helena Lighthouse and its grounds, the entire island is the St. Helena Island Nature Preserve, owned by Little Traverse Conservancy, and the island is accessible only by private watercraft. To the east of the bridge are three islands, two of which are accessible by ferry.

Mackinac Island, just under 19 square miles (49 square kilometers) and an island on which motor vehicles are not permitted, is serviced by three passenger ferry lines, with departure points from both Mackinaw City in the Lower Peninsula and St. Ignace in the Upper Peninsula. Bois Blanc, just over 40 square miles (104 square kilometers), has a vehicular ferry that runs from Cheboygan in the Lower Peninsula to the island. In between these two islands is Round Island, comprised of 378 uninhabited acres, almost all of it the Round Island Wilderness Area, part of the Hiawatha National Forest. The only building on the island, the Round Island Lighthouse, is the iconic lighthouse one sees when aboard a ferry coming into Mackinac Island's Haldimand Bay. The only way to get to Round Island is by private watercraft, and the lighthouse is off limits to any island visitors.

The Straits of Mackinac are five miles (eight kilometers) wide at their narrowest point, approximately 30 miles (48 kilometers) long, and only 120 feet (37 meters) deep. Given their narrowness and shallowness, the Straits often freeze in the winter. The winter ice bridge across the Straits is a cause for celebration for all islanders because it connects them to the mainland for some of the time during the months the ferries do not run. The U.S. Coast Guard's icebreaker, USCGC *Mackinaw,* keeps the Straits open as a shipping lane.

Although the flow of the Straits is generally eastward—the strong currents of the Straits do tend to reverse direction every few days—the average water levels of both lakes are the same (rising toward 580 feet in 2015); there is no drop in elevation between these three bodies of water as there is between every other two of the one dozen major bodies of water that make up the Great Lakes Basin. Not surprisingly, then, the Straits of Mackinac connect two bodies of water that are—"hydrologically"—considered one: Lake Michigan-Huron (aka "Lake Huron-Michigan"). This makes sense when you think of Michigan as two peninsulas and the two lakes as being a newer version of what is referred to by geologists as Lake Algonquin, which included a part of Lake Superior as well.

The Frenchman Jean Nicolet was the first European to paddle through the Straits, in 1634, searching for the Northwest Passage, a new way to reach China. While he didn't find the Northwest Passage, he did find Lake Michigan, and he did see many beaver in the area, and so the story of the fur trade began. This profitable trade brought European settlement to the region and, ultimately, shipping to the Great Lakes. Today, the Straits of Mackinac Underwater Preserve is a testament to the dangers of navigating through the Straits, with their rocky shoals and shallows and the potential for storms that enter the Straits and dramatically change the wind and wave conditions. For more information about the preserve, visit www.michiganpreserves.org/straits.htm.

Mackinac Island, Michigan

THE MOST HISTORIC SPOT AND THEN SOME

October 4, 2013, 5:45 p.m.
Mustang Lounge

Here is the place to sneak away from the present—and the past—at Mackinac: the Mustang Lounge. To get away from the overriding island concerns of time and flags: What century is it? Who's in possession of the island? The French? The British? The Americans? Or is it the islanders? The seasonal cottagers? The Jamaican hospitality staff? The photographers, painters, and small entrepreneurs? The day-trippers?

I'm guessing that all who can may have taken the locals' advice at some point to "hang at the 'Stang," drinking a beer (and it would be a Bud, not some sort of fudge stout, I'm guessing).

The Mustang Lounge started as a barn (one of the original walls was left standing when it was renovated), and the first owner flew a Mustang prop plane in World War II. So the name Mustang works on more than one level.

As do many of those supporting the island's tourist infrastructure. The bartender waiting on me used to come here seasonally (at one time, when he was 19, he played the bugle at the fort) before becoming a year-rounder. Firefighter patches are tucked up on the beam over the bar. We raise a glass and toast the Detroit Fire Department Junction Boys.

GETTING THERE: Passenger-only ferry; private boat or plane

GETTING AROUND: No cars allowed; bring your own bike; bicycles, kayaks, paddleboards, and horses (with/without carriages) available to rent; horse-drawn carriage tours

OVERNIGHT ACCOMMODATIONS: Resorts, hotels, historic inns, and B&Bs; rental cottages and vacation condos; no camping

FOOD: Restaurants; groceries

DAY TRIP? Yes, but you could easily fill a long weekend with island adventures!

STATE / PROVINCIAL / NATIONAL PARK? Mackinac Island State Park

If you plan a visit to the famously car-free Mackinac Island and you are at all interested in history or in getting a great view of the Straits of Mackinac, you will want to visit Fort Mackinac, a fort that was built and successfully defended by the British but claimed by the Americans twice, once after the American Revolution and again after the War of 1812. But that is a thread of this island's story we'll pick up in a bit.

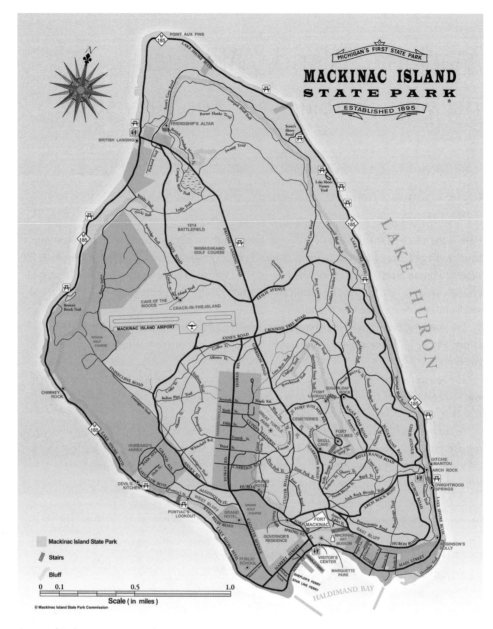

Courtesy of Mackinac State Historic Parks

First, we are more interested in the wide stretch of ground below the fort, between the 150-foot limestone bluff on which the fort is built and Haldimand Bay. When soldiers were posted at Fort Mackinac, this wide swale was where they planted their vegetable gardens. Today, as a landscaped city park of wide lawn and lilacs (in bloom in June), it is a perfect place for a picnic, especially given the convenient proximity of Doud's Market, America's oldest family-owned grocery store (1884), which is just across Fort Street from the park on Main Street.

This park, Marquette Park, is named after Père (Father) Jacques Marquette (1637–75), the French Jesuit missionary and Great Lakes explorer who is remembered for many things, chief among them founding the very first European settlement in the Midwest at Sault Ste.

Marie. He later established a mission at St. Ignace and then, with French Canadian explorer Louis Jolliet, was the first European to explore and map the Mississippi River.

Given its size, you'll be hard-pressed to miss the bronze statue of Jacques Marquette, which claims center stage in the park. The statue was designed by Italian sculptor Gaetano Trentanove in 1909 and is a duplicate of a bronze statue of Marquette in Marquette, Michigan, which itself is a duplicate of a marble statue in the National Statutory Hall Collection in the U.S. Capitol Building in Washington, DC. How many of the names of the 16 explorers memorialized on a bronze plaque on one side of the stone base of the statute do you recognize?

You'll probably also notice the replica of the Missionary Bark Chapel set up as a historical display on the west edge of the park. Father Claude Dablon built the original on the island in 1671; it was his report that resulted in Marquette arriving on the island with a group of refugee Hurons. The poor soil could not support their agricultural needs, and hence the mission of St. Ignace was founded on the mainland we now refer to as the Upper Peninsula. But that, too, is another story.

You may be distracted by the white marble bench, by the wooden cross, by the appearance of a snow goose in the midst of a flock of Canada geese, as I was. After lunch, you may wander over to the tourist information kiosk, right past a perfect monument for Mackinac Island, the one that is so oddly shaped and relatively small that seen up above from the fort in the fog it might be mistaken for a small pyramid of cannonballs.

The Daughters of the American Revolution of Michigan dedicated this monument in Marquette Park below Fort Mackinac, declaring Mackinac Island Michigan's "most historic spot" in 1931.

On August 16, 1931, the *Ludington Daily News* included an Associated Press story regarding this monument:

> Climaxing a 10-day tour of Michigan, the Daughters of the American Revolution of Michigan, headed by Mrs. James H. McDonald of Ypsilanti, state regent, today dedicated at Mackinac Island a monument erected by them, designating the island as Michigan's main historic spot.
>
> The monument is made from honeycomb stone found on the island, and bears a bronze tablet, the face of which represents the wall of a log cabin with a bear skin hanging, on which is inscribed "Michigan's most historic spot," and "erected by the Daughters of the American Revolution—1931."

The AP reporter got a few things wrong. The "honeycomb stone" found on the island is the brecciated limestone that, over the centuries, has formed all of the natural stacked stone wonders of Mackinac Island. And there are a few features missing from his description of the bronze plaque affixed to the limestone. Can you see what they are?

How to Get There

There are two departure points for Mackinac Island from the mainland, both off Interstate 75 by car: Mackinaw City, the northernmost tip of Michigan's Lower Peninsula, and St. Ignace, the southernmost tip of the eastern half of Michigan's Upper Peninsula. The Mighty Mac spans the full five miles (eight kilometers) between these two cities, so no matter what peninsula you are approaching the bridge from, you have a choice. St. Ignace is the shorter ride: five miles (eight kilometers) versus eight miles (13 kilometers) from Mackinaw City on the ferry and 16 versus 30 minutes.

Once you decide from which city you want to depart, another decision awaits you: from which dock? Three ferry companies ply the Straits of Mackinac—Arnold Transit, Shepler's Ferry, and Star Line Ferry—and they each leave from either Mackinac City or St. Ignace. Each ferry service has its own promotional slant:

Arnold Transit—Mackinac's oldest ferry service ("Ride the Classic") operates three catamarans, five ferries, and three freight service boats.
Shepler's Ferry—Started by Captain Shepler in 1945, this family-owned business offers "tradition" and provides freight service as well.
Star Line—This company boasts "the only Hydro-Jet Ferry."

You can also choose to fly a 15-minute Great Lakes Air Delta flight from Pellston Regional Airport (PLN) in Pellston, Michigan, to Mackinac Island Airport (horse-drawn service is available from the island airport).

What to Expect

Eighty-two percent of the island is owned by the State of Michigan and managed by the Mackinac Island State Park Commission as part of Mackinac Island State Park. In 1875, it became the country's second national park; it was established as Michigan's first state park in 1895.

No overnight camping is allowed on Mackinac. Camping is available at Wilderness State Park near Mackinaw City in Michigan's Lower Peninsula and at the Straits State Park in St. Ignace in the Upper Peninsula (where some sites have terrific views of the Mackinac Bridge) as well as at a number of other campgrounds on the mainland.

No private motor vehicles are allowed on the island, but that certainly won't prevent you from getting around and seeing the island—and in ways so much more fun than driving. You can bring your own bike (ferry boats charge a nominal additional fee per bike) or rent one from a number of rental businesses on the island. Electric carts and wheelchairs are also available at Ryba's Bikes. You can take an island carriage tour, rent your own horse-drawn buggy, or enjoy guided or unguided trail horseback riding. Perhaps best of all, you can use your feet—the over 140 miles (225 kilometers) of road and trails make Mackinac Island a great place to hike. That's a lot of ways to do a lot of exploring.

And expect a lot to explore: boreal forest, beautiful coastline, dramatic geological curiosities, and many historical sites, both in town and out.

Paths to Adventure

Begin planning your adventures by equipping yourself with the Mackinac Island Overview Map (available at www.mackinacisland.org/wp-content/uploads/2011/04/mackinacisland-map_printable.pdf).

NATURAL SITES

Lake Shore Nature Trail—If you take the Lake Shore Drive (aka M-185) loop around the island, be sure to stop at the sign on the east side of the island to walk the 200-yard interpretive trail that traverses several of the island's habitats: from Great Lakes beach over a wetland and into a northern boreal forest.

British Landing Nature Trail—An interpreted nature trail loop by the British Landing Nature Center on the northwest end of the island.

Croghan Water—An area off of the British Landing Road created by a very small cold spring coming from between the limestone and named after Colonel George Croghan, who was in command of the American troops against the British forces on Mackinac in 1814; the trail may be damp, and the area may be waterlogged seasonally.

Brown's Brook Nature Area—An interpreted nature trail loop beginning at Brown's Brook State Roadside Park west of M-185 (aka Lake Shore Drive), between Griffin Cove and Heriot Point.

Check out the often dramatic—and generally created from breccia limestone—natural formations on the island:

- Arch Rock
- Sugar Loaf
- Skull Cave (Native American burial site)
- Crack-in-the-Island
- Cave of/in the Woods
- Devil's Kitchen
- Robinson's Folly

- Lover's Leap
- Chimney Rock
- Friendship's Altar
- Scott's Cave
- Eagle Point Cave

HISTORY PRESERVED

One could write, and many have written, entire books just on the history of Mackinac Island, and history buffs may want to arrive armed with one or more such volumes that detail each of these historic sites. Here are the places you can go to begin exploring the history of the island. You'll find many of these sites offer good interpretive displays to help you wend your way through island, state, and national historic events.

Fort Mackinac—Consisting of 14 restored buildings located atop the 150-foot limestone bluff overlooking the City of Mackinac Island and the Haldimand Bay, the fort itself is

Arch Rock, one of Mackinac Island's distinctive geological features, is a natural arch composed of limestone breccia, an unusual formation in the Great Lakes Basin.

the oldest surviving building in Michigan, built by the British in 1780, during the American Revolution, to control movement on the Straits. The fort was not relinquished to the Americans until 15 years after independence had been won. At the start of the War of 1812, the fort was attacked by a force of British and Native Americans before the small U.S. garrison knew war had been declared, and the fort was surrendered to avoid bloodshed. The Americans failed to retake the fort in the Battle of Mackinac Island in 1814. Following the Treaty of Ghent, the Americans reoccupied Fort Mackinac in July 1815. The fort served a number of different purposes in the next 60 years before becoming the headquarters for Mackinac National Park, the country's second national park (after Yellowstone). During that time the troops stationed there served as park rangers. In 1895, the National Park was closed and the fort and park were transferred to the State of Michigan. The island became Mackinac Island State Park, Michigan's first state park.

Cemeteries—The three cemeteries on Mackinac Island are located in the interior of the island off Garrison Road and are open to the public during daylight hours.

- Fort Mackinac Post Cemetery—Located .5 mile (.8 kilometer) north of Fort Mackinac, this military cemetery of 108 gravesites—some of which date back to the 1820s and 69 of whose occupants are unknown—is surrounded by a white picket fence and maintained by the Department of Veterans Affairs with oversight by the Great Lakes National Cemetery. It is believed that the cemetery was used from the War of 1812 and that both British and American soldiers from that conflict are buried there. The last burial in the Post Cemetery was in the 1890s; the last military funeral on the island was in 1891. The cemetery flag continually flies at half-mast, as it does at only three other national cemeteries. The cemetery is designated as a National Historic Landmark.
- Protestant Cemetery—Referred to by islanders as the Mackinac Island Cemetery, graves were moved here in 1850 from a downtown cemetery behind the Mission Church. A section of this cemetery has been reserved for Jewish burials.
- St. Ann's Catholic Cemetery (aka St. Anne's)—Founded in 1924, this is the largest cemetery on the island. Near the south entrance is a Native American burial mound, created in 2012 after construction in the downtown area on the island in 2011 disturbed an older cemetery with Native graves. The Sault Ste. Marie Tribe of Chippewa Indians donated $2,000 to the project, and two tribe members restored a totem pole and a wooden turtle carving that were installed, flanking the mound, in 2013.

Fort Holmes—Built on the highest point of the island by British troups in 1814 during the War of 1812 and originally called Fort George, this was a small wood and earthen fort that has recently been restored (dedicated August 16, 2015). This project was a part of Michigan's bicentennial celebration of the War of 1812. The fort is open to visitors year-round, and a visit to this site is well worth it for the view.

Historic Downtown Mackinac (on Market Street) offers a number of places to dip into the island's history:

- Biddle House
- Benjamin Blacksmith Shop
- American Fur Company Store and Dr. Beaumont Museum
- McGulpin House
- Robert Stuart House
- American Fur Company Warehouse
- Michilimackinac County Courthouse

Grand Hotel—Completed in 1887, this hotel ranks in *Travel+Leisure*'s 500 World's Best Hotels and *Conde Nast Traveler*'s Top 5 Midwest Resorts. The hotel boasts the world's

On Mackinac Island, where cars have been banned since 1898, a horse and carriage approach a side entrance of St. Ann's Catholic Cemetery.

longest porch, from where one can enjoy some of the best views of the Straits. The Grand hosts a number of annual weekend events, including the October *Somewhere in Time* Weekend, which commemorates the 1979 filming of the classic movie (1980), starring Christopher Reeve and Jane Seymour, at the Grand Hotel and other locations on Mackinac Island.

Historic churches

- Mission Church—This Congregational church, located at the corner of Huron and Tuscotts Streets and built in 1829, is the oldest surviving church in Michigan.
- St. Anne's Catholic Church—This church, at 6836 Huron St., houses a free museum.
- Little Stone Church—This Congregational church is at 1580 Cadotte Ave.
- Trinity Church—This Episcopal church is at 472 Fort St.

Historic East Bluff and West Bluff cottages

Mission Point Observation Tower and maritime exhibits

CULTURAL ATTRACTIONS

Richard and Jane Manoogian Mackinac Art Museum (7070 Main St.)—Displays a collection of Mackinac-related art and photography in the historic Indian dormitory building (www.mightymac.org/mackinacartmuseum.htm).

Michigan Governor's Summer Residence (Wednesdays, early June–late August)—Free two-hour tour of the 1902 cottage at the corner of Forest Street Hill and Huron Road that has been used by Michigan governors and their families in the summer since 1943.

Downtown Main Street

OTHER ISLAND THINGS TO DO

Hike some of the 140 miles (225 kilometers) of trails and roads. You can get a detailed map of Mackinac Island's hiking trails at Mackinac Island State Park Visitor's Center, across from Marquette Park between the marina and the Chippewa Hotel on Main Street.

Bike the 8.2-mile (13.2-kilometer) perimeter route around the island. Bikes can be rented at a handful of spots along Main Street or, for a nominal additional ferry charge, you can bring your own.

Mountain bike on the trails.

Take a carriage ride and settle into clip-clop rhythm.

Kayak/paddleboard in the Haldimand Bay, just off Main Street, or take a kayak tour (see Great Turtle Kayak Tours: www.mackinackayak.com).

See where you are, and where the island's been, by visiting the Observation Tower and Museum at Mission Point Resort.

Get "fluttered by"—Visit the two island butterfly attractions: the Original Mackinac Island Butterfly House and Wings of Mackinac Butterfly Conservatory

Practice being a true "Fudgie" (the islanders' name for an island tourist)—There's been fudge on Mackinac Island since 1887. At last count there were six (seven if you count Sanders Candy's hot fudge topping) different fudge companies plying their wares on the island, four with multiple locations on Main Street. Sample them all, pick your favorite, and take some home for friends and family. According to one source, over 10,000 pounds of fudge leave the island every *day*.

Take the self-guided tour of the Grand Hotel shops and/or the Grand Hotel flower gardens, depending on your inclination.

Play golf at the nine-hole Wawashkamo Golf Course or Grand Hotel's Jewel Course "Grand Nine."

Go horseback riding at the Mackinac Community Equestrian Center.

Go to the library—Visit the Mackinac Island Public Library. The Mackinac Collection, which contains historic information about Michigan and the Michilimackinac area, is housed in the Rosa Webb Room. You may check out a book as a visitor if your home library is a participant in Michicard and you have your library card on you. If not, the library hosts a used-book sale every day. For a view of the Straits and the Round Island Lighthouse, the vantage point of a rocking chair on the library's back deck is hard to beat!

Put an impromptu picnic together from Doud's Market and enjoy it on the grounds of Marquette Park.

Have a beer and chat up the bartender at the (year-round) Mustang Lounge, "where the locals drink."

Investigate the paranormal on the island with Haunts of Mackinac's night walking tours.

SPECIAL ISLAND EVENTS

Twilight Turtle Trek and Great Turtle Chili Cook-off (February 14)—Follow a two-mile (3.2-kilometer) lantern-lit cross-country ski and snowshoe trail and end the night by sampling and scoring the entries in the annual chili cook-off in town.

Memorial Day Observance at the Fort Mackinac Post Cemetery (May).

Mackinac Island Lilac Festival—A 10-day festival, held since 1949, beginning the first weekend in June and ending with the horse-drawn Lilac Parade.

Vintage Baseball Game (July)—Played barehanded on the old Fort Mackinac ball field, the oldest continually used ball field in Michigan.

Mackinac Island Festival of the Horse (August)—Sponsored by the Mackinac Horsemen's Association at the Mackinac Community Equestrian Center.

Mackinac Island Fudge Festival (August).

Mackinac Island Music Festival (October).

Women's Wellness and Wee Bit o' Wine Weekend (October).

***Somewhere in Time* Weekend** (October)—Held at the Grand Hotel.

Foot races (www.runmackinac.com).

- The Lilac 10K (June)—10K run/walk and kids' race.
- Mackinac Eight Mile (September)—Run/walk and kids' fun run.
- Great Turtle Trail-Run (October)—5.7-mile (9.2-kilometer) trail run/walk and half marathon on island's last open weekend of season.

Boat races

- Pink Pony 4th of July Sailboat Race (July 4)—Family fun race.
- Round the Island Race (July).
- Horn's Bar Labor Day Regatta (September).

For More Island Information

Mackinac Island State Park website—www.mackinacparks.com/parks-and-attractions/mackinac-island-state-park.

Mackinac Island State Park Visitor Center (7165 Main St.).

Mackinac Island Tourism Bureau information booth.

Inside Mackinac—A free publication available on the island (and online) and published by the Mackinac Island Tourism Bureau that provides maps and information on accommodations, shopping, and island dining options: www.mackinacisland.org.

Town Crier—Mackinac Island community's weekly newspaper.

We Live on Mackinac Island—Booklet created by Mackinac Island Public School students as a fund-raiser for the school. In it, they answer some of the questions they receive as island residents.

Historic Mackinac Island Visitor's Guide: Tours, History, Maps, by Phil Porter (Mackinac Island, MI: Mackinac State Historic Parks, 2013).

Mackinac: An Island Famous in These Regions, by Phil Porter (Mackinac Island, MI: Mackinac State Historic Parks, 1998)—This book has an excellent list of suggested further readings.

Mackinac Connection: The Insider's Guide to Mackinac Island, 3rd ed., by Amy McVeigh (Mackinac Island, MI: Mackinac, 1998).

Explore Michigan—Mackinac: An Insider's Guide to Michigan, by George Cantor (Ann Arbor: University of Michigan Press, 2005).

"Mackinac Island," in *Biking the Great Lakes Islands,* by Kathleen Abrams and Lawrence Abrams (Wausau, WI: Entwood, 1985), 50–67—Includes four Mackinac Island cycling routes: Circle Tour, Bike Route, Interior Historical Tour, and Grand Hotel & Market Street.

Mackinac Island Bike Shop offers self-guided tour maps and tour descriptions as well as bike rentals (www.bikemackinac.com).

Lore of the Great Turtle: Indian Legends of Mackinac Retold, by Dirk Gringhuis (Mackinac Island, MI: Mackinac Island State Historic Parks, 1970).

How You Can Support the Island

Mackinac Associates
"Friends Preserving and Sharing Mackinac's Heritage"
PO Box 567
Mackinaw City, MI 49701
231-436-4100
  Members support programs through this 501(c)(3) nonprofit and share in benefits at Mackinac State Historic Parks sites.

Parting Thoughts

October 6, 2013, 9:00 a.m.
Mackinac Island

We're waiting at Shepler's baggage claim for our bags to arrive from the Harbour View Inn B&B. We'll head back to St. Ignace on the 9:30 ferry.

  The clop of horse hooves and the jangle of their tack as they pull maroon-covered carriages back from the Grand, a pair of dapple grays switching their tails, their shoulder flesh quivering, a snickering and a neigh as another of the Grand's carriages comes out of a side street and heads up Main Street in the other direction.

  The American Breed's "Bend Me, Shake Me" plays over the dock speakers, mixing with passenger confusion about the Mackinaw City and St. Ignace half-hour departure difference.

  Looking up and down the rainy Main Street, I can see in one direction Pontiac Lodge, the Loon Feather, Bicycle Street Inn, and Main St. Inn, and in the other Goodfellows Wine Cellar, Lakeview Bicycle Rental, and Mackinac Bike Shop. And in both directions, a surprising number of dogs visiting the island with their owners: one riding in a bike basket and two walking on leashes, one on each side of a bike right in front of me.

  9:30 a.m.—On Shepler's *Hope* in the fog. The forecast is for a rough ride in eight- to 10-foot waves until we get around the breakwater. Passengers look nervously toward the breakwater as we turn around. The boat speeds up more quickly and much faster than expected as the captain of 30 years, from Cheboygan, moves us quickly out into the current. The last of Mackinac Island's buildings retreat, ghosts shrouded in the fog.

  Mackinac is just the latest setting for a familiar cast of island characters I'm beginning to get more familiar with: the glacier, the Native people, the explorers, the Jesuits, the fur traders, the fishermen, the captains of industry, the tourists, the historical societies, the environmentalists, the preservationists. And some of these characters weren't playing the roles I expected. How did each of them contribute to the island's journey to today? And what role will today play in the island's future?

  As we chug through the fog hovering over the lake, the next 50 yards of waves become visible, one series at a time. How far will this fog follow us off the Straits? What tendrils of it will weave themselves into my mainland life?

Bois Blanc Island, Michigan

THE OTHER OF A PAIR IN A STRAIT

July 8, 2013, 6:33 p.m.
Bois Blanc Island

The foghorn sounds out over the lake. Just north of the Snake Island–Mud Lake Conservation Area, Barb and I catch sight of a pair of sandhill cranes going over the ridge to the beach. We follow.

GETTING THERE: Car ferry; private boat or plane

GETTING AROUND: Bring your car; bring your own bike (no rentals)

OVERNIGHT ACCOMMODATIONS: Limited options: one B&B; a few vacation home rentals; rustic camping (no electricity, restrooms, showers, or water)

FOOD: Two restaurants; limited groceries

DAY TRIP? Possible, but not recommended

STATE / PROVINCIAL / NATIONAL PARK? No, but much of the island is a part of the Mackinac State Forest

You may think you know the rhythm of the Straits of Mackinac if you've danced to the Mackinac Island vibe, but there's another drumbeat happening in these Straits. Surrounded by the same waters, this other drumbeat is as distinctive as a frozen shot of Yukon Jack downed at the Bob-Lo Tavern is from a Mackinac Fudge Martini sipped at the Grand Hotel's Gate House Restaurant. That different island drumbeat comes from Bois Blanc Island, southeast of and just visible, around Round Island, from Mackinac Island.

Only eight miles (13 kilometers) from the mainland, a 40-minute ferry ride, 34 square miles (88 square kilometers) of pristine beauty and a rich, quiet history await you. Bois Blanc is where Native Americans from Mackinac tapped maple syrup in the spring. Bois Blanc supplied historic Mackinac with wood for its fires, lime for plaster and log chinking, the dolomite from which the best lime kilns could be built, a hideout for its general, and hunting grounds for its sports hunters.

Both Bois Blanc and Mackinac Island were once part of the peninsula that reached its finger out from where Cheboygan is today into the ancient Algonquin Lake. In more recent centuries, Mackinac was settled; Bois Blanc was left more wild. You can see the layers of European and American settlement at Mackinac. On Bois Blanc, layers of the Native American use of the island are apparent. Artifacts from a civilization of Native Americans earlier than

those the French or English came upon—the Late Woodland people—have been discovered at the Juntunen archaeological site on Bois Blanc. Later, the Ojibwe, migrating from the east, became the prominent tribe in the area and were the people encountered by the waves of French fur traders and voyageurs, English settlers, and American victors as they arrived in the Great Lakes Basin. On August 3, 1795, Ojibwe Chief Matchekewis ceded Bois Blanc to the United States as part of the Treaty of Greenville.

Most of Bois Blanc Island was once used as a military reservation for the troops at Fort Mackinac. During the War of 1812, U.S. Navy captain Arthur Sinclair's fleet took shelter at Bois Blanc, the low island, while waiting to attack the British at Fort Mackinac on the island of bluffs. After the war, Bois Blanc experienced a period of lumbering, with much of the lumber going to Mackinac Island. This was followed by the tourism of the resort era; people came from Chicago, Detroit, and Columbus to escape the hay fever season. Now, as on many other Great Lakes Basin islands, there are acres of state-owned and conservancy-owned land and land trusts to preserve what remains for future generations to enjoy.

And here, now, are miles of gravel roads and trails to explore. However, at the end of an adventure-filled day, there are not a lot of choices about where to lay one's head. There is a remote, rustic campground with no facilities and no charge (electrical or monetary). There are no motels on the island, but some of the privately owned cottages are available to rent; check online for possibilities that coincide with your needs. And there's one very unusual bed-and-breakfast, currently run by Shelby Newhouse, an Emmy Award–winning retired documentary filmmaker, and Christi Newhouse, a former film editor and an intrepid knitter. They've built a very large European-style home full of artistic and architectural surprises, located just off the lake and buffered from the forest of towering Norway and white pine and spruce by a meadow on which deer materialize out of morning fog. Insel Haus is a place that you can retreat to, too.

Why so relatively few accommodations options? Bois Blanc Island, at 34 square miles (88 square kilometers), is almost *10 times bigger* than Mackinac Island, at 3.8 square miles (9.8 square kilometers), yet Mackinac has over 10 times more year-round residents (according to the 2010 census, 492 to Bois Blanc's 47), to say nothing of their respective number of annual tourists: Mackinac Island's 900,000 to Bois Blanc Island's 200.

Which, absolutely, does not imply that there's nothing to do on the island. As the French, who visited both Mackinac and Bois Blanc and left their imprint in the island's name ("White Wood") would say, *au contraire!* The experience that awaits you is simply different.

Although this pair of islands in the Straits have the same waters lapping at their shores, share the same wonderful breezes in the summer, were once parts of the same peninsula, belong to the same county—Mackinac—and are in the same state forest—Mackinaw—they are very different. Consider, for instance, the price of those two drinks I mentioned earlier: on Bois Blanc, one frozen shot of Yukon Jack, the 100-proof honey-based Canadian whiskey sometimes referred to as "the Black Sheep of Canadian Liquors," is *free* to first-time visitors at the Bob-Lo Tavern; the Grand Hotel's Mackinac Fudge Martini will set you back $12.50.

You just don't really know the Straits until you've visited Bois Blanc Island, too.

How to Get There

Head for Cheboygan, very near the tip of Michigan's Lower Peninsula, southeast of Mackinaw City and just 20 minutes east of I-75 via Riggsville Road or E. Levering Road. At the Cheboygan City Marina, on the Cheboygan River, you'll find:

Plaunt Transportation Company
412 Water St.
Cheboygan, MI
231-627-2354; 888-PLAUNTS
www.bbiferry.com

Kristen D, a 16-vehicle ferry (which does not accept credit cards at this time) provides passenger/vehicle ferry service to the island, eight miles (13 kilometers) and 40 minutes away, every day of the week, May to November, weather permitting. Check the schedule online during the season (the ferry's online account may be suspended off season).

Given the size of Bois Blanc (12 miles long, six miles wide, and approximately 34 square miles/19 kilometers long, 10 kilometers wide, and approximately 88 square kilometers), you may want to bring your car (note that the speed limit island wide is 25 miles per hour/40 kilometers per hour) as well as a bike along (there is no bike rental on the island). You need a ferry reservation for a vehicle.

Look for the boat with the colorful logo of a gull flying across the sun. The Plaunt's route includes as nice a beginning to an island ferry trip as you'll experience in the Great Lakes Basin: you'll cruise down the Cheboygan River, going under a drawbridge, watching the activity on the riverbanks. If you're lucky, you'll see larger ships as the ferry moves out to Lake Huron (we were fortunate enough to see the *Michigan* tug, which operates in tandem with the barge *Great Lakes,* a tanker with an unusual bow shape). Look for the Cheboygan Crib Light, first built in 1884, in Lake Huron, now at the west pier head where river meets lake at Cheboygan's Gordon Turner Park.

Great Lakes Air Service provides flights from Cheboygan or St. Ignace to the unattended public airstrip of Bois Blanc Island Airport, K6Y1.

What to Expect

The ferry lands at the one town on the island: Pointe Aux Pins, French for "Pine Point." Be prepared to hear islanders and cottagers refer to the island as "Bob-Lo," an early English attempt to pronounce the French "Bois Blanc." Many believe that the white wood referred

A curious buck. If Mackinac Island is all about history, Bois Blanc Island is all about nature. It's been said that deer outnumber permanent island residents by 20 to 1.

to in the name is the white inner bark of the American basswood tree, which was used by both the Native Americans and French as a source for fiber, used to make rope, in the construction of canoes, and for the webbing on snowshoes. The Native Americans' name for island was Wigobiminiss, *wigobi* signifying "tying bark" and *miniss* "island."

We saw a deer soon after we left the ferry, not far from our first (but not last) sighting of a wood lily. Much of Bois Blanc Island is heavily forested, with 200-foot white and Norway pine, cedar, and birch. There is very little development; over 50 percent of the island is owned by the State of Michigan. Besides deer, wildlife includes beaver, rabbit, loons, sandhill cranes, and hummingbirds.

Paths to Adventure

NATURAL SITES

Nature Conservancy Bois Blanc Preserve (established in 1987)—Includes the 244-acre Snake Island/Mud Lake Nature Study and Natural Area. Low water has connected Snake

Island—named for the eastern massasauga rattlesnakes that make their home there at the northernmost edge of their range in Michigan—to Bois Blanc. Hine's emerald dragonflies have also been sighted here.

Little Traverse Conservancy Vosper Nature Preserve (established in 2003, added to in 2007)—Created when Jim and Betty Vosper donated a total of 114 acres, including 654 feet of Lake Huron shoreline, for protection as a nature preserve.

Six inland lakes:

- Lake Mary—Here you will find rock bass, brown bullhead, yellow perch, smallmouth bass, and pumpkinseed sunfish. Bois Blanc Township Park is located on the north-central shore and has a boat launch and fishing pier.
- Twin Lakes (the eastern basin is known as Lake Duncan, the western as Echo Lake; they are attached by Twin Lake Creek)—Here are pumpkinseed sunfish, rock bass, yellow perch, largemouth bass, northern pike, smallmouth bass, and walleye.
- Mud Lake—A part of the Snake Island–Mud Lake Conservation Area; osprey feed here.
- Thompson Lake—Home to perch.
- Deer Lake—Located at the base of Lighthouse Point peninsula, this is the smallest of the major inland lakes on the island and has no structures on its shores.

Snow Beach—One of the only sandy—not rocky—shores on the island.

HISTORY PRESERVED

According to legend, notorious gangster John Dillinger once hid out on the island. But there's more history here than legend.

Bois Blanc Island Historical Society Museum—Open July through Labor Day, Tuesday, Thursday, and Saturday, between 10:00 and 2:00. Pick up a self-guided tour map of the island.

Pointe Aux Pins—The only town on the island. Here you'll find a neighborhood—referred to as "The Pines"—of beautiful historic Victorian homes, including one built by Mr. H. Earl Hoover of vacuum cleaner fame.

Church of the Transfiguration—The church was built in 1905. Check out the stained glass rose window, designed by Alaskan artist Eustace Ziegler (1881–1969)—who also painted the center portrait—and constructed in Detroit by the firm Friederichs and Wolfram in 1905. Ziegler's father, Paul Ziegler, founded the church with Rev. William Bulkley, and Eustace Ziegler's brother was the minister of the church for many years.[27] "The history of the window above the altar is elusive. The [church] *Register* briefly notes it as (a donation?) from the Mariner's Church of Detroit, a parish [also] served by Paul Ziegler. Other sources are sure it was made from bottoms of bottles collected from a tavern (in the Upper Peninsula or Cheboygan or downstate), thus its 'bottle window' name."[28]

Woodland Glade Township Cemetery—A cemetery on the edge of town set in—the name doesn't lie—a beautiful woodland glade.

Coast Guard Station—In 1890, the U.S. Coast Guard established a life-saving station at Walker's Point. The building is still there and in regular use during the summer for a variety of events, including the island's Historical Society's Memory Nights and nondenominational Sunday church services.

Bois Blanc Lighthouse—Originally built in 1829 and reconstructed three times between 1839 and 1867, the lighthouse, which is listed on the state registry of historic structures, is now privately owned and has been restored. It includes an old life-saving station, a

Bois Blanc has provided a perfect hideout for people needing one, including, perhaps, the notorious John Dillinger. These are the ruins of one of three cabins purportedly used by Dillinger and his gang. You, too, may find Bois Blanc Island a good place to hide away from the rest of the world.

brick outhouse, a brick oil shed, and a cement boathouse. The lighthouse can be viewed best by private boat or on Shepler's Ferry's "Eastbound Tour" lighthouse cruise out of Mackinac City.

CULTURAL ATTRACTIONS

On such a big island with so many acres of beautiful wilderness, it is easy to understand that anything other than that beautiful wilderness could be considered a "cultural attraction."

U.S. Post Office—Bois Blanc Island has its own zip code: 49775.

Coast Guard Chapel—Offers seasonal nondenominational worship and "Tuesday Fun Nights" in July and August and serves as a venue for special events.

Church of the Transfiguration—Offers Episcopal services and facilitates the use of the Hoover Community Building next door.

Hoover Community Building—Built by an island resident in 1967, funded by and named for H. Earl Hoover (former chairman of Hoover Company, a vacuum cleaner manufacturer), and owned by the Episcopal Diocese of Northern Michigan, the building hosts square dances, meetings, receptions, slide shows, and art exhibits.

Hawk's Landings General Store & Deli—Sells food and drink (in a restaurant setting), ice cream, ice, gas, select groceries, souvenirs, hunting and fishing licenses, ORV stickers, fishing tackle and bait. The establishment also rents movies, provides wireless Internet, and serves as the site of Bois Blanc Island Real Estate.

Look for the cross at the end of the single-lane Bible Road (named after the Bible family farm, aka Weiner Road), which runs from Lime Kiln Point Road to North Shore Road. Free camping is available here at the primitive Bible Beach Campground.

Bob-Lo Tavern—Features the aforementioned shots of frozen Yukon Jack, a vintage table shuffleboard, Taco Tuesdays, and occasional appearances by northern Michigan singer-songwriter Dan Reynolds, who has produced two full-length albums about Bois Blanc Island: *This Ain't the Mainland* (2010) and *Bob-Lo Style* (2013).

Pines School—This smallest one-room schoolhouse in Michigan serves kindergarten through eighth grade from a converted maintenance shed. In 2010, the school had five students in three grades with one teacher.

Insel Haus—Unique 7,800-square-foot retreat center and European-style B&B that is currently for sale.

OTHER ISLAND THINGS TO DO

Hike—Miles of trails await exploration on the island. Start off with a map from the Bois Blanc Island Historical Society Museum and see what you can discover.

Bike—Follow the winding dirt shore road around much of the perimeter of the island. When you come to Bible Road, you may want to head farther west down Lime Kiln Point Road to see the spectacular view of the Mackinac Bridge.

Follow the Bois Blanc Island Landmark Trail—Pick up a copy of this self-guided island tour from the Bois Blanc Island Museum and see the 24 attractions by bike or car.

Kayak/canoe—The coastline or any one of the six inland lakes await exploration by paddle.

Go birding—Sandhill cranes and hummingbirds were plentiful during my July visit. The Mackinac Straits Raptor Watch in the Straits begins in mid-March and continues through the beginning of May and tracks 16 raptor species. The Straits Area Audubon Society's most recently published (2014) annual spring bird count lists 147 species spotted in the area and can be found at www.straitsareaaudubon.org/page6.html.

Hunt for wildflowers—The Michigan state wildflower, the rare dwarf lake iris, found only in the Great Lakes region, is here, as are approximately 340 other species of wildflowers. Some rare-plant surveys of the island have found Houghton's goldenrod, beauty sedge, Lake Huron tansy, limestone fern, pitcher's thistle, butterwort, and pale Indian plantain.

Watch the water traffic—Freighters, sailboats, and yachts.

Grab your camera—Snap some spectacular photographic shots.

Imagine the Pines Hotel—View the exhibit at the Bois Blanc Island Historical Society Museum and then take the historic walk in the Pines neighborhood, checking out the Association dock, the gazebo, and the Pines Hotel site.

Fish—See above for the many varieties of fish to be found in the inland lakes; you might catch salmon in Lake Huron.

Camp—Bible Beach Campground in the Mackinaw State Forest, located on the north shore, has several rustic sites with a fire pit but no electricity, water, or restrooms. However, the beach has fantastic views!

SPECIAL ISLAND EVENTS

Bois Blanc Island Historical Society's Memory Nights—Come hear some oral histories from islanders and cottagers about what they remember of times past.

Bob-Lo Tavern's Taco Tuesdays—Have your free shot of Yukon Jack, eat some tacos, and try your hand at table shuffleboard.

For More Island Information

Bois Blanc Island Historical Society Museum (www.facebook.com/bbihs)—Full of all things Bois Blanc: artifacts from earlier times, nature photographs, exhibits of island attractions and eras with educational text and historic photos, maps. The museum also serves as the site of the island's lending library. Island maps and copies of the self-guided Bois Blanc Island Landmark Trail are available here.

Bois Blanc Island Landmark Trails—Lists 24 island attractions and is available from the Bois Blanc Island Historical Society Museum.

Michigan DNR Bois Blanc Trail Map—www.uptrails.org/michigan-trail-maps/bois-blanc-island.pdf.

A Short History of Bois Blanc Island, by Chris McAfee, 2001 (based on the research of Mike White and Helen Crouch)—Available from the Bois Blanc Island Historical Society Museum.

Boyhood: A Memoir, by Jim Vosper (Milwaukee: Stone Beach Books, 2001).

The Bibles of Bois Blanc, John Franklin and Mildred Lenora: Their Life and Times on Bois Blanc Island, by Thomas W. Pfeiffelmann (Boyne City, MI: Harbor House, 2003).

Military Buttons, War of 1812 Era, Bois Blanc Island, Straits of Mackinac, Michigan, by Michael J. White (Amazon Digital Services, 2012).

Wildflower Photo Field Guide: Straits of Mackinac Region, Northern Michigan, by Michael James White (Amazon Digital Services, 2013)—Describes over 340 species of wildflowers found in the Straits region of northern Michigan.

Wild Violets Identified in the Straits of Mackinac: Bois Blanc and Round Islands, by Michael J. White (Amazon Digital Services, 2012)—A reference to the 10 species of wild violets that grow on two islands in the Straits of Mackinac.

The Juntunen Site and the Late Woodland Prehistory of the Upper Great Lakes Area, by Alan McPherron (1967; repr., Ann Arbor: University of Michigan Museum, 2001)—Available at the Bois Blanc Island Historical Society Museum.

Bois Blanc Island (www.bois-blanc.com)—"A website for islanders and island lovers."

How You Can Support the Island

Bois Blanc Island Historical Society
c/o Betty Hutchinson
HCR1, #189
Bois Blanc Island, MI 49775
www.facebook.com/bbihs

Bois Blanc Island Community Foundation (BBICF)
PO Box 907
Pointe Aux Pins, MI 49775
www.bbicf.com
www.bbicf.org

    Established in 1999 to improve the long-term well-being of the community by promoting tourism, improving roads and communications, and preserving the beautiful surroundings. Donations are used to establish endowed funds.

TWO OTHER ISLANDS IN THE STRAITS

Round Island is an uninhabited island, not accessible by bridge or ferry, located between Bois Blanc Island and Mackinac Island. Most of it constitutes the Round Island Wilderness Area, part of the Hiawatha National Forest. The red and white Round Island Light (aka Old Round Island Point Lighthouse) is the iconic structure visible as you enter the harbor in Mackinac Island's Haldimand Bay.

    St. Helena Island is the only one of the four Straits of Mackinac islands to be located to the west of the Mackinac Bridge, 10 miles (16 kilometers) from Mackinac Island. At one time a thriving community of over 200 people, this island is not accessible by bridge or ferry. Of the island's 266 acres, 263 represent the St. Helena Island Nature Preserve, which is owned by the Little Traverse Conservancy. The other three acres are owned by the Great Lakes Lighthouse Keepers Association and are the site of a still-operating lighthouse, the St. Helena Island Lighthouse, which Shepler's Mackinac Island Ferry service includes in its "Westbound Cruise."

Parting Thoughts

July 11, 2013, 3:00 p.m.
On the Kristen D *between Bois Blanc Island and Cheboygan*

We've missed him this time. Dan Reynolds, the singer-songwriter who's produced two solo albums solely celebrating Bois Blanc and who often performs at Barb's Bob-Lo Tavern.

The lyrics to his "Bible Road" (from *This Ain't the Mainland*) nail our sentiments perfectly as we head back to the mainland:

> Heaven's going ta have ta look a helluva a lot like Bob-Lo,
> And if it don't, I don't want to go . . .
> Not Detroit, not Chicago . . .
> Heaven's going ta have ta look a helluva a lot like Bob-Lo,
> And if it don't, I don't want to go.

Lake Huron Islands

An Introduction to Lake Huron

Along with Lake Michigan and the Straits of Mackinac, Lake Huron was part of the pre-historic and proglacial Lake Algonquin. Today, Lake Huron is attached in the northwest to the Straits of Mackinac, the St. Marys River drains into the northernmost part of the lake, and in the south, Lake Huron drains into the St. Clair River.

Ontario, Canada, claims the east shore of the lake, and Michigan claims the west shore as well as some of the north, along the south shore of the Upper Peninsula. The international border begins in the deepest lobe of the lake's southern shore, alongside the outside of Michigan's "Thumb."

By surface area, Lake Huron is the second largest of the Great Lakes and the third largest by volume. The lake is 183 miles (295 kilometers) from north to south and 206 miles (332 kilometers) across. It has an average depth of 196 feet and is about 750 feet at its deepest point. The elevation of Lake Huron is the same as Lake Michigan, which is why they are considered today, hydrologically, to be two parts of the same lake. The lakeshore is 3,827 miles (6,159 kilometers) around and is characterized by both shallow sand beaches, such as those in the Thumb area of Michigan and the Pinery area of Ontario, and the rocky shores of Georgian Bay.

Lake Huron was the first of the five Great Lakes European explorers stumbled upon in the beginning of the seventeenth century. Samuel de Champlain, founder of Quebec and "Father of New France," paddled out of the mouth of the French River and into Georgian Bay. The lake was given several different European names in succession. The French explorers, who had no idea there were more huge freshwater lakes on this continent of the New World, named the lake La Mer Douce, meaning "the Sweet (or Freshwater) Sea." Father Zenobius Membré and Father Louis Hennepin called it Lake Orleans, and cartographer Guillaume De L'Ilse's map of 1700 identified it as L. des Hurons, while his maps of 1703 and 1718 named it Lac Huron ou Michigane.

Before the arrival of the Europeans, this area had been the land of the Huron, also called Wyandot or Wendat, the "People of the Peninsula." "Huron" refers to a confederacy of four or more tribes of people who spoke Wyandot, an Iroquoian language. Village dwellers, they relied on agriculture for the majority of their food. In 1535, French explorer Jacques Cartier was the first European to make contact with the Huron. Over half of their population of 20,000 to 40,000 members died in the space of six years (1634–40) of European diseases (such as measles or smallpox) for which they had no immunity. In the 1640s, in the conflict referred to as the Beaver Wars, the Huron were attacked by the Iroquois, who wanted to interrupt the Huron's fur trade with the French. In 1648, the Seneca and Mohawk were successful in their effort to destroy the Huron trading network. Wyandotte, Michigan, the Wyandot First Nation reserve in Quebec, Canada, and especially Lake Huron, where the

Huron Confederacy was centered before the Europeans arrived, are reminders of the people of this confederacy.

The islands of Lake Huron are many. Georgian Bay, such a large bay of Lake Huron that it was initially mistaken for a sixth Great Lake and given the name Lake Manitoulin, is known for its tens of thousands of islands, referred to as the Thirty Thousand Islands. A number of the islands in Lake Huron, both in and outside of Georgian Bay, can be accessed by bridge, passenger ferry, or vehicular ferry.

Les Cheneaux Islands—A Michigan archipelago of 36 islands. Two small islands—Hill Island and Island No. 8—are accessible by bridge, and the remaining islands are accessible by kayak, canoe, or private motorboat.

Drummond Island—A 249-square-mile (645-square-kilometer) Michigan island accessible by the (vehicular) Drummond Island Ferry. From De Tour Village at the far eastern edge of the Upper Peninsula of Michigan, it's a 30-minute ride across the mile (1.6 kilometers) or so of the De Tour Passage, a round trip made at least hourly from early morning to the wee hours of the next morning, 365 days a year.

St. Joseph Island—An Ontario island that, at 227 square miles (588 square kilometers), is the second-largest island on Lake Huron (and the third largest in the Great Lakes). The island is accessible by Highway 548, which is carried from mainland Ontario, across Lake Huron's North Channel by the Bernt Gilbertson St. Joseph Island Bridge.

Manitoulin Island—The largest freshwater island in the world, 1,068 square miles (2,766 square kilometers), is in Ontario's Georgian Bay and accessible by the Little Current swing bridge (via Highway 6 from Espanola, Ontario) or by ferry from Tobermory, Ontario, at the tip of the Bruce Peninsula. From Manitoulin Island a number of other Ontario islands are accessible by bridge.

Flowerpot Island—A 490-acre (two-square-kilometer) Canadian island inside Fathom Five National Marine Park and accessible by passenger ferry from Tobermory, Ontario.

Parry Island—This 30-square-mile (78-square-kilometer) island with 78 miles (126 kilometers) of shoreline is home to the Wasauksing First Nation (formerly Parry Island First Nation), an Ojibwe, Odawa, and Potawatomi First Nation band government reserve. Parry Island is accessible by bridge from Parry Sound, Ontario.

Beausoleil Island—The largest of 63 islands in the Parks Canada Georgian Bay Island National Park (total park area is just over five square miles, or 13.5 square kilometers) and the only one accessible only by passenger ferry from Honey Harbour. Beausoleil Island is just under five miles (eight kilometers) long and about one mile (1.6 kilometers) wide.

Christian Island—This large forested island is accessible by vehicular ferry from Cedar Point, Ontario, at the northwest tip of the Penetanguishene Peninsula. Christian Island is one of three islands that make up part of the Beausoleil First Nation Reserve (the other two islands, not accessible by bridge or ferry, are Beckwith Island and Hope Island).

For more information on Lake Huron, visit www.great-lakes.net/huron.html and consider looking for a used or library copy of the American Lake Series volume *Lake Huron,* by Fred Landon (Indianapolis: Bobbs-Merrill, 1944).

Les Cheneaux Islands, Michigan

PADDLING *LA MER DOUCE*

July 21, 2014, 9:40 p.m.
Woodside Room, Dancing Waters B&B

In the evening our bed-and-breakfast hosts, Jim and Betty, accompanied by Emma the basset hound (aka Her Lowliness), take Nancy and me out on their pontoon boat for a ride through the channels. We admire the wooden boathouses, sample the Jersey Mud ice cream on the mainland where we dock, and then, back on the water, enjoy—no surprise here—the incredible sunset.

After experiencing such an evening, I can easily imagine the connection people have made over the centuries with their boats in this part of the lakes, where, on the map, the islands look like scratches made by bear claws, the channels between them tantalizing to anyone with even the littlest bit of explorer in her.

We come back to Dancing Waters to be greeted by the sight of a doe grazing on the lawn, a mink frolicking in a boathouse.

GETTING THERE: Bridges from mainland Cedarville to Hill Island and from Hill Island to Island No. 8; private boat, kayak, or canoe to the other 34 islands in archipelago

GETTING AROUND: Bring your car; bring your kayak/canoe; canoe and kayak rentals

OVERNIGHT ACCOMMODATIONS: Vacation home rentals throughout the Les Cheneaux Islands (a private boat may be necessary for access); one B&B and two resorts on Hill Island; leave-no-trace camping on Government Island, accessible only by kayak, canoe, or motorboat

FOOD: Restaurants and groceries on mainland in Cedarville and Hessel

DAY TRIP? Yes

STATE / PROVINCIAL / NATIONAL PARK? Government Island is part of the Hiawatha National Forest

The area of the Les Cheneaux archipelago was once a "strategic international northern outpost and center of early exploration."[29] Native Americans and French explorers, on their way to and from the Straits of Mackinac and St. Marys River, navigated this area, protected by the safe harbors of the many channels between the islands. Since the latter part of the nineteenth century, the shores and islands of Clark Township have become a favorite summer resort.

How to Get There

The Les Cheneaux Islands are 35 miles (56 kilometers) north and east of the Mackinac Bridge, just off the south shore of Michigan's Upper Peninsula, in the northwestern tip of Lake Huron.

Two of the 35 private islands in the Les Cheneaux Archipelago—Hill Island and Island No. 8 (the latter so christened during the government surveys of 1840 and 1845 when the surveyors ran out of names), are accessible by bridge: Hill Island from the mainland at Cedarville and Island No. 8 from Hill Island. These are both residential islands with private cottages. However, on Hill Island, you will find two longtime family resorts and one B&B (with perhaps a better location than any cottage on the island: at the southern point of the island, where one can see both sunrise and sunset, a place of "dancing waters" for sure!).

If you are approaching the islands from Michigan's Lower Peninsula, after crossing the Mackinac Bridge to the Upper Peninsula, you drive on I-75 beyond the exit for M-123 to exit 359 for M-134 toward De Tour Village/Drummond Island. Head east on M-134 for 16 miles (26 kilometers), stopping in Hessel if you are in need of a kayak and/or guide, and then on to Cedarville, a 3.5-mile (5.7- kilometer), five-minute drive. If you'd like to drive across the causeway to Hill Island and/or on to Island No. 8, look for South Hill Island Road's intersection on M-134, one mile (1.6 kilometers) past Cedarville. To get to Island No. 8, continue onto Hill Island and turn onto South Forest Lane, which leads onto the bridge between the two islands and ultimately onto Island No. 8.

The view from Dancing Waters B&B, at the south end of Hill Island, looks down the Les Cheneaux channel made by Coryell Island, Boot Island, and Gravelly Island to the west and Lakeside (part of a mainland peninsula), Fisherman's Point, and Strongs Island to the east toward the "East Entrance" and beyond to Lake Huron.

GOVERNMENT ISLAND

Only one of the 36 islands in the Les Cheneaux archipelago is public land: the federally owned Government Island. Part of the Hiawatha National Forest, this uninhabited wooded island is within paddling distance of the mainland (4.5 miles from Cedarville). If you don't have a kayak or canoe, you can rent one from Woods & Water Ecotours, an outfitter and guide service (WoodsWaterEcotours.com) on the mainland at Hessel (at the intersection of Highway M-134 and S. Pickford Avenue), and glide into the water, with or without a guide.

Government Island was once the location of a Coast Guard Station (building foundations are still visible). Today, up a hill from the shore, a few established campsites with fire rings and picnic tables offer good vantage points overlooking the water, and farther into the center of the island are two outhouses. Leave-no-trace camping rules are in effect. Camping permits are not required, but notify the U.S. Forest Service if you intend to camp with a group. For more information, see www.thegreatwaters.com/member-profile/65/48/.

Two boat landings are on the shore, one on the east (channel) side by the campsite, and the other on the south side facing Lake Huron. As beautiful as the island is as a day-use park, I can only imagine how fine the camping would be here with water encircling the dark forest.

You can also reach the islands by private watercraft: many local public marinas and boat launches dot the shoreline of the Les Cheneaux area.

Alternatively, you can fly to the area: the Albert Lindberg Airport (K5Y1), with a paved 3,700-foot runway, is located in mainland Hessel, Michigan.

What to Expect

Here's a wonderful opportunity for kayaking, whether you've never kayaked before or whether it's your regular "go-to" travel activity. "Les Cheneaux" (pronounced *Lay-Shen-O*) is French for "the Channels" (because of the pronunciation, it is also occasionally referred to in English as "the Snows"). It is the perfect name for an archipelago of 36 small islands that radiate out from 12 miles (19 kilometers) of the southern shore on the eastern end of Michigan's Upper Peninsula, resembling, some say, the claw marks of a bear left in Lake Huron. And between those 36 islands are miles of sheltered channels and bays to explore, perfect for kayaking.

Only 35 minutes from the Mackinac Bridge or 45 minutes from the Soo Locks, two villages anchor the Les Cheneaux area: Hessel on the west end and Cedarville on the east. These two villages have been included with the Les Cheneaux archipelago on the Nature Conservancy's "Last Great Places in the Western Hemisphere" list, due to the area's pristine water, air, and woodlands.

Paths to Adventure

NATURAL SITES

The Channels—The 36 islands of the Les Cheneaux Archipelago provide a kayaking/canoe-ing/boating paradise.

Government Island—Once the site of a Coast Guard station (1874 to 1939) and now a part of the Hiawatha National Forest, this two-mile-long (three-kilometer-long) island

The kayaks we rented from Woods & Water Ecotours in Hessel to paddle with a guide to Government Island.

represents the only public land in the entire archipelago. The uninhabited island is a popular day-use/picnicking spot for boaters—sandy beach stretches for .33 mile (.5 kilometer) along the west shore—and both the east and south shores offer a landing. Two outhouses are on the island. The island is also open for leave-no-trace camping (that is, proper waste disposal, no cutting of trees for campfires). Cleared campsites include a fire ring and picnic table. While neither a camping permit nor fee is required, if you plan to camp with a group, you must notify the U.S. Forest Service of your visit. (Contact the National Recreation Reservation Service [NRRS] at 877-444-6777 or go to Hiawatha facilities listed on the NRRS system at www.recreation.gov.)

HISTORY PRESERVED

Les Cheneaux Historical Museum

On Meridian Road, one block south of the M-129 and M-134 intersection.

Open Monday–Saturday, 10:00–5:00 and by appointment.

Winner of the Superior Award for an outstanding museum by the Historical Society of Michigan, this museum includes exhibits of Native American crafts, tools from logging times, a model of a lumber camp, and photos from the frontier life of early settlers and the summer resort hotels and tourist era.

Les Cheneaux Maritime Museum

On M-134, four blocks east of the traffic light in Cedarville.

Open Monday–Saturday, 10:00–5:00 and by appointment.

The O. M. Reif Boathouse (circa 1920) houses displays of vintage boats, marine artifacts, and antique outboard motors as well as historic photos of area boating, a boatbuilding workshop, and a gift shop.

Old Mission Indian Cemetery

Next to the parking lot of Our Lady of the Snows Catholic Church (261 South Island View Rd., Cedarville, Michigan).

On the banks of the mainland, opposite Marquette Island, is a historical burial ground for members of the Sault Ste. Marie Tribe of Chippewa Indians, formerly known as the Father Marquette Indian Cemetery and believed to date to the early 1700s. Chief Shab-wa-way of Marquette Island may be buried here. The Native American Society for Historic Preservation (NASHP) maintains the cemetery. Of the 134 known graves, 90 are marked only by a plain white wooden cross. A spirit house marks one grave.

CULTURAL ATTRACTIONS

Tassier Sugar Bush

2875 E. Swede Rd.

Cedarville, MI 49719

888-744-5024

www.tassiersugarbush.com

Tassier Sugar Bush makes maple syrup products and welcomes visitors to tour the family-owned operation, three miles (five kilometers) north and three miles (five kilometers) east of Cedarville.

Great Lakes Boat Building School

485 South Meridian St.

Cedarville, MI 49719

906-484-1081

www.glbbs.org/

The school's mission statement is: "A non-profit educational center that seeks to provide quality traditional and composite wooden boat building skills to preserve and continue the rich maritime heritage of the Great Lakes." Public tours are offered daily June–August, Monday–Friday, at 10:00 a.m. and 2:00 p.m. (or by appointment).

Les Cheneaux Culinary School

186 S. Pickford Ave.

Hessel, MI

Located across from the Hessel Marina, this boutique culinary school is a state-of-the-art facility where students with a passion for cooking take part in an in-depth, one-year program with an open lesson plan devoted to hands-on experience in learning all aspects of a professional kitchen as they occur in a real environment. Mid-May through mid-September, they practice what they've learned in the Hessel Bay Inn, a full-service restaurant and catering facility featuring local seasonal produce.

OTHER ISLAND THINGS TO DO

Get out on the water—bring along a camera—to view the colorful historic boathouses dotting the shorelines of Les Cheneaux's channels.

Kayak, canoe, boat—This is the way to see Les Cheneaux! Kayaks, canoes, and stand-up paddle boards can be rented from Woods & Water Ecotours in Hessel.

Hike or bike—Helpful information on where to explore by foot or bike can be found on the Les Cheneaux Bike Path Map and Activity Guide (www. http://lescheneaux.org/wp-content/uploads/2013/07/LCBikeTrails.pdf) of the Eastern Upper Peninsula Bike Map offered by the Michigan Department of Transportation or obtained from the Les Cheneaux Islands Welcome Center (aka Les Cheneaux Visitor Center) in Cedarville or

Les Cheneaux Islands, a boater's, canoist's, and kayaker's paradise. And where there are boats, there are boathouses. These are of the historic wooden variety.

Woods & Water Ecotours in Hessel. Mountain bikes, cruisers, and children's bikes as well as cross-country skis and snowshoes can be rented from Woods & Water Ecotours.

Bird-watch—Rich in marshes, rocky peninsulas, sandy coves and ridges, wetlands, bogs, and sedge meadows as well as forests of cedar, fir, birch, and aspen onshore and sugar maple and beech farther inland, the Les Cheneaux region is an excellent birding area, serving as a migratory stopover site and and nesting area for over 250 bird species. You can pick up a free *Birds of Les Cheneaux Islands Area* brochure from the welcome center and find more birding information at www.lescheneaux.org/things-to-do/birding.

Fish—"Collectively, the near shore fishing experience at Les Cheneaux is as good as any we have to offer in Lake Huron," said fisheries research biologist Dave Fielder of the Michigan Department of Natural Resources.[30] Local catch includes yellow perch, northern pike, and smallmouth bass.

Visit some of the Les Cheneaux Area Artisan Cooperative artists—Access an artist directory at www.lescheneauxartisancoop.weebly.com.

Golf—Eight golf courses are within 40 miles (64 kilometers) of the Les Cheneaux area.

Drive the Lake Huron Circle Route.

Take the Fall Color Tour Route by bike or car in the fall.

Cross-country ski in the winter.

SPECIAL ISLAND EVENTS

Snowsfest (February)—Held annually over Presidents' Day weekend at Hessel, offering a variety of winter events for snowmobilers, snowshoers, cooks, kids, and more.

Michigan Maple Syrup Weekend at Tassier Sugar Bush (March).

Islands Wildlife Pike Fishing Contest (May).

Les Cheneaux Islands Antique Wooden Boat Show & Festival of Arts (second Saturday in August)—The largest antique wooden boat show in the world is sponsored by Les Cheneaux Historical Association and held at the Hessel Public Marina, including travel-lift and launch ramps, nautical exhibits, live entertainment, boat excursions of the islands, food concessions, and 70 juried Midwest artists.

For many more events, see www.lescheneaux.net.

For More Island Information

Les Cheneaux Islands Welcome Center (aka Les Cheneaux Visitor Center)
680 West M-134 (on the north side of the highway)
PO Box 301
Cedarville, MI 49719
888-364-7526
http://lescheneaux.org
The welcome center, supported by the Les Cheneaux Chamber of Commerce (www.lescheneaxu.net), the Tourist Association, and the Watershed Council, is stocked with a wide variety of maps and informational brochures about the area, including information on businesses in Les Cheneaux, the Upper Peninsula, and nearby Ontario.

Les Cheneaux Historical Association
PO Box 301
Cedarville, MI 49719
906-484-2821
www.lchistorical.org
Responsible for both the Les Cheneaux Historical Museum and the Les Cheneaux Maritime Museum.

Les Cheneaux Community Library
75 E. Hodeck
Cedarville, MI 49719
906-484-3547
uplibraries.org
lcclib@uproc.lib.mi.us
Houses special collections of materials related to Michigan history and nautical books and nautical charts.

A Brief History of Les Cheneaux Island: Some New Chapters of Mackinac History, by Frank R. Grover (Evanston, IL: Bowman, 1911).

The Les Cheneaux Chronicles: Anatomy of a Community, by Philip McM. Pittman (Cedarville, MI: Les Cheneaux Venture, 1985).

Ripples from the Breezes: A Les Cheneaux Anthology, by Philip McM. Pittman (Cedarville, MI: Les Cheneaux Venture, 1988).

Martin Reef Lightship to Lighthouse: Another Chapter in Les Cheneau History, by John J. Sellman (Cedarville, MI: Les Cheneaux Historical Association, 1995).

Government Island Campground—www.thegreatwaters.com/member-profile/65/48/.

How You Can Support the Island

Friends of Les Cheneaux Community Library (FLCCL)
PO Box 332
Hessel, MI 49745
906-484-2919

Parting Thoughts

My only regret is that I didn't trust my apparently inherent skills enough to carry my camera with me the first time I kayaked on a Great Lake. Instead, I gave it over to Mary, our guide from Woods & Water Ecotours who carried it in a waterproof pouch in her kayak. I was reunited with it when we stopped paddling and had lunch, as we'd planned, on Government Island, once the location of a Coast Guard station and now part of the Hiawatha National Forest.

What we'd not expected was the magnificent bolt of lightning suddenly connecting sky and water, which prompted us to begin paddling "like the dickens," as my Grandpa Klotzbach might have said, through the labyrinth of water grass that is Flower Bay to return to Hill Island, from where we'd launched.

Just as well that my camera was not with me, for despite the feeling of imminent danger and the urgency to get off the water, I might have been compelled to drift just for a bit instead of digging my paddle into that last mile of water. I would have been tempted to try to visually capture the excitement of being so small on such an expanse of water, so small, as wind and waves picked up.

Drummond Island, Michigan

KICK BACK, RENT A CABIN, WATCH THE SUN SET

July 22, 2014, 10:05 p.m.
Drummond Island Resort and Conference Center

What I remember liking best the first time I visited Drummond Island on a day trip a few years ago was the Maxton Plains Preserve: snowflakes of lichen on rocks; dark, pointy balsam fir and the shining, fluttery leaves of aspen; the limestone "paving" fractured by both prairie grasses and artic tundra plants. A different kind of very diverse "simplicity." And I need to get back out there, pronto, first thing tomorrow morning!

This Drummond Resort and Conference Center feels like a ghost town. Maybe no one plays golf in July? It feels like there's something about this place everybody else knows and I should too, but don't. Have I missed something in the news?

I suppose the décor of our room is supposed to be "North Woods," but it feels more like the "Robert Redford–Sundance Catalog" version of "Southwest," and I find it disconcerting. I guess I believe that "Up North," Michigan's version of "North Woods," should look like a Houghton Lake log cabin from the 1950s and 1960s, like the places I stayed on vacation as a kid.

But to be fair, my discontent began before we even set foot on the island. It began during the 4:40 ferry crossing of the De Tour Passage, the entire 10-minute ride dominated by the view of the dolomite-processing plant on the island, which only got larger the closer we got. Then a jarring array of advertising signs greeted us when we disembarked, and the 10-minute, eight-mile drive on a highway to get to this third-largest Great Lakes island's one traffic light, which marks Four Corners, was the beginning of what didn't feel like much of an island adventure. I already felt grumpy by then, ready to move on to another island. This island has 99 miles of ORV trails, for goodness' sake.

On the other hand, things did improve at Four Corners, where there was the biggest-I've-ever-seen puddingstone out front and where we were cordially welcomed by Gerry and Betty Bailey in the Drummond Island Welcome Center; even though I'd met them only briefly a few years back, they felt like old friends. We checked in here at Tom Monaghan's once-upon-a-time place, and then, when we couldn't find Chuck's Place, settled for a disappointing fried whitefish dinner in town. But our subsequent search for a cell phone signal to confirm future accommodation reservations led to an unplanned stop at the cemetery at St. Florence Catholic Church, which made up for it all. There Nancy and I, fed and watered and free of any other commitments for the evening, both slid into our island selves as we walked around the cemetery, discovering, in addition to other interesting markers, that a member of the Drummond Gable family is buried there under a Drummond puddingstone boulder. Buoyed by our island cemetery walk, we aimed toward sunset and ended up on the peninsula east of Seastone Point just in time to watch the sun flame the edges of clouds as cold and dark as the lake before us.

GETTING THERE: Car ferry; private boat or plane

GETTING AROUND: Bring your car; bring your own bike; bicycle, pontoon, fishing boats, canoe, and kayak rentals

OVERNIGHT ACCOMMODATIONS: Resorts with rental cabins, hotel resort and conference center, inn, and B&Bs; vacation rental homes; camping

FOOD: Restaurants; groceries

DAY TRIP? Yes, but a longer trip is recommended

STATE / PROVINCIAL / NATIONAL PARK? No, but State of Michigan Wildlife Management Areas constitute 68 percent of the island

You may have heard of folks who go to Drummond to rack up holes-in-one on the greens or to bag a white-tailed deer or even to participate in the lottery to hunt a black bear. But this large Lake Huron island, reached by easy ferry access and dotted with inland lakes, offers much more than the ideal golfing or hunting experience. Sure, the State of Michigan owns over two-thirds of the island, perfect if you'd like to hunt, and there's always the Drummond Island Resort and Conference Center if golf is your game, but if you want to experience the vibe of the real Drummond Island, select a housekeeping cottages resort—there's a directory listing of cottages to rent that goes from A to W, all on the water, some of which allow RV or

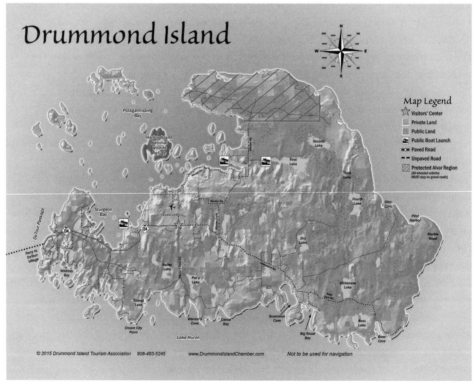

Courtesy of the Drummond Island Tourism Association

One of many cottages for rent on Drummond Island, this one is at Papin's Resort, on the sunset side of the island.

tent camping as well. With enough time and good weather, you'll be able to look forward to snagging a sunset or two.

Meanwhile, while the sun's high in the sky, find a beach or hike around some overturned earth in the forest and look for puddingstones. Drummond Island's Chamber of Commerce positions Drummond as the "Gem of the Huron," advertising that "at the center of her crown is the Puddingstone."

One advantage of hunting puddingstones on Drummond is that before you start looking, just 3.5 miles (5.6 kilometers) from where you disembark from the Drummond Island Ferry, you can get a bit of an education on puddingstones at the Puddingstone Rock Shop at North Haven Gifts. You may be fortunate enough to stop by on a tour day, when you can watch puddingstones being cut and made into handcrafted art and jewelry. For more information, see www.northhavenonline.com/.

How to Get There

Head north or south on I-75, depending on your departure point, to the Upper Peninsula of Michigan. Then head east on M-134, if you're coming from the south, or "stair-step" your way south and east if you're coming from the north.

De Tour Village, the point of departure for the Drummond Island Ferry, is at the very easternmost tip of the Upper Peninsula; in fact, M-134 on the mainland ends at the ferry dock (and picks back up on the island).

PUDDINGSTONES

While we may think of pudding as a creamy dessert, closely related to custard, nineteenth-century British puddings were boiled, often contained suet, and, as a finished product, resembled a cake. Plum pudding (Christmas pudding) was sweet and contained nuts and all kinds of dried fruit (but no actual plums), making it a chunky affair. When the newly arrived British in the Great Lakes area found specimens of this rock, relatively rare outside of the area and known to geologists as jasper conglomerate, the British dubbed them puddingstones because they resembled such a pudding.

A jasper conglomerate consists of subrounded pebbles of different colored chunks of jasper, black chert, white quartzite, dark, silvery-gray hematite, and semitransparent quartz in a coarse-grained quartzite matrix. The conglomerate specimens can range in size from a small pebble to a large boulder.

The jasper chunks in puddingstones come in shades of red, orange, pink, maroon, purple, tan, and brown, and they were deposited over an east-west band of only about 50 miles (80 kilometers) that lies mainly in Ontario but also touches a small area of Michigan's Upper Peninsula—Drummond Island in particular. The puddingstones found in these Great Lakes areas are also known as Drummond Island puddingstone, Michigan puddingstone, and St. Joseph Island puddingstone.

For more about puddingstones and how they have helped explain the glacial movement in the Great Lakes Basin, see "The Jasper Conglomerate, an Index of Drift Dispersion," by Chester B. Slawson of the University of Michigan: www.jstor.org/discover/10.2307/30067310?uid=3739728&uid=2&uid=4&uid=3739256&sid=21104772371621.

Drummond Island Ferry
Drummond Island Yacht Haven, Inc.
33185 S. Water St. (PO Box 148)
Drummond Island, MI 49726
800-543-4743/906-493-5232
www.diyachthaven.com/gettinghere/ferryschedule.html
marina@diyachthaven.com

May 1 through November 30, the ferry leaves mainland De Tour Village hourly, between 6:40 a.m. and 11:40 p.m., crossing the De Tour Passage of the St. Marys River, and then, between 11:40 p.m. and 6:40 a.m., it makes two trips during the week and three on Friday and Saturday. The ferry leaves Drummond Island at 6:10 a.m. and follows an hourly schedule until 11:10 p.m., and then makes similar return trips to the mainland between 11:10 p.m. and 6:40 a.m. Check the Drummond Island Yacht Haven website for schedules and fares.

On the short—about 10-minute—ride across the De Tour Passage, you'll see the quarrying operations of Drummond Dolomite, Inc., on the island's western shore. If you look south between De Tour Village and Drummond Island in the distance in Lake Huron, you'll see the De Tour Reef Light.

Drummond's central business district is approximately a 10-minute, eight-mile (13-kilometer) drive on M-134, also known as East Channel Drive, from the ferry landing. The Drummond Island Tourism Association, located at the Four Corners in town, is a very helpful place to begin your time on the island. Be sure to check out the large puddingstone boulder in front. If you're fortunate, you'll meet Gerry and Betty Bailey, who can answer just about all your questions about the island.

Drummond Island Airport (KDRM) is less than one mile (1.6 kilometers) northwest of Drummond Island's central business district.

What to Expect

Drummond Island is a very big island, with approximately 250 square miles (650 square kilometers) to explore. Deer, sandhill cranes, and coyote are more common, but black bear and the occasional lone wolf call Drummond their home, too, along with a variety of rare flora and fauna.

Don't let your first impression of the island—the Drummond Dolomite operation at the end of the island where the ferry lands—put you off. You won't see it again until you're back in line to leave the island.

Keep in mind, too, that Drummond is so big and its 150-mile (240-kilometer) coastline is so full of peninsulas and bays that very rarely does a road run along the coast, so when you're driving, you are not going to see the water like you may on a smaller island or an island with a less irregular shoreline.

Given the island's 133 square miles (345 square kilometers) of forest and 34 inland lakes, and the fact that 68 percent of the island is owned by the Department of Natural Resources, Drummond is paradise for hunters and anglers. And with 99 miles (160 kilometers) of ORV trails, you can understand how that may appear to be the preferred manner of getting around. Areas of darker boreal forest, thick woods with mature birch trees rising above impenetrable brush, acres of wetlands spreading out from lake and river may feel a bit foreboding.

Learn from my experience: plan to spend more than two or three days on Drummond; rent a cabin for a week in a resort with some waterfront. When you get off the ferry, head for Four Corners and begin your stay on the island by dropping in at the Drummond Island Tourism Association office. Consider visiting the Drummond Island Museum and the Maxton Plains Preserve. Hike to the fossil ledges. Come sunset, find a spot on the west coast. Try the Bear Track Inn for breakfast, and when the sun gets low in the sky, check out Chuck's. In between, spend a day looking for a puddingstone. Slow down, and let the island work its magic on you.

Paths to Adventure

NATURAL SITES

Drummond Island Township Park Heritage Trail—Hike or snowshoe this trail, also good for bird-watching.

The Fossil Ledges—Get a map from the tourism office or directions online at www.drummondislandchamber.com/index.php?page=Fossil_Ledges. When we hiked to the ledges, we found the road rutted, and there were some areas where we were stepping from stone to stone and placing our feet very carefully on the grass along muddy banks, but it was quite the adventure, and the fossils at the ledges were worth the walk. Or you could say that having the destination of the ledges gifted us with a wonderful walk.

Maxton Plains Preserve—A rare ecosystem that supports a large number of wildflowers.

HISTORY PRESERVED

Drummond Island Historical Society and Museum—Museum exhibits focus on the history of the Native Americans and the early settlers on the island, including: Finnish artifacts; Fort Drummond from the time of the British, 1815–28; the early lumbering era; and marine and sportsmen's exhibits. The museum itself is a spacious, beautiful building made of hand-hewn logs from the island, located about 10 miles (16 kilometers) from the ferry

The Fossil Ledges, on the north shore of Drummond Island, are accessible by a two-track hard-packed gravel road (map directions read, "First rt. turn after swamp"). Puddingstones aren't the only thing to look for on this island.

dock. The museum is open Memorial Day through Labor Day, from 1:00 p.m. to 5:00 p.m. daily. Admission is free; donations are appreciated.

Betsy Seaman Memorial Park—Across from the museum, this is a good place to pay homage to a woman of the oldest family still on the island. Becoming a widow 10 years after arriving from Beaver Island, she finished raising her 15 children here alone. Needless to say, Seaman is a common name on the island.

Drummond Island Cemetery—The cemetery is at St. Florence Catholic Church. Look for puddingstone grave markers.

CULTURAL ATTRACTIONS

North Haven Gifts—includes the Puddingstone Rock Shop. If you don't know what to hunt for, this is a good place to learn the finer points of puddingstone identification from the shop's owner, Jim Kelley.

Bear Track Inn—This is where you'll find locals and conversation, directions, answers to all of your questions, and hardy big breakfasts among newfound friends.

Papin's Resort—A perfect example of the best Drummond Island holds for families, couples, friends, and individual travelers. Enjoy a cottage, a dock, a sunset over the lake.

OTHER ISLAND THINGS TO DO

Go bird-watching—The Maxton Plains, Bald Knobs, and Sheep Ranch Road are all favored areas for spotting birds. In addition to birds migrating through, Drummond Island is the summer home of a large population of sandhill cranes. Year-round residents include bald eagles, ospreys, ravens, and pileated woodpeckers.

Hunt morels—The elusive morel—both white and black—can be found in the spring, typically around Mother's Day weekend.

SPECIAL ISLAND EVENTS

Fall on the Island Festival (October)—Includes a golf outing, "Taste of Drummond," artisan fair, pub crawl, and a 5K walk/run.

For More Island Information

Drummond Island Tourism Association
At Four Corners (the one traffic light on the island)
PO Box 200
Drummond Island, MI 49726
800-737-8666
www.drummondislandchamber.com

Drummond Island Historical Museum
Water St.
Drummond Island, MI 49726
906-493-5746
www.drummondislandchamber.com/index.php?page=Historical_Museum

A pair of sandhill cranes on the Maxton Plains Preserve. This Nature Conservancy preserve on Drummond Island contains a number of unique habitats including alvar, rich conifer swamp, boreal forest, bedrock beach, and Great Lakes marsh.

Drummond Island Digest—A monthly, at least in summer, publication that touts itself as "News and views that inform, inspire, and connect the Drummond Island and De Tour Village communities and points west."

Drummond Island: The Story of the British Occupation, 1815–1828, by Samuel F. Cook (Lansing, MI: Robert Smith, 1896).

Drummond Island: History, Folklore and Early People, by Jill Lowe Brumwell (Saginaw, MI: Black Bear, 2003).

Growing up on Drummond Island, by Jill Lowe Brumwell (Saginaw, MI: Black Bear, 2005).

Drummond Island's Part in the War of 1812, by Jill Lowe Brumwell (Saginaw, MI: Black Bear, 2012).

The North Channel and St. Mary's River: A Guide to the History, by Andrea Gutsche, Barbara Chisholm, and Russell Floren (Toronto: Lynx Images, 1997).

"Drummond Island," in *Biking the Great Lakes Islands,* by Kathleen Abrams and Lawrence Abrams (Wausau, WI: Entwood, 1985), 68–83—The four Drummond Island bike routes detailed are Circle Tour, Big Shoal Bay Beach, Waterfowl Nesting Site, and Quarry Route.

Michigan DNR Drummond Island Map—www.michigandnr.com/publications/pdfs/huntingwildlifehabitat/sga/Reference-map_all_Drummond_Island_map.pdf.

How You Can Support the Island

Drummond Island Historical Society and Museum
PO Box 293
Drummond Island, MI 49726

A nonprofit educational and cultural institution founded in 1958 and dedicated to "collecting, preserving, and sharing local rich and fascinating historical collections at the Society's Museum with all those interested in understanding and appreciating our American heritage." Donations are tax deductible.

Parting Thoughts

July 24, 2014, 9:33 p.m.
Cabin 6, Papin's Resort
Drummond Island

It's just after sunset and I'm sitting in a purple velvet armchair with caned sides. Decidedly not a rustic piece of furniture, although this is a most rustic cottage with beautiful log rafters. There is nothing like a cabin on a Great Lake to change one's mind about an island. I'm glad Nancy talked me out of leaving yesterday. She said to sleep on it. I did and we had a wonderful island day yesterday. My opinion of Drummond Island has changed significantly over the last 24 hours.

Yesterday we followed a cryptic hand-drawn half-page map that indicated some landmarks I'm not sure we ever really found. But we hiked all the way to the fossil ledges and found plenty of adventure along the way, some of it involving figuring out how to ford, on foot, the washed-out road. After we'd made it back to relative civilization, we finally found Chuck's

Place (Chuck's "lac," to be exact; the P and the E were missing). When the waitress, Gartha-lene, heard about our disappointment in our island accommodations, she made a few calls, right then and there. And before we'd drained our drafts, she'd worked out a one-night stay for us at a cottage in Papin's Resort (note that cottages on Drummond are rented by the week in the summer; this case involved a last-minute cancellation by another guest and some sort of family connection—second cousin, perhaps—between the waitress and the resort owners).

On our way to our home for the night, we passed a sign along the road: "If you don't talk to your cat about catnip, who will?" We were downright giddy ourselves at this point with our good fortune. Two more wonderful Baileys, Michael and Amy, run Papin's Resort. (Turns out that most people on the island are either a Seaman, a Bailey, or related to one or the other; John T. Nevil, who wrote a series of articles about the Seaman family of Drummond Island that was published in the *Evening News*, also wrote a poem that begins, "If you live on Drummond Island / And Seaman's not your name, / You'll likely be a Bailey. . . .")

After we'd checked in and spent some time talking to Amy and Michael, we had a glass of wine on our porch, hung out on the resort's dock while the sun set, and had a great sleep in a log cabin that reminded me of an updated version of my Houghton Lake ideal.

July 24, 2:00 p.m.
On the Drummond Island II

We started this day with the sight of a pair of sandhill cranes on our way to the Maxton Plains Preserve. Then we bought sandwiches at the Bear Track Inn restaurant while the owners and some regulars fielded some of our island questions, visited the Drummond Island Historical Museum, and were taken on a tour of the Puddingstone Rock Shop at North Haven Gifts by owner Jim Kelley. His were the only puddingstones we saw on this island, but we hadn't really looked; we'd been too busy having other types of fun. Maybe on a visit back or on some other island someday.

By the time we pulled up to wait in line for the ferry, or "The Pulse," as it's known, for its back and forth hourly trips discharging and taking up passengers, we were pulsing ourselves with good cheer for Drummond Island.

St. Joseph Island, Ontario

STAGING SITE FOR THE WAR OF 1812

July 24, 2014, 9:50 p.m.
Sunnyside B&B
Sailors Encampment, St. Joseph Island

It's interesting how following the history of one or two families on an island, or the way in which a family name intersects with an island, sometimes provides a window into the island's history, a focal point from which to look around. The prevalence of the name Rains (sometimes written Raines) has been noticeable to me on St. Joseph Island today, beginning when we started up the long drive to our bed-and-breakfast, Sunnyside, in the northwestern area of the island known as Sailors Encampment (this western shore edges the St. Marys River, despite the island being considered a Lake Huron island). A large white sign on the long hill of the front lawn states that Sunnyside was settled in 1853 or 1854 by Owen Roland Rains, whose family farmed the plot until 1966.

Later, Owen Rains turns up in the pioneer cemetery, which is within walking distance of Sunnyside up Highway 548 on the grounds of the first church built on St. Joseph Island, in 1876, the Church of Mary. Rains lived to be 97 (1830–1927). He's sharing a headstone with his wife, Victoria (1841–1909). There is also an Owen T. Rains (1875–1967) and then an entire large plot of Rains: Arthur M. Rains, died June 19, 1926, aged 87 years, three months; his wife, Frances Melvina, died December 23, 1910, aged 66 years, eight months. There's also a tall Rains memorial with stones around it. Given that Owen and Victoria had 13 children, it should not be surprising that there are two large family plots, and then some, in such a small cemetery.

Across the St. Marys River from Sailors Encampment is a small American island attached to Neebish Island. Americans call it Little Neebish Island, but I've noticed that a number of Canadians call it Rains Island. Why?

At 36, Owen R. Rains's father, Major William Kingdom Rains (Kingdom was his mother's maiden name), left his first wife in England after the Peninsular Wars and came to the New World. On his way across the Atlantic, he met the two daughters of a friend, Frances, 16, and her younger sister, Eliza Doubleday, who had lost their parents and would each become Rains's wife, Frances his second and Eliza his third, resulting in Rains being married to three women. Rains and the sisters settled first at Lake Simcoe in Ontario. In 1835, Rains tried to start a colony on St. Joseph with several others, but becoming estranged from his fellow investors in 1838, he relocated first to the southwest of the island and then to Little Neebish, which for a time officially bore his name: Rains Island. There he built a home for each of his New World families. Frances and Eliza bore 19 of Rains's 25 children, many of whom, apparently, remained in the area. Some might say, given all of the unusual alliances that developed in the area to bring us to how things are today, that the story of this man with two wives on this side of the

Atlantic and one on the other and 25 children is an interesting place to begin in considering the French-British-American-Canadian history of St. Joseph Island.

Another Rains connection: at the St. Joseph Historic Museum, out in the barn, an old sign reading "Rainsmere" hangs from the rafters. According to the timeline of the St. Joseph Historical Society (founded in 1963), the Rainsmere Hotel, built between 1892 and 1896, "had 20 bedrooms, several dining rooms, sitting rooms and kitchens. It catered to river travellers and was one of the first hotels to be managed by a woman," Mrs. Clara (Rains) Robinson. The hotel was demolished in 1989.

In current times, Jackileen Rains, married to a descendant of Major Rains and an island historian, is one of the coauthors of *St. Joseph Island: A Tour and Historical Guide* and *St. Joseph Island: Images of the Past* (both written with Elsie Hadden Mole).

Tonight, in my lakeside bed, I raise the shade to look across to Rains Island. Instead, I see a large lit building, as big as a hotel, headed directly for the front of the B&B. A freighter, of course, making a late-night pass by the island.

GETTING THERE: Bridge; private boat or plane

GETTING AROUND: Bring your car; bring your bike; bicycle rentals available

OVERNIGHT ACCOMMODATIONS: Motel, inn, and B&Bs; resort with cabins; vacation rentals; camping

FOOD: Restaurants; groceries

DAY TRIP? Yes

STATE / PROVINCIAL / NATIONAL PARK? No, but Fort St. Joseph, at the southernmost point of the island, is a National Historic Site of Canada operated by Parks Canada

---

The westernmost of the Manitoulin chain of islands in the North Channel, the body of water between Georgian Bay and the St. Marys River along the north shore of Lake Huron, St. Joseph Island, for a time, was also the most westerly point of Upper Canada. Then Fort St. Joseph, at the southwest tip of the island, was the center of a robust community of soldiers, Native people, and fur traders from its construction in 1796 until the outbreak of the War of 1812.

Fort St. Joseph was built as a replacement for Mackinac Island's Fort Mackinac, built by the British during the American Revolutionary War and lost in the American victory of 1783 but not turned over to the United States until 1796. The site of Fort St. Joseph was chosen for its proximity to Fort Mackinac and the most established navigation routes.

The U.S. Congress declared war on Great Britain on June 18, 1812, and the commander of Fort St. Joseph was ordered to attack Fort Mackinac, which was then known as Fort Michilimackinac. On July 17, a cobbled-together army of approximately 50 British soldiers, 150 French Canadian or métis voyageurs, and perhaps 400 Native people (although it is said their number may have been overestimated) arrived in a flotilla made up of one armed schooner, 70 canoes, and 10 bateaux at what is now called British Landing at the northern end of Mackinac Island and made for the fort, two miles (three kilometers) away.

Garrisoned at the fort were approximately 61 Americans with seven guns—they were significantly outnumbered and taken completely by surprise, unaware that war had been declared. The Americans surrendered after the firing of a single cannon round followed by a demand to surrender. The demand was emphasized by the presence of three captured villagers. Later, Lieutenant Porter Hanks, the commander of the fort, was facing a court-martial at Fort Detroit, charged with cowardice for surrendering Fort Michilimackinac, when the British initiated the siege of Detroit and "a cannonball ripped through the room where he was standing, cutting him in half and killing the officer next to him as well before he could be tried."[31]

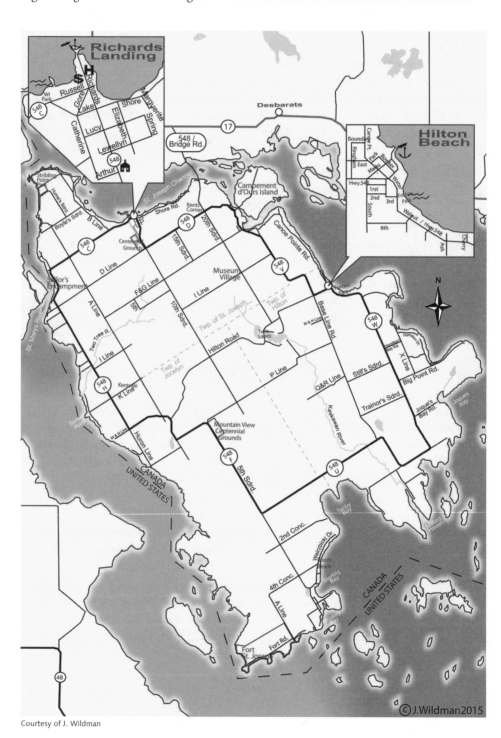

Courtesy of J. Wildman

Fort St. Joseph was abandoned as British soldiers and traders moved into Fort Mackinac. In 1814, an American expedition led by Captain Arthur Sinclair burned the abandoned fort on the way to destroy a number of British targets farther north in the St. Marys River.

The Treaty of Ghent, ratified by the English Parliament on December 30, 1814, before the Americans won the decisive Battle of New Orleans on January 8, 1815, restored the borders of American and British land to their original configuration before the war: Mackinac Island went back to the Americans, and St. Joseph remained under British control. Later, in 1867, with the formation of the Dominion of Canada, St. Joseph Island became Canadian.

Today, Fort St. Joseph is a National Historic Site run by Parks Canada. However, the fort is just one of a number of interesting sights on this island.

How to Get There

St. Joseph Island is accessible by the Bernt Gilbertson Bridge on Highway 548, off Highway 17, about 30 miles east of Sault Ste. Marie, Ontario. Take the Trans-Canadian Highway, known as Ontario Highway 17 here, to Highway 548, an intersection about 12 miles (19 kilometers) west of Bruce Mines, Ontario. Highway 548 runs across the Bernt Gilbertson St. Joseph Island Bridge and continues on the island as the major perimeter road.

What to Expect

St. Joseph Island, 19 by 12 miles (31 by 19 kilometers), is the second-largest island in Lake Huron and the third-largest island in the Great Lakes Basin, behind only Isle Royale and Manitoulin Island. The island feels big and settled, with its three townships, Hilton, Jocelyn, and St. Joseph; two villages, Richard's Landing (in the township of St. Joseph) and Hilton Beach (in the township of Hilton); and a year-round population of almost 2,000 people. In the middle of the island is the "mountain," which contributes the lures of mountain biking and "mountain" products (St. Joseph Island is the largest center of maple syrup in Ontario) to an island visit. The mountain provides an explanation of how multiple settlements grew up on the island; this geographical feature, unlike inland lakes (the Twin Lakes, Deer Lake, and Caufield Lake are the only ones large enough to have names), separates parts of the island from each other.

Paths to Adventure

NATURAL SITES

The Women's Institute Park—Located in Richards Landing, the park features a sandy public beach, a swimming area, playground equipment, picnic pavilions, and tennis courts.

Forbes Community Park—A sand beach in Hilton Beach with a marked swimming area, a raft for diving, public restrooms, changing rooms, picnic tables, and playground equipment. The Hilton Beach boardwalk, which follows a mile-long (1.6-kilometer-long) scenic walk, runs the length of this park.

Big Point Park—Sand beach with picnic tables, public restroom, and playground equipment. Sandhill cranes frequent the reeds along the shoreline.

Beech Beach—A sandy beach located in Jocelyn Township on the southern end of the island, close to the St. Joseph Island Bird Sanctuary.

Twin Lakes Park—A warm inland lake in Hilton Township with a sand beach, picnic tables and a picnic pavilion shelter, public restrooms, and changing rooms.

St. Joseph Island Marine Park at Stribling Point—The park has a number of forest trails (which double as snowshoe trails in the winter), a waterfront, and a viewing station. Stribling Point is a good place to watch ships heading upstream to Lake Superior.

St. Joseph Island Bird Sanctuary—In the southwest corner of the island, near Fort St. Joseph.

St. Joseph Island Nature Reserve—Ontario Nature's northernmost nature reserve and a part of the Jocko Bay Provincially Significant Wetland. In addition to northern bird species (such as the black-throated green warbler) and small mammals (such as beaver, muskrat, and mink) a number of northern orchid species can be found in the reserve. Please consult www.ontarionature.org/protect/habitat/PDFs/St Joseph Island Nature Reserve.pdf before making plans to visit.

HISTORY PRESERVED

St. Joseph Island Museum—Located at the intersection of I Line and 20th Sideroad on St. Joseph Island, the museum complex includes historic buildings. See if you can complete

St. Joseph Island Museum, established in 1963, offers visitors a "Museum Quest," a scavenger hunt to complete while exploring a village of six historic buildings, and over 7,000 artifacts that span more than 200 years of island history.

Chimney ruins at Fort St. Joseph. The ruins are a mystery: archaeologists have found no surrounding building foundation, nor have historians discovered any record of a building at this location.

the "Museum Quest," correctly identifying artifacts. For a further challenge, try the scavenger hunt. The museum is open daily, except Tuesdays, from 9:30 a.m. to 4:30 p.m., mid-June through Labor Day. It's open other days and times by appointment; for group or custom tours, call for reservations: 705-246-2672.

Fort St. Joseph—A National Historic Site of Canada, the fort offers a visitor center, museum, gift shop, theater, tours, an archeological site, nature trails, and picnic grounds.

Old Town Jail—A stone structure built in the early 1900s and used until the 1920s, located in the center of Richards Landing.

Church of Mary and Cemetery—The first church built on the island, in 1876, with a pioneer cemetery on the grounds.

CULTURAL ATTRACTIONS

Gilbertson's Maple Products—Ontario's largest producer of pure maple syrup and a family-run business in Richards Landing since 1936. Spring season begins after the first week of March and runs to the latter part of April. In addition to guided tours through the

The 1,000-footer *American Spirit* upbound on the St. Marys River, slipping past the northwest side of St. Joseph Island at Sailors Encampment and Johnson Point on Little Neebish Island— aka Rains Island—one of the narrowest points of the Great Lakes shipping system, and the view from Sunnyside B&B.

production facility and old-fashioned kettle-syrup-making Saturday events, Gilbertson's runs the Pancake House Restaurant and Gift Shop on the weekends. For more information, see www.gilbertsonsmaple.com.

Adcock's Woodland Gardens—Features native and imported plants, flowers, shrubs, and water lily ponds with iris and other shore plants, all set in the forest with several kilometers of hiking.

OTHER ISLAND THINGS TO DO

Watch the ships go by.

Ride your bike three seasons of the year; bike rentals are available at the Richards Landing Marina.

Cross-country ski the Mountain View cross-country ski trails in winter.

Hunt for puddingstones.

SPECIAL ISLAND EVENTS

Maple Syrup Festival in Richards Landing (first two weekends in April).

Tractor Trot (July).

Canadian Arts Festival in Richards Landing (July).

Arts on the Dock in Hilton Beach (July).

Heritage Tea Day at the St. Joseph Island Museum (second Sunday in July).

Teddy Bear Picnic at the St. Joseph Island Museum (fourth Sunday in July).

Arts and Artifacts at the St. Joseph Island Museum (second Sunday in August).

Children's Day Camp at St. Joseph Island Museum (second Wednesday in August).
Community Days.
Fort St. Joseph Ghost Walk (August).

For More Island Information

St. Joseph Island Museum
RR#2
Richards Landing, ON P0R 1J0
705-246-2672
www.stjoemuseum

Fort St. Joseph
PO Box 220
Richards Landing, ON P0R 1J0
705-246-2664
www.pc.gc.ca/eng/lhn-nhs/on/stjoseph/index.aspx

St. Joseph Island Chamber of Commerce
www.sjichamber.ca
www.facebook.com/stjosephislandchamberofcommerce

Island Clipping, a weekly newspaper published since 1995 (archived online at www.island-clippings.com).

History of Fort St. Joseph, by John Abbott, Graeme S. Mount, and Michael J. Mulloy (Toronto: Dundurn Group, 2000).

Historic St. Joseph Island, by Estelle and Joseph Bayliss (Cedar Rapids, IA: Torch, 1938).

OTHER ONTARIO ISLANDS IN THE ST. JOSEPH CHANNEL

- **Pine Island**—A small island of primarily seasonal cottages in the channel and accessible by bridge across Maskinonge Bay via Pine Island Road, located in the township of Tarbutt and Tarbutt Additional, in the Algoma District.
- **Brown's Island**—An even smaller island of a handful of seasonal cottages, between Pine Island and the mainland, accessible by a short one-lane wooden bridge—minus railings—across rock and a bit of the channel via Browns Island Road (Islandview Drive connects Townline Road West and Browns Island Road closer to the water).
- Other small islands are accessible by bridge from St. Joseph Island.
  - **Bamford Island**—The Bernt Gilbertson Bridge is supported by and crosses over this small island, which is used as a picnic spot—picnic tables and portable restrooms are on-site—and fishing site between the mainland and St. Joseph Island.
  - **Twyning Islands**—The Bernt Gilbertson Bridge is supported by and crosses over these tiny islands, which are used as fishing sites.
  - **Munroe Islands**—These small islands support and are accessed by the Bernt Gilbertson Bridge. They, too, are popular fishing sites.
  - **Campement d'Ours ("Den of Bears") Island**—Accessible by bridge from the northeast tip of St. Joseph Island, this heavily forested island has one road running up the middle of it, flanked by seasonal cottages. All property, including the riverbanks, is privately owned.

St. Joseph Island—A Tour and Historical Guide, by Elsie Hadden Mole and Jackileen Rains (Sault Ste. Marie: Journal Printing, 1988).

St. Joseph Island—Images of the Past, by Elsie Hadden Mole and Jackileen Rains (ebook published by the Trailing Arbutus, 2014).

The North Channel and St. Mary's River: A Guide to the History, by Andrea Gutsche, Barbara Chisholm, and Russell Floren (Toronto: Lynx Images, 1997).

"St. Joseph Island," in *Biking the Great Lakes Islands,* by Kathleen Abrams and Lawrence Abrams (Wausau, WI: Entwood, 1985), 84–101—The five St. Joseph Island bike routes detailed are Lighthouse Tour, Sailors Encampment Circle Tour, Fort St. Joseph, Museum Tour, and Big Point Beach.

How You Can Support the Island

St. Joseph Island Historical Society
PO Box 82
Hilton Beach, ON P0R 1G0
705-246-2089

Parting Thoughts

July 25, 2014
St. Joseph Island

Much more than plentiful history, good ship watching, and beach fun is to be found on St. Joseph Island. Nancy and I went looking for puddingstones at two sites recommended by our B&B host, with excellent results. At the first, in the hot morning sun, we found our very first ones, some small pebble-sized jasper conglomerates, but at the second, later in the day, just before the rain came at 6:00, we hit the jackpot.

Near what may have been an abandoned gravel pit, on a hill of sand covered in sweet white clover and a few stalwart milkweed plants, and under a threatening sky, we found a number of pieces of quartz pebbles with evidence of jasper that made them puddingstones. I caught sight of what at first looked like just a softball-size piece of quartz embedded in the hill, but as rain-drops started to sprinkle it, I realized there were more than rain speckles to be seen. Big, bold, beautiful chunks of brick red, rich chocolate brown, pure white, deerskin tan, and a deep, deep purple. I picked up its heft from the side of the hill of sand. I'd finally found a perfect specimen of puddingstone on a pretty—and pretty perfect—island.

Manitoulin Island, Ontario

HOME OF THE OJIBWE CULTURAL FOUNDATION

October 27, 2013, 9:30 a.m.

Jeanne and I drove through scarves of mist twisting beneath a bright half moon hung low in the sky almost the entire length of the Bruce Peninsula to Tobermory, where we were to take the *Chi-Cheemaun* ferry the next day to Manitoulin Island. Perhaps the skunk trundling out of my high-beam lights and into the illusions of light and reflection on the two-lane road could have been construed as a caution of events to come: a too-late night arrival, a hurried morning departure, clothes accidentally left hanging on a hook behind the door, a fuse blown, a misunderstanding before breakfast. But the magic of the moon and the mist between shoulders of forest was all I saw. And, in the end, was the perfect introduction to the wildness of Manitoulin, Mnidoo Mnis, Island of the Great Spirit.

GETTING THERE: Car ferry from the south or bridges from the north; private boat or plane

GETTING AROUND: Bring your car; bring your own bike and/or kayak; bicycle and paddle sports rentals; boat and motor rentals at many resorts/vacation rentals

OVERNIGHT ACCOMMODATIONS: Motels, resorts, cottages, apartments, and B&Bs; vacation rentals; camping

FOOD: Restaurants; groceries

DAY TRIP? Yes, but not recommended; one could weave a month of island adventures on this largest freshwater island in the world!

STATE / PROVINCIAL / NATIONAL PARK? Misery Bay Provincial Park, a day-use-only park, provides access to the Lake Huron coastline and educational programming

Before you head off for Manitoulin Island, you may want to consider its size as you make your plans. The largest freshwater island in the world, Manitoulin is located in Lake Huron between Georgian Bay (Manitoulin Island's east coast and the Bruce Peninsula create this bay) and the North Channel (located between Manitoulin and the Ontario mainland). In terms of size, it feels like a small state although, as it is in Canada, a small province would be more like it.

In actuality, the island is 80 miles (129 kilometers) long and from 2.5 to 30 miles (four to 48 kilometers) wide. It has a number of bays to explore and over 80 inland lakes; the three largest are Lake Manitou, Lake Kagawong, and Lake Mindemoya. It has a number of communities as well, including Little Current, Sheguiandah, Manitowaning, South Baymouth,

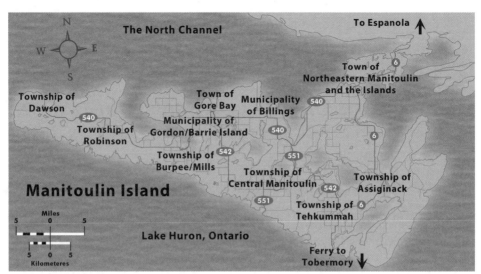

Courtesy of Dylon Whyte

Tehkummah, Sandfield, Mindemoya, Providence Bay, Spring Bay, Kagawong, Gore Bay, Evansville, Silver Water, and Meldrum Bay.

How to Get There

In getting to Manitoulin Island, you have a choice. You can take the MS *Chi-Cheemaun* vehicle ferry from Tobermory, Ontario, at the end of the skinny finger of the Bruce Peninsula and land at South Baymouth on the island. Or you can drive across multiple bridges—and several other islands—from the village of Whitefish Falls, Ontario, on the north shore of the North Channel of Lake Huron, via Highway 6.

If you take the ferry, you'll have the opportunity to put your car in line (and taking your car is recommended, given the size of the island) and take some refreshment at the Lakeside Restaurant and Patio Bar, within sight of your car; it seems to be the thing to do. Or you can wait and dine on whitefish (or make another choice from a large menu) in the dining room of the largest ferry sailing the Great Lakes.

The Gore Bay–Manitoulin Airport (CYZE) provides fly-in access to the island.

What to Expect

Water! Forest! And a number of small communities and First Nation reserves with interesting museums and galleries. There are many island things to do; having a general plan about what you want to do or what one or two areas you'd like to explore on the island will allow you to relax into the adventure mode that makes for a successful island trip.

Paths to Adventure

Manitoulin Island seems to have endless paths of adventure to follow. Here are a few.

NATURAL SITES

Bridal Veil Falls—A beautiful waterfall that one can actually walk behind. There are easy-to-walk trails on both sides of the Kagawong River. If you're there in the fall, you may see the salmon swimming up—they are so dense in places, you feel you could step across the river on their backs. The Bridal Veil Falls trail comes off of Highway 540 at the entrance to Kagawong.

Lake Kagawong—Camping on Lake Kagawong, a place my in-laws told us about before they were my in-laws, was my introduction to Manitoulin Island four decades ago. After staying at Norm's Tent and Trailer Park in the "honeymoon site" on that first trip, my husband and I took our daughters back to camp there when they were young.

Gore Bay—A lovely town on a beautiful bay. Years ago, I came home with a small woven basket filled with horn coral I'd found on its shore. This is a different type of "Lucky Stone" than the ones you find on Pelee Island; these are prehistoric rugosa coral fossils. You can find out more about these special fossils at the Gore Bay Museum.

Cup and Saucer—11 miles (18 kilometers) west of Little Current at the intersection of Highway 540 and the Bidwell Road, the Cup and Saucer is the highest point on Manitoulin Island, and the Cup and Saucer Trail is one of the most popular trails in Ontario, with its two kilometers of dramatic 70-meter (230-foot) cliffs. With up to 7.5 miles (12 kilometers) of hiking trails plus a 1.25-mile (two-kilometer) adventure trail, the hike can take from one and a half to four hours.

The M'Chigeeng Hiking Trails—Off Highway 551, just south of Highway 540, the entrance to the trails is behind the M'Chigeeng First Nation Ballpark. The M'Chigeeng includes two

Manitoulin Island, the largest freshwater island in the world, can be accessed by the MS *Chi-Cheemaun* ("Big Canoe") ferry from Tobermory, Ontario, or by the Little Current Swing Bridge (*above*) from Goat Island, Ontario.

Bridal Veil Falls, where the Kagawong River falls over a 35-foot limestone bluff between Lake Kagawong and the North Channel of Lake Huron on Manitoulin Island. The Ojibwe term *kagawong* means "mists rising from falling water."

trails, one along the bottom of the bluff and one that goes to the very top. The Bear Caves and Fossil Rock Point are two spots of interest, in addition to the height of the bluff, which offers outstanding views of the North Channel. The walk through thick forest is appropriate for families—children who like to hike should be able to complete it—and takes two to three hours. For more information on the trails and other points of interest, call the M'Chigeeng Economic Development Office at 705-377-5362.

HISTORY PRESERVED

Ojibwe Cultural Centre in M'Chigeeng First Nation territory (West Bay)—Committed to the revitalization and growth of the language, culture, arts, spirituality, and traditions of the Anishinaabe people, the center includes an elders' room, arts and craft retail outlet, museum, art gallery, healing lodge, classroom and presentation area, AV studio, resource center, and administration offices.

Lighthouses:

- Mississagi Lighthouse (Meldrum Bay)
- Janet Head Lighthouse (Gore Bay)
- Manitowaning Lighthouse (Manitowaning)
- Strawberry Island Lighthouse (Little Current)
- Little Current Lighthouse (Little Current)
- South Baymouth Range Lighthouses
- Kagawong Lighthouse (Kagawong)

Museums galore! Eight Manitoulin museums offer a glimpse at the era of European settlement and beyond:

- Little Schoolhouse and Museum (South Baymouth)
- Assigninack Museum Complex (Assigninack)
- Centennial Museum of Sheguiandah (Sheguiandah)
- Pioneer Museum (Mindemoya)
- Old Mill Heritage Centre and Post Office Museum (Kagawong)
- Gore Bay Museum (Gore Bay)
- Net Shed Museum (Meldrum Bay)
- Jack Seabrook's Farm Museum (Mindemoya)

CULTURAL ATTRACTIONS

MS *Chi-Cheemaun*—Taking the largest ferry that plies the Great Lakes, with its outdoor decks, indoor dining, full bar, and occasional musical entertainment, is an experience in itself. For more information, visit www.ontarioferries.com/ontarioferries/English/index.asp.

The Ojibwe Cultural Centre in M'Chigeeng First Nation (aka West Bay) on Manitoulin Island. The Ojibwe Cultural Foundation is the identity center of the Anishinaabe people.

Great Spirit Circle Trail—Seven First Nation reserves dot Manitoulin Island. The Great Spirit Circle Trail offers nature-based and cultural tourism from the perspective of the Anishinaabe people—the Ojibwe, Odawa, and Potawatomi—on Manitoulin Island (also in the Sagamok region of northeastern Ontario on the Canadian mainland). Experiences range from educational interpretive tours to "soft adventure" to wilderness eco-adventures.

> Great Spirit Circle Trail
> Manitoulin Island–Sagamok Region
> 5905 Hwy. 540, PO Box 469
> M'Chigeeng, ON P0P 1G0
> www.circletrail.com

St. Gabriel Lalemant Catholic Church—on nearby Birch Island, home of the Whitefish River First Nation.

Lillian's Crafts & Museum (in M'Chigeeng)—Features porcupine-quill and birch-bark baskets (www.lillianscrafts.ca).

Manitou Studio and Gallery (on Lake Manitou)—Showcases work by Moira Elsley in watercolor, acrylic, and oil (705-377-4104).

Clearly Vintage Studio (Gore Bay)—Headlines stained glass and métis beadwork work by Maggie King (www.maniotoulin-island.com/clearly-vintage-studio/.

Christie Best Pearson (Evansville; virtual gallery)—Here you'll find watercolors, pen and ink drawings, and colored pencil drawings of local scenes (www.christiebestpearson.com).

Hettmann Studio (Dominion Bay)—Features the work of Ursula Hettmann in jewelry, clothing, and paintings (www.hettmannstudio.com).

Perivale Gallery (Spring Bay)—Exhibits fine paintings, sculpture, woodwork, photography, and glasswork by three dozen or more artists (www.perivale-gallery.manitoulin-island .com).

Southbay Gallery and Guesthouse (South Bay)—A bed-and-breakfast featuring artwork and handmade gifs created by Canadian, aboriginal, and local artists (jewelry, pottery, hot glass, quilts, clothing, furs, quill boxes, prints, paintings, beeswax candles, and fresh Manitoulin preserves) (www.southbayguesthouse.com).

OTHER ISLAND THINGS TO DO

Hike—Besides trails at the Bridal Veil Falls, up the Cup and Saucer, and through a part of the M'Chigeeng First Nation reserve, there are seven other well-recognized trails on Manitoulin Island. For a description of each, visit www.manitoulin-island.com/hikingtrails.html.

Cycle—For a few pointers and a description of the location of the two highest hills, see www .manitoulin-island.com/activities/activities.

Camp—A full description of available camping sites is found at www.manitoulin-island .com/accommodation/campgrounds.html.

Fish—Besides, by one count, having 108 lakes, Manitoulin Island has three rivers: the Kagawong, the Manitou, and the Mindemoya, which are spawning grounds for Atlantic salmon and trout. For specifics, visit www.manitoulinislandfishing.com/.

Go horseback riding—Try Honora Bay Riding Stables (west of Little Current on Highway 540) or Kicking Mule Ranch (south of Manitowaning on Highway 6).

Golf—You have your choice of three: Brookwood Brae Golf Club (9-hole, par 36); "Manitoulin's Old Course" in Mindemoya; Manitoulin Island Golf and Country Club (9-hole, par 36 and 18-hole, par 72) in Gore Bay; and Rainbow Ridge Golf Club (18-hole, par 72) championship course in Manitowaning.

OTHER ISLANDS ACCESSIBLE FROM MANITOULIN ISLAND

- **Birch Island**—A part of the 21-square-mile (54-square-kilometer) Whitefish River First Nation Reserve, this island is accessible on Highway 6 between the city of Espanola on the Ontario mainland and Great La Cloche Island. The island is home to Dreamer's Rock, a promontory atop a high bluff, where for generations Native youths have gone for a rite of passage to fast, pray, and receive a vision of guidance in understanding their life's purpose.
- **Great La Cloche Island**—An Ontario island named by French explorers for the Bell Rock, a huge boulder located on a limestone plain dotted with glacial erratics that when hit with a rock rings like a bell. Great La Cloche Island is located between Birch Island and Goat Island, accessible by Highway 6. (Little La Cloche Island, accessible from Great La Cloche Island by bridge, is the site of a limestone quarry and currently privately owned by a cement company.)
- **Goat Island**—A small Ontario island located in the municipality of Northeastern Manitoulin and the Islands. Highway 6, which traverses the island, crosses from Manitoulin Island via the Little Current swing bridge. A fixed bridge at the other end of the island crosses to Great La Cloche Island. Goat Island's only community is called Turner.
- **Barrie Island**—A 31-square-mile (80-square-kilometer) island in the north-central region of Manitoulin Island, just west of Gore Bay, that was established in 1878. At one time, this rural island had both a church, Barrie Island United Church (1913–70), and a school, Barrie Island School (1896–1969). Today, a part of the municipality of Gordon/Barrie Island, it still has farms, a community center, and several well-maintained daytime-use waterfront parks: Goosegap West Park and Salmon Bay Park (and boat launch). Highway 540A crosses over a causeway linking Barrie Island with Manitoulin Island.
- **Twilight Isle**—A tiny island in Manitoulin Island's Evansville area entirely occupied by the Twilight Isle Resort, which contains housekeeping cottages for tourists interested in fishing or hunting. Twilight Isle is reached by Highway 540 on the southern approach to the Indian Point Bridge that divides Lake Wolsey from the Campbell Bay (aka the Bayfield Sound) off North Channel.
- **Burnt Island**—A small island accessible by causeway on the southern shore of Manitoulin Island (nearest to the town of Silverwater), home to the fifth-generation family-owned and family-operated Purvis Fisheries. The island is off Manitoulin Island's Queen Elizabeth The Queen Mother Mnidoo Mnising Provincial Park (aka "Queen Mum"), a 6,500-hectare Natural Environment Provincial Park owned by the Crown and the Nature Conservancy of Canada.

Go bird-watching, go on an "Owl Prowl," and look to the stars—Gordon's Park Eco Resort in Tehkummah, winner of the Attraction Canada Award, offers these activities and more. You don't have to be a guest of the resort to participate in astronomy nights, fossil hikes, moonlight hikes and wolf howls, night hikes, or geocaching. The public is also welcome to use the pool, play miniature golf, practice archery, hike the educational trails, and visit the nature interpretive center. Activity fees apply to non-overnight guests. More information is at www. gordonspark.com.

SPECIAL ISLAND EVENTS

Manitoulin Annual Art Tour (July).
Haweater Weekend (August).
Perseids Meteor Party (August).

For the what, where, and when of these and other special island events, visit www.manitoulintourism.com/events-calendar/.

For More Island Information

www.manitoulin-island.com.

Misery Bay Provincial Park—www.ontarioparks.com/park/miserybay.

Exploring Manitoulin, 3rd ed., by Shelley J. Pearen (Toronto: University of Toronto Press, 1992).

"Manitoulin Island's North Shore," in *The North Channel and St. Mary's River: A Guide to the History,* by Andrea Gutsche, Barbara Chisholm, and Russell Floren (Toronto: Lynx Images, 1997), 51–87.

"Manitoulin Island," in *Biking the Great Lakes Islands,* by Kathleen Abrams and Lawrence Abrams (Wausau, WI: Entwood, 1985), 102–15—The two Manitoulin Island bike routes detailed are Providence Bay Circle Route and the Eastern Shore.

Nishnabe Delights, by Mary Lou Fox (M'Chigeeng, ON: Ojibwe Cultural Foundation, n.d.)—This book, available from the Ojibwe Cultural Foundation in M'Chigeeng, is a compilation of recipes collected from the Ojibwe and Odawa people of Manitoulin Island and reserves on the north shore of Lake Huron.

How You Can Support the Island

The Ojibwe Cultural Foundation
PO Box 278
15 Hwy. 551 (corner of 551 and 540)
M'Chigeeng, ON P0P 1G0

"Committed to the revitalization and growth of the language, culture, arts, spirituality and traditions of the Anishnaabe People of the First Nations of the Robinson Huron Treaty area."

Manitoulin Streams Improvement Association
25B Spragge St., PO Box 238
Manitowaning, ON P0P 1N0

"Restoring water quality and the fisheries resource on Manitoulin Island and the Great Lakes that surround it."

The Manitoulin Conservatory for Creation and Performance
2758 Union Rd.
RR 1
Evansville, ON P0P 1E0

"The Manitoulin Conservatory for Creation and Performance (MCCP) is a unique facility for research, training, creation and performance in all areas of the performing arts."

Parting Thoughts

September 30, 2013

Our trip to the island coincided with the M'Chigeeng First Nation's annual invitation to visitors to come to the Ojibwe Cultural Foundation to hear the stories of the "Original People," as told by Leona Nahwegahbow, all of which emphasize the role of the Ojibwe as stewards of the land.

And how beautiful the land and waters of this island are! The spectacular sight of salmon swimming upstream at the Bridal Veil Falls is only one example.

But there's more than visual beauty here and on nearby islands. Yesterday, we visited St. Gabriel Lalemant Catholic Church on Birch Island just before the Sunday services started, a place where "Everyone is Welcome," according to the sign. And that inclusivity was in evidence at the altar, where two statues of First Nation members, dressed in tribal dress and with raised arms, were in place on a rock ledge below a mural of the Crucifixion. Whitefish River First Nation welcomes visitors to Birch Island, identifying it as "a place of Visions and Dreams."

I have climbed up to Dreamer's Rock on Birch Island and lain in the great boulder's shallow depression twice in my life. By no means, either time, was I a First Nation boy entering puberty: the first time I was in early adulthood, the second pregnant with my second daughter. Was there a guardian spirit present who advised me with respect to my calling? I would say there was. Perhaps it was "just" all a dream, a vision. But the very vivid memory of that experience and of this place has never left me and has only intensified on my latest visit to this Island of the Great Spirit.

Flowerpot Island, Ontario

CALL OF THE FATHOM FIVE

September 27, 2013, 12:10 p.m.
Beachy Cove

We have disembarked from our tour boat, after having viewed the shipwrecks in Big Tub Harbor through its glass bottom and cruised along the shore of Flowerpot Island to see the Flowerpots, the natural rock formations from the water, and trekked with a handful of fellow passengers up the boardwalk over cobble beach. It is a hot end of September. Georgian Bay is flat calm. The cloud of a daytime half moon floats above Flowerpot Island. Jeanne and I hatch the ambitious plan to hike to the Flowerpots, the cave, and the lighthouse and take the rest of the Loop Trail back before we must return to catch the last boat of the day off the island.

GETTING THERE: Passenger-only ferry; kayak or private boat

GETTING AROUND: No cars allowed; foot traffic only; paddle or motorboat around the island

OVERNIGHT ACCOMMODATIONS: Limited options: camping only (just six campsites at Beachy Cove)

FOOD: Bring your own food *and* drinking water

DAY TRIP? Yes

STATE / PROVINCIAL / NATIONAL PARK? Island is part of Parks Canada's Fathom Five National Marine Park

---

Flowerpot Island, with its two iconic sea stacks, natural rock pillars, represents an important historic vantage point from which to consider two common Great Lakes island features: lighthouses and shipwrecks. The Fathom Five National Marine Park, an over 40-square-mile (104-square-kilometer) preserve, encompasses the island, protecting 22 shipwrecks as well as three of the 32 historic lighthouses of Georgian Bay.

How to Get There

Flowerpot Island makes a wonderful day trip—filled with "rich and strange" sights—by private tour boat from Tobermory, Ontario. Tobermory is reached by following Highway 6 north, up the finger of the Tobermory Peninsula, until it reaches the waters of Georgian Bay.

From Tobermory, two private tour boat companies operate 4-mile (6.5-kilometer) round trips between Tobermory and Flowerpot Island from mid-May to mid-October, weather permitting.

Bruce Anchor Cruises (www.bruceanchorcruises.com)—Offers three glass-bottom boats with a new viewing technology and UV-resistant canopies as well as mainland accommodations.

Blue Heron Company (www.blueheronco.com)—Offers a two-hour cruise through the Fathom Five National Marine Park on "Canada's largest glass-bottom boat" or on a jet boat cruise as well as mainland accommodations and three retail shops.

Check the tour companies' websites for schedules, rates, and more information.

Kayaking or canoeing to the island is recommended for experienced paddlers only.

What to Expect

Expect to pay a fee for national park admittance in addition to the cost of the tour boat ticket. Valid for 24 hours, the fee also includes entry to the Bruce Peninsula National Park Visitor Centre in Tobermory.

What you'll find on the island:

- Choice of hiking trails (loops)
- Picnic shelter at Beachy Cove, where you disembark from the tour boat
- Composting toilets at Beachy Cove (main dock) and the lightstation
- Historic lightstation maintained by the Friends of Bruce District Parks
- Garter snakes and red squirrels (feeding the latter is illegal)
- Rare plants

What you won't find on the island:

- Massasauga rattlesnakes (or any other kind of venomous snake)
- Bears, chipmunks, or any other animal that is hibernating during the time the ice bridge forms between the mainland and the island.

What to bring to the island:

- Sturdy footwear (hiking shoes/boots)
- Sunscreen and hat
- Full water bottle—no tap water is available on the island; during the summer, drinks and snacks *may* be available at the lightstation
- Camera

Note: Plan to take everything you brought back with you, as there are no garbage facilities on the island.

Camping is available in just one location on Flowerpot Island. Near Beachy Cove, the island's main dock, are six tent sites, each with a wooden tent platform. Reservations are suggested; preregistration is required. Camping reservations can be made starting in May by calling 519-596-2233, ext. 221, or in person at the Parks Canada Bruce Peninsula National Park Visitor Centre in Tobermory; this is where you pick up your permit. Carry your own water onto the island or plan to purify the bay water. When planning a camping trip to Flower-pot Island, be aware that bad weather may leave you stranded on the island for an extra day or two. For more information, go to www.pc.gc.ca/eng/amnc-nmca/on/fathomfive/activ/activ1.aspx.

Paths to Adventure

NATURAL SITES

Small Flowerpot and Large Flowerpot—These rock formations—naturally formed "sea stacks"—are what give the island its name. You may notice their layers have been shored up. The Ottawas' legend of the origin of the Flowerpots (printed in the *Owen Sound Sun Time* in 1944) can be found at www.flowerpotisland.ca/page.php?page=rockformations.

Beachy Cove—Where the passenger boats land and the kayakers launch their craft.

Castle Bluff—The island's highest point, at the northeast end of the island, where the light-house is located.

Loop Hiking Trail—Beginning at Beachy Cove, this trail goes past the Small and Large Flowerpots to one of the island's caves and then on to the island's lightstation. One can return by the same route or follow the rest of the loop through the more rugged interior of the island.

Marl beds—Visible from Marl Trail, the one other trail on Flowerpot Island besides the Loop Trail and a popular one for orchid hunters, this hiking destination is about 45 minutes

The Small Flowerpot, one of two natural "sea stack" formations on Flowerpot Island.

Flowerpot Island Lightstation is accessible by the island's Loop Trail. The Lightkeeper's House currently serves as a museum staffed by volunteers. Out on the water, a Bruce Anchor Cruises glass-bottom boat is providing passenger ferry service to the island from Tobermory, Ontario.

southwest from where the tour boat lands. The marl beds have been described as a "curious shallow pond of orange water."[32] The *American Heritage Science Dictionary* defines *marl* as "a crumbly mixture of clays, calcium and magnesium carbonates, and remnants of shells that form in both freshwater and marine environments." Marl is used for fertilizer.

Caves—The caves on Flowerpot Island formed after the last ice age, approximately 12,000 years ago, when the glacial Lake Algonquin completely covered the island. As the lake levels fell in stages, island cliffs were exposed to the eroding effects of the lake for varying amounts of time. This phenomenon caused numerous caves to form in the cliffs.

HISTORY PRESERVED

Flowerpot Island Lightstation Museum—The century-old Lightkeeper's House provides a pleasant destination on the Loop Trail as well as cold drinks, souvenirs, and tours when a Friends of Fathom Five Lightkeeper's Host Program volunteer is available.

Fathom Five National Marine Park of Canada—According to Parks Canada, "Fathom Five offers some of the best freshwater diving opportunities in the world. Clear, clean water, submerged geological formations (cliffs, caves, overhangs), and more than 20 historical shipwrecks offer a variety of underwater experiences." If you plan to dive in Fathom Five, you must first register and purchase a dive tag at the park visitor center.

CULTURAL ATTRACTIONS

The Tobermory, Ontario, website (www.explorethebruce.com/tobermory) lists a variety of "quaint shops, art galleries, ship chandlers, and a wonderful array of restaurants serving fresh whitefish [that] line the harbour."

The Flowerpot Loop Trail from Beachy Cove.

OTHER ISLAND THINGS TO DO

Picnic—You will need to bring food with you to the island.

Swim in the refreshing waters of Georgian Bay—While there are no sand beaches on the island, Beachy Cove and the area around the Flowerpots is suitable for swimming and snorkeling if you use appropriate caution with respect to the cold water, the rocky surfaces, the underwater ledges, and the drop-off in depth.

Look for wildflowers and ferns—From mid-May to early June, Flowerpot Island is the place to see the calypso orchid (also known as fairy slipper). According to one flower enthusiast on the Explore the Bruce website, "Flowerpot Island is best know among floral enthusiasts for its small population of Round-Leaved Orchids. Many other orchid species, including Large Round-Leaved Orchid and Heart-Leaved Twayblade, can be found here. Flowerpot is also renowned for its ferns, notably the Wall Rue Fern, Ostrich Fern, and Northern Holly Fern." The site reminds visitors to stay on the trails and avoid trampling plants, never to pick or dig up wildflowers, and that orchids can be viewed with binoculars and photographed with a telephoto lens.

Sail or kayak the waters of Georgian Bay—A number of outfitters are available in the Tobermory area to supply you with everything you might need.

SPECIAL ISLAND EVENTS

Volunteer Lightkeeper's Host Program at Flowerpot Island Lightstation—This program, which provides opportunities to Friends of the Bruce District Parks Association to become modern-day lightkeepers, began in 1998. Applicants who are accepted must join the Friends organization and pay a minimal fee for the privilege of performing the day-to-day duties of a lightkeeper. Learn more at www.castlebluff.com/volunteer_lightkeeper_host_progr.htm.

For More Island Information

www.flowerpotisland.ca

Fathom Five National Marine Park—www.pc.gc.ca/eng/amnc-nmca/on/fathomfive/index
.aspx.

Fathom Five National Marine Park and Bruce Peninsula National Park of Canada Visitor Centre—This interactive visitor center serves both national parks. It features exhibits for all ages (here, for example, you can learn about massasauga rattlesnake), a theater program about the parks (*Life on the Edge* gives you a sneak peek of special places in the parks), and 112 steps will take you up the 66-foot (20-meter) lookout tower. Park staff members are on-site to answer your questions. Hike the beginning of the 524-mile (843-kilometer) Bruce Trail right outside the center. The visitor center is located right next to the village of Tobermory, just a short walk/drive from downtown:

If you are traveling north on Highway 6 into Tobermory, turn right (east) onto Chi sin tib dek Road, across from the Royal Bank of Canada. Follow the road approximately one kilometer to the visitor center.

If you are traveling south on Highway 6 from Tobermory, turn left (east) onto Chi sin tib dek Road, across from the Royal Bank of Canada. Follow the road approximately one kilometer to the visitor center.

If you are walking from downtown Tobermory (on the Bruce Trail), start at the Bruce Trail monument across from the Liquor Control Board of Ontario. Follow the beaver signs to the visitor center, a five-minute walk.

Fathom Five National Marine Park of Canada website—www.pc.gc.ca/eng/amnc-nmca/on/fathomfive/index.aspx.

Land and Lake Newsletter—Provides updates on Fathom Five National Marine Park and Bruce Peninsula National Park. Available at www.pc.gc.ca/eng/amnc-nmca/on/fathom-five/ne/news4.aspx.

How You Can Support the Island

Friends of Bruce District Parks Association
PO Box 66
Tobermory, ON N0H 2R0
www.castlebluff.com

"Friends of Fathom Five and Friends of Bruce Peninsula . . . promot[e] awareness of the natural, historic and cultural resources of the park and surrounding hinterland . . . through educational publications and programs, volunteer service, facility and display development and planning, research assistance and community service."

Parting Thoughts

September 27, 12:20 p.m.
Flowerpot Island

We stop for lunch after exploring the area around the two remaining Flowerpots (three sea stacks graced the shoreline when the island was named; the third tumbled in 1903), the waves-carved cave, the lighthouse and the keeper's house, now a museum. Sun warms the wood of our picnic table, the side of my face.

From this island hike, I am taking home memories of: the mushrooms as red as chili peppers, pushing up through the evergreen-like moss, that we stepped over and around, and then the knobby flutes and flukes of their opened caps becoming a kaleidoscope of deep orange, yellow and, yes, pink; that pair of ravens in silhouette that lifted from the towering evergreens on the cliff above us at the site of the original lighthouse where we'd stopped to look out; and the ridged colors of the water as the underwater limestone cliffs drop from the Caribbean turquoise of 15 feet to the piercing sea blue of 85 feet.

Where we know, even on this perfect September day, spread below, the remains of ships, and we can imagine in their holds the memories of many others who saw these shores. How many of those, in the midst of November's wind and storm, suspected that "Ariel's Song" from Shakespeare's *The Tempest* would ever apply to him?

> Full fathom five thy father lies;
> Of his bones are coral made;
> Those are pearls that were his eyes;
> Nothing of him that doth fade,
> But doth suffer a sea-change
> Into something rich and strange.
> Sea-nymphs hourly ring his knell:
> Ding-dong.
> Hark! Now I hear them—Ding-dong, bell.

Beausoleil Island, Ontario

THE GEORGIAN BAY ISLANDS
NATIONAL PARK VERSION

June 2, 2013, 10:45 p.m.
Picnic Island Resort
Honey Harbour

On a piece of Great Lakes Basin mainland near my home in Michigan, running across the historic site of the John Almon Starr property, you can still see a small remnant—less than 75 feet—of the original Sagana (Saginaw) Trail, the trail that Native Americans used to travel from the Detroit River to the Saginaw Bay. The trail is only about 20 inches, maybe two feet, wide, as was typical of trails on which Native Americans and their horses moved single file, touching the land relatively lightly as they traversed the continent. When Europeans began claiming ownership of the land that, until this time, had primarily been imprinted by human inhabitants moving seasonally across it, trails were widened to accommodate wagons and teams of horses.

Today, on Canada's Beausoleil Island, Val and I found relatively wide trails, wide enough that the Georgian Bay Islands National Park Welcome Centre rents bicycles to ride them. And ride we do. On Beausoleil Island, one can find visible remnants of earlier "versions" of the intersection between human civilization and the island, a story similar to that told by other Great Lakes Basin islands. One can also run into inhabitants and aspects of Beausoleil's habitat that have most likely been here during all the human stories that have transpired on this island.

GETTING THERE: Passenger ferry; private boat (docks available on a first come, first served basis)

GETTING AROUND: No cars allowed; bring your own bike (day visitors only); bicycle rentals; canoe and kayak rentals on mainland (crossing is not for novice paddlers)

OVERNIGHT ACCOMMODATIONS: Waterfront rustic cabin rentals; nine campgrounds; accessible camping at Cedar Spring campground

FOOD: Bring your own

DAY TRIP? Yes

STATE / PROVINCIAL / NATIONAL PARK? Georgian Bay Islands National Park of Canada

Beausoleil Island is one of the largest islands in the "30,000 Islands" region of Georgian Bay, the world's largest freshwater archipelago. These islands once provided safe haven for the Huron from their rivals, the Iroquois, to whom Beausoleil Island was known as

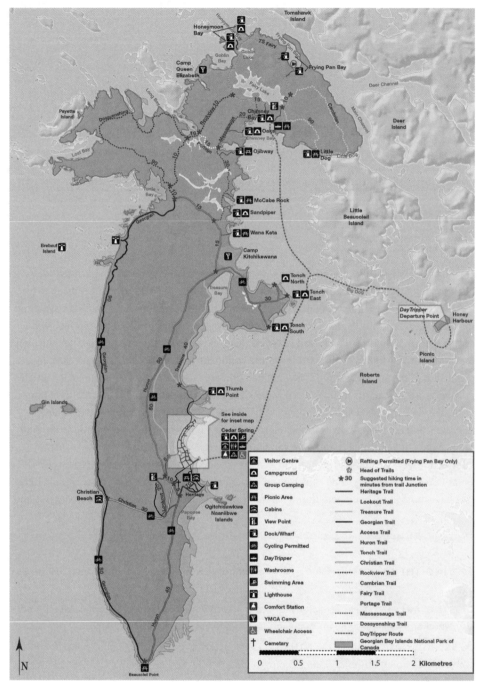

Courtesy of Parks Canada

Schiondekiaria, or "This Land to Appear Floating Afar." Georgian Bay Islands National Park, established in 1929 and managed by Parks Canada, consists of 63 islands, covering about five square miles (13 square kilometers), and a visitor center that is located on Beausoleil Island.

Many beaches, inhabited by diverse Ontario wildlife, line both the shores of the Honey Harbour peninsula and the many surrounding islands, most of the latter available only by

THREE HONEY HARBOUR ISLANDS

- **Picnic Island**—Home to a campground, rental cottages, a grocery store, and a marina.
- **Brandy's Island**—The site of a marina.
- **Potato Island**—Of the several homes on this small island, at least one is a vacation rental.

private boat. However, three other small Ontario islands are accessible by bridge from Honey Harbour.

For more information on these three islands and a tale of a Honey Harbour quest, visit http://greatlakesislandescapes.com/2013/06/10/a-taste-of-honey-honey-harbour-islands-2/ for "A Taste of Honey Harbour Islands."

How to Get There

Honey Harbour, Ontario, serves as a launching point to the 30,000 Islands region of the Georgian Bay. One of a cluster of 14 communities comprising the township of Georgian Bay, Honey Harbour is a part of the district of Muskoka in south-central Ontario. The district's municipal offices are at Port Severn, from which Honey Harbour is about a 30-mile (48-kilometer) drive northwest.

DayTripper, a passenger ferry run by Parks Canada, leaves from the park dock in Honey Harbour. Reservations for the three-mile (five-kilometer), 15-minute ride are recommended: 705-526-8907. No pets are allowed, but if the shuttle is not too crowded, you can bring your own bike.

DayTripper, a passenger ferry operated by Parks Canada, runs between Honey Harbour, Ontario, and Beausoleil Island. If there are few enough passengers, your bike can ride, too; if not, bikes are available to rent on the island.

What to Expect

On Beausoleil Island, in addition to the Georgian Bay Islands National Park Welcome Centre, Parks Canada manages 9 campgrounds with 120 sites in total, including the Cedar Spring Campground (36 sites), primitive campgrounds, group camping sites, and equipped campsites as well as rustic waterfront rental cabins.

In addition, the island is also the site of two YMCA campgrounds: YMCA Camp Kitchikewana (YMCA of Simcoe/Muskoka) and YMCA Camp Queen Elizabeth (YMCA of Western Ontario)

Beausoleil is one of the last refuges for the threatened and generally timid (but venomous) eastern massasauga rattlesnake. Parks Canada is committed to the long-term protection of the snake and has presented a proposed recovery strategy to the public for input.

Black bears have been known to startle campers on the island and relieve them of their unsecured food. Stash your food and cooking supplies in food lockers where provided.

Poison ivy can be found along trails and in other disturbed areas like campgrounds and day-use areas. Be alert to "leaves of three"!

Black-legged ticks (aka deer ticks), which can carry Lyme disease, may be present. Follow protection guidelines: www.health.gov.on.ca/en/ms/lyme/public.

Paths to Adventure

NATURAL SITES

Trails—Beausoleil Island has 12 marked and groomed trails, from the less than .5-mile (.6-kilometer) Heritage Loop to the 4.4-mile (7.1-kilometer) Georgian Trail, which is an advanced mountain biking trail created by a mountain bike trail designer from Europe. Two of Canada's recognized bioregions are represented on the island:

- The six Southern Beausoleil Trails pass through hardwood and mixed forest representative of the Great Lakes St. Lawrence lowlands (imagaine leaf-shaded trails through towering hardwood forest).
- The six Northern Beausoleil Trails introduce you to the bedrock and wetland beauty of the Canadian Shield (imagine pink granite and leaning stunted white pine).

Lakes—The island has two small lakes in its northernmost rocky part. Both lakes can be circled using the Fairy Trail, listed as a "must-hike" trail on Parks Canada website. The trail offers spectacular views from the island's rocky shores as it approaches Chimney Bay, Frying Pan Bay, Honeymoon Bay, and Goblin Bay.

- Fairy Lake—Information plaques placed along this easy trail tell the Natives' Fairy Lake story. Beausoleil First Nation Ojibwe artist William Anthony Monague retells the story of Fairy Lake (as told by Parks Canada) as "the story of [the] 'Lady of the Blueberry Moon' on Beausoleil Island and the great protector 'Nanaboozhoo' who hear[s] her cries for help. A long furious battle was fought with a dreadful beast from another world; all were mortally wounded. The spirit of the woman forms the outline of Beausoleil Island. Nanaboozhoo's body [was laid] to rest on a small island near Giants Tomb. Rock-stained blood on Fairy Lake forms the eye of the beast. Today, the spirit of this beautiful young woman can sometimes be heard singing or seen as she walks about her beloved island."[33]
- Goblin Lake—Smaller and farther north than Fairy Lake, this lake is close to Goblin Bay.

The Canadian Shield landscape of Beausoleil Island's west shore, near the Beausoleil Island Rear Range Light. The Brébeuf Island Lighthouse, which served as the front range light, is in view across the water and rock.

HISTORY PRESERVED

Camp Kitchikewana—A YMCA camp that has also been the site of an archaeological dig allowing archaeologists to piece together the cultural record of the First Nations' history on the island. Before Beausoleil Island became an attraction for tourists, it was "visited and inhabited by many distinct Aboriginal peoples. Artifacts from as far back as the Middle Archaic period, 7,000 years ago, have been found. ... Archeologists [have] determine[d that] ... over the years, Point Peninsula and Saugeen groups ... and the Odawa ... then the Algonkian and Huron, and finally, Ojibwe have succeeded each other in calling Beausoleil Island home."[34]

Ngohkaan (aka Beausoleil Island Cemetery, Red Oak Cemetery, and Cemetery of the Oak)— Located along the Heritage Loop Trail—which was created around the time the island was designated a National Historic Site of Canada (2001) for representing a cultural landscape of the Anishinaabe—this small cemetery site tells a sad story:

> Beausoleil Island was an Ojibwe reserve from 1836 to 1856, and the settlement was under the leadership of Chief John Assence [also spelled "Assance"]. The Anishinaabek people (i.e., Ojibwe/Chippewa, Potawotamie, Odawa) who moved here had

traditionally live a hunter-gatherer lifestyle but were being converted to a settled, agricultural way of life under colonial policy.[35]

Life was very difficult for the Beausoleil Band. The island proved to be quite difficult for farming; the sandy barren soil caused repeated crop failures despite their efforts. Although the fishing was very plentiful, they could not sustain themselves there, and the once independent band was forced to rely on the government for staples such as flour and pork. In 1856, the band moved west to another island in Georgian Bay, [taking] with them the name Beausoleil First Nation.[36]

Beausoleil Island became a part of the Georgian Bay Islands National Park in 1929:

When George Lynn [the first warden appointed to Georgian Bay Islands National Park in 1931] first came to Beausoleil Island, there was a small cemetery where the graves were marked only with sticks. Over several years, Indians and local residents came to the island to identify the gravesites. Lynn marked each one with a shingle and over the winter months made and inscribed white wood crosses to be placed in the Cemetery of the Red Oak. On May 24, 1934, Lynn was made an honorary Ojibwe chief for his work in having the graves identified. An altar was required for the ceremony so he had one erected at the cemetery entrance using the remains of brick chimneys found in a nearby clearing. A feast was essential and drew nearly a thousand people from Rama Township, Christian Island, and many other reserves.[37]

The Ngohkaan (Anishinaabe cemetery), aka the Beausoleil Island Cemetery, Red Oak Cemetery, and Cemetery of the Oak, on Beausoleil Island (1836–1939) contains 58 graves, including that of Ojibwe Chief John Assance.

THE BEAUSOLEIL FIRST NATION ON CHRISTIAN ISLAND

Ojibwe Chief John Assance left the failed Coldwater Reserve (1834–42) in the area of what is today Severn, Ontario, with one of three Ojibwe bands to settle on Beausoleil Island. By all accounts, Beausoleil was unable to sustain them, and in 1856, the tribe resettled on Christian Island, where the Beausoleil First Nation lives today.

Christian Island is a beautiful forested island accessible by the car ferry *Sandy Graham* or the passenger ferry *Indian Maiden;* the Christian Island Ferry service makes its run from Cedar Point, Ontario. Island residents, cottagers, and campers alike enjoy beautiful beaches with banded and tumbled stones magnified in the clear, clear water. The dunes of Big Sand Bay are an example of the few remaining ancient dunes in Georgian Bay.

At the southern tip of the island is the Christian Island Lighthouse (1857)—the first of the "Imperial Tower" lighthouses to be completed and the first official lighthouse on Lake Huron's Georgian Bay. Although it no longer provides light out on the lake (it was replaced by an off-shore buoy in 1922), today it presents a wonderful photo opportunity. St. Francis Xavier Catholic Church (1999), a limestone hexagon with cobblestone pillars, has unique and beautiful stained glass doors and windows at the entrance and provides another such opportunity.

You may recognize some names associated with Christian Island (aka Christian Island Indian Reserve No. 30). The novelist Joseph Boyden (of Irish, Scottish, and Anishinaabe heritage) writes about First Nation heritage and culture. He describes Christian Island as "that special place from my childhood where [my mother] allowed all of us children to run wild."* Other times he's suggested he was on Beckwith Island, one of the other two islands (Hope Island is the third) in the archipelago, looking across to Christian Island. Boyden is the author of an awarding-winning trilogy of novels: *Three Day Road* (2006), about two Cree soldiers serving in the Canadian military during World War I, was inspired by Ojibwe Francis Pegahmagabow, legendary sniper in the war; *Through Black Spruce* (2009) follows the story of one of the characters in *Three Day Road;* and *The Orenda* (2014) is a seventeenth-century story told in three voices, that of a Huron warrior, an Iroquois girl, and a French Jesuit. The story ends on Christian Island.

Another artist, the musician Gordon Lightfoot, wrote a song, "Christian Island," in 1962 about the protection afforded his sailboat *Silver Heels* by the long arm of land that extends toward the mainland:

> I'm sailin' down the summer wind,
> I got whiskers on my chin,
> And I like the mood I'm in,
> As I while away the time of day
> In the lee of Christian Island . . .
> And when summer ends we will rest again,
> In the lee of Christian island.**

* Joseph Boyden, *Globe and Mail*, May 22, 2013.
** Gordon Lightfoot, "Christian Island," *All Live* (Rhino Records, 2012).

Frying Pan Bay—They say a lilac bush still blooms on the shore of the bay at the spot where French voyageur Joe Corbière and his wife, Susan, lived even after the park came into existence, at least as late as 1929.

OTHER ISLAND THINGS TO DO

Hike—There are one dozen trails.

Bike—If there's room you can transport your own on *DayTripper;* if not, mountain bikes are rented at the Cedar Spring Visitor Centre.

Camp—There are nine campgrounds, with accessible camping at Cedar Spring.

Picnic—There is no food available on the island, so you'll want to bring food with you from the mainland; Honey Harbour Towne Center or Picnic Island Resort grocery and general store are the places to go for stocking up.

Swim—There are some sand beaches amid all of the granite of the Canadian Shield, primarily on the eastern shore and in a few sheltered bays in the northern section of the island. On Beausoleil, the best beaches are at the Cedar Spring Campground and day-use areas, the Wana Keta picnic and docking area, and Sandpiper, Oaks, and Honeymoon Bay campgrounds. None of the beaches or swimming areas are guarded. While swimming is possible at many points around the island, the smooth flat rock along much of shoreline makes for a dangerously slippery time.

Kayak/canoe—Although there are no kayaks or canoes available to rent on the island, you may be able to rent a canoe from the Honey Harbour Boat Club or the Picnic Island Resort. Georgian Bay often has a lot of motorboat traffic and tends to be choppy. In addition, storms can blow up quickly. Guides are available for hire in the area.

Boat—If you don't have your own, it's easy to rent a water taxi in the Honey Harbour area.

Fish—While fishing is not permitted in any inland lake on the island, a wide variety of fish live in Georgian Bay, from small perch to record-size muskie, and people do fish along the shore of the bay. An Ontario fishing license is required to fish from the waters surrounding the island.

Geocache—On its website, the park provides a link to a geocaching website: www.geocaching.com.

Photograph—Take 10, take 100, take 1,000 shots; then consider posting your best to Parks Canada's Facebook display page.

SPECIAL ISLAND EVENTS

Aboriginal Youth Week—"Partners in History, Culture, and Environment at Georgian Bay Island National Park of Canada," held annually since 2000 at Camp Kitchikewana on Beausoleil Island, allows "Grade 7 and 8 Aboriginal children, teachers and resource people to gather for a week each September. Students are taken on a journey through activities designed to enhance their knowledge of, and appreciation for, their history and culture. Archeology plays a role in helping that happen."[38]

Beausoleil Island Artist-in-Residency—Does the opportunity to spend a week in the iconic Canadian landscape of Georgian Bay making art appeal to you? If so, Parks Canada invites you to submit your application. For more information on the program and on how to apply, visit www.parkscanada.gc.ca/gbi or call 705-527-7200.

For More Island Information

Georgian Bay Islands National Park of Canada, the Parks Canada, www.pc.gc.ca/eng/pn-np/on/georg/index.aspx.

"Beausoleil Island," in *A Taste of Honey Harbour: The Area and Its People,* edited by Su Murdoch (Honey Harbour, ON: Honey Harbour Historical Committee, 1999), 31–45.

Up the Shore: The History and Changes Time Has Brought to Eastern Georgian Bay, by Juanita Rourke (Midland, ON: Up the Shore Enterprises, 1994)—While not about Beausoleil Island per se, this memoir of life on Minnicognashene Island, nearby by boat, just northeast from Beausoleil's Pirates Cove or Lost Bay, provides insight into the area.

How You Can Support the Island

Georgian Bay Biosphere Reserve (GBBR)
17 George St., PO Box 337
Parry Sound, ON P2A 2X4
705-774-0978
www.gbbr.ca

The 30,000 Islands of the Eastern Georgian Bay are unique on the planet and have been identified as a UNESCO World Biosphere Reserve. GBBR, Inc., is a nonprofit organization that works to protect the environment, build a healthy economy, and create vibrant communities with help of supporters through memberships, donations, and bequests.

Georgian Bay Land Trust (GBLT)
www.gblt.org.

"The GBLT is a not-for-profit registered charity supported by people who love and want to protect the wilderness of Georgian Bay for current and future generations."

Georgian Bay Osprey Society (GBOS)
c/o Ian and Meta Ferguson
130 Courtland Crescent
East Gwillimbury, ON L9N 0B1
www.gbosprey.ca

With the help of the Georgian Bay Osprey Society, a volunteer organization that performs five important osprey-related tasks, and a responsive public, the bay is again becoming one of the ospreys' important summer breeding areas. Besides becoming involved in monitoring and protection and/or financially contributing to their protection, you can help by keeping your distance: don't approach closer to ospreys than 220 yards (200 meters) and keep moving if you come to a nest while boating to avoid unduly disturbing them.

Parting Thoughts

June 2, 2013, 10:45 p.m.
Picnic Island Resort

Val and I have seen some things on this island I have never seen before—and yet they are remarkably like other things I know.

When we stopped to have picnic on a small Canadian Shield boulder at the shoreline of the Wana Keta picnic area, a northern watersnake—just as curious but smaller and thinner than a Lake Erie watersnake, with which I'm very familiar (but this watersnake was black, not brown or patterned as those in Lake Erie)—swam to our rock to investigate what we were up to.

After a bit more riding, Val and I parked our bikes to hike to the Beausoleil Island rear range light, a skeletal white metal tower with a red roof that looks more like a fire tower than a lighthouse, but it apparently serves the purpose for which it was intended when paired with the Brefeuf Island Lighthouse. There are so many small islands and large boulders in this part of the Georgian Bay that it's hard to imagine there'd be any hope of figuring out where one was and what to avoid by the time the range lights were in view. But I'm no sailor. We got mixed up enough in the daylight as passengers on a boat when we were on our quest looking for the island that turned out not to be one.

But I digress. Below the range light, from its perch atop an informational sign, we rescued what I think—because of its large toe pads—might have been an eastern gray tree frog. (Although who is to say this frog needed rescuing? According to the DNR, these frogs have a penchant for clinging to the windows of houses at night.) When I set the frog down on a lichen-covered rock, the frog and rock seemingly became one, blending perfectly not only in color but also in pattern. We had to add leaves between the two to separate them so we could admire the frog's cleverness.

Leaving the frog and the range light to go back to our bikes, we decided to take a shortcut, tiptoeing across the tops of rocks above the water's surface of a shallow cove. Midway across, having already gotten a "soaker," I stopped to pick up a rock that had caught my attention. Hardball-sized but much heavier, this dense rock has concentric pink circles of feldspar girding its layers of black granite, shot with gold mica that sparkles in the sun. In its totality, this rock is an exact tiny replica of an island of the Canadian Shield, one that fits as perfectly in my hand as those true Georgian Bay islands we lost ourselves amidst fit in my memory.

St. Clair River Islands

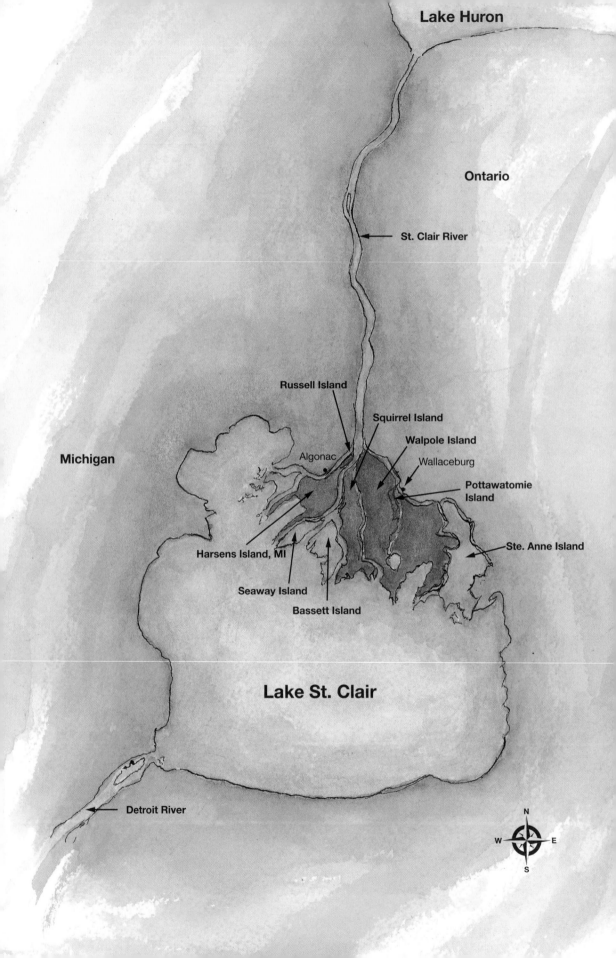

Lake Huron

Ontario

St. Clair River

Russell Island

Squirrel Island

Walpole Island

Wallaceburg

Michigan

Algonac

Pottawatomie
Island

Ste. Anne Island

Harsens Island, MI

Seaway Island

Bassett Island

Lake St. Clair

Detroit River

N
W   E
S

An Introduction to the St. Clair River

The St. Clair River connects Lake Huron at its northern end and Lake St. Clair, a secondary lake of the Great Lakes Basin, at its southern end, dropping a relatively "gentle" five feet in elevation over its course of 41.5 miles (67 kilometers). The river is 800 feet wide at its narrowest point and forms, in its entirety, a portion of the international boundary between the United States and Canada.

The St. Clair River carries more freighter traffic than the Suez Canal and the Panama Canal combined. Over 1 billion gallons of fresh water per day flow down the river, past Stag Island (between Marysville, Michigan, and Corunna, Ontario) and Fawn Island (just south of the Sombra, Ontario–Marine City, Michigan, Bluewater Ferry crossing), and out through its delta region—the largest freshwater river delta in the world—known as the "St. Clair Flats" by Michiganders to the west of it.

The delta is known as Bkejwanong (Where the Waters Divide) by those to the east, the Walpole Island First Nation, a combined nation of Ojibwe, Potawatomi, and Odawa who reside on the unceded Walpole Island, which is composed of Walpole and five additional islands: St. Anne, Potawatomi, Squirrel, Bassett, and Seaway Islands.

The U.S. portion of the river delta includes Harsens Island, Russell Island, The Gold Coast, Anderson Island, and—inaccessible by bridge or ferry—Sand Island, all of them separated by cuts at the northern neck of land above Harsens Island. Other U.S. islands in the delta include Dickinson Island, North Island, Middle Island, Strawberry Island, Bruckner Island, Club Island, Green Island, Gull Island, McDonald Island, and Muscamoot Ridge, all of which can be accessed only by personal watercraft.

RUSSELL ISLAND: OPEN TO THE PUBLIC SIX HOURS A YEAR

Just a cut or two north of Harsens Island—on the other side of Sand Island and what at least a few on Russell Island call "Snake Island" (both inaccessible by ferry or bridge)—is Russell Island, a small private Michigan island in the St. Clair River that is open to the public just one day a year—from noon to 6:00 p.m. on the last Sunday in July—for an authentic old-fashioned family picnic. Guests take a passenger ferry—a converted bus that departs from Algonac, Michigan—and reach the island in under 10 minutes. There, you will find approximately 120 cottages on Russell Island and its two attached islands: Anderson Island (northwest extension) and The Gold Coast (southeast extension). Golf carts are the only motorized vehicles allowed on the island.

For more information about the annual picnic, see www.facebook.com/Russell-Island.

Three wider channels cut through the U.S. side of the river delta: the South Channel (or Shipping Channel, also the route that the international border follows), the Middle Channel, and the North Channel.

Two separate vehicle ferry companies have routes here, just north of the delta, crossing the St. Clair River, one from Algonac to Harsens Island and the other from Algonac to Walpole Island (the latter of which is also accessible by bridge from Wallaceburg, Ontario). A passenger ferry—a converted bus—transports property owners to the private Russell Island; bridges from Russell access Anderson (in the northwest) and The Gold Coast (in the southeast).

Harsens Island, Michigan

THE "VENICE OF AMERICA" AND
THE DAYS OF TASHMOO

June 3, 2014, 11:45 a.m.
HISCF Historical Society Museum

It's an easy hour drive northeast from the Detroit area to the ferry at Algonac. Ten minutes later we're on Harsens Island and headed for the Harsens Island St. Clair Flats Historical Society Museum in the former Harsens Isle Fire Department in the one town, Sans Souci, truly a place as carefree as the name (Without Cares) implies.

This fire hall was originally dedicated in 1938; 73 years later, on Memorial Day 2011, the museum held its grand opening in the vintage building. In 2012, the Society held a First Nations Festival, under the guidance of Susan Wrobel, longtime Harsens Island resident of Ojibwe heritage, and Dr. Evelyn White-Eye of the First Nation of Walpole Island, which included powwow dancers, drummers, singers, and First Nation food and crafts.

In 2013, a Tashmoo Day video was produced featuring the story of the steamer that made daily trips from Detroit to Port Huron 100 years ago. The graphic artist on that project was the granddaughter of the man who ran Tashmoo Park, a popular amusement park on the island between 1897 and 1951. And in 2014, Tashmoo Days became an annual July event.

GETTING THERE: Car ferry; private boat or plane

GETTING AROUND: Bring your car and/or bike; canoe, kayak, and paddleboat rentals on mainland

OVERNIGHT ACCOMMODATIONS: Limited options: vacation home rentals; one B&B; no camping

FOOD: Restaurants; groceries

DAY TRIP? Yes, recommended

STATE / PROVINCIAL / NATIONAL PARK? No, but the Michigan Department of Natural Resources manages 3,355 acres of waterfowl habitat on the island

Harsens Island is one of a dozen islands in the delta region called the St. Clair Flats, the only major river delta in the Great Lakes Basin and the largest freshwater river delta in North America. The delta is located where the St. Clair River, running just over 40 miles (65 kilometers) from Lake Huron, empties into Lake St. Clair, a secondary lake in the Great Lakes Basin.

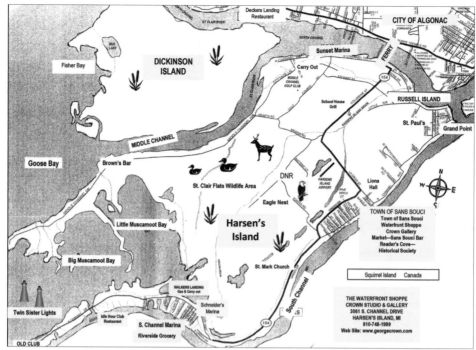

Courtesy of Crown Studio and Gallery and the Waterfront Shoppe

Harsens Island, like other Great Lakes islands, was, for a time, a destination for hotel and resort guests and amusement park visitors. First launched on December 30, 1899, from June 1900 to June 18, 1936, the White Line Star sidewheeler steamer *Tashmoo*, with a 4,000-passenger capacity (which on one trip included the passenger President Theodore Roosevelt), made the trip daily from Detroit to Port Huron, bringing overnight guests to a number of resort hotels on this delta island of canals, known as the Venice of America, and dropping day-trippers off at Harsens Island's 60-acre Tashmoo Park.

Tashmoo Park began as a place to enjoy a day's summer outing, graced by a picnic grove, a casino pavilion, two baseball diamonds, and a bicycle track. To these attractions were added a dance pavilion with a 10,400-square-foot unobstructed dance floor (and a band to play there as well as during the trip both to and from the park on the boat), swings and slides, and a beach house and bathhouse to take advantage of the river. Food was served at the casino pavilion, and souvenir tents were added to the park's delights. Then there was the popular merry-go-round, with a steam calliope, and a very tall waterslide. Boats could be rented at the park, as could swim attire (featuring swim cap, stockings, and laced boots) and towels. Footraces and tug-of-war competitions, company outings, and church picnics were all common events at the park.

When the steamer *Tashmoo* sank just before the start of the park's summer season in 1936, the White Star Line chartered boats from other companies to carry park-goers, but attendance was in decline, and the park was closed in 1951. See historian and Harsens Island resident Arthur Woodford's *Tashmoo Park and the Steamer* Tashmoo for wonderful photos and information about Tashmoo Park and the steamship named after it.

What to Expect

Expect friendly and helpful people; the small town of San Souci to explore; low, flat land perfect for biking, with great views of the water on at least one side almost always in view; plenty of cool-looking canals (that would be your water on the other side); a strong local interest in preserving island history; and a commitment to destroying the island's population of phragmites.

Also plan to see freighters up close in the shipping channel on the east side of Harsens—you won't need binoculars—and Coast Guard boats zipping along the international border of the river, with exotic Walpole Island directly across the river.

How to Get There

Make for Algonac, Michigan, a relatively direct shot from I-94 whether you're heading north from the Detroit area or south from the U.S.-Canadian border crossing at Sarnia, Ontario. If you are coming from the south, you will head east from I-94 on M-29 around Anchor Bay and cross the North Channel on Champion's Auto Ferry, which runs 24 hours a day, seven days a week, 365 days a year.

Champion's Auto Ferry
810-748-3757
www.michigan.org/property/harsens-island-champion-s-auto-ferry

If you're coming from Canada, you do have the choice of a less used border crossing that involves crossing the St. Clair River on the Bluewater Ferry at Sombra, Ontario, which lands you at Marine City, Michigan, and allows you to follow M-29 south along the St. Clair River to Algonac for your second ferry ride.

Bluewater Ferry
519-892-3879
www.bluewaterferry.com

Harsens Island Airport (KZ92) has a grass runway and no controllers.

THE PROBLEM WITH PHRAGMITES

Phragmites australis is a common reed found in wetlands and native to the Great Lakes area. However, there is a nonnative, invasive strain of phragmites (frag-MY-teez) that has become a major invasive problem in the Great Lakes Basin, "threatening both the ecological health of wetlands and the Great Lakes coastal shoreline. [The invasive species] creates tall, dense stands which degrade wetlands and coastal areas by crowding out native plants and animals, blocking shoreline views, reducing access for swimming, fishing, and hunting and can create fire hazards from dry plant material."* In 2007, Harsens Island became a Great Lakes island leader in working to control phragmites. For more information, see www.stewartfarm.org/phragmites.

* http://www.michigan.gov/deq/0,4561,7-135-3313_8314-178183--,00.html.

Paths to Adventure

NATURAL SITES

Like many Great Lakes Basin islands, Harsens Island is best seen from the seat of a bicycle. Pedal the length of the island by the perimeter road and down the peninsulas along South and Middle channels. You'll probably have lots of opportunity, depending on the time of year, to spot turtles and waterfowl. At the turnaround, if the wind is right and you're fortunate, you may see kiteboarders doing their thing in Muscamoot Bay.

HISTORY PRESERVED

Harsens Island St. Clair Flats Historical Society (HISCFHS) Museum—This vintage Harsens Isle Fire Department building is graced with interesting exhibits that lovingly reveal layers of the island's history.

Harsens Island/St. Clair Flats Historical Society Home and Historic Building Walking Tour— Walk the tour of the San Souci's historic homes and businesses, including the Tashmoo Park Marina, located on the property that was Tashmoo Park (where the dance and casino pavilions are used today to store boats). You can pick up a copy of the walking tour description at the HISCFHS Museum or find it online at www.hiscfhs.org or at www.bluewater.org.

St. Mark Catholic Church (4190 Green Dr.)—Located off South Channel Drive, right on the river, this church (part of the Our Lady on the River Parish) with the graceful bell tower celebrated its centennial in 1997. In earlier times, when the church was known as St. Mark by-the-Sea, people would come to Mass by boat or chartered tugboat. At one point in

Many visitors to Harsens Island come to fish, kayak, or canoe the St. Clair River, but this flat island calls to bicyclists and joggers, too. Others, attracted by the island's many canals and marshes, come to hunt waterfowl or to take advantage of this birding hot spot.

Harsens Island St. Clair Flats Historical Society Museum is in the former fire hall in the town of San Souci.

history, St. Mark might have been lost to a plan to straighten the shipping channel. But islanders protested, and South Channel was dredged instead. Of the church's stained glass windows, Marie Eidt wrote in the *Delta News:* "The windows do tell the story of how a devout group of Germans came to Harsen's Island as the resorts were evolving in the late 1800s, [and] joined forces with the earlier French settlers to build the lovely little mission church of St. Mark."[39]

Riverside Gas Dock and Grocery (7650 S. Channel Dr.)—A place to stop for a snack or something to drink on your bike ride or from your boat. New owners in 2014 have added some spice: Michigan-made products, boat knots, hand-packed ice cream, and an espresso machine; they may add skis, stand-up paddleboards, and kayak rentals in the future.

The Old Club (9900 S. Channel Dr.)—You can only get as close as the entrance gates unless you're a member of this private club, which began as the Lake St. Clair Fishing and Shooting Club seven years after the American Civil War ended and is connected to Harsens Island by a bridge, but you can see more of it here: www.theoldclub.com.

CULTURAL ATTRACTIONS

San Souci Bar and Restaurant—Stop for refreshments along the South Channel and watch the international and domestic freighters go by. In the early 1880s, Captain William LaCroix built a dock and pavilion in Sans Souci for the White Star Line steamers. The pavilion was enclosed and became in succession an ice-cream parlor, a dance pavilion, Beaudoin's Tavern and, today, the Sans Souci Bar. Islanders today recall water washing under the floorboards of the bar in the 1970s before a steel seawall was installed and the ground underneath San Souci was filled in. Choose the outdoor seating area, covered or not, if the weather is nice, or sit at a booth inside next to the big plate glass window if it's

Watching the freighters go by with a ringside seat at Harsens Island's San Souci Bar and Restaurant on the South Channel of the St. Clair River, part of the international border between the United States and Canada. Across the channel is the unceded territory of Walpole Island.

not. This is perhaps the best vantage point from a commercial establishment for watching the freighters pass on the St. Clair River.

George Crown Studio and Gallery—At the back of the Waterfront Shoppe (a "nautical gift resort store,") located on the river—where artist George Crown has another great view— you can view and buy, from the artist himself, nautical watercolor paintings and prints of natural and shipping scenes of the Great Lakes and Lake St. Clair.

Harsens Island Schoolhouse Grille—Come see what can happen at a schoolhouse that served the island's children from 1934 to 2005 when it's turned into a fine restaurant with a creative chef at the helm. There is such a nice vibe here (and great fish tacos) that I'd drive from metro Detroit to experience it again if there were overnight accommodations, as opposed to only weekly rentals, available on the island (maybe someday).

Engel's Fish Camp—One of a number of interesting cottages to notice as you pass through cottage land; some cottages have their own access bridges over a channel.

Browns (6630 Middle Channel Dr.)—A local landmark since 1946; boaters dock right out in front of this seasonal tavern on the water (although patrons in cars are welcome, too) to enjoy fish, burgers, and beer while sitting out on the patio over the water of the Middle Channel of the St. Clair River flowing between Harsens and Dickinson islands.

OTHER ISLAND THINGS TO DO

Go birding—Harsens Island is touted as a birding hot spot in southeast Michigan, known to be particularly good for wintering and migrant waterfowl.

Go fishing—In addition to fishing from private boats and chartered trips, shore fishing is available at the South Channel Drain, a small channel leading from the center of the island out to Muscamoot Bay. Fish species available include bullhead, carp, largemouth bass, northern pike, sunfish, and yellow perch.

Go hunting—Harsens Island has 3,355 acres of strictly managed waterfowl habitat—including flooded agricultural, marsh, and open-water areas—with mallards as the most prevalent species, but black ducks, pintail, wood ducks, and Canada geese are also present.

Go golfing—Try Middle Channel Golf and Country Club, an 18-hole public golf course.

SPECIAL ISLAND EVENTS

Tashmoo Days (July), including "Return to Tashmoo" 5k and 10k runs (www.tashmoodays .com).

Harsens Island Bluegrass Festival (August).

Harsens Island Lions Annual Turkey Shoot Festival (Labor Day weekend)—A tradition since 1950, the event includes the Antique Boat Parade (Saturday morning), Annual Lions Parade (noon), trapshooting, a competition for (frozen) turkeys, music, dancing, food, casino gambling, bingo, kids' games, the Diabetes Testing Program (free diabetes screening for adults and children) and KidSight Program (free vision testing for children six months to five years), and the Annual Turkey Trot (5K run/walk) (Monday).

For More Island Information

Harsens Island St. Clair Flats Historical Society Museum
PO Box 44
Harsens Island, MI 48028
www.hiscfhs.org

For a list of links to Harsens Island websites, see www.stewartfarm.org/links.php.

The Harsens Island Flyer—Published by an islander weekly from Memorial Day through Labor Day, this includes island news, information, and advertising.

The Society Pages—Published monthly by the Harsens Island St. Clair Flats Historical Society. As a benefit to HISCFHS members, past issues are archived online at www.hiscfhs .org.

Delta News—An annual publication of the Harsens Island St. Clair Flats Association, the largest property owners' group in Michigan, which was started in 1943 (www.hiscfa .org).

The Turkey Shoot Book—An annual publication that promotes and commemorates the Labor Day Harsens Island Lions Turkey Shoot Festival.

www.stewartfarm.or/hiscfhs/docs/hotel.pdf—Provides information about early clubs, hotels, and resorts on Harsens Island, as well as the South Channel Range Lights and the U.S. Ship Canal.

TO WHOM DID TASHMOO REALLY BELONG?

One of the photos in historian Arthur M. Woodford's *Tashmoo Park and the Steamer* Tashmoo shows a row of tables set up under trees bearing the caption: "Indian Souvenir Stand. Shopping for souvenirs was a popular attraction at Tashmoo Park, and this was especially true if it was a souvenir from one of the stands belonging to the Indians from Walpole Island."

A number of Great Lakes Basin islands are currently involved in unresolved Aboriginal/Native land claims. In February of 2007, "there [were] more than 1,300 land claims filed against Canada, by native groups—hundreds more filed against provinces—and the list, and frustration, [was] growing longer under a system plagued with decade-long delays." Itself involved in more than 100 such Native land claims in Ontario, the Walpole Island First Nation claims that Harsens Island is also unceded Anishinaabe territory and properly belongs to them.*

* John Miner, "Powder Keg," *London Free Press*, February 17, 2007, www.caledoniawakeupcall.com/updates/070217lfp.html.

Tashmoo Park and the Steamer Tashmoo, by Arthur M. Woodford (Charleston, SC: Arcadia, 2012).

Life at the Flats: When Bedore Was King, by Michael M. Dixon (Grosse Pointe, MI: Mervue, 1985).

The Flats Golden Era: An American Venice, by Michael M. Dixon (Grosse Pointe, MI: Mervue, 1987).

Marshland Memories: Sketches from Life at the Flats, by Michael M. Dixon (Grosse Pointe, MI: Mervue, 1989).

The Life and Times of Minnie Harm: Dairy [sic] *Entries from 1938–1976 about Her Life on Harsens Island,* compiled by Michele Komar (Westland, MI: self-published, 2009).

A Kid on the Flats: The Stumbling, Bumbling Exploits of a Kid Growing Up in the 1940's, in a Primitive Utopia Called the Flats of Harsens Island, Michigan, by Commodore Mushrat Robert B. Coulter (St. Clair, MI: Commodore Books, 1993).

How You Can Support the Island

Harsens Island St. Clair Flats Historical Society
3058 S. Channel Dr.
San Souci, Harsens Island, MI
www.hiscfhs.org

Parting Thoughts

June 4, 2014, 6:00 a.m.
Carriage House on South Channel

I can only imagine what this Venice of America must have been like in the heyday of steamers and resorts, clubs and hotels, when it was an escape for the wealthy from Detroit. The islanders' carriage house in which Carol and I spent the night—the view of the freighters on the river during the night was spectacular—was comfortable and cozy, our host's hospitality overwhelmingly generous, the price way below the going rate for vacation rentals on the island, of which there are a number.

But I woke up finding myself wishing that more people could easily spend the night on Harsens Island. The Harsens Island St. Clair Flats Historical Society has put together a wonderful document titled "Hotels in the St. Clair Flats and Harsens Island Then and Now." Currently, with only one B&B on the island (which had been a boathouse back in 1892, and today only accommodates known guests), I'm more interested in the "then."

Then, the Maple Leaf dock, after which the one B&B on the island is apparently named, was used by the White Star Line to drop off some of the 250,000 visitors and 100,000 cottagers who came to Harsens Island every summer in the late 1800s and early 1900s. Where did all of those visitors stay? The steamer made additional stops at many of these accommodations: the Old Club, Hotel Mervue, the Rushmere Club, the Star Island House, the Marshland Club, Riverside, Kehl's Public House, Joe Bedore's Hotel, the Muir House, and the Grande Pointe Hotel.[40]

Today, Harsens Island has, among other attractions, an excellent historical museum, a gifted resident artist, fine dining at the Schoolhouse Grill, wonderful flat biking roads surrounded by water, a great place to watch freighters pass on the shipping channel at the San Souci Bar—a number of charms that go well beyond the island's local reputation for excellent duck hunting.

I would imagine for this beautiful, easily accessible island new life, a writing retreat center, perhaps. Until then I'll be back for long days pedaling, watching the freighters, spending summer and fall days the way they were meant to be experienced.

Although I wasn't able to get a reservation at Harsens Island's one B&B, I did receive the gift of a few lines of a perfectly true island poem from the establishment's website:

Oh! you won't know why and you can't say how
Such a change upon you came,
But once you have slept on an island,
You'll never be quite the same.[41]

Walpole Island

THE UNCEDED TERRITORY OF BKEJWANONG

May 21, 2014, 10:55 a.m.

It's a sunny spring morning, delicate mist on the river. *Bkejwanong* ("Where the Waters Divide") lies to the south of us. I am glad I decided to cross the St. Clair River at Marine City, Michigan, 15 miles north of the standard crossing at Algonac. Noreen and I watch the *John D. Leitch*, an Algoma Companies ship, approach down the middle of the St. Clair River as a couple of small fishing boats power out of its way. Our ferry docks on the other side of the river at Sombra, Ontario. This approach allows us to drive along the river down the St. Clair Parkway and to cross over to Walpole Island by bridge.

And when we do, we order lunch at Papa's Place Coffee Shop in Thunderbird Plaza. While we wait for our food to be prepared, we can't help noticing we're the only people who could not be classified as members of a First Nation in this thrumming business at this Wednesday noon hour. We admire an islander's brand-new grandchild. A grandbaby is a grandbaby is a grandbaby.

GETTING THERE: Car ferry from west or bridge from east; private boat

GETTING AROUND: Bring your car; bring your own bike (best on paved roads; beware of island dogs that may be interested in pursuing bikes)

OVERNIGHT ACCOMMODATIONS: Limited options: camping only (at Chematogan Camp)

FOOD: One coffee shop/restaurant

DAY TRIP? Yes, recommended

STATE / PROVINCIAL / NATIONAL PARK? No, but all six of the islands in the St. Clair River delta between the United States and Canada constitute the Walpole Island First Nation reserve

Despite its appearance on Canadian maps, Walpole Island does not belong to Canada. Nor does it belong to United States. Walpole Island is unceded territory. This means that this First Nation island, located at the border of the United States and Canada—specifically, between Ontario and Michigan—has never relinquished title to its land to either the U.S. or Canadian government by treaty or in any other manner. Walpole Island was not included in any of the land cessions of 1790, 1796, 1819, 1822, or 1825. Today, it remains Walpole Island First Nation land.

Boozhoo (Welcome) to the unceded Bkejwanong (Where the Waters Divide) Territory of the Anishinaabe on Walpole Island.

The First Nation people's name for their island, Bkejwanong, "Where the Waters Divide," refers to the island's location in the delta area at the mouth of the St. Clair River. Walpole Island First Nation Reserve (Indian Reserve No. 46; both names are misnomers in terms of the use of the word *Reserve*) includes five other unceded islands: Seaway Island, Bassett Island, Squirrel Island, Potawatomie Island, and St. Anne Island. The people who call this island home have formed a political and cultural confederacy, the Council of Three Fires: the Ojibwe, the Potawatomi, and the Ottawa. Over the last 200 years, although there are a few dissenters, many have claimed that the bones of the great Native American leader Tecumseh are buried here, on this beautiful island of Bkejwanong.

In 1995, the Walpole Island First Nation received the We the Peoples 50 Communities award from the Friends of the United Nations for the community's exemplary record with respect to the environment and sustainable development. According to the award panel, "Walpole Island has influenced not only its own members, but also the policies of the Province of Ontario. The Walpole Island First Nation has maintained their cultural heritage and traditional knowledge of the environment, while interacting effectively with the non-indigenous population and western environmental scientists to everyone's mutual benefit."[42]

How to Get There

You can take the Walpole-Algonac Ferry (in operation for over 100 years) from Algonac, Michigan, across the St. Clair to Walpole Island, from which it originates.

Walpole-Algonac Ferry
100 Tahgahoning Rd.
Walpole Island, ON N8A 4K9
519-365-5183
www.walpolealgonacferry.com

Alternatively, you can cross on the Walpole Island Bridge from Wallaceburg, Ontario, onto Walpole Island on Lambton County Road 32, which is also called Dufferin Avenue in Wallaceburg and Tecumseh Road on Walpole Island.

What to Expect

Expect to be welcomed, if you arrive by bridge, by a beautiful piece of art on a sign reading "Boozhoo, Bkejawanong Territory," closely followed by a second with the translation "Welcome to Walpole Island First Nation, Unceded Territory."

Right across the bridge is the Thunderbird Plaza, the location for businesses including the First Nations Bank, the Walpole Island First Nation Pharmacy, Sands-Keller Law Office ("Criminal, Family, Aboriginal Issues, Wills"), Bkejwanong's Coffee Shop (aka Papa's Place), the Pit Stop ("Open 7 days, Lotto, magazines, cigarettes"), JJ's Coin Laundry ("Feathers & Smokes"), 3-Fires Grafix ("Printing, vinyl signs, Native designs"), Discount Smokes, and Dot's Naame Nangoog ("Gifts from under the Stars") Native Gift Shop.

Expect the delta's native habitat, a habitat that you may have never seen anywhere before. Walpole Island supports a unique ecosystem with some of Ontario's greatest biological diversity, featuring remnant tallgrass prairie, one of the most rare and endangered ecosystems in the world. Colicroot (*Aletris farinose*), a species threatened by habitat destruction and a member of the lily family, is one rare prairie plant found on Walpole Island.

Expect to feel a strong sense of community on the island from Papa's Place to the Heritage Centre and captured for all time in all of the monuments and memorials in between. (Be advised that Walpole Island is also home to a community of excellent watchdogs that can make bike riding on the island an adventure.)

Paths to Adventure

NATURAL SITES

Walpole Island is a part of the Carolinian Life Zone. In the summer of 2004, the Ontario Trillium Foundation posted an information sign on the island that reads, in part:

> In 1984, Carolinian Canada identified 38 sites in a study of critical natural areas. Walpole Island First Nation was the only one that fulfilled all 10 criteria in the selection of the sites.

Walpole Island First Nation supports some of the most biologically diverse natural areas remaining in Canada. It has one of the largest tracts of forest cover in southwestern Ontario, species-rich coastal waterways, one of the largest wetland systems in the Great Lakes Basin, and extensive areas of rare tallgrass prairie and oak savanna. These ecosystems provide habitat for many rare plant and animal species such as small white lady's slipper, southern flying

Nin.Da.Waab.Jig ("Those Who Seek to Find"), the Walpole Heritage Centre.

squirrel, king rail, and channel darter. Some, such as lace grass and white prarie gentian, occur nowhere else in Canada.

For more on Walpole Island First Nation's Carolinian nature, see http://carolinian.org/legacy/Publications/Oct-20-06-Dean%20Jacobs.pdf.

For the story of the collaborative 65-foot circular environmental art installation *Three Fires Prairie* created by Canadian artist and naturalist Karen Miranda Abel (based in Toronto) in 2004 and 2005 to celebrate the natural heritage of Walpole Island First Nation and the community members who have protected and honored the ecological significance of this unique territory for generations, see www.karenabel.ca/projects/three-fires-prairie/.

The biggest activities on Walpole Island for recreational tourists are hunting, fishing, and trapping. As this is First Nation land, these activities can only be done with a guide who is a member of the Walpole Island First Nation.

HISTORY PRESERVED

St. Anne Island Treaty Monument—The brass plaque mounted below the beautiful piece of granite, itself bearing letters spelling out "St. Anne Island Treaty," reads: "On August 30th 1796, a treaty council fire was lit on St. Anne Island. A large gathering of Chippewa and Ottawa people circled the fire and listened to a speech made by Colonel Alexander McKee, who was the representative of King George III. McKee, on behalf of the Crown affirmed the 'rights and independence of all the Indian Nations,' including the rights to be 'free and unmolested in their trade and hunting grounds and to pass and repass freely undisturbed to trade with whom they please.' McKee also confirmed that the Chenail Ecarte Reserve (present-day Sombra Township) [was] to be set apart for the exclusive use of the Chippewa, Ottawa, and other First Nations."

Walpole Island Heritage Centre (River Rd.)—Nin.Da.Waab.Jig., meaning "Those Who Seek to Find," is the name of the Walpole Island Band's Research Center, established in 1973 to conduct the band's land claims research. "Since 1982, when much of the basic claims research was complete, the Heritage Centre expanded its mandate to include environmental, socio-economic, resource development, and historical research."[43] Since 1989, it has evolved into a multidepartmental unit that provides historical and environmental research and consulting for the Walpole Island First Nation, with the mission "to preserve, interpret, and promote the natural and cultural heritage of the Walpole Island Community." Open to both residents and visitors, the center boasts an extensive collection of legal and Native history books as well as a small display area of artifacts and photographs. It also now houses a natural heritage program, an environmental program, a research department, and an external projects program while continuing to serve as an archival building for land claims and research.

One particularly notable aspect of the Heritage Centre is its great emphasis on environmental education and awareness, both inside and outside the community. Walpole Island First Nation "has been recognized internationally for its work with a variety of partners to facilitate natural heritage protection and restoration efforts within the traditional territory." For an example of the types of projects Walpole Island First Nation has recently embarked upon outside the community, consider the Rt. Hon. Herb Gray Parkway (www.hgparkway.ca), where "traditional knowledge and respect for prairie have been integrated into the project through the involvement of Walpole Island First Nation, who have been stewards of Tallgrass Prairie and Oak Savannah. . . ." Danshab Enterprises, a Walpole Island–based business, [undertook] a significant component of the species-at-risk plant relocation work and restoration efforts within the Parkway.[44]

Residential School Memorial Monument—Erected in 2002, this monument is dedicated to all the children from Walpole Island who attended residential schools throughout Canada and the United States. An amendment to the Canadian Indian Act of 1876 made school attendance mandatory for First Nation children. The schools were funded by the Canadian government's Indian Affairs and Northern Development and were administered by Christian churches. The Canadian Residential Schools network was based on the U.S. government's cruel system of American Indian boarding schools designed for the stated purpose of "civilizing," "making Christian," and "assimilating" Native Americans into the dominant Euro-American culture. According to *Wikipedia*, "There has long been significant historiographical and popular controversy about the conditions experienced by students in the residential schools. . . . [A] new consensus emerged in the early 21st century that the [residential] schools did significant harm to Aboriginal children who attended them."[45] Approximately 400 of the 550 children from Walpole listed on this beautiful and sad monument were taken from four generations between 1873 and 1996.

On May 8, 2006, the Canadian government passed the Indian Residential Schools Settlement Agreement (IRSSA) that established a $2 billion compensation package for the approximately 86,000 people who were forced to attend these schools, the largest class action settlement in Canadian history, and on June 11, 2008, Prime Minister Stephen Harper, on behalf of the Government of Canada, offered a public apology to the former Canadian students of the Indian residential schools. Although President Obama signed an Apology to Native Peoples of the United States into law on December 19, 2009,

On October 5, 2015, 80 years after a memorial to contain the bones of the great leader of the Shawnee and of a large tribal confederacy was begun, the statue of Tecumseh, created by the sculptor Georgina Toulouse Bebamikawe, was raised onto the stone cairn, unveiled, and dedicated on Walpole Island.

the U.S. has not compensated the attendees for the devastation the schools wrought on Native communities.[46]

War Memorial—Dedicated to "Warriors Killed in Action," the memorial lists Walpole Island First Nation casualties from the American Civil War, World War I, and World War II.

Walpole Island Cemetery—Formerly known as High Banks (also Highbanks) Cemetery, this is the final resting place of members of island families, including the Aquash, Blackbird, Kicknosway, Nahdee, Sands, and Soney families, among others. There is a grave of someone born in 1825, another of someone who died in 1907.

Stone Cairn Monument to Tecumseh—The question remains as to whether Walpole Island is the final resting place of Shawnee chief Tecumseh, the nineteenth-century leader who formed a large First Nation confederacy and allied his warriors with the British during the War of 1812. Tecumseh helped capture Fort Detroit, but he died on the battlefield in 1813.

Statue of Tecumseh—By Ontario sculptor Georgina Toulouse Bebamikawe, this statue at the intersection of Tecumseh Highway and River Road was unveiled atop the stone cairn on October 5, 2015.

CULTURAL ATTRACTIONS

Dot's Naame Nangoog (Gifts from under the Stars) Native Gift Shop—Located in the Thunderbird Plaza, the shop features authentic Native crafts.

Papa's Place Coffee Shop—Also in the Thunderbird Plaza, this is a place to nurture friendships as well as the body.

OTHER ISLAND THINGS TO DO

Fish—You'll need a Walpole Island fishing permit.

Go duck hunting—You must be accompanied by a Walpole Island band member as a guide.

SPECIAL ISLAND EVENTS

Bkejwanong Spring Gathering Pow Wow (Victoria Day weekend in May)—Features singing, dancing, food, and crafts for sale.

Bkejwanong Fall Fair—In 2013 this event coincided with the Rekindle Tecumseh's Vision Gathering, in 2014, with the celebration of the twenty-fifth anniversary of the Walpole Island Heritage Centre, and in 2015 with the unveiling of the Tecumseh statue.

For More Island Information

Walpole Island First Nation website—www.walpoleislandfirstnation.ca.

Walpole Island Heritage Centre
2185 North St Clair River Rd., RR 3
Walpole Island, ON N8A 4K9
Joyce Johnson, Director
519-627-1475
www.walpoleislandfirstnation.ca/operations/heritage-centre

Minishenhying Anishnaabe-aki, Walpole Island: The Soul of Indian Territory, by Nin. Da.Waab.Jig, the community-based research arm of the Walpole Island Band Council (Walpole Island, ON, 1987).

Earth, Water, Air and Fire: Studies in Canadian Ethnohistory, edited by David T. McNab for Nin.Da.Waab.Jig (Waterloo, ON: Wilfrid Laurier University Press, 2012)—The book presents several chapters on Walpole Island from May 1994 conference papers:

"*Bkejwanong*—'The Place Where the Waters Divide': A Perspective on Earth, Water Air and Fire."

"'Water Is Her Life Blood': The Waters of Bkejwanong and the Treaty-Making Process."

"'Under the Earth': The Expropriation and Attempted Sale of the Oil and Gas Rights of the Walpole Island First Nation during World War I."

"The Reverend Simpson Brigham (1875–1926): The Worlds of Henry Ford and Simpson Brigham Collide."

How You Can Support the Island

Walpole Island Land Trust
Postal Box 22032
Dufferin Ave. Postal Outlet
Wallaceburg, ON N8A 5G4
walpolelandtrust.com

Parting Thoughts

October 5, 2015
Walpole Island

On my first visit to the island in 2014, Joyce Johnson, director of the Walpole Island Heritage Centre, assures me that Chief Tecumseh is indeed buried on the island. I hadn't thought to ask. But as I stand in the May-green grass outside the Heritage Centre, looking down a path through trees to a sparkling delta ribbon of the St. Clair River, running between the island's area called Highbanks and the Ontario mainland, I feel certain she's right.

On October 5, 2015, I return to Walpole Island on the 102nd anniversary of Tecumseh's death in the Battle of the Thames. The Bkejwanong Territory is hosting a dedication of the bronze sculpture of the great leader created by Georgina Toulouse Bebamikawe. This is the final piece of the memorial that was begun in 1934 with a sod-turning ceremony and a cornerstone-laying ceremony. In 1941, the rock cairn was completed and the ceremonial interment of Tecumseh's bones accomplished.

Today the bronze statue that has been installed atop the rock cairn is unveiled. The statue is silhouetted by the brightest of October sun against a blue sky. Tecumseh looks across the shipping channel of the St. Clair River to the United States, a spear in his left hand, a tomahawk in his right. It seems fitting that the great leader whose vision was that all of the tribes of the continent would unite in a confederacy would finally be laid to rest on an island that itself is the home of a successful confederacy, one of Ojibwe, Odawa, and Potawatomi people comprising a political pact known as the Three Fires Confederacy. Tecumseh said, "A single twig breaks, but the bundle of twigs is strong."

Below and behind his statue is a limestone memorial for the first of the island's war dead who fought alongside Americans: Oliver Ar-Pe-Targe-Zhik, a sharpshooter in the Civil War, buried in Arlington National Cemetery, topped by two inscribed granite stones, the one on the left in honor of the 10 Walpole Island men killed in World War I and the one on the right commemorating the four Walpole Island men who gave their lives in World War II.

Tecumseh also said, "Love your life, perfect your life, beautify all things in your life. Seek to make your life long and its purpose in the service of your people."

Detroit River Islands

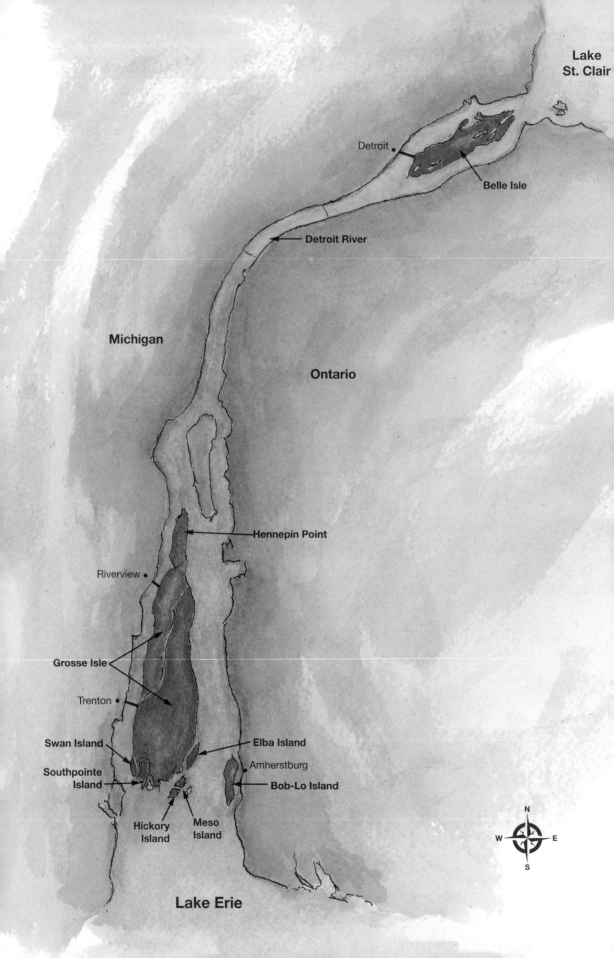

Lake
St. Clair

Detroit •

Belle Isle

Detroit River

Michigan

Ontario

Hennepin Point

Riverview •

Grosse Isle

Trenton •

Swan Island

Elba Island

Amherstburg •

Southpointe
Island

Bob-Lo Island

Hickory
Island

Meso
Island

N
W   E
S

Lake Erie

An Introduction to the Detroit River

The Detroit River was named Détroit by the French, meaning "the Strait" and referring to the nautical waterway that drops only three feet on its way down the 32-mile (51.5-kilometer) stretch between Lake St. Clair—a secondary lake in the Great Lakes Basin system—and Lake Erie. Here there has never been any need for locks or dams. From oceangoing freighters to the Detroit Boat Club crew sculling their shells, this is a stretch of boat-friendly water to navigate.

The river is only .5 mile (.8 kilometer) to 2.5 miles (four kilometers) wide, and the entire river serves as a part of the U.S.-Canadian border, with Windsor, Ontario, to the south and east and Detroit, Michigan, to the north and west. The river and the international border are crossed by the Ambassador Bridge and the Detroit-Windsor Tunnel, the latter of which goes under the river. In 2013, an inebriated man swam across the river and back. He was fortunate to be charged only with fines (Canadian regulations prohibit swimming in a shipping channel) and rescue costs, as the river's current and undertow make it a dangerous place to swim other than at properly designated and protected swimming beaches like the one on Belle Isle.

However, there are other ways than swimming to get "in" the river. Many islands dot the river, and three of these are accessible without private watercraft: the two American islands—Belle Isle and Grosse Ile—by bridge and the Canadian Bob-Lo Island by ferry from Amherstburg, Ontario.

At one time the river was extremely polluted due to the city of Detroit being so heavily industrialized, particularly in the downriver area, where the River Rouge plant is located on the riverbank. Beginning in the 1960s, steps were taken to clean up the river. Today, one of the groups committed to taking care of the river is the Friends of the Detroit River (FDR), an environmental group that watches and protects the river, inspired by the vision of an ever-improving quality of life for people, plants, and animals in southeast Michigan and

THE DETROIT RIVER TRIO

The Detroit River Trio may sound like the name of a jazz group, but it is a most appropriate group name for three easily accessible—and very different—islands in the Detroit River. Each island is worthy of a day trip. Exploring their differences will give you an idea of just how different island adventures can be.

This adventurer found Bob-Lo Island—that once-upon-a-time playground—barely eking out its formerly sizzling brushwork, Grosse Ile continuing to provide the steady walking bass of community, and Belle Isle augmenting its centuries of melodic musings with new uplifting improvisation. What do you think of the music made by this Detroit River trio of islands?

southwest Ontario. At the heart of the FDR's mission is the Detroit Riverkeeper Program, which pays a staff member—the "riverkeeper"—to patrol the river in the FDR boat, being the eyes and ears of the Detroit River community. Two annual events are the Riverkeeper Dinner and the Lower Detroit River Clean-up.

Friends of the Detroit River (FDR)
20600 Eurka Rd., Suite 313
Taylor, MI 48180
www.detroitriver.org

All three of these islands' names appear to show the French influence in the settlement of the region (although only in one case did English speakers actually get it right).

Pronounced "bell-aisle," *Belle Isle* is most commonly—and wrongly—believed to be French for "Beautiful (Small) Island."

Grosse Ile, pronounced "grow-zeal" with the accent on the "zeal," is French for "Big Island," and big it is, in several ways.

Bob-Lo, pronounced "bob-low," is an attempt to duplicate the French Bois Blanc, the original name of this Canadian island, meaning "white wood" and pronounced "bwa-bla(n)" (with a very nasal second syllable). "Bob-Lo" was as close as most English speakers could get to the French.

At least two of this trio of islands evoke sweet summertime memories for many native metro Detroiters. Regardless of where you hail from, a trio of island adventures awaits you!

For stunningly beautiful views of the Detroit River, peruse *A Year on the River,* by Joseph Crachiola (photographs) and Robert McGowan (poems) (Clarkston, MI: St. Clair Press, 2011), and for more information about the Detroit River's heritage (and from the Canadian side), check out *Heritage along the Detroit River,* by Dr. Trevor Price (Windsor, ON: Essex County Historical Society, 2010).

BELLE ISLE: WHAT'S IN A NAME?

Belle Isle *is* a beautiful small island, but that's not how it acquired its name. Stepping back in time, the island that is now called Belle Isle has been many things to many people over the years, and the sequence of names the island has borne over the centuries reflects its history.

To the Ojibwe and the Odawa, the island was known as Wah-na-be-zee (Swan Island), perhaps because trumpeter swans made their nests on the originally marshy island or because migrating tundra swans rested there. Other sources say Native Americans later called the marshy island Rattlesnake Island because of the number of snakes they found there. (Swans, but not rattlesnakes, occasionally visit the island today.)

French explorer Antoine de la Mothe Cadillac initially named the island Isle La Marguerite, in honor of one of his daughters. Cadillac decreed that the island be used as a common grazing area in the 1700s, and the French settlers eventually first renamed it Isle Au Ste. Clair, possibly due to its proximity to Lake St. Clair. Later the settlers renamed it Ile aux Cochons. The island was known by the English translation, Hog Island, as late as 1840. (Hogs were grazed there, possibly to kill the rattlesnakes and/or to protect the hogs from mainland wolves.)

In 1845, the island was renamed Belle Isle by Barnabas Campau in honor of Isabelle (Belle) Cass, the daughter of Michigan's then territorial governor (and later U.S. senator), Lewis Cass. In 1881, Belle Isle became Belle Isle Park—the name it has today—by an ordinance of the Detroit Common Council.

A TRIO OF MAINLAND "LAUNCHES"

Add a mainland adventure to your trip to each of the Detroit River islands, and double your adventure.

- Belle Isle—Pewabic Pottery (10125 E. Jefferson Ave., east of the MacArthur Bridge leading to Belle Isle, Detroit)—A National Historic Landmark, this ceramic studio was founded in 1903 by Mary Chase Perry Stratton, artist and teacher, who experimented with iridescent glazes. Pewabic tile graces many well-known buildings. Pewabic pottery is on display in many galleries worldwide, including the Louvre. For more information, see www.pewabic.org.
- Grosse Ile—Elizabeth Park (Slocum's Island, on Jefferson St. just north of the Wayne County Bridge leading to Grosse Ile, in Trenton, Michigan)—This county park—the oldest county park in Michigan and located primarily on an artificial island—features over 1,300 feet of river walk for fishing or just taking in the river. A perfect spot for a picnic, the park also accommodates softball, cycling, in-line skating, hiking, cross-country skiing, and ice-skating. For more information, see www.trentonmi.org.
- Bob-Lo Island—Town of Amherstburg, Ontario (half an hour south of Windsor on King's Highway 20)—A National Historic Site; in 1796, Fort Malden was built here. In addition to the fort, there are a number of other attractions nearby, including the Amherstburg Freedom Museum, Park House Museum, the Commissariat in the King's Navy Yard Park, the Marsh Collection Society, several galleries, three award-winning wineries, and a number of parks and public gardens. For more information, see www.amherstburg.ca.

Belle Isle, Michigan

A FAVORED PLACE

October 9, 2013, 12:10 p.m.
Scott Memorial Fountain

On this beautiful October day, my mom and I watch two Asian couples, one older, one younger, take turns photographing each other posed next to the larger-than-life bronze sculpture of a man seated in an armchair, his view of Detroit's skyline partially obstructed by the monument erected in his honor, the James Scott Memorial Fountain. I take a photo of the four of them together around the sculpture. Of all the many stories of Belle Isle, the one behind the sculpture of James Scott may be one of the weirdest—although maybe not; there's a lot of history to consider here. Certainly it's one of the stories involving the greatest hubris.

Unseen in the tourists' photographs will be the question of Belle Isle's future, undecided at this moment in time in 2013.

GETTING THERE: Bridge

GETTING AROUND: Bring your car and/or bike; bicycles, kayaks, canoes, pedal boats and paddleboard rentals

OVERNIGHT ACCOMMODATIONS: None (park closes at 10:00 p.m.)

FOOD: Bring your own

DAY TRIP? Yes, only option

STATE / PROVINCIAL / NATIONAL PARK? Belle Isle Park became a Michigan State Park in 2014 as part of a lease agreement with the City of Detroit, which owns the island

"The island is the priceless jewel in the crown of Detroit; woods of green and waters of blue—art and nature—moving waves and waving grass—stillness and activity—vistas and broad views—beautiful flowers and lofty trees—the white sails of numerous vessels, and the swift motion of great steamers, all alike are combined in the captivating beauties of this favored place."[47] So the prolific Michigan historian Silas Farmer rapturously described Belle Isle before 1899. Belle Isle became in need of more than surface polish, requiring some major care, toward the end of the twentieth and into the twenty-first century. Enter the Belle Isle Conservancy.

The island was purchased by the City of Detroit from the descendants of Barnabas Campau in 1879 for $200,000. Frederick Law Olmsted, the landscape architect who had

Belle Isle Park

SHELTERS (numbers on map correlate to shelter numbers)
- - - HIKING TRAILS
FISHING SITES
SWIMMING BEACH
DISC GOLF
GOLF
HANDBALL
PADDLING
SOCCER FIELDS
TENNIS COURTS
BASKETBALL
PLAYGROUND
BASEBALL FIELDS
MODEL BOAT BASIN
PARKING LOT
RESTROOM
CONCESSIONS
BIKE RENTALS
WATERCRAFT RENTALS
BUS STOP
* Carriage rides and Pedi-cabs pick up at Shelter 7

Ⓐ SUNSET POINT
Ⓑ SCOTT MEMORIAL FOUNTAIN
Ⓒ CASINO (event center)
Ⓓ DETROIT BOAT CLUB
Ⓔ FLYNN MEMORIAL PAVILION
Ⓕ REMICK MUSIC SHELL
Ⓖ NANCY BROWN PEACE CARILLON
Ⓗ GIANT SLIDE
Ⓘ ANNA SCRIPPS WHITCOMB CONSERVATORY

Ⓙ DOSSIN GREAT LAKES MUSEUM
Ⓚ WHITE HOUSE / ADMINISTRATION
Ⓛ AQUARIUM
Ⓜ ATHLETIC SHELTER / REFECTORY
Ⓝ BEACH HOUSE
Ⓞ DETROIT YACHT CLUB (private)
Ⓟ NATURE ZOO
Ⓠ U.S. COAST GUARD STATION
Ⓡ LIVINGSTONE MEMORIAL LIGHTHOUSE

Courtesy of the Michigan Department of Natural Resources

co-designed New York's Central Park (1858) and would go on to create Chicago's Wooded Island for the 1893 Columbian Exposition, was commissioned on August 29, 1881, to design a true city park on Belle Isle. The park was opened to the public in 1884, although this initial development continued through 1908, as roads, bridges, lakes, shelters, and gardens were added. Belle Isle Park became the place to promenade and picnic, to paddle a canoe down a lagoon and listen to a concert (sometimes at the same time), to swim in the river in the summer and ice-skate on the lagoons in the winter.

Over the years, Belle Isle has witnessed a lot of Detroit—and national—history. The island's location in the Detroit River, with the border of the United States and Canada just south of the island's south shore (yes, Ontario here is south of Michigan), made it a natural station on the Underground Railroad for slaves escaping to freedom in Canada between 1810 and 1850. From 1920 to 1933, rumrunners used the island to bring in booze during Prohibition.

Houdini's jump from the old Belle Isle Bridge on November 27, 1906, was breathlessly reported by a *Detroit News* headline: "Jump Manacled from B.I. Bridge; Handcuff King Houdini Performs Remarkable Feat and Comes out Safely; Had a Rope Tied around His Waist and Tied to Bridge to Safeguard against Accident."

The Detroit race riot of 1943 began on Belle Isle on June 20, fueled by two rumors: one that a white woman had been raped and murdered by an African American man on the Belle Isle Bridge and another that an African American mother and child had been thrown into the Detroit River by a mob of whites. Three days later, 34 people were dead and 433 wounded, and $2 million worth of property had been destroyed. During the Detroit race riot of 1967, the Belle Isle bathhouse was used as a detention center—a use that led to its destruction.

Suburban families still picnicked on Belle Isle in the 1960s and 1970s. I remember picnics that followed visits with both sets of my grandparents to the Belle Isle Children's Zoo, where shaggy llamas freely wandered among visitors. Later in life, my soon-to-be fiancé and I took his nephew to Belle Isle for a breakfast picnic cooked on our camp stove at Sunset Point. In the 1980s, friends who lived in our Detroit neighborhood were joined in wedlock near the Livingstone Memorial Lighthouse on the island.

In 1992 the Detroit Indy Grand Prix moved to Belle Isle. In more recent years, Chevrolet has sponsored the Detroit Belle Isle Grand Prix over a three-day period at the end of May. The annual September Tour de Troit biking event has included Belle Isle since 2007.

In 2014, months after my visit, Belle Isle became a Michigan State Park under a 30-year lease agreement signed by the City of Detroit. Under the agreement, the city maintains ownership of the 982-acre park—the largest city park in the United States—while the Michigan Department of Nature Resources manages the park. Today, the park's grass is mowed again while plans abound regarding just what type of polish should be applied to this "priceless jewel in the crown of Detroit."

How to Get There

Three miles (4.8 kilometers) east of downtown Detroit, cross the Douglas MacArthur Bridge (aka the Belle Isle Bridge) from East Grand Boulevard at Jefferson Avenue to access Belle Isle.

A Michigan Recreation Passport is required when accessing the island by vehicle. You can purchase one on Belle Isle. For the current cost of a Recreation Passport as well as answers to FAQ about Belle Isle Park, visit www.michigan.gov/dnr/0,4570,7-153-10365_67024_67025---,00.html.

Note: No public marina exists on Belle Isle; if you arrive by private boat, you need to dock at a mainland marina and cross the bridge by foot, bike, or taxi.

What to Expect

Expect a lot of park and many opportunities to indulge in leisure activities, sightseeing of historic park structures, and doing some serious river watching. If you have been to Belle Isle before, you can expect things to look different on the island as the City of Detroit and the State of Michigan work with the Belle Isle Conservancy to polish the park.

Paths to Adventure

NATURAL SITES

The canals—Now a part of the natural landscape, construction of the canals and lagoons took place between 1893 and 1910. My mom remembers island-goers canoeing on these canals. The canoers, often courting couples, could drift along the canals, listening to concerts (Loop Canal, at one time, had a music pavilion situated on a bridge). Canoe rentals were discontinued in the 1980s. However, in the summer of 2015, as one of the new state park's offerings, a rental vendor offered bikes as well as canoes, kayaks, and stand-up paddleboards from the Flynn Pavilion, and the word is that by the 2016 season, two canoe and kayak launch areas will be built and ready for use, one on the Detroit River at Belle Isle Beach and the other on Lake Muskoday.

The lagoons—There is a large lagoon, the Scott Fountain Lagoon, at the western end of the island located by the Scott Fountain. The other lagoon, the 42-acre Blue Heron Lagoon at the eastern end, was until recently enclosed; a recent restoration project has breached the lagoon to the river by removing the former land bridge and infrastructure at the old pump station discharge channel and replacing these features with a 100-foot opening spanned by a pedestrian bridge. This new opening allows river flow containing fish larvae into the lagoon's nursery habitat.

The woods—230 acres of forested wetlands (along with three lakes and the Blue Heron Lagoon) make up more than half the island. Identified as a rare wet-mesic forest, the island features "specimens that mimic the Detroit ecosystem of hundreds of years ago. Forests like this were found throughout southeastern Michigan after the glacial period."[48] The DNR hosts one-hour nature hikes through the woods, departing on a trail from the Belle Isle Nature Zoo parking lot.

The shore—Approximately seven miles (11 kilometers) of island shoreline front the Detroit River on all sides. Don't miss Sunset Point, where you'll get the best view of the Detroit skyline. This westernmost point of the island was created using fill from construction sites in downtown Detroit in 1915 to increase the size of the island in order to provide a location for the Scott Fountain and Lagoon.

HISTORY PRESERVED

Douglas MacArthur Bridge (Belle Isle Bridge)—Built in 1923, the Douglas MacArthur Bridge connects mainland Detroit to Belle Isle with a reinforced, cantilevered concrete arch structure with a 2,356-foot span and a roadway width of 61 feet. Nearly .5 mile (.8 kilometer) long, it features 19 arches, five lanes for traffic, and two sidewalks for pedestrians. This bridge replaces a wooden bridge, built in 1889 for $315,000, that burned in 1915 as well as a ferry service begun in 1870 and discontinued in 1957.

Interior island bridges—Crossing over the canals are more than a dozen small bridges. (Some have been lost; the fourteenth annual report by the commissioner of parks and boulevards of the City of Detroit in 1903 describes 22 such bridges.) Today, those bridges include one long covered bridge off Oakway Drive in the Belle Isle Disc Golf Course and the Inselruhe Bridge (aka Inselrue Bridge or Bridge No. 11), which spans the Nashua Canal. The latter is the only island bridge featuring decorative brickwork and carved stonework.[49] For photographs of this bridge, see www.loc.gov/pictures/.

The White House—This white frame structure is the oldest building on Belle Isle and has been used by Belle Isle administrators since the mid-twentieth century. The house was built in 1864 by Alexandrine (Macomb Sheldon) Campau, the widow of John Barnabas Campau—who drowned in the Detroit River in 1859 and whose father (Barnabas) had purchased the island from David Macomb in 1817 (Barnabas was the younger brother of Joseph Campau, who at the time of his death in 1863 was the largest landowner in Michigan and one of the wealthiest Detroiters)—and Campau's second husband, R. Storrs Willis, a Detroit real-estate developer who developed what is now the Willis-Selden Historic District. The house was later named Inselruhe (Island Tranquility) in the 1870s. In the twentieth century, the house has served as the park manager's residence and then,

The William Livingstone Memorial Lighthouse at the east end of Belle Isle, designed by renowned Detroit architect Albert Kahn, can be seen from up to 15 miles away and is the only lighthouse in the country built of marble.

from 1941 to 1957, housed the offices of the Detroit Garden Center, which focused on island landscaping.

William Livingstone Memorial Lighthouse—Measuring a total of 80 feet high, including the bronze lantern room that houses the light set atop a 58-foot shaft of Georgia marble with exquisite green and purple coloration, this is the only lighthouse in the country built entirely of marble. Situated at the head of the Detroit River facing Lake St. Clair, its light (11,500 candlepower) can be seen 15 miles (24 kilometers) away. The renowned Detroit architect Albert Kahn designed the lighthouse, which is named after William Livingstone, a prominent and popular Detroit resident who was president of the Lake Carriers' Association, the trade association representing U.S.-flag vessel operators on the Great Lakes from 1902 to 1925. The lighthouse was first lit on April 8, 1930.

Dossin Great Lakes Museum—Opened in 1960, this Detroit Historical Society museum (at 100 Strand Drive on the island's south shore) is open on weekends only and is free of charge. The museum's mission is to showcase the story of the Great Lakes and the Detroit River, particularly with respect to Detroit's role in regional and national maritime history over the last 300 years. Permanent exhibits include *Miss Pepsi,* a championship hydroplane raced by the Dossin family in the 1950s; the SS *William Clay Ford* pilothouse; the bow anchor of the legendary *Edmund Fitzgerald;* the restored Gothic Room from the SS *City of Detroit III;* the ship model showcase; and the exhibition *Built by the River,* which explores the link between Detroit and the Detroit River. For more information, see www .detroithistorical.org/about-us/our-museums/dossin-great-lakes-museum.

CULTURAL ATTRACTIONS

Belle Isle Aquarium (900 Inselruhe Ave.)—Originally opened in 1904, the aquarium had been the oldest continually operating aquarium in North America until 2005, when it closed. The aquarium reopened in 2012 through the fund-raising efforts of the Friends of the Belle Isle Aquarium, one of the four organizations that merged to become the Belle Isle Conservancy. Designed by architect Albert Kahn, the aquarium's oft-photographed Beaux-Arts–style entrance is decorated with a stone facade incorporating two spitting fish on either side of the the official seal of the City of Detroit, which is a representation of the Detroit fire of 1805 that burned all of the city but one building: one figure weeps over the destruction, and the other figure gestures to the new city that will rise from it. The two Latin mottos are *Speramus Meliora* (We hope for better things) and *Resurget Cineribus* (It will rise from the ashes).

The Belle Isle Aquarium is open on weekends, and admission is free. For more information, visit www.belleisleconservancy.org/visit-the-park/belle-isle-aquarium/.

One of a pair of Commodore Oliver Hazard Perry's Victory Cannons captured from the British at the 1813 Battle of Lake Erie, in front of the Dossin Great Lakes Museum on Belle Isle.

The Anna Scripps Whitcomb Conservatory on Belle Isle (aka the Belle Isle Conservatory).

Anna Scripps Whitcomb Conservatory and Botanical Gardens (7000 Inselruhe Ave.)—
Better known as the Belle Isle Conservatory, this centerpiece on the island encompasses
13 acres of green along with the 85-foot domed greenhouse built by Albert Kahn in 1904.
The woman for whom the conservatory is named left her collection of 600 orchids to
Detroit, among other donations. Highlights include the Palm House, the Tropical
House, the Cactus House, the Fernery, and the Show House. Also look for the Levi L.
Barbour Fountain set among the formal gardens out front, and visit the lily pond—home
to koi and turtles—situated between the conservatory and the Belle Isle Aquarium.

The Anna Scripps Whitcomb Conservatory is open Wednesday through Sunday, and
admission is free. For more information, visit www.facebook.com/pages/Anna-Scripps
-Whitcomb-Conservatory/234289544427.

Belle Isle Nature Zoo (176 Lakeside)—"Bringing the 'wilds' of Michigan to the heart of
Detroit" is the nature zoo's tagline, and the institution is committed to increasing environmental awareness by providing educational programs to the community, students, and
teachers. Attractions include an operating beehive; an observation window from which
to view native and migratory bird species at feeders; exhibits featuring Michigan amphibians, fish, invertebrates, and reptiles; and the "Deer Encounter," which allows visitors to
feed fallow deer.

The Belle Isle Nature Zoo is open Wednesday through Sunday, and admission is free.
For more information, visit www.belleislenaturezoo.org/.

Belle Isle Beach and Waterslide—Be sure to take in the .5-mile-long (.8-kilometer-long)
swimming beach; this is the only public beach in Detroit and the only one along the river,
at least on the U.S. side. Lifeguards are on duty, and the beach is groomed daily. Next to
the beach is the popular water slide, on which kids can ride all day with a pass obtained
for a minimal cost.

OTHER ISLAND THINGS TO DO

Take the Belle Isle Self-Guided Tour, which includes buildings, monuments, and other distinctive features and attractions. Download the tour at www.belleisleconservancy.org/wp-content/uploads/BELLE-ISLE-Self-Guided-Tour.pdf.

See how many of these sights on Belle Isle you can find:

Floral Clock

Scott Memorial Fountain

Belle Isle Casino

The Carillon, aka the "Nancy Brown Peace Carillon Tower—Dedicated in 1940 to honor Nancy Brown, the nom de plume of Annie Louise Brown Leslie, a *Detroit News* columnist whose "woman's" column, which debuted in the paper in 1919 and ran until February 1942, was titled "Experience."

The Monument Builders of America's International Peace Memorial—"With this everlasting witness we keep peace with our neighbors as they have kept peace with us throughout the years."

Remick Music Shell

U.S. Coast Guard

Model Yacht Basin

Fishing Piers

Blue Heron Lagoon Restoration Project

Detroit Yacht Club—The building is on its own island, accessible by bridge off Riverbank Drive on Belle Isle.

Detroit Boat Club—The Rowing Crew, established in 1839 and today known as the Detroit Boat Club Crew, is still attracting members.

Monuments and historical markers, including:

- Two of Commodore Perry's "Victory Cannons" from the decisive 1813 Battle of Lake Erie.
- Spanish American War Memorial—"Cuba, Puerto Rico, Erected by the People of Wayne County, MI in commemoration of the service of her Volunteer Sons in the Army, Navy and Marine Corps during the War with Spain 1898–1902."
- Major General Alpheus Starkey William, 1810–78.
- James Scott, 1831–1910—Coming from a number sources, a battalion of negative charges marches through this wealthy Detroiter's biography. He has been described as "a prankster," "a rapscallion," "a womanizing scoundrel," "a combative gambler," "a man-about-town," "a scurrilous misanthrope," and "lazy," "eccentric," "irascible," and "vindictive" to boot. He left his vast fortune to the City of Detroit to build a monument "for the people." The catch was that the monument had to include a life-size statue of James Scott himself.[50] Notice that while the monument does include a life-size statue of Scott, the statue is of him seated, and it is placed inconspicuously behind a fountain with a large lower bowl, the diameter of which takes up 510 feet, and a central spray that shoots up 125 feet. It is possible to visit the fountain and not notice the statue.
- Ransom Eli Olds Commemorative Marker—In 1899, Olds relocated his business from Lansing to Detroit, establishing Olds Motor Works on West Jefferson by the MacArthur Bridge.
- General O. M. Poe Memorial Marker—General Orlando Metcalfe Poe was a U.S. Army officer and engineer in the Civil War who was responsible for much early

lighthouse construction on the Great Lakes as well as the design of the Poe Lock at the Soo Locks.

- James J. Brady Memorial (1928)—Founder of the Old Newsboys Goodfellow Fund of Detroit ("No child without a Christmas").
- Newsboy Water Fountain and the sculpture *Partners: A Newsboy and His Dog* (1897).
- Johann Christoph Friedrich von Schiller Monument (German dramatist, poet, philosopher, historian)—Commemorates the heritage of Detroit's German American community.
- Bust of Dante Alighieri (Italian poet, 1265–1321)—Commemorates the heritage of Detroit's Italian American community.

20 picnic structures—Some are quite photogenic:

- Newsboy Picnic Structure
- Shadynook Picnic Structure
- Police Area Picnic Structure
- Pony Area Picnic Structure
- Bus Stop Picnic Structure
- Bath Lunch Picnic Structure
- Fishing Pier Picnic Structure
- Schiller Picnic Structure
- Daisy Dock (east)
- Daisy Dock (west)
- Picnic Structures 3, 4, 10, 11, and 13–18

"Comfort Stations," including some old photogenic ones and the renovated restroom at Sunset Point.

Note the names of the island's streets, for example, "Loiter Way," "The Strand," "Muse."

Athletic field and sports complex

Cricket field

Belle Isle (Golf) Practice Center—Features a driving range, putting greens, chipping greens, and five-hole short course.

Handball, tennis, and basketball courts

Disc golf course (18 holes)

Playscape

Harbor Master's House and Dock

Flynn Memorial Skating Pavilion—Accommodates canoeing in summer and ice-skating in winter.

SPECIAL ISLAND EVENTS

Grand Prixmiere (May)—Kicks off the Grand Prix weekend on Belle Isle and supports the island.

Scott Fountain Pewabic Party (June)—Held at the Pewabic Pottery, this event raises funds through purchases made from Pewabic's House and Garden Show to help restore the Scott Fountain's Pewabic tiles.

BLISS (Belle Isle Summer Saturdays)—Advertised as "summer fun for everyone," these events are offered on the last Saturdays of July, August, and September, each with a different theme (for example, Sports and Fitness, Nature and History, Arts and Culture).

Garden Party on Belle Isle (September)—Cocktails, hors d'oeuvres, and music; ticket revenue benefits the Ann Scripps Conservatory and the Belle Isle Aquarium.

Polish the Jewel (October)—This annual luncheon, honoring Belle Isle individual and corporate sponsors, "historically attracts more than 400 of the region's most prominent women wearing their favorite shoes and chapeaus, for an afternoon of networking and support of [the] island gem."[51]

Light Up the Aquarium (December)—A holiday fund-raiser to support the Belle Isle Aquarium involving hors d'oeuvres, beer and wine, and a silent auction.

For information on annual events as well as onetime events on the island, see www.belleisle conservancy.org/calendar.

For More Island Information

Belle Isle Self-Guided Tour—Includes buildings, monuments, and other distinctive features and attractions. Download the tour at www.belleisleconservancy.org/wp-content/uploads/BELLE-ISLE-Self-Guided-Tour.pdf.

Michigan DNR "Recreation Search"—www.michigandnr.com/parksandtrails/Details.aspx ?id=736&type=SPRK.

Island in the City: How Belle Isle Changed Detroit Forever, by Janet Anderson (Detroit: Friends of Belle Isle, 2001).

Detroit's Belle Isle: Island Park Gem, by Michael Rodriguez and Thomas Featherstone (Mount Pleasant, SC: Arcadia, 2003).

Fourteenth Annual Report of the Commissioner of Parks and Boulevards of the City of Detroit: One Thousand Nine Hundred and Three (free Google e-book).

The Park for Detroit: Being a Preliminary Consideration of Certain Prime Conditions of Economy for the Belle Isle Scheme, by Frederick Law Olmsted (1882; repr., Whitefish, MT: Kessinger Legacy Reprint Series, 2010).

For a timeline of Belle Isle projects, visit http://voiceofdetroit.net/wp-content/uploads/2012/07/BELLE-ISLE-HISTORY.pdf.

To read more about Belle Isle, go to http://greatlakesislandescapes.com, click on "Blog," and select "Belle Isle Breezes."

How You Can Support the Island

Who's looking after and "polishing" Belle Isle these days besides the City of Detroit and the Michigan Department of Natural Resources? That would be:

The Belle Isle Conservancy
300 River Place Dr., Suite 2800
Detroit, MI 48207
www.belleisleconservancy.org

Four volunteer organizations came together to form the Belle Isle Conservancy: the Friends of Belle Isle (founded in 1972), the Belle Isle Botanical Society (1988), the Belle Isle Women's Committee (2004), and the Friends of the Belle Isle Aquarium (2005).

The Belle Isle Conservancy is a 501(c)(3) nonprofit organization working to restore, preserve, protect, and enhance Detroit's Belle Isle. Working in partnership with the State of Michigan's Department of Natural Resources and the City of Detroit, the Belle Isle Conservancy's mission is to bring additional resources to the island, including planning and funding improvements; providing extra hands to do work that the city cannot afford to do otherwise; being an advocate to protect the park; and marketing Belle Isle as a place for everyone to enjoy. Annual dues start as low as $10. Members receive e-newsletters and print newsletters to keep them informed about Belle Isle projects and important issues affecting the park as well as invitations to Belle Isle events.

Great Lakes Restoration Initiative (GLRI)
www.greatlakesrestoration.us

Funded by the Environmental Protection Agency, this initiative supports many Great Lakes projects, including the ongoing projects involving restoring wetlands and other habitats on Belle Isle.

- The South Fishing Pier—Installation of barriers to protect a newly created aquatic nursery habitat from freighter wake and ice floes.
- The Blue Heron Lagoon—Enhancement of the entire wildlife community, providing reproduction and nursery habitat for fish, herpetofauna, migrating birds, and waterfowl.
- Lake Okonoka Habitat Restoration—Reconnection of the island's internal waterways with the river to enhance habitat for a greater diversity of animal and plant species.
- Invasive species prevention and control.

Parting Thoughts

October 9, 2013, 3:00 p.m.
Belle Isle

My mom and I, the two of us together, walk to Livingstone Lighthouse. Blue sky, blue river, two blue herons at the Blue Heron Lagoon. October's highbush cranberry leaves touched with red and sporting bold red berries. Yellow cabbage butterfly lights on purple-stemmed aster. Chicory in bloom next to a single shaggy mane mushroom. Atop the fluted shaft of white marble—dwarfed by a towering poplar, whose leaves glint in the sun and shiver in the breeze—the light is lit yet, serving still as a beacon on the water.

Grosse Ile, Michigan

A WONDER WELL OF HISTORY

April 26, 2012, 3:05 p.m.
Grosse Ile

I came to Grosse Ile, this big island in the Detroit River, as one of my first island trips on this project. The island is relatively close, it was relatively familiar—I'd been here once before—and, really, how much adventure could there be on this island, generally labeled a "downriver bedroom community"?

Woo-hoo, was I off the mark! I came back the next week just to check out the very fine Grosse Ile Historic Museum and then got caught up in pursing the historic site markers and the experience of history "coming alive," as they say.

And then I came back again with my friend Val, who'd grown up on the island, with our bikes to pedal around the island. We had such a good time, and there was still so much to explore—we hadn't made it to the alpaca farm or Westcroft Gardens yet—that we came back this weekend, too. It was then, today, we saw the twin fawns in the road pause as we pedaled toward them. Twins, a good symbol for this island, with its equally strong adventure attractions: rich island history and a wonderful biking environment.

GETTING THERE: Bridges; private boat or plane

GETTING AROUND: Bring your car and/or your bike; bring your own kayak/canoe

OVERNIGHT ACCOMMODATIONS: Limited options: one inn, one B&B; no camping

FOOD: Restaurant; groceries

DAY TRIP? Yes, recommended

STATE / PROVINCIAL / NATIONAL PARK? No, but a number of Michigan Historic Site markers are posted around the island

Notable things have happened on Grosse Ile in the past.

There was the day, July 23, 1701, that French explorer Antoine de la Mothe Cadillac, traveling from Montreal, camped with his convoy of 25 canoes carrying 50 soldiers and 50 Canadian voyageurs (farmers, traders, and artisans) on the shore of Grosse Ile. The next day, he headed back upriver to look for another place to build Fort Ponchartrain du Détroit, claiming French possession of the territory for King Louis XIV and creating the settlement of Detroit. Thus did Grosse Ile "almost" become Detroit.

Then there was the day, July 6, 1776, that Native Americans and Europeans met on Grosse Ile. Native American tribes used Grosse Ile as a fishing and hunting ground before they sold the island. That meeting and its historical aftermath were described in the early years of the twentieth century:

Two days after signing the Declaration of Independence . . . Grosse Ile was sold to Alexander and William Macomb by the resident Indian tribes. The Fox, the Sacs, the Kikapoos and the Potawatomies are all spoken of, the former tribes inhabiting the ravine, which lies between the Edward Lyon and Horace Gray farms. . . . The old council tree, the silent witness of many negotiations between the white settlers and the Indians, had braved the elements for over a century when a severe storm, July 3, 1901, snapped the weather-beaten trunk. . . . It was under this tree, upon the knoll just above the old boat landing at Gray's dock that the treaty [had been] signed by the Potawatomie Indians which made Alexander and William Macomb the owners of the island. This treaty was ratified by the American government, June 1, 1811, when President James Madison granted by patent the land to John W., William, and David Macomb, heirs of William Macomb. . . . From the roots of the old treaty tree, a fine young sapling has sprung. To . . . preserve historical landmarks, an organization called the Woman's Improvement Association of Grosse Ile determined a year ago [1905] to mark the site. A large bowlder [*sic*] bearing a bronze tablet has been erected.[52]

The woman presiding over this ceremony was Miss Madeleine Macomb Stanton, a direct descendant of both Alexander and William Macomb. In attendance was the chief of the Potawatomi, Joseph Warren of Amherstburg, Ontario. Clare Koester of the Grosse Ile Historical Society further describes the actual signing of the treaty: "On July 6, 1776, 18 Potawatomi Indian chiefs signed a deed. . . . Each Indian chief signed by drawing his totem along side of a wafer of sealing wax upon which he left his thumb print."[53]

Between 1927 and 1969, Grosse Ile was influential in the nation's military history. Operating from 1927 until 1969, Naval Air Station Grosse Ile was one of the largest primary flight-training stations for both U.S. Navy and the United Kingdom's Royal Air Force pilots during World War II. Thousands of navy pilots began their careers here, including former president George H. W. Bush and Donald Rumsfeld. You can learn more about this period in Grosse Ile's history at the island's Naval Air Station Museum.

You can explore this history of Grosse Ile by car or on foot, but it's a great island to bike. You will need to bring your own bike or rent one before you cross to the island. Either way, if you park your car at Elizabeth Park on the mainland, it is advised that you walk your bike across the Wayne County Bridge as a safety precaution; there was a bicycle fatality on the bridge in 2012. Grosse Ile Parkway, coming off the Wayne County Bridge, has a paved shoulder bike route that runs the 2.5 miles (four kilometers) from west to east at the widest width of the island.

Taking advantage of the paved trail system on Grosse Ile, you can plan a comfortable and safe bicycle excursion. If you were to plan to head north on East River Road, you would have to ride on the edge of the two-lane roadway, so the recommended route is to begin at the northernmost end of the paved trail, just north of Bridge Road, riding south on Meridian to Horsemill and then counterclockwise around the eastern half of the island, heading east on Horsemill. At the Detroit River, Horsemill curves onto East River Road. You can ride down its entire length on the west shoulder to Groh, or beyond onto the three smaller inhabited islands of Grosse Ile Township clustered around Gibraltar Bay and connected by bridge: Elba Island (which cuts off from East River, the last turnoff before Groh Road), Meso Island (aka Upper Hickory), and (Lower) Hickory Island. Then back to Groh and across to the west side, where you can cross onto South Pointe and then from that island to Swan Island. And finally, back east on Groh Road and north on Meridian.

There are over 12 miles (19 kilometers) on this bike trail if you remain on Grosse Ile proper, without forays in the southern realms to the five other islands.

How to Get There

Grosse Ile is about 25 miles (40 kilometers) south on I-75 from downtown Detroit. Take I-75 south to exit 32A, then take West Road east toward Trenton/Grosse Ile. Turn right on Allen Road. Take the first left on Van Horn, and then turn left on W. Jefferson. From here you have two options.

The free option is to take your first right onto Grosse Ile Parkway, which crosses the Trenton Channel of the Detroit River on the Wayne County Bridge (aka the Free Bridge). Formerly the Michigan Central Railroad's rail bridge built in 1873, this swing bridge connects Grosse Ile to mainland Trenton.

Your other option, the northernmost, is to take the Grosse Ile Toll Bridge, built between 1912 and 1913 (at the time of writing, the toll was $2 one way). The bridge crosses to the island on Bridge Road, also off Jefferson, about 3.7 miles (6 kilometers) farther north in Riverview, Michigan.

Grosse Ile is the only Detroit River island with an airport, the Grosse Ile Municipal Airport (KONZ).

Paths to Adventure

NATURAL SITES

There are three nature trails on Grosse Ile:

Grosse Ile Wildlife Sanctuary Trail—350 yards in length and partially covered with woodchips, this trail is through a heavily forested area and affords a view of the Thorofare Canal. This trail can be accessed from Horsemill Road or Morkland Avenue; both entrances are east of Thorofare.

80-Acre Woods Trail—This trail, 400 yards long, has low spots and logs and cuts through a heavily forested area. It is accessible near Meridian Road, across the street from Meridian Elementary School. You may see deer and encounter poison ivy.

Playscape Trail—This trail, about 280 yards and covered with woodchips, is heavily forested and has deer runs crossing the trail. The trail is accessed from the parking lot behind the post office on Macomb Street. It is west of the Adventure Island Playscape.

Courtesy of the Grosse Ile Garden Club, you can download the *Grosse Ile Township Nature Trails Guide* (2009), which features these trails, at www.grosseile.com/document_center/ GI_Township_Nature_Trail_Guide.pdf.

There are also two nature preserves on Grosse Ile:

The Grosse Ile Nature Area

www.ginlc.org/nature_area.html

A 40.5-acre marsh and upland area that was previously a navy seaplane base (1927) and a NIKE missile base (1954–63). In 1972, the Defense Department turned it over to the

Environmental Protection Agency (EPA) for use as a wetlands research area. In 1993, the EPA granted stewardship of the area to the Grosse Ile Nature and Land Conservancy. In 2009, the nature area was made part of the Detroit River International Wildlife Refuge.

Detroit River International Wildlife Refuge

Large Lakes Research Station

9311 Groh Rd.

Grosse Ile, MI 48138

734-365-0219

www.fws.gov/refuge/Detroit_River/about.html

"On December 21, 2001, President [George Walker] Bush signed legislation establishing the first International Wildlife Refuge in North America. The refuge, which includes islands, coastal wetlands, marshes, shoals, and riverfront lands along 48 miles (77 kilometers) of the Detroit River and western Lake Erie, will protect and restore habitat for 29 species of waterfowl, 65 kinds of fish, and 300 species of migratory birds in Michigan and Ontario, Canada. . . . In the first five years, the refuge has grown from 304 acres to 4,982 acres. The refuge is managed by staff at the refuge office in Grosse Ile, Michigan."[54]

HISTORY PRESERVED

The Grosse Ile Historical Society's information and displays found at the **Grosse Ile Historical Museum** (25000 East River Rd.) can help you wend your way through Grosse Ile's history. The Grosse Ile Historical Society is a nonprofit corporation established (ahead of its time) in 1959, governed by an elected board of trustees, and run by volunteers. The society operates a historical museum in the old Michigan Central Railroad Depot at the corner of East River Road and Grosse Ile Parkway and has also acquired the 1871 Grosse Ile Customs House (hours by appointment only), which was moved from Macomb Street to behind the depot.

These two buildings are located within the East River Road National Historic District, which includes six historic private homes as well as the chapel (1867) at St. James Episcopal Church.

WONDER A BIT

The geological feature Grosse Ile used to be best known for was the Wonder Well, the largest artesian well east of the Mississippi, discovered when Sinclair Oil struck water instead of oil in 1903. It's now dry, but in its heyday, it gushed 2 *million* gallons of 52-degree water 22 feet in the air *every day*. The pungent mineral water was bottled for its "medicinal properties" (consumers claimed it helped abate "stomach troubles, constipation and rheumatism") and sold in Michigan and Ohio until 1957.

The Wonder Well became a major tourist attraction, featured in *Ripley's Believe It or Not* and listed in the AAA tour guide. However, in the late 1950s both the flow of water and interest in the well began decreasing. The well ran dry in 1994, and the property where it had been located, at the south end of the island, was sold at the end of 2012 for $80,000.

To read more about this interesting story, go to www.americantrails.org/resources/benefits/NatureKinBene.html, where you'll find "Pathways to Nature Kinship," presented by James A. Swan, PhD, at the Fifteenth National Trails Symposium in Redding, California, September 21–24, 2000, sponsored by American Trails.

Grosse Ile Historical Society (founded in 1959) maintains a museum in the old Michigan Central Railroad depot.

At the Grosse Ile Historical Museum, one can purchase the *Tour Guide to Grosse Ile*, which provides a map and a guide to 74 spots of interest on the island. One can also see a copy of the deed for Grosse Ile signed by the Potawatomi chiefs at the Grosse Ile Historical Museum (the original deed is in the Burton Historical Collection at the Detroit Public Library).

There is a second historical museum on the Grosse Ile, the Naval Air Station Museum, located in the Grosse Ile Township Hall (9601 Groh Rd.). The Naval Air Station Grosse Ile Virtual Museum is at http://nasgi.net. This museum was organized by a group of Naval Air Station Grosse Ile veterans, and the online version is a collection of stories about and pictures of the Naval Air Station on Grosse Ile from the 1920s until it was decommissioned in 1969.

The Treaty Tree Marker (the large boulder bearing a bronze table) on East River Road at the foot of Gray's Drive, between Ferry and Macomb Streets.

Grosse Ile North Channel Front Range Lighthouse—Built in 1894, this was the first and northernmost structure in a series of channel range lights constructed by the federal government to help ships avoid shallow areas in the Detroit River. The lighthouse was rebuilt in 1906 as a 40-foot octagonal white tower with an eight-sided lantern room. Deactivated in 1963, it is now under the Grosse Ile Historical Society's protection. The lighthouse is located on private property and is open to the public to tour only one day each year, usually in September. Visitors must be escorted by a historical society member. Call 734-671-6269 for reservations. For further information, see www.lighthouse.boatnerd.com/gallery/Detroit/grosseile.htm.

The chapel of St. James Episcopal Church on Grosse Ile. The red main entrance doors are dedicated to Lisette Denison Forth, born a slave in 1786, who crossed into Canada to gain freedom. When she died in 1866, she left $3,000 in her will to build a chapel.

St. Anne's Chapel of Sacred Heart Parish (East River Rd. and Church Rd)—In 1679, the Catholic missionary Father Louis Hennepin accompanied French explorer Robert de La Salle on the ship *Le Griffon* in exploring the Great Lakes. Father Hennepin came ashore and said Mass on the east shore of the island near the present site of St. Anne's Chapel, whose congregation dates back to 1869. In 1914 and 1915, islanders of all denominations brought back Livingston Channel stone from Stony Island to replace a little frame church with this charming permanent building.

Chapel at Saint James Episcopal Church (25150 East River Rd.)—Built in 1867 with a bequest from Elizabeth (Lisette) Denison Forth, who was born a slave in 1786 on a farm in the area that is now Macomb County in Michigan. In her lifetime, Forth crossed into Canada for five years to gain freedom. (Augustus B. Woodward, the first chief justice of the Michigan Territory, had declared that every "man coming into this Territory is by law of the land a freeman."[55] Under the ruling, this apparently was true for women as well, but Lisette had to first escape to Canada and then return to qualify as "coming into" the territory.) Upon her return, Forth saved her money and became an investor with the knowledge she had gained from her employers, Solomon Sibley and John Biddle. "In 1825, Elizabeth Denison ... purchased 48.5 acres of land from ... the Pontiac Company [chaired by Soloman Sibley] ... [and] became Pontiac's first black property owner."[56] Forth also developed a friendship with Biddle's wife Eliza. The two women, both Episcopalians, vowed to build a chapel. Forth died in 1866, remembered as a philanthropist for leaving half of her estate to build a church "where blacks and whites, poor and rich, could worship together."[57] Even on overcast days, light permeates into the beautiful Gothic-style wooden chapel through a large Tiffany window, called "Angel of Praise," which was installed in 1898.

Bishop's Cottage Bed and Breakfast

7573 Macomb St.

734-671-9191

www.bedandbreakfast.com/michigan-grosse-ile-bishopscottagebedbreakfast.html

www.facebook.com/pages/Bishops-Cottage-Bed-Breakfast/103143090655

Built in 1886 and located in the island's business district, Bishop's Cottage was originally the summer home of the Episcopal Reverend Gershom Mott William (he and Eliza Bradish Biddle were married in St. James Church in 1879). Today, this year-round B&B, surrounded by a beautiful garden, is operated by innkeeper Kathy Brockmiller, who grew up on Grosse Ile. One of just two establishments offering overnight accommodations on the island, Bishop's Cottage is also used for executive retreats, family gatherings, and special occasions such as bridal showers, dinner parties, and small weddings.

The B&B seasonally operates Bishop's Cottage Outdoor Garden Café, which often offers musical entertainment on Thursday evenings in the summer.

Grosse Ile Pilot House Hotel

9645 Groh Rd.

734-395-5195

www.gipilothouse.com/

www.facebook.com/pages/Grosse-Ile-Pilot-House/333881685706

Overnight accommodations are also available at the Pilot House, whose proprietor is Jim Cortis. "Built by Curtiss-Wright Aeronautical Corporation in 1929 as a part of a[n] . . . expansion program, the Grosse Ile Pilot was designed as a dining area and barracks for the flight school students the company was training at the Grosse Ile Air Field."[58] The base closed in 1969, and Arthur Cortis, Jim's father, established the Grosse Ile Pilot House in 1981.

This historic **World War II Officers Club** near the Grosse Ile Airport offers 12 hotel-type rooms equipped with kitchenettes, for overnight or long-term guest lodging. The upper floor is used for private dinner dances, weddings, and banquets, and the original dance floor and two original natural fireplaces are still in use.

Grosse Ile Memorial Cemetery (aka Island Memorial Cemetery) (10026 Groh Rd., by the airport).

Rucker Cemetery (aka Rucker-Fox Cemetery) (22775 West River Rd.).

Sacred Heart Catholic Cemetery (aka Grosse Ile Cemetery, Saint Anne Chapel of Sacred Heart Church Cemetery) (21526 East River Rd., at the corner of Church Rd. and East River Rd., behind the church).

ANOTHER INFLUENTIAL ISLANDER: CAMERON BEACH WATERMAN

While at Yale Law School, Cameron Beach Waterman, captain of the Yale University Rowing Crew, got the idea for the first outboard motor while working on a motorcycle engine. He took the plans he'd drawn up to a Detroit machine shop and with the result made a successful crossing from Grosse Ile to Trenton, Michigan, in 1905. Look for the historic plaque honoring Waterman and the first gas outboard motor near where he launched it in the Detroit River near the Angus Keith House at Horsemill and West River Road. And check out the 1915 Waterman engine at the Grosse Ile Historical Depot Museum, on display since its 2008 purchase and subsequent restoration by collector and authority on Waterman engines Robert Skinner.

Ten island historic sites are listed on the Michigan State Register of Historic Sites, and there are five additional Grosse Ile local **historic sites and war memorials**.

CULTURAL ATTRACTIONS

Enjoy some unusual flora and fauna on Grosse Ile. Here you can enjoy the unusual pairing of azaleas and alpacas (although you'll find them at different ends of the island).

Westcroft Gardens

21803 West River Rd.

734-675-1671 (call for hours)

www.westcroftgardens.com

Free admission

Established in 1776, Westcroft Gardens is the oldest family-owned and family-operated (currently by a seventh-generation family member, a descendant of the Macombs) farm in Michigan. Westcroft—meaning "West Farm"—Gardens is a plant nursery specializing in azaleas and rhododendrons, including hybrids created at Westcroft by former owner Ernest Stanton, but also offering trees, shrubs, perennials, annuals, wildflowers, herbs, and vegetable plants. The four-acre botanical garden is open to the public year-round, from dawn to dusk, and is available for weddings and other events.

Gibraltar Bay Alpaca Farm

8545 Groh Rd.

734-675-6220

www.facebook.com/pages/Gibraltar-Bay-Alpacas/165341756810556

Owners: Richard and Gail Steffke

Visitors are welcome from 10:00 a.m. to 4:00 p.m., Wednesday–Sunday. There is no admission fee; donations are accepted.

Gibraltar Bay breeds, sells, and boards huacaya (prounounced "wuh-kai-ya") alpacas (related to llamas). In 2012, 53 alpacas (and one dog alert to local coyotes; we watched him in action!) lived at the farm.

Alpacas are periodically shaved for their fleece, which is then made into yarn. Yarn made from alpaca wool is particularly warm and soft, not prickly. It is naturally water repellent and, having no lanolin, is hypoallergenic. The farm sells alpaca yarn as well as a number of items of made from it.

OTHER ISLAND THINGS TO DO

Hike—In addition to the nature trails, the bike trails are shared with walkers on the island; one can get in a lot of steps on this island.

Go birding—Check out the Detroit River International Wildlife Refuge's "Byways to Flyways," a driving tour of featured birding locations in the Windsor–Detroit metropolitan region, to see just how fine a location Grosse Ile is for birding: www.fws.gov/uploaded Files/Byways%20to%20Flyways%20-%20PDFMap.pdf.

The Detroit Audubon Society (www.detroitaudubon.org/bird_hotspots.html) considers Grosse Ile a birding hot spot of southeastern Michigan: "Great view of waterfowl along perimeter roads (East and West River Roads) and now there are a few places to stop and park and use an observation platform. The Grosse Ile Nature Area near the airport is open for public tours occasionally (contact the Grosse Ile Nature and Land Conservancy). Westcroft Gardens is great for songbirds in the winter. . . . Common Terns are now nesting on the piers on both the north and south bridges."

Some 50 huacaya alpacas roam at the Gibraltar Bay Alpaca Farm on Grosse Ile.

Other birds observed at the island's Westcroft Gardens include bald eagle, osprey, great gray owl, great horned owl, screech owl, kite, peregrine falcon, marsh hawk (aka northern harrier), red-tailed hawk, Cooper's hawk, and woodcock.

Go fishing—The Detroit International Wildlife Refuge, which includes islands, coastal wetlands, marshes, shoals, and riverfront lands along 48 miles (77 kilometers) of the Detroit River and western Lake Erie, is protecting and restoring habitat for 65 kinds of fish in Michigan and Ontario, Canada. Fisherman Dan Boileau, writing for *Angler's Digest*, claims, "The Detroit River provides some of the finest year-round fishing that Michigan has to offer," and he recommends, "[I]f you are interested in fishing for Northerns or Largemouth, try your favorite presentation in the bays, or cuts around Grosse Ile."[59] For some other advice about fishing the Detroit River, see http://tightlinecom.com/Anglers_Digest/fishing_river.htm.

Go waterfowl hunting—More than 3 million waterfowl are estimated to migrate through the Great Lakes area annually. The Detroit River International Wildlife Refuge opened three designated and managed hunt zone areas within the Brancheau Unit (across the

Trenton Channel of the Detroit River, on the mainland portion refuge) to hunt water-fowl in 2012, based on a plan written by the Department of Natural Resources and the U.S. Fish and Wildlife Service to allow waterfowl hunters to utilize some of the marsh on the refuge. For a copy of the U.S. Fish and Wildlife Service Detroit River International Wildlife Refuge hunting map and regulations, see www.fws.gov/uploadedFiles/DTR .Hunt12web(2).pdf.

Drink some island wine—

Island Winery

8400 Concord Rd.

Grosse Ile, MI 48138

734-818-1501

www.enjoyislandwines.com

www.facebook.com/Islandwinerymi/info?tab=overview

Founded in 2012 by two island couples, the winery makes, bottles, and sells wine made from fruit concentrate for $10 a bottle from the owners' island home. Their first website quoted Galileo: "Wine is sunlight held together by water"—much like Grosse Ile, one might add. You can order the wine for drinking on-site at Sharkey's Tavern on West River Road and can find Island Winery's Island Red as well as their fruit varieties of Blackberry Breeze, Dragon Fruit Sunset, Strawberry Tidal Wave, Pomegranate Breeze, and White Cranberry Shipwreck available for sale at a number of local stores.

SPECIAL ISLAND EVENTS

Islandfest (June)—A three-day festival (formerly called the Azalea Festival) is typically held the weekend after Memorial Day weekend and includes a parade and fireworks as well as events such as a pancake breakfast, steak dinner, crab races, a car show, and lots of music (www.grosseile.com/html/community/Islandfest.html).

Tour of the Grosse Ile North Channel Lighthouse (September)—The Grosse Ile North Channel Light is located on private property and is open to the public only one day each year (www.gihistory.org/).

Phantom Forest Halloween Hayrides (October)—At Halloween, Westcroft Gardens transforms 13 acres of the 27-acre farm into the Phantom Forest, the perfect place for a hayride (ww.westcroftgardens.com/halloweenhayrides).

Holiday Gift Boutique (November and December)—Featuring the work of Grosse Ile artisans and crafters, the Grosse Ile Historical Society sponsors a holiday store in the Customs House on weekends before Christmas (www.gihistory.org/shopping.html).

Boar's Head Festival (December)—Begun in 1980 and presented six times in December every four years (most recently performed in 2015), the Boar's Head Festival is produced by five churches and involves over 600 community members in the cast and production. The festival includes the Christmas story; the Twelve Days of Christmas presented as a singing, dancing, and acting routine; and various choral and orchestral presentations. The arrival of the king and queen of the realm, the presentation of the boar's head, and the Yule log ceremony are all reenacted during the festival (http://boarsheadgi.com/).

For More Island Information

Grosse Ile Historical Society

25000 East River Rd.

Grosse Ile Township, MI 48138

734- 675-1250

www.gihistory.org

Hours: Thursday, 10:00 a.m.–noon; Sunday, 1:00 p.m.–4:00 p.m.

Naval Air Station Museum

(Located in the Grosse Ile Township Hall)

9601 Groh Rd.

Grosse Ile Township, MI 48138

734-675-1250

http://nasgi.net (Naval Air Station Grosse Ile Virtual Museum)

Monday–Friday, 8:00 a.m.–5:00 p.m.

Official Grosse Ile Township website—www.grosseile.com.

Grosse Ile Nature and Land Conservancy—www.ginlc.org.

The Ile Camera—Grosse Ile was still served by a weekly (Friday) newspaper when I visited. Started in April 1945 "by and for kids," it was initially published biweekly by two teenage girls; it was taken over by neighbors when, after a year and a half, there were 100 subscribers in the community. It became a weekly newspaper in 1979. (Update: In July 2015 the newspaper folded, and Grosse Ile news and information began appearing in the digital and print editions of the *News-Herald.*)

Grosse Ile Then and Now: An Island Sketchbook and Tour Guide (Grosse Ile Historical Society, 2010)—A series of historic views of Grosse Ile from the *Ile Camera,* 1948–53, prints by William Thomas (Tommy) Woodward with commentary by Barbara Woodward, available from the Grosse Ile Historical Depot Museum. The work includes a map to 50 historical sites.

Grosse Ile, by the Grosse Ile Historical Society (Mount Pleasant, SC: Arcadia, 2007).

The Treaty Tree and Memorial Tablet (Lansing, MI: Women's Improvement Association, 1907).

U.S. Naval Air Station Grosse Ile, by Kenneth M. Keisle, Grosse Ile Historical Society (Mount Pleasant, SC: Arcadia, 2011).

The Deep Roots: A History of Grosse Ile, Michigan, to July 6, 1876, by Isabella E. Swan (Grosse Ile: self-published, 1976).

Lisette, by Isabella E. Swan (Grosse Ile: self-published, 1965).

Looking for Lisette: In Quest of an American Original, by Mark F. McPherson (Dexter, MI: Mage Press in conjunction with Thomson-Shore, 2001).

A Fluid Frontier: Slavery, Resistance, and the Underground Railroad in the Detroit River Borderland, edited by Karolyn Smardz Frost and Veta Smith Tucker (Detroit: Wayne State University Press, 2016).

"Cameron Waterman and His Waterman Marine Motor Co.," by W. J. Webb, *Antique Outboarder,* January 1970.

Our Little Island Grosse Ile, by Julie J. Keith (1931; repr., Grosse Ile Historical Society 1962)—Although out of print, this book is available in the original 1931 edition online through HathiTrust Digital Library at the University of Michigan. The 1962 reprint is available at the University of Michigan's Bentley Historical Library in Ann Arbor and the Library of Michigan in Lansing.

The Ark of God: A History of the Episcopal Church, Grosse Ile, Michigan by Isabella E. Swan (1968).

How You Can Support the Island

Grosse Ile Historical Society
25000 East River Rd.
Grosse Ile Township, MI 48138
734- 675-1250
www.gihistory.org

Naval Air Station Museum
9601 Groh Rd.
Grosse Ile Township, MI 48138
734-675-1250
http://nasgi.net (Naval Air Station Grosse Ile Virtual Museum)

Grosse Ile Nature and Land Conservancy
PO Box 12
Grosse Ile, MI 48138
www.ginlc.org

The Grosse Ile Nature and Land Conservancy (GINLC) mission statement reads, "To promote, for public benefit, the preservation, stewardship, and understanding of the natural resources in the Township of Grosse Ile and surrounding areas." The conservancy "works to achieve its goal of protecting land through land acquisition, conservation easements, and educational projects. . . . Through gift or purchase, [the conservancy members] secure ownership of natural land needed to protect our [area's] beauty and fragile habitats." Formed in 1993, the GINLC has no paid positions; all donations are applied directly to projects.

Gibraltar Bay Unit of the Detroit River International Wildlife Refuge
Large Lakes Research Station
9311 Groh Rd.
Grosse Ile, MI 48138
734-692-7608
www.fws.gov/midwest/detroitriver/

Established on December 21, 2001, the Detroit River International Wildlife Refuge is the first international refuge in North America and one of the few urban ones in the nation. The refuge, with Grosse Ile at its center, is one of over 540 such refuges managed by the U.S. Fish and Wildlife Service.

Parting Thoughts

April 26, 4:45 p.m.
Grosse Ile

In the afternoon, with the wind off the river at our backs, Val and I pedaled up to St. James Church. The redbuds were in bloom against the sandstone brick walls of the church, against the brown paneling of the chapel, and in glorious contrast to the bright-red Lisette Denison doors. We rode around back, dismounted from our bikes, and found Val's mom's name on the

Memorial Garden plaque: Vivian B. Lewis (1913–2009). Dwarf iris of a gorgeous purple shot with maroon veins and fuzzed with bright lavender stamens bloomed against the warmth of the garden wall.

This island, such a place to grow up. Val tells me about her dad, who died when she was in high school, taking her ice-skating in Elizabeth Park when she was young, before he was sick. The ice rink, the cold off the river, the hot chocolate—it feels like my friend's memory has become one of mine, the house of her childhood on the West River Road, where I photographed her wedding, a place I could return to and call home.

Bob-Lo Island, Ontario

ONCE UPON A TIME

August 21, 2014, 1:17 p.m.
Bob-Lo Island Beach House Restaurant

My most memorable visit to Bob-Lo Island, before today, was in June 1968. On that trip, my companions on the Bob-Lo Excursion Line steamer were other ninth graders from Livonia's Holmes Junior High. We were participating in a totally sanctioned, transportation-provided-by-the-school-district, ship-them-off-to-the-biggest-and-best-amusement-park-around "Ninth-Grade Skip Day." I'd never heard of Cedar Point Amusement Park in Sandusky, Ohio, back then, and the only other amusement park I knew of, Edgewater Park on Detroit's west side, was less than one-tenth the size of Bob-Lo—and you took a boat to get to Bob-Lo.

We would have boarded either the *Ste. Claire* or the *Columbia*, but no cell phone cameras documented that embarkation, and carrying a Kodak Instamatic simply would not have been cool. After a 20-mile cruise on the Detroit River, almost an hour and a half of music, talking and yelling, flirting and laughing, we arrived. On that visit, the very air between the Wild Mouse and the Whip was fraught with hormones dancing to a top 10 soundtrack, which included "Sitting on the Dock of the Bay" and "Grazing in the Grass."

Over four decades later, on my last island research trip, I am spending an afternoon exploring what is left of Bob-Lo today—a few ruins sparking lots of memories—with my husband, Craig.

GETTING THERE: Car ferry; private boat

GETTING AROUND: Cars allowed only at the northeast end of the island by the ferry dock, in the condominium parking lot, and in the residential development; bring your own bike

OVERNIGHT ACCOMMODATIONS: Limited options: one vacation rental only

FOOD: Limited options: one restaurant

DAY TRIP? Yes, recommended

STATE / PROVINCIAL / NATIONAL PARK? No

In this century, when you disembark from the five-minute ride on the very small, pretty empty ferry, which departs from Canada, you find yourself adjacent to a private, very well-to-do residential area. North of the road leading from the ferry dock is the north-end subdivision of mini-mansions and duplexes, with an emphasis on stone and heavy on Victorian-style turrets. On the south side of the road leading from the ferry dock is a five-story condominium.

Paved or gravel trails that at one time accommodated visitors to the Bob-Lo Amusement Park and are suitable for bike riding or hiking, cover all of the island, with two exceptions. One is the north-end subdivision, the only place where motor vehicles are allowed and where you'll find three paved streets, Gold Coast Drive, Crystal Bay Drive, and Whitewood Ridge Boulevard, in addition to Bob-Lo Island Boulevard, which leads to and from the ferry. People who live in the residential areas use golf carts to get to the community pool in the center of the island. The other exception is White Sands, the Essex region conservation area, a popular boating area located at the south end of the island and traversed by trail.

One can easily see why Bob-Lo Island is now billed as a "Marina Resort Community," but Bob-Lo exhibits the most profound split personality of any island—perhaps any place—I've ever been. Which may not be surprising, given that it's been many things to many people over the centuries, including a camp for European explorers, the site of a French Catholic mission, within reach of a British fort, headquarters for Shawnee chief Tecumseh during the War of 1812, an invasion site for Canadian patriots during the Upper Canada Rebellion and, more recently, a picnic spot, a dance venue, an amusement park, and a suburban retreat. We know from recorded history that four Algonquin and Iroquoian tribes, the Ojibwe, the Ottawa, the Potawatomi, and the Wyandot (Huron) used this island. One source claims the original Wyandot name of the island was Etiowiteedannenti (which one writer claims means "Peopled Island of White Wood Guarding the Entrance"), presumably the entrance to Lake Erie or the Detoit River.[60] The first recorded passage to the island, which was named Bois Blanc ("White Wood") by the French, dates from 1670. After the French explorers came, in succession, the Jesuits, the British, Canadians, slaves (traveling the Underground Railroad), American and Canadian pleasure seekers, and investors.

How to Get There

If you're not familiar with international geography in the Detroit River area, it may seem odd that Bob-Lo Island, although it belongs to Canada, is the *southernmost* of the three Detroit River islands accessible by bridge or ferry. To get to Bob-Lo Island in the twenty-first century, you take a ferry from Amherstburg, Ontario, instead of from the old dock on Jefferson Avenue in Detroit.

The ferry leaves every 20 minutes from a dock next to the Bob-Lo Discovery Centre at 340 Dalhousie in Amherstburg, Ontario. The center serves as sales office for Amico Properties, which has developed a "Marina Resort Community" of approximately 200 units and 70 people at the north end of the island and whose draft plan for a subdivision of 209 lots at the south end received unanimous support from the town of Amherstburg in August 2014.

The ride across the Amherstburg Channel takes five minutes (instead of the 80 minutes it used to take when one departed from the other side of the border) and is courtesy of the 16-car ferry *Ste. Claire V*[61] owned by Amico (aka the Bob-Lo Island Ferry Service and the Amherstburg Ferry Company).

Visit www.boblo.ca/amherstburg-ferry-company for the current ferry fare; special rates for pedestrians, restaurant patrons, or potential real-estate investors may apply.

Boaters can dock at the Bob-Lo Wharf on the west side of the island.

What to Expect

Expect not a lot of activity outside of the quiet north-end development or the west-side marina and restaurant area. Expect to see few other people outside of those two areas if you walk or ride your bike around the island. If it's a pleasant day for boating on the river, you may see other people at the restaurant on the west side of the island and boaters at the south end's White Sands Conservation Area. If you have been to the island before in the last decade, expect to see fewer remains of the amusement park. And if the developer's dreams come true, expect to see plenty of construction activity, eventually over just about every inch of the island other than the conservation area (and one would hope the lighthouse and blockhouse would be protected as having some significant historical value).

Paths to Adventure

NATURAL SITES

White Sands Conservation Area—Bob-Lo Island once ended at the lighthouse. The white sand beach was created in 1957 when a bar of sand in the mouth of the river was dredged by the U.S. Army Corps of Engineers as they deepened the Amherstburg Channel to meet St. Lawrence Seaway standards. Today, a spit of sand extends over a mile (1.6 kilometers) toward the mouth of the river and Lake Erie: perfect for a hike! For more information, see www.erca.org/conservation-areas-events/conservation-areas/white-sands.

If you get lucky, you may see a bit of nature in the ruins of Bob-Lo Island Amusement Park, as we did: wild turkey in the brush and deer in the soybean field. Fields are being

Buck in the soybeans: nature's and agriculture's attempt to reclaim Bob-Lo Island.

Bob-Lo Island's Dance Pavilion, a 35,000-square-foot building of stone and steel that opened in 1913, the largest dance pavillion in North America until 1925.

cultivated in the middle of the island these days, and at least one six-point buck seemed pretty happy about that development.

Most exciting was the coyote on the path. Riding my bike on a trail that runs up the middle of the island, with the carousel building on my left and the powerhouse on my right, I came upon a T-intersection buried amid tall, tall grass. Suddenly, without warning, in the middle of the trail, directly in the line of my front bike tire was a relatively large mammal. The animal had trotted out into the intersection, clearly not expecting anyone to be on the trail. Encountering me, the coyote froze for a moment, then turned and shot back up the path, hind legs trying to gain purchase on the crushed limestone path.

HISTORY PRESERVED

American-Canadian Friendship Memorial (aka the Sailor's Monument)—Look for the anchor set atop a concrete monument between the condominium building and river.

Remains of Bob-Lo Island as summer playground—Play amateur archaeologist and search for what remains from times past: the old dance hall pavilion (attributed to Albert Kahn, it was actually built by John Scott in 1913), the washrooms building, the miniature golf course, the Amherstburg and Gibraltar dock terminal, the barge dock, Bob-Lo Island Sky Tower, the dodgem car building, the powerhouse, and the carousel building.

1836 Bois Blanc Island Lighthouse—A National Historic Site of Canada, at the south end of the island, this is not open to the public.

1839 Bois Blanc South British Army blockhouse—Near the lighthouse at the south end of the island. For the story of its recent restoration, see http://blogs.windsorstar.com/news/restored-boblo-island-blockhouse-a-labour-of-love-for-retired-school-teacher.

Visible from the White Sands Conservation Area: (*right*) the Bois Blanc Island Lighthouse, built in 1836; (*center*) the roof of the 1839 British block-house, rebuilt in 2014; and (*left*) the Bob-Lo Sky Tower, a relic from the island's amusement park era.

CULTURAL ATTRACTIONS

Bob-Lo Island Beach House Restaurant—Located at the Bob-Lo Island Marina, you'll find this the perfect place for refreshment. If you chose to sit at an outdoor table, you may see the top of a down-bound freighter as it goes through the Livingstone Channel, which lies between Grosse Ile and Bob-Lo Island.

Captain Bob's Ice Cream Shack—For dessert, enjoy an ice cream cone.

For More Island Information

Boblo Development, Inc.—www.boblo.ca.

Summer Dreams: The Story of Bob-Lo Island, by Patrick Livingston (Detroit: Wayne State University Press, 2008).

Bob-Lo: An Island in Troubled Waters, by Annessa Carlisle (Royal Oak, MI: Momentum Books, 2005).

Bob-Lo Revisited, by Bill Rauhauser (Chicago: Lorentz, 2003)—A collection of 100 photographs of the Bob-Lo amusement park.

To read more about Bob-Lo Island, go to http://greatlakesislandescapes.com, click on "Blog," and select "Bob-Lo Island Ghosts."

How You Can Support the Island

Each of these institutions (*not* on Bob-Lo) could also provide an interesting adventure in and of itself! Check the websites for more information, including the days and hours of operation.

Dossin Great Lakes Museum
100 Strand
Belle Isle, Detroit, MI
313-833-5538
www.detroithistorical.org/dossin-great-lakes-museum
    Bob-Lo Island artifacts such as swan boats, midway games, maps, and signs are on permanent display.

Marsh Historical Collection
235A Dalhousie St.
Amherstburg, ON, Canada N9V 1W6
519-736-9191
www.marshcollection.org
    According to the website, "The Marsh Collection Society is a non-profit organization established in 1983. It was initially based on the collection of local historic papers, books and artifacts gathered throughout their lives by the late Arthur W. Marsh (1872–1940), his son John A. Marsh (1901–1993) and his daughter Helen M. Marsh (1900–1986), editors and publishers of the Amherstburg Echo for over 80 years. It was their wish and mandate of the Society 'to collect, preserve and encourage research into the heritage of Amherstburg and the lower Detroit River district' and to maintain a facility and staff who would assist researchers of local history and genealogy."

Parting Thoughts

August 21, 2014
Back on the mainland

Before biking around the island, Craig and I rode to the Beach House Restaurant, parked our bikes, and ordered perch baskets and beers, a day-after birthday celebration for him. We chatted with our waitress, Shelley, from mainland Amherstburg, watched the top of a freighter move through the Livingstone Channel, and then set off to explore the island.

    After we'd checked out the restored blockhouse and the remains of the lighthouse, we locked our bikes and hiked to the end of the White Sands Conservation Area, to the mouth of the Detroit River. Out on Lake Erie, we saw the *Lake Guardian*, a research vessel that is owned by the U.S. Environmental Agency and serves on the Great Lakes. After we'd walked back along the mile of sandy trail, and with the sky becoming overcast, we started off on our bikes again. We saw two bucks in a soybean field and a wild turkey in the brush, and when we had ridden past what remained to be seen, we had ice cream at the marina.

Biking through the sterile north-end "island community," we noticed a white wood-frame two-story house on the river, screened off by woods from the unattractive-to-my-eyes "luxury" houses of the development. Could this be the cottage of Dorothy Tresness, the last summer resident, known as the "longest-residing private citizen" of Bob-Lo? She had built the cottage in 1956 with her husband, Orin, and she was still there in October 2004 when—for the first time in 64 years, she finally had electricity—having fought one developer after another for her right to remain.[62] She died in 2009 in Florida, far away from her "slice of island paradise." A paradise that clearly is no more.[63]

And then we hightailed it to the ferry, leaving the island with no regrets, with the uncertainty of a storm brewing behind us.

Lake Erie Islands

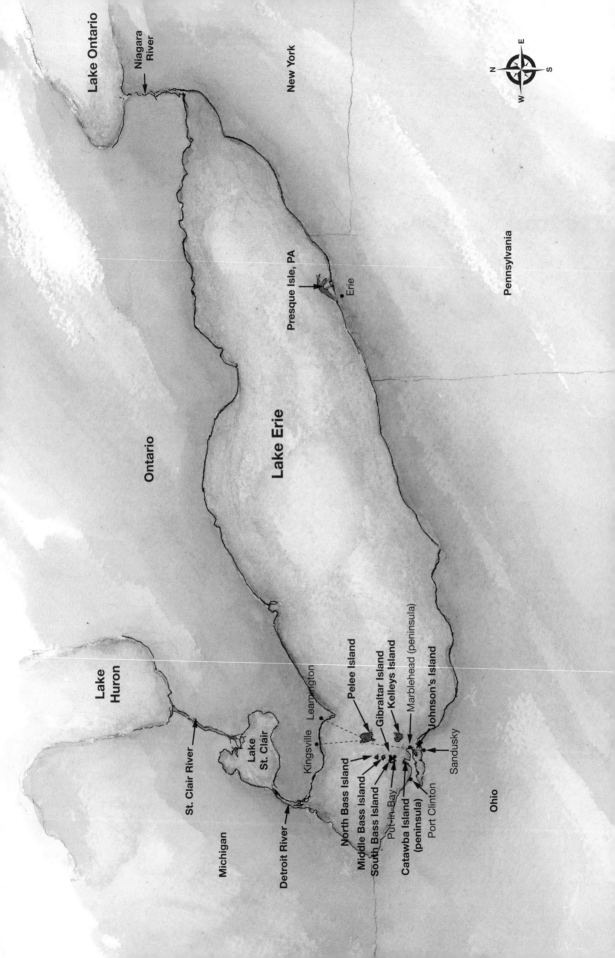

An Introduction to Lake Erie

Lake Erie is the fourth-largest lake of the Great Lakes by surface area, with just under 10,000 square miles (25,900 square kilometers) of lake and 871 miles (1,402 kilometers) of shoreline. The lake measures 241 miles (388 kilometers) from east to west and 57 miles (92 kilometers) from north to south. In terms of volume, however, Lake Erie is the smallest of the Great Lakes, with an average depth of only 62 feet and a deepest point of 210 feet. The lake's shallow depth makes it particularly prone to storm surges, which may alter the water level by eight to 10 feet at its western and eastern ends, and to dangerous navigation conditions, particularly in November storms. Lake Erie has seen more than its share of shipwrecks since La Salle set sail on it in *Le Griffon* in 1679.[64]

The border between the United States and Canada just about splits the shoreline in half: Lake Erie's north shore is in Ontario, and its south shore is primarily in Ohio. The western tip of the lake touches southeastern Michigan where the Detroit River flows into Lake Erie, and at the eastern end, after the lakeshore has extended into Pennsylvania (for a length of only about 51 miles/82 kilometers) and New York, the lake drains into the Niagara River. The eastern end of the lake "tilts" in a northerly direction. This is the first incidence in the Great Lakes system (other than in the case of the Lake Michigan portion of Lake Michigan-Huron) that the "bowls" of the Great Lakes Basin on the gentle downward slope, in terms of elevation, begin to tip northward. Lake Erie's average elevation is 569 feet, only eight feet lower than Lake Michigan-Huron.

The name of the lake came from the Erie tribe's Iroquoian word *erielhonan,* meaning "long tail." The Erie tribe, also called Chat (French for "cat"), Cat Nation, or People from the Place of the Puma, lived on the south shore of the lake in agricultural villages in what is now northern Ohio, northwestern Pennsylvania, and western New York. The Erie tribe's demise—caused by great war casualties and by the fact that those who survived were "adopted" into the opposing tribe as refugees—came at the hands of other Iroquoian tribes, like the Seneca, who were punishing the Eries for their support of the Huron in their fur trade with the French during the seventeenth-century Beaver Wars.

A number of islands in Lake Erie's Western Basin are accessible by ferry or bridge.

Kelleys Island—A 4.4-square-mile (11.4-square-kilometer) Ohio island (the largest American island in Lake Erie) about five miles (eight kilometers) offshore from Marblehead, Ohio (at the tip of the Marblehead Peninsula) via a 20-minute ride on one of the Kelleys Island Ferry Boat Line's vehicular ferries.

South Bass Island (aka Put-in-Bay, the name of the large bay on the northern side of the island)—A 2.5-square-mile (6.5-square-kilometer) Ohio island three miles (five kilometers)

THE BASIN'S WATER IGNITES, THE GREAT LAKES ARE INVADED, AND ERIE BLOOMS

Lake Erie's basin has been more densely populated than the areas around the other four Great Lakes. By the 1960s, Lake Erie was very polluted as a result of heavy industry in Cleveland and other rust belt cities along its shores. Factories dumped pollutants into the lake and into the rivers that flow into the lake. One of these, the Cuyahoga River, caught fire on June 22, 1969.

This was not the first time or the worst time the river had caught fire from pollutants. Since 1868, the river had burned at least 13 times; the worst fire, which caused over $1 million in damage to boats, a bridge, and a riverfront office building, was in 1952. The 1969 fire was different in its outcome however, as it prompted the federal government to address water pollution throughout the country. In 1972, Congress passed the Clean Water Act, and the United States and Canada signed the Great Lakes Water Quality Agreement to lower the amount of pollutants entering all of the Great Lakes.

The first sign of the invasion of nonnative zebra mussels, believed to have been carried in the ballast tanks of ships from Western European ports traveling the St. Lawrence Seaway, showed up in Lake St. Clair in June 1988; soon after they were found in Lake Erie. These small freshwater mussels are believed to be responsible for a number of bad things: a major decrease in the concentration of both oxygen and chlorophyll in some bodies of water, an avian botulism that has killed tens of thousands of birds in the Great Lakes in the last 20 years, and the near extinction of many species in the Great Lakes system, as the invasive species bests native species in the competition for food and suffocates native clams and mussels by growing on top of them.

Nonetheless, there was an upside to the introduction of zebra mussels: they have increased the population and size of smallmouth bass in Lake Erie (and yellow perch in Lake St. Clair) by cleansing the lakes, which has resulted in better sunlight penetration and increased growth of native algae at deeper levels, increased water visibility, and the filtering out of pollutants. There is no doubt that while costing businesses—particularly power companies—and municipalities over $5 billion since they arrived in our waters, zebra mussels have also significantly helped to clean up Lake Erie.

In June 2014, Canadian conservation authorities announced that a test performed in a lakefront harbor in Manitoba using liquid fertilizer to kill invasive zebra mussels was successful.

Today, the pollutant issue in Lake Erie is related to extensive shoreline farming throughout the lake's basin of fertile soil. This heavy agriculture has resulted in a significant amount of phosphorus runoff from manure, which feeds the blue-green algae (cyanobacteria) growing in shallow Lake Erie. These algae can produce microcystin, a toxin that can cause nerve and liver damage in people and animals. In August 2014, Toledo's water was deemed undrinkable for two days due to an algae bloom in Lake Erie's Maumee Bay. In 2015, two legislative bills were introduced to ban the practice of spreading manure on frozen or rain-soaked fields. Environmental groups claim these bills are not enough, that Ohio's response is too slow and too weak and won't achieve the recommended 40 percent reduction in phosphorus runoff.

from Catawba, Ohio (at the tip of the Catawba Island peninsula) via a less-than-20-minute ride on one of the Miller Boat Line vehicular ferries.

Middle Bass Island—An 805-acre Ohio island less than two miles (three kilometers) from South Bass Island aboard the *Sonny S* passenger ferry belonging to Middle Bass Ferry or about five miles (eight kilometers) from Catawba, Ohio, via the Miller Boat Line (45 minutes).

Pelee Island—A 16-square-mile (42-square-kilometer) Ontario island, the largest island in Lake Erie, accessible via an hour-and-a-half vehicular ferry boat ride on the MV *Jiimaan* or the MV *Pelee Islander* run by the Pelee Island Transportation Company out of either Kingsville or Leamington, depending on the time of year, and the MV *Pelee Islander* from Sandusky, Ohio (during some of the sailing season).

Johnson's Island—Located in Lake Erie's Sandusky Bay, this small 300-acre Ohio island is accessible by bridge, connected to the mainland at the west end of Marblehead Peninsula's south shore by the Johnson's Island Causeway. This island contains seasonal cottages and is all private land except for the Confederate Civil War Cemetery, which is just on the island side of the causeway.

In addition, there are two former islands that are currently peninsulas in Lake Erie:

Catawba Island—An Ohio peninsula that branches off north from the east-west Marblehead Peninsula, Catawba was an island proper at one time in relatively recent history. For more about Catawba Island, in the way of stories told about the Catawba Cliffs area in the northwest part of the island, pick up a copy of *Legends of Catawba,* edited by Don Rhodes (2008); the original edition was created to help sell lots in the area by Henry W. Prescott for the J. H. Bellow Company in 1922. For more about Catawba Island today, visit http://greatlakesislandescapes.com, click on "Blog," and select to read "The 'Non-Island' of Catawba Island."

Presque Isle—Today, Pennsylvania's Presque Isle State Park covers the entire peninsula. As recently as 1864 Presque Isle (French for "almost island") was a true island. Only by the strenuous efforts of the Army Corps of Engineers has the island remained attached to the mainland over the last 150 years. The work involves shoring up maintenance at the neck of the peninsula where Pennsylvania Route 832 becomes Peninsula Drive as well as a series of other alterations that prevent the sand ridge peninsula from migrating farther westward than it is already in the process of doing.

For more information on Lake Erie, visit www.great-lakes.net/erie.html and consider looking for a used or library copy of the American Lake Series volume *Lake Erie,* by Harlan Hatcher (Indianapolis: Bobbs-Merrill, 1945).

Other books on the Lake Erie islands include:

Explore the Lake Erie Islands: A Guide to Nature and History along the Lake Erie Coastal Ohio Trail, by Art Weber and Melinda Huntley (n.p.: Lake Erie Coastal Ohio Trail National Scenic Byway, Ohio Chapter of the Nature Conservancy, Ohio Sea Grant, 2009).

Lake Erie Islands: Sketches and Stories of the First Century after the Battle of Lake Erie, edited by Michael Gora (Put-in-Bay, OH: Lake Erie Islands Historical Society, 2004).

The Beginnings and Tales of the Lake Erie Islands, by Jessie A. Martin (n.p.: J. A. Martin, 1990).

Ohio's Lake Erie Islands: A Brief History in Words and Pictures, by Chad Waffen (Bay Village, OH: Westfalia, 2010).

1812: A Traveler's Guide to the War That Defined a Continent, by National Geographic (Washington, DC: National Geographic, 2013).

The War of 1812: Official National Park Service Handbook, edited by the Northeast Regional Office of the National Park Service (Fort Washington, PA: Eastern National, 2013)—Contains a timeline of the war and 10 brief essays written by experts in the field.

For more information on the challenges that invasive species pose to the Great Lakes, read *Lake Invaders: Invasive Species and the Battle for the Future of the Great Lakes,* by William Rapai (Detroit: Wayne State University Press, 2016).

Pelee Island, Ontario

FOR THE BIRDS AND FOR WRITERS

August 17, 2013, 10:50 a.m.
Aboard the Pelee Islander

A hot August day. Today's 11:00 ferry from the Kingsville dock is the *Pelee Islander*, the "little" ferry, put in service in 1960. The Canadian flag, twisted once around its pole, flaps in a slight breeze. Up on deck are families, couples—some young and some retired—and dogs. Passengers lean over the rails, watch goods being loaded onto the ferry behind their cars, snap pictures of the piles of sand and gravel alongside the fishing docks adjacent to the boat at the Kingsville Coal and Dock Company, leaf through their tourist guides to Essex County. There is nervous laughter from those passengers who jump at the sound of the ferry's five-minute warning blast.

Most passengers are seated under the portion of the upper deck shaded by laced-on canvas awnings. A few are scattered in the hot sun at the back, preparing to see where we've already been. While docked, however, those of us so seated are watching a fisherman on the breakwater and looking out toward the island, just an hour and a half's transit in this fine weather but barely discernible in the haze of this hot summer day.

The second the pull-away blast sounds, the engines power up, and the boat glides from the dock. The calm lake, wavelets glistening, invites us to relax.

In French, *pelée* means "bare." Some say that the word was employed as a warning to sailors, followed by an exclamation point: "Pelée!" The warning was not about the island but referred to what could not be seen *around* the island. Although there *appears* to be a wide stretch of water between the end of Point Pelee and the closest point of Pelee Island, geologically, the island is an extension of the point. While above the water the limestone surface is tree covered on both the mainland and island ends, beneath the lake the bare limestone lurks. This limestone formation connecting peninsula and island extends underwater, where it is "bare" (of trees, that is) and very dangerous. Only in one marked passage—the Pelee Passage— is the trough between the peninsula and the island deep enough for ships to go through, and today they line up to do so in single file. In the past, ships that did not head the "*Pelée!*" warning were likely candidates to be involved in one of the more than 200 shipwrecks that lie between Point Pelee and Pelee Island.

If I am asked—as I just was on the ferry—how to proceed in exploring Pelee, I suggest that regardless of whether one plans to get around by foot, bike, or motor vehicle, Pelee explorers can best begin their discovery of the island at the Pelee Island Heritage Centre, located in the old Township Hall in the town of West Dock, directly across from where the ferry docks. There you will learn a lot about what you'll be seeing on the island in addition to some history of the island (including information on the numerous nearby shipwrecks) and descriptions of the flora and fauna. The best selection of books about Pelee is available for sale at the Heritage Centre, many by Ron Tiessen, founder and former director.

Once you leave the Heritage Centre, you are presented with a number of choices. The Pelee Island Winery's Wine Pavilion is within easy walking distance of West Dock, south along the west shore. The other town on the island is Scudder, across the island on North Bay, held between the arms of Lighthouse Point and Sheridan Point. In the twentieth century, the ferry left year-round from Kingsville and docked at Scudder, or North Dock, as it is called. A bike ride around the island will get you to Scudder as well as to many of the natural and historic sites that await you. There are bikes for rent near the ferry dock in West Dock if you didn't bring your own. Consider heading to one, or to all four, of the peninsulas of the island: hike to the water at Fish Point through the Carolinian forest, check out Mill Point with its limestone shelf beach, go to Lighthouse Point for the historic lighthouse, and visit the cemetery on Sheridan Point.

Stretched out on my back on the ferry's warm bench in the sun, I could nap. Now that we've passed the end of the over-four-mile-long peninsula that is Point Pelee, the site of Point Pelee National Park, other than distant lined-up freighters and the helicopter pad in the middle of the Pelee Passage, here's what's on the lake: cormorants (black "sea crows"), the occasional seagull looking for a handout, a pleasure boat or two.

As the ferry continues to head south, the long length of the Point Pelee Peninsula finally disappears from our eastern view, and at about exactly the trip's halfway point, we enter the Pelee Passage marked by the helicopter pad off in the distance, and the island's most northern point appears to the east across the expense of North Bay: Lighthouse Point. In the summer, it's difficult to distinguish the Pelee Lighthouse from the trees, mainly poplar, at the farthest point north on the island. Next, the private, historic Pelee Club with its broken dock appears on the western side of North Bay, on the west shore of the Sheridan Point, the shorter of the two arms that form the North Bay. The town of Scudder is between Lighthouse Point and Sheridan Point. Hulda's Rock is just off of Sheridan Point. Before the ferry ties up at West Dock, it will pass cottages in the Vin Villa Estates and more along West Shore Road, the strip of sand at Sunset Beach, and the airport runway.

On the west side of the ferry, other islands of the Lake Erie Archipelago, of which Pelee Island is the largest, appear. In the distance are North Bass, Middle Bass, South Bass (Put-in-Bay), and farther south are Kelleys Island and Middle Island.

If you take the 11:00 *Pelee Islander*, as I have, you will likely pass the 12:00 MV *Jiimaan* as it heads back to the mainland between the smaller ferry and the islands to the west, another good photo op. (The *Islander*, which has a small counter selling coffee and snacks, provides a different experience from that of the *Jiimaan*, which has a cafeteria serving beer and wine as well as burgers and fish-and-chip fare.)

You could plan to eat dinner at the Anchor and Wheel Inn, preferably on the lovely screened-in porch, or on Scudder Beach Bar and Grill's deck, or visit Conorlee's Bakery and order a pizza or put together a picnic from the full deli case. Whatever you do, make sure you've found a spot on the west shore by sunset. Sunset Beach is a good choice if you're not staying overnight on the west shore or North Bay (from where you can see both sunrise and sunset).

Sit outside after sunset. The breeze of the lake generally carries away mosquitoes or flies. (If you experience either, just go around to the other side of the island; they generally won't be on both sides at the same time.) Slow down, enjoy what's important in the moment: watch the colors in the sky streak and change, the lake below shifting them again, wave by wave.

GETTING THERE: Car ferry; daily air service; private boat or plane

GETTING AROUND: Bring your car and/or bike and/or kayak; bicycle rentals; tours

OVERNIGHT ACCOMMODATIONS: Inns, motel, B&Bs; vacation rentals; campgrounds

FOOD: Restaurants and wine pavilion; groceries

DAY TRIP? Yes, but you could easily fill a week with island adventures!

STATE / PROVINCIAL / NATIONAL PARK? No, but two provincial nature reserves are on the island:

Fish Point Provincial Nature Reserve

Lighthouse Point Provincial Nature Reserve

Pelee Island, at 28 square miles (73 square kilometers), is the largest island in Lake Erie. It is also the southernmost inhabited landmass of Canada.

Pelee Island lies between the peninsula of Point Pelee National Park in Leamington, Ontario, on the north shore of Lake Erie and the Marblehead Peninsula, just north of Sandusky, Ohio, on the south shore. The island is located about 10 miles (16 kilometers)—an hour-and-a-half ferry ride—from Kingsville or Leamington, Ontario, and is a part of Lake Erie's archipelago of 22 islands in the Western Basin. The island population of approximately 275 year-round residents ("islanders") swells to over 1,000 with seasonal residents ("cottagers") during the summer months.

Another time when the population annually swells is for Springsong weekend. There are some annual events on Great Lakes Basin islands that are so wonderful visitors return to enjoy them year after year. The best such event I know of is Springsong weekend on Pelee

WHAT'S FARTHER SOUTH IN CANADA THAN PELEE ISLAND?

Middle Island has always been located in Canadian waters since there have been waters designated as "Canadian." The island's history includes the Middle Island Lighthouse (first lit in 1872 and deactivated in 1918, the structure later burned to the ground); visits by the bootlegging Purple Gang of Detroit, with its connection to Al Capone; and private ownership by an American citizen from Ohio. There was a runway, now grown over, and a mansion with intrigue attached to it that met the same fiery fate as the lighthouse.

"Interest in preserving the island prompted a 1982 Parks Canada study, which recommended naming it a national natural landmark. Its ecological, historical, and aesthetic value led Essex County to include it on its list of Environmentally Sensitive Areas and an Area of Natural and Scientific Interest. A conservation group, Carolinian Canada Coalition, named the island as one of the 38 critical unprotected sites in its effort to preserve remnants of Ontario's southern forests."[*]

The island was purchased by the Nature Conservancy of Canada in 1999, and ownership was transferred to the government of Canada in 2000. In 2001, the island became a part of Point Pelee National Park, but it is not officially open to visitors (and not accessible by bridge or ferry). Inhabited today by only double-crested cormorants and Lake Erie watersnakes, Middle Island is the only piece of Canadian land farther south than Pelee Island.

[*] "Middle Island (Lake Erie)," *Wikipedia*, www.en.wikipedia.org/wiki/Middle_Island_(Lake_Erie).

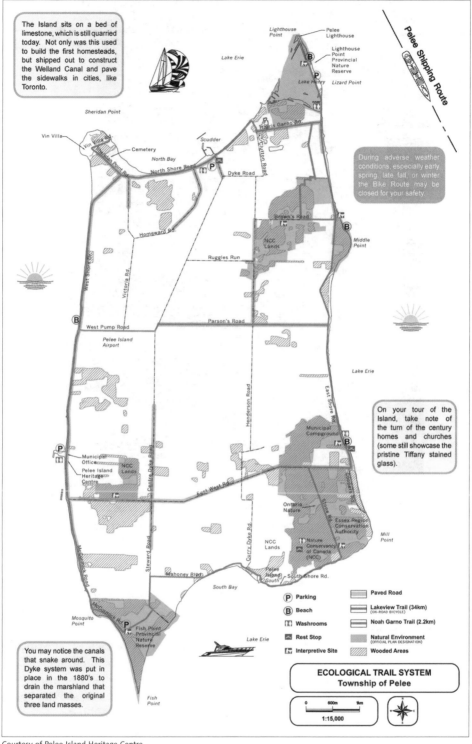

The Island sits on a bed of limestone, which is still quarried today. Not only was this used to build the first homesteads, but shipped out to construct the Welland Canal and pave the sidewalks in cities, like Toronto.

During adverse weather conditions, especially early spring, late fall, or winter the Bike Route may be closed for your safety.

On your tour of the Island, take note of the turn of the century homes and churches (some still showcase the pristine Tiffany stained glass).

You may notice the canals that snake around. This Dyke system was put in place in the 1880's to drain the marshland that separated the original three land masses.

Pelee Shipping Route

Lighthouse Point
Pelee Lighthouse
Lighthouse Point Provincial Nature Reserve
Lake Henry
Lizard Point

Lake Erie

Sheridan Point

Vin Villa
Vin Villa Rd.
Sheridan Point Road
Cemetery
North Bay
North Shore Road
Scudder
Dyke Road
Harris Garno Rd.
Crutton Road

Brown's Road
Middle Point
NCC Lands
Ruggles Run

Homeward Rd.

West Shore Rd.
Victoria Rd.

Parson's Road

West Pump Road

Pelee Island Airport

Lake Erie

Henderson Road

East Shore Rd.

Municipal Campground

Municipal Office
Pelee Island Heritage Centre
NCC Lands

East West Rd.

Centre Dyke Road

Ontario Nature
Essex Region Conservation Authority
Mill Point

Steward Road

Curry Dyke Rd.

NCC Lands
Nature Conservancy of Canada (NCC)

Mahoney Blvd.
Pelee Island South
South Shore Rd.
South Bay

McCormick Road

Mosquito Point

Fish Point Provincial Nature Reserve

Lake Erie

Fish Point

Legend	
P Parking	Paved Road
B Beach	Lakeview Trail (34km) (ON-ROAD BICYCLE)
Washrooms	Noah Garno Trail (2.2km)
Rest Stop	Natural Environment (OFFICIAL PLAN DESIGNATION)
Interpretive Site	Wooded Areas

ECOLOGICAL TRAIL SYSTEM
Township of Pelee

0   500m   1km
1:15,000

Courtesy of Pelee Island Heritage Centre

Baltimore oriole (*Icterus galbula*) on the annual Pelee Island Springsong weekend, feasting on half an orange nailed to a hackberry tree.

Island. But that may be because I love birds and books. Traditionally held on Mother's Day weekend, Springsong is a celebration of both. The event was first held in 2002 as a fund-raiser for the Pelee Island Heritage Centre (one of the very *best* island museums) with the help of the Pelee Island Bird Observatory and internationally acclaimed Canadian writer Margaret Atwood, who also owns a cottage on Pelee. The weekend includes the Botham Cup Bird Race (a "green" race—contestants look for birds by foot or bicycle; the Pelee Island Bird Observatory checklist includes 311 species) and the Springsong banquet at the Pelee Island Winery, which concludes with a reading by an award-winning Canadian writer.

Springsong 2012's "Celebrity Birder," Ian Davidson, now director of Bird Conservation at the National Fish and Wildlife Foundation in DC, posted for *Nature Canada* on May 11, 2012: "The island is a globally important bird area and a critical staging area for migratory birds. Over 300 species have been recorded on the island, including some of Canada's rarest breeding species—Prothonotary Warblers, Acadian Flycatchers, and Yellow-Breasted Chats."

Besides the migratory birds, who show up every year—twice actually; we get to see them both coming and going—Springsong attendees are treated to readings by very fine Canadian writers: Margaret Atwood, Farley Mowat, Alistair MacLeod, Jane Urquhart, Alice Munro, David Suzuki, Vincent Lamb, Joseph Boyden, Brian Brett, Nino Ricci, Wayne Grady and Merilyn Simonds, Elizabeth Hay, Linden MacIntyre, and Lawrence Hill.

How to Get There

The Pelee Island Transportation Company services the island from mid-March until mid-December, offering passenger, vehicle, and goods transportation services on its two ferries, the MV *Pelee Islander* and the MV *Jiimaan*. Ferry service is available from both Canadian and U.S. ports: Leamington, Ontario (mid-March until the end of July), Kingsville, Ontario (August until mid-December), and Sandusky, Ohio (May until the end of September).

For directions, schedules, fares, and reservations, see www.ontarioferries.com/en/mv-jiimaan-mv-pelee-islander. You can make reservations or get the status of the current sailing schedule by calling 800-661-2220.

The three terminal locations are: Leamington Terminal, 500 Erie St., Leamington (519-326-2154); Kingsville Terminal, 25 Dock Rd., Kingsville (519-733-4474); and Sandusky Terminal, 109 W. Shoreline Dr. (800-661-2220). If departing from a Canadian location, be sure to double-check your departure location to ensure you end up at the correct dock before the ferry departs.

There are no motorized vehicle rentals on Pelee Island. If you plan to take a vehicle to the island, make a reservation for it as soon as you know your travel dates because ferry vehicle space, especially for weekends and special events, sells out quickly. For vehicle ferry reservations, call 800-661-2220 (from the United States) or 519-724-2115 (from Canada). (Note: Gas is available at the Pelee Island Co-operative only during business hours, which vary depending on the time of year.)

The idea of a Pelee taxi service at one time was only a rumor, but these days, you generally are able to get one if you need it, especially if you make arrangements in advance; call Anne Marie Fortner at 519-325-8687 or Moe Hape at 519-977-9477.

Private watercraft can dock at Scudder Marina, located on North Bay and owned and operated by the Township of Pelee. For information, visit www.pelee.org/i?page=watercraft&sid=101382116778BO or call 519-724-2377.

Both private aircraft and commercial flights use the Pelee Island Airport (CYPT), the southernmost international airport in Canada. The Pelee Island Airport is an official port of entry into Canada.

The Griffing Flying Service offers daily year-round service from Sandusky, Ohio, to Pelee Island. For reservations, call 419-626-5161. For more information, see www.griffingflyingservice.com/islandflights.html.

The Pelee Island Transportation Company offers regularly scheduled flights during the winter months, when the ferry is not running, and can be contacted at 800-661-2220 or 519-724-2115 for more information.

Visitors flying private aircraft should contact the airport manager Monday to Friday 9:00 a.m. to 5:00 p.m. at 519-724-2931 for more information. The Pelee Island Airport features a 3,300-foot paved runway.

What to Expect

Expect islanders, cottagers, and regular visitors to wave to you as they pass you driving on the road. (Also expect drivers to "brake for snakes.")

Expect a rural community with a fringe of shoreline cottages and two small settlements: West Dock and Scudder (aka North Dock). In 2005, Pelee Island was featured in the *New York Times* in a half-page story titled "An Island unto Itself, Loved for What It Lacks." The island is indeed often loved for what it lacks: stoplights, cable television, newspapers, Wi-Fi, and lattes.

Expect to slow down. The spotty cell phone service on the island may help by keep you in the here and now; you may find yourself really seeing what you happen to be looking at in the moment.

You may slow down enough that even if you are not an amateur birder, you will likely notice gulls and terms, cormorants, and perhaps a blue heron or an egret. You may see a wild turkey amid all the green, as I have while working on this chapter. Having survived the annual turkey hunt, he fans his tail feathers and struts; the cat at the window is not amused. In the fall after the annual pheasant hunt, you may see pheasants scurrying across the road, into the woods, across a lawn outside your window. At the beach, you may see an endangered Lake Erie watersnake making its way in or out of the water, or see the "bellyprint" record one has left on the sand. You may wake at dawn from a dream of amazing birdsong and discover you weren't dreaming before you dip back into a Pelee-profound sleep.

Expect the opportunity to create your own adventures—and memories—here.

(Full disclosure: I am a Pelee Island cottager. Pelee Island, home to islanders who have become my good friends, is the island I know best in the Great Lakes Basin; we've had a relationship for over 20 years now. It's the first Great Lakes Basin island I visited to look for a cottage two decades ago and ended up being the only island on which I looked. Within my first hour on Pelee, I was hooked.)

Paths to Adventure

Pelee Island Heritage Centre—Directly across from the ferry dock, this the best start to a visit on Pelee Island. Here you'll find information, displays, and books on the human and natural history of Pelee Island. Here you can view items ranging from a 370-million-year-old Devonian fish to the island *Bird Sightings* book (and perhaps contribute to the latter before you leave the island). For more information, visit www.peleeislandmuseum.ca.

Consider taking the *100 Gateways to Pelee* self-guided out-of-doors audio tour, available at the Pelee Island Heritage Centre, to be taken on your own time and at your own speed (via bike or motor vehicle). It's a wonderful way to see the island while learning about its past and people.

NATURAL SITES

Approximately 35 species of flora and fauna found on Pelee Island are on Ontario's and/or Canada's list of species at risk—including the nodding onion, the yellow-breasted chat, and the gray fox—and several species on the island are found nowhere else in Canada. There are three rare (and nonvenemous) snake species on the island: blue racer, Lake Erie watersnake, and the eastern fox snake. (Snakes like to bask in the sun, often on roads; remember to "brake for snakes!")

A PERFECT PAIR: PELEE ISLAND'S FLATNESS AND BICYCLING

Ronald Tiessen's *A Bicycle Guide to Pelee Island,* for sale at the Pelee Island Heritage Centre, maps and describes 62 sites around the island. Bikes can be rented at:

Comfortech Bicycle Rentals and Retail Store
North of Westview Tavern in West Dock
www.peleebikerentals.com

Short, medium, and long bike routes as well as an island map are provided in Comfortech's brochure.

There are a number of places to go on the island and ways to encounter its wealth of flora and fauna:

Pelee Island's Eco Biking and Walking Trail—The trail system encompasses 21 miles (34 kilometers) of on-road bicycle trails, 6 miles (10 kilometers) of ecological multiuse trails, and 3 miles (5 kilometers) of walking trails. Combined, these trails provide access to unique natural heritage environments on the island. The township is proposing to extend the Trans Canada Trail to Fish Point.

Pelee Island Bird Observatory (PIBO)—Established in 2003 to collect data on migratory birds, study and preserve Pelee's unique nesting bird communities, serve as an education center, and encourage ecotourism on the island.

Fish Point Provincial Nature Reserve, Ontario Parks—Fish Point, the southwestern point of Pelee Island, is a 110-hectare nature reserve geologically characterized by "gently rolling shallow sand over a limestone plain, typical of the Great Lakes lowlands, with lacustrine nearshore features including an excellent example of a sand spit and dune system extending south into Lake Erie."[65] The reserve has almost two miles (over three kilometers) of sandy and forest trails.

The area's near-virgin southern deciduous forest shelters several plants and animals that are rare in the province, including eastern prickly pear cactus, hoptree, eastern fox snake, Lake Erie watersnake, and giant swallowtail butterfly. The reserve also contains approximately 15 percent of Ontario's plant species.

Fish Point is an important stopover for migrating birds and a bird-watcher's paradise. Black-crowned night herons and an array of other bird species frequent a lagoon along the trail (I saw my first warbler here some years ago), while the beach here is popular with numerous shorebirds.

Follow trails through a Carolinian forest to the sand spit that is Fish Point, at the southernmost tip of the southernmost inhabited point of Canada. Because of currents, it is dangerous to swim (or even wade) off this spit, which can extend out into the lake for a mile (1.6 kilometers). However, the nearby beach of Mosquito Bay, which makes for a good return hiking route, is good for swimming (and I've yet to encounter a mosquito there, even though Peregrine's Pond—aka the Maple Swamp—is just up the road).

Lighthouse Point Provincial Nature Reserve—At the northeast point of the island, this destination offers a hike through marsh on land trails. Look for the rare eastern spiny soft-shelled turtle and the many different species of birds in the remnants of deciduous forests, savannas, and wetland. The trail leads to a public beach and the original 1833 Pelee Island Lighthouse, which was restored in 2000. Look for the blue racer snake and the smallmouth salamander. Lake Henry, a wetlands area on the west side of Lighthouse Point, is a good place to find blue herons and egrets.

Stone Road Alvar near Mill Point—This area is protected by three conservation groups: Nature Conservancy of Canada (100 hectares), Ontario Nature (42 hectares), and Essex Region Conservation Authority (36.4 hectares). The Stone Road Alvar on Pelee Island is a designated Area of Natural and Scientific Interest (ANSI) of Ontario, one of more than 1,000 such areas. While most are on private land, the Stone Road Alvar is for the public to enjoy and protect. A truly outstanding array of rare habitats and species is packed into this ANSI: oak-hickory woodland, oak savanna, red cedar savanna, old-field thicket, prairie, and open alvar communities. It is said that this mix of communities occurs nowhere else in Canada or in any of the adjacent U.S. states.

Most of the open area in the Stone Road Alvar is characterized by scattered shrubs and limestone outcroppings. Here visitors may find small elusive plants such as conobea, smaller skullcap, false pennyroyal, and narrow-leafed vervain.

From late July to early September, all the open areas are filled with a bright cacophony of yellow gray-headed coneflower, purple nodding wild onion (a provincially imperiled species in Ontario), and white whorled milkweed.

The scattered oaks are predominantly chinquapin—despite their stunted appearance, they are often well over 100 years old. On the open savanna, visitors can find red cedar and the provincially rare hoptree as well as blue ash. Of special note is the local abundance of downy wood mint, a plant that in Canada is confined to Pelee Island.

In the open oak-hickory woodlands near the road, visitors may also find Miami mist, a rare member of the waterleaf family, blooming in profusion in late May. The alvar has several plant species that occur nowhere else in Canada, such as corn salad, yellow horse gentian, and Leavenworth's sedge.

Stone Road Alvar also provides a prime habitat for the endangered blue racer snake. Five rare butterflies make frequent appearances here as well: giant swallowtail, tawny emperor, Acadian hairstreak, hackberry butterfly, and sachem skipper.

Carolinian bird species such as the yellow-breasted chat, the orchard oriole, and the blue-gray gnatcatcher all find reasons to enjoy this habitat. Whereas the orchard oriole prefers open areas, look for the other two species in the dense thickets.

Glacial Grooves at Mill Point—Off Cooper's Road, Mill Point (where the island's virgin red cedar was milled and sent off by ship to Cleveland for railroad ties, or so I've heard) is a good spot to check out the striations, grooves, and erratics left behind from the Canadian Shield and the Quaternary period. Among the most dramatic glacial grooves found on Pelee Island are these at Mill Point. Here you can see how the ice moved along the length of Lake Erie, not across it—as previously recorded on the rocks—and left grooves aligned east to west.[66] Mill Point is a great place to picnic, but the slippery algae on the limestone

---

ALVAR

Alvar is an Estonian word that describes a limestone plain covered with scattered vegetation that endures extreme wet and dry conditions. Alvars have their own unique flora that takes advantage of the extreme variations in moisture and the highly calcified soil and bedrock openings. You can learn more about alvars at www.natureconservancy.ca/en/where-we-work/ontario/our-work/alvars-of-ontario.html.

November sunset as seen from a Pelee Island beach.

shelf that extends from the beach into the water makes this a dangerous place to swim or wade. I know from personal experience that a concussion may be the consequence.

Ivey-Red Cedar Savanna—Located on East-West Road, this Nature Conservancy of Canada site features stands of centuries-old red cedars.

Brown's Point—Located on the east side of the island, this Nature Conservancy of Canada site features wildflowers in Brown's Woods and shorebirds at the shore.

Brown's Road Alvar—A 300-hectare area owned by the Nature Conservancy of Canada, this alvar is a "mosaic of savanna, open woodlands, meadows, and thickets. The site contains one of the few known occurrences of Chinquapin Oak and Nodding Wild Onion Savannas in the world.[67]

Public beaches—Check out East Park Beach on East Shore Road, across from the campground and just north of East West Road; Sunset Beach on West Shore Road north of West Dock; the beach at Mosquito Bay (aka Fish Point Beach; dangerous currents surround the sand spit at the tip of Fish Point proper), and Lighthouse Point Beach. It is also permissible to swim at any beach that is at the end of a public road.

Note: On Pelee Island, as on many other Great Lakes Basin islands, among the wealth of species can be found invasive species. In the past few years the Nature Conservancy of Canada (NCC) has been implementing garlic mustard control measures on the island, and at Middle Point Woods, on the island's east side, the NCC is removing the invasive common reed (*Phragmites australis*) from the shoreline.

HISTORY PRESERVED

Indian Grinding Stone—According to archaeologists, this large flat boulder was left on Pelee by glacial ice, and given that it has been identified as Oriskany sandstone, it was most likely moved by the glacier to the island either from near Hagersville, Ontario, or from New York State. The boulder is distinguished by its abraded depressions. Ron Tiessen suggests, "Some native inhabitant, between 7500 B.C. and the more recent past, us[ed] the sandstone as an abrader. What [was] being ground is likely food found on the island. Acorns, like [those] from the white oak were eaten by the Indians to supplement their normal diet. The collection of depressions on one stone may suggest a commercial or social activity."[68] Currently, the stone is located north of Westview Tavern and south of the island's municipal offices on the east side of West Shore Road.

There is much further evidence of Native prehistoric use of Pelee Island. At the Pelee Island Heritage Centre, you can see other artifacts that have been found—smoking pipes, tools, and decorated ceramic vessels—primarily from the east side of the island, where the Indian grinding stone was originally located.

Hulda's Rock—There is a story passed down by the island's earlier Native inhabitants. Hulda was a young métis woman who jumped from this rock to her death after receiving a letter informing her that her young English husband would not be returning to her. "The rock marking the meeting of two . . . cultures and the tragic end of a young . . . woman is Hulda's Rock."[69] You can read a version of Hulda's story in Ladislaus Segers's *The Song of Hulda's Rock: The Indian Legend of Pelee Island*. This rock is off the end of Sheridan Point across from the shore of the Vin Villa property and can be seen (if one knows where to look) as the ferry approaches the island. What one might find on Hulda's Rock now would be plants bearing tiny sweet strawberries and the surprise of a coiled Lake Erie watersnake basking in the sun. The rock, however, is no longer accessible from land, as the beach across the water from it is privately owned property.

Pelee Island Lighthouse—Built in 1833 to help ships navigate the treacherous Pelee Passage (between the Pelee Peninsula and Pelee Island), this is the second-oldest Canadian lighthouse on Lake Erie. William McCormick, who in 1823 purchased Pelee Island—which he had previously been leasing from Alexander McKee (in 1788, the Ojibwe and Ottawas gifted Thomas McKee, the then current Indian Department official's son and Alexander's father, an agricultural lease for Pelee Island for 999 years in exchange for an annual rent payment of three bushels of Indian corn)[70]—for £100, provided both the land and the stone for the lighthouse. McCormick was appointed the first lighthouse keeper. When he died in 1840, his son Alexander succeeded him. There were an additional five keepers until the lighthouse was decommissioned in 1909.

Vin Villa Winery (ruins) at Sheridan Point—The home of the McCormick family was on Sheridan Point. Thomas McCormick sold a parcel of 40 acres to D. J. and Thomas Williams and Thaddeus Smith. In 1868, Smith finished the stone house and wine cellar and made Vin Villa his home. Smith's subsequent leadership in experimenting with native vintages made "Pelee Island the first place of major commercial wine manufacturing in

Pelee Island Lighthouse, built in 1833 by John Scott of Detroit and last lit in 1909. Ninety years later, the island Relight the Lighthouse committee was awarded a Canadian federal grant that provided the additional funding needed to complete restoration of the lighthouse, which was rededicated in August 2000.

Ontario."[71] The ruins of Vin Villa are on private land, on the west side of Sheridan Point Road where the road curves toward North Bay. They can be viewed from the road.

Pelee Island Cemetery—The cemetery is located on Sheridan Point, the second site of the island cemetery, which was moved from the shoreline back to the center of the point (which once was called Graveyard Point) in the 1890s. A number of historic figures found their final resting place in this cemetery: "William McCormick, who died in 1840, is buried here. Nearby is the grave of Frederick Fisher, Chief of the Chippewa Nation. The Schulthies family who accompanied Thaddeus Smith to Pelee from Kentucky is buried here."[72] There is a second island cemetery located at Our Lady Star of the Sea Church.

Historic churches—By 1900, Pelee island had four churches; all four of them are still in existence, three in their original locations, and all are still used in some capacity today:

- St. Mary's Church—The oldest church on the island, St. Mary's was built using limestone from an adjacent quarry. The first recorded baptism was that of a McCormick daughter in 1863. Today, the parish is a part of the Anglican Church of Canada. The church is located on East West Road adjacent to the Pelee Art Works.
- Calvary Anglican Church—Built of island limestone, this Methodist church was dedicated in 1898. In 1942, it became Calvary Anglican Church. In 1946, the south-end Methodist church, which had been on East West Road and was the first Methodist church on Pelee, built in 1882, was moved to this location to serve as the parish hall.[73] Calvary Anglican Church is located on North Shore Road at Victoria Road.

- Our Lady Star of the Sea Church—The lighthouse keeper Jack Cummins, who arrived on the island circa 1850, was the first Catholic resident of Pelee. By 1887 there were 13 Catholic families, and plans were made to build a chapel. The first Mass was celebrated in the partially completed building in 1887 with the arrival of a donated 300-pound bell. By June 1944, the present rectory was rebuilt on the property.[74] A second island cemetery is located in the churchyard. The church is located on East West Road, east of Stewart Road.

CULTURAL ATTRACTIONS

Pelee Island Wine Pavilion—The first grapevines were planted on Pelee around 1854, and winemaking had begun on the island by 1873. Today, Pelee Island Winery, Canada's largest estate-owned winery, makes ecologically conscious wine at its Kingsville Winery from 17 varietals grown on almost 700 acres of vineyards on the island—and every year, a number of the wines win awards.

At the Wine Pavilion—within walking distance of the ferry dock—you can learn about winemaking, participate in a wine tasting, buy unique gifts for all of the oenophiles in your life at the shop, indulge in snacks or "you BBQ" items purchased from the Deli Hut, and sip some fine wine while enjoying the view. The winery is one of the Nature Conservancy of Canada's conservation partners. For more information, see www.peleeisland.com/island/island_pavillion.php.

Pelee Art Works (82 East West Rd., east of the Pelee Island Wine Pavilion)—This non-profit organization features the works of local painters, photographers, potters, weavers, woodworkers, jewelers, textile artists, writers, and more. Pelee Art Works also offers a seasonal program of craft workshops and beginner art classes. Open May–October; call 519-724-9916 for days and hours of operation. For more information, see www.pelee.org/i?page=artworks.

Conorlee's Bakery, Deli, & Pizzeria—*And* art gallery! Ricki Oltean (baker Matt is her husband) is a fine artist with a studio—Blackbird Studio—on the island. She exhibits her work at Muse Gallery in Toronto, the Nancy Johns Gallery in Windsor, and Pelee Art Works on the island; some of her pieces can also be found for sale on the walls and shelves of the bakery at 5 North Shore Drive. You will most likely be pleased with any gustatory treats you order at Conorlee's: sweet or savory, pizza or soup and sandwiches, and any of the traditional or more creative bakery goods. If you happen to be on the island during one of the multicourse Wine and Dinner Series events often held at the Pelee Island Wine Pavilion and can get a ticket, you'll have an evening to remember. For more information on all of these delights, see rickolte.wix.com/bakery.

Township of Pelee Pheasant Farm—"The ring-necked pheasant was introduced to the United State from China in 1880. In early December of 1897, four pair of pheasants were introduced to Pelee Island."[75] Thousands of pheasants are raised at the farm for the three two-day hunts every fall. In 2012, the township celebrated the eightieth annual pheasant hunt. The farm—you can see the beautiful birds in their pens—is located on Centre Dyke Road.

OTHER ISLAND THINGS TO DO

Enjoy an ice cream cone—Stop by Pelee Island Coneheads in West Dock, just north of the ferry dock on West Shore Road, or the Filling Station in Scudder, across from the Pelee Island Co-op on North Shore Road.

Go birding—Pelee is located at the junction of two migratory flyways, the Atlantic and the Mississippi, and an estimated 2 million migrant birds pass through during each migration in May and August/September. You can get a checklist of what you might see at http://pibo.ca/en/keeping-track/checklist-of-the-birds-of-pelee-island/.

Go fishing—Walleye, smallmouth bass, and yellow perch abound. If you don't have your own boat and equipment, options for arranging a chartered fishing excursion include Chanté Sport Fishing Charters of Kingsville, Ontario, April through November (www.chante charters.com) or Char-Tom Charters from Port Clinton, Ohio (www.chartomcharters .com).

Go camping—East Park Campground (1362 East Shore Rd.) has 25 individual wooded sites for tents or tent trailers as well as a group camping area. The sandy public East Beach is right across from the park. No electricity is available, but there are washroom and shower facilities and a campground store. Anchor and Wheel Family Campground at 11 West Shore Road has sites for tents and camper trailers with electrical hookups and washroom and shower facilities.

Explore Pelee . . . with Explore Pelee!—Choose from daily motor tours, a south shore or lighthouse bike tour, or a birding tour. Customized school field trips can also be arranged. While you're making up your mind, you can get a feel of Pelee from the Explore Pelee blog. For more information, visit www.explorepelee.com/.

Essex County Tours—Beginning in June, look for the Big Blue Bus to be at the ferry dock. If you come over on the 10:00 ferry, you'll be in time for the noon Pelee Island tour. Learn some island history, see the sights and unique points of interest, and have some fun as you tour the island. This tour includes an optional nature hike to the old lighthouse. For more information, see www.peleeislandtour.com.

SPECIAL ISLAND EVENTS

Pelee Island hosts a number of annual special events, which you may want to take into consideration in planning your visit to Pelee—either because you're interested in participating in one of them or because you'd rather *not* be there when an event is going on. Remember that vehicle reservations on the ferries may be more difficult to get at the time of these events.

Springsong (second weekend in May)—The *particularly* Pelee celebration of birds, birding, and Canadian literature.

Victoria Day (last Monday before May 25)—Victoria Day, observed since before Canada was formed, called Fête de la Reine (formerly and unofficially known as Fête de Dollard—check it out, you history buffs) in French, is a federal Canadian public holiday celebrated in honor of the birthday of Queen Victoria (May 24, 1819). Like Memorial Day in the United States, it is sometimes informally considered as marking the beginning of the summer season in Canada.

Pelee Island Music Series (Sundays in June, July, and August)—Defined on the website of the organizers, the Windsor Feminist Theatre (WFT), as an "eclectic series of concerts and other artistic events featuring the spoken word, live performance and visual arts" and held at the "Quarry" (a former limestone quarry on East West Road). An artist workshop precedes some of the concerts. For more information, visit, www.windsorfeministtheatre .ca/pelee-island-music-series.

Total Recall Retreat: A Time to Gather the Women Again (early June)—Begun in 2003, this weekend retreat for women has a yearly theme (for example, "exuberance"). In 2015 it was held at the Pelee Island Winery and involved yoga and movement, good food, workshops and speakers, a healing tent, and a marketplace. For more information, visit www.total recallretreat.com.

Canada Day (July 1)—Previously named Dominion Day and called Fête du Canada in French, this federal public holiday marks the 1867 joining—into the autonomous federal Dominion of Canada—of the three British North American colonies of Nova Scotia, New Brunswick, and the Province of Canada, the latter of which was, at unification, split into Ontario and Quebec. The British Parliament kept limited rights of political control over the new country thus formed until 1982, when the Constitution Act (which is the name replacing the British North America Act of 1867) was signed by Elizabeth II, queen of Canada, as the culmination of the political process that led to Canadian sovereignty. Canada Day inspires activities similar to those characterizing American Fourth of July celebrations, and Pelee Island generally hosts a fireworks display in honor of both holidays on the weekend closest to Canada Day.

(Note: The first cottagers on Pelee Island were Americans from Lorain, Ohio, who boated or ferried over from Sandusky and built cottages on the east side of the island, primarily on a small road that forks off of East Shore Road called Lorain Lane. Because of the number of cottagers who hail from the States, there is often more than a nod given to the American holidays on Pelee Island.)

The Island Unplugged (first weekend in August)—This family-friendly music and arts festival is a well-received new island event. For more information, see www.theisland unplugged.org.

Heritage Weekend (second weekend in September)—Sponsored by the Pelee Island Heritage Centre. Every year, one weekend of activities is devoted to the history of a different topic related to Pelee Island (for example, the history of fishing on Pelee). To read the account of one Heritage Weekend, go to http://greatlakesislandescapes.com, click on "Blog," and select "Pelee Island Heritage Weekend 2011."

Heritage Centre Harvest Dinner (mid-September)—A community dinner of friends, neighbors, and island visitors is held at the Pelee Island Wine Pavilion celebrating the harvest.

There are numerous other events on Pelee Island. The following are only a sampling:

Pelee Island Winery Half-Marathon (May)
Pelee Island Artists' Studio Tour (July)
Pelee Art Works Lobsterfest (July)
Heritage Centre's Southernmost Canadian Chili Cook-off (August)

Note: Confirm dates for all special events at www.pelee.org (click on "Events" to get to the "Calendar of Events").

For More Island Information

www.pelee.org—The official website of the Township of Pelee.

The Pelee Grapevine: Living on the Edge—Published every two weeks, this community newsletter highlights current events on the island. It is available on the ferry and at select island establishments for only 50¢.

Discover Pelee—www.pelee.com.

Pelee Island Heritage Centre—https://www.facebook.com/PeleeIslandHeritageCentre and www.peleeislandmuseum.ca (most of the books below are available from the Pelee Island Heritage Centre).

Pelee Island: Human and Natural History; a Guide to a Unique Island Community, by Ron Tiessen (Pelee Island, ON: Wilds of Pelee, 2003).

A Bicycle Guide to Pelee Island, 2nd ed., by Ronald Tiessen (Pelee Island, ON: Pelee Island Heritage Centre, 1992).

A Guide to Exploring Pelee Island Wildlife, by Ethan Meleg and Ron Tiessen (Pelee Island, ON: Pelee Island Heritage Centre, 1996).

The Vinedressers: A History of Grape Farming & Wineries on Pelee Island, 2nd ed., by Ron Tiessen (Pelee Island, ON: Pelee Island Heritage Centre, 1997).

Shipwrecks, Pelee Island, and The Life Saving Service, by Ron Tiessen (Pelee Island, ON: Pelee Island Heritage Centre, 1992).

Point au Pelee Island: A Historical Sketch of and an Account of the McCormick Family, Who Were the First White Owners on the Island, by Thaddeus Smith (Amherstburg, ON: Echo, 1926).

The Story of Pelee, by Noah Garno (n.p., 1954).

The Song of Hulda's Rock: The Indian Legend of Pelee Island, by Ladislaus Segers (1960; repr., Whitefish, MT: Literary Licensing, 2013).

The Pelee Island Lighthouse, by Ronald Tiessen and Irena Knezevic (Pelee Island, ON: Pelee Island Heritage Centre, 1999).

Mennonite Memories of Pelee Island, 1925–1950: A Virtual Museum Exhibit, compiled by Anne Fast and Astrid Koop (Leamington, ON: Essex-Kent Mennonite Historical Association, 2011), www.virtualmuseum.ca/sgc-cms/histoires_de_chez_nous-community_memories/pm_v2.php?id=exhibit_home&fl=0&lg=English&ex=00000777.

Wildflowers of the Canadian Erie Islands, by Mary Celestino (Windsor, ON: Essex County Field Naturalists Club, 2002).

The Pelee Project: One Woman's Escape from Urban Madness, by Jane Christmas (Toronto: ECW Press, 2002).

Uncle Lawrence: The Story of a Young Englishman's Visit to a Long-Lost Relation on a Remote Island in Lake Erie, by Oliver Warner (New York: Random House, 1939)—This book is out of print, but used and duplicated copies can be found for sale online, and it is well worth the search if you become interested in "all things Pelee."

How You Can Support the Island

Pelee Island Heritage Centre
www.peleeislandmuseum.ca/donations/

Pelee Island Bird Observatory
http://pibo.ca/en/getting-involved/funding-pibo/

Pelee Art Works
www.peleeartworks.org/

The Nature Conservancy of Canada
ontario@natureconservancy.ca

Parting Thoughts

I've spent more than 20 years of spring, summer, and fall weekends on Pelee Island. Our two daughters were 5 and 11 when we bought our first cottage here; now they're both married and busy with demanding careers. This year with the birth of our first grandchild, I imagine where a crib might fit in our second cottage come summer.

We've had two cottages during our time here and collected so many island memories. Each daughter had a group of her best girlfriends spend a summer weekend when she turned sweet 16. My parents have celebrated birthdays and several Mother's and Father's Days here with us. My dear Grandma Klotzbach came with us after she was widowed. Baron, our beagle, spent many weekends of his life—almost 15 years—sniffing the island, inch by inch.

My husband and I have walked the length of beach on our slight bay countless times, as the ferries pass, as Old Hen Island floats and shifts on the horizon, as the sun sets, as we watch with our neighbors Heinz and Ulli for a green flash to follow as it sometimes does, as the blue heron lifts from the point, and we finally come in for the night, to empty our pockets of fossils and "lucky stones." We, surely, have been lucky.

Pelee prompted, perhaps in many ways, the beginning of this island project for me, and there will never be another island I know or love so well. My island friend Ron summed up the "island thing" well:

Islands are special microcosms,
Places of fascinating surprises,
Neighbourhoods of difference,
Forever entertaining!*

And Pelee certainly is all that.

* Ron Tiessen in *100 Gateways to Pelee* (Pelee Island, ON: Pelee Island Heritage Center, 2012).

South Bass Island, Ohio

"DON'T GIVE UP THE SHIP!"

June 28, 2014, 5:35 p.m.
The Wine Garden at Heineman's Winery

The "Crystal Cave" is cool, literally and figuratively. As Carol and I descend the steep flight of steps into the dark, the temperature cools and we arrive where artificial light illuminates the walls, which begin to look, well, cavelike but oddly thick and disordered. And then as our eyes adjust and we get closer, we make out what composes this jumble—incredible big, thick, and milky-blue crystals. "Celestite!" our guide informs us. There is something celestial about it even here under the ground, especially when I can begin to see, to actually understand, that we are standing in the interior of a huge geode. Of course, we can't see, can only imagine, the plain outside, but generally one thinks of holding a geode in the hand, of turning it to the light to admire the sparkle of the crystal, not of being contained underground in one with a small group of sightseers and a guide.

This is the story as I understand it: in 1887, a Mr. Gustav Heineman emigrated from Baden-Baden, Germany, to Put-in-Bay, Ohio, where he started a winery that is still functioning today. In 1897, two men digging a well for him discovered what they thought was a cave, but it turned out to be a geode, the largest of its kind in the world. Crystals line the limestone walls of the cave, which is 37 feet below the ground and 12 feet below lake level, and maintains a temperature of 54 degrees Fahrenheit. The eight-sided crystals are made of the milky-blue mineral celestite. The geode's dense crystals are as wide as 18 inches to three feet across and estimated to weigh up to 300 pounds each.

This story goes that the men who found the geode thought they had discovered diamonds and would be rich. No diamonds, but it was soon discovered that the mineral (formed from a sulfate of the element strontium) would ignite when crushed and would then produce a bright red flare, so it could be used for flares. Crystals from the geode were harvested and sold for manufacturing fireworks. The original cave was much smaller than it is today; as much of the celestite was mined for the manufacturing of fireworks, the cave has opened up considerably. However, at some point, Heineman decided to stop the mining and turn the property into a tourist attraction. It was a wise move—the resulting tourism revenues helped Heineman's Winery survive Prohibition.

Visitors today can enjoy both the Crystal Cave and Heineman's Winery.

GETTING THERE: Passenger-only and car ferries; daily air service; private boat or plane
GETTING AROUND: Bring your car and/or bike and/or kayak; downtown bus; tour train; golf cart, bicycle, canoe, kayak, boat, and jet ski rentals

OVERNIGHT ACCOMMODATIONS: Hotels, resorts, B&Bs, conference centers, and retreats; vacation condo, home, cottage rentals; camping

FOOD: Restaurants; winery; brewery; groceries

DAY TRIP? Yes, but you could easily fill a week with island adventures!

STATE / PROVINCIAL / NATIONAL PARK? South Bass Island State Park and Oak Point State Park

At the beginning of the War of 1812, much of which was fought on the Great Lakes, Britain had the upper hand thanks to a much stronger navy. South Bass Island—also called Put-in-Bay—served as the base of military operations for 27-year-old Commodore Oliver Hazard Perry once he had supervised the building of a fleet of two large brigs and seven smaller ships in Erie, Pennsylvania. He sailed from this harbor to defeat the British in the Battle of Lake Erie—also sometimes called the Battle of Put-in-Bay—on September 10, 1813. When the entire British squadron surrendered, this decisive victory turned the tide in favor of the Americans in the war.

It is from this battle that we get two oft-quoted proclamations. "Don't give up the ship" flew on a blue battle flag from Perry's brig, the USS *Lawrence*. These words were a paraphrase of the dying words of Captain James Lawrence, Perry's friend for whom the ship was named. After the British had surrendered and Perry's victory was clear, his battle report to General William Henry Harrison was succinct: "We have met the enemy and they are ours."

Today on South Bass Island at the harbor of Put-in-Bay stands Perry's Victory and International Peace Memorial, a Doric column of granite rising 352 feet over Lake Erie. Constructed 100 years after the war, it was built to honor those who fought in the Battle of Lake Erie and to celebrate the long-lasting peace between Britain, Canada, and the United States. The site became a national park in 1936.

How to Get There

Head for the tip of the Catawba Island peninsula in Ohio. Miller Boat Line ferry will take you across in under 20 minutes, landing at the Lime Kiln Dock in Put-in-Bay at the south end of South Bass Island. On the skyline, in one direction, you can see the tall, slender Perry peace monument on the island and, in the other, the Davis-Besse Nuclear Reactor cooling tower, belching steam, southwest of the island in Oak Harbor, Ohio. If you have not brought your vehicle or your own bike, the Island Bike Rental is just across the road and to the north

PERRY'S VICTORY TIMES TWO

A smaller, similar-looking 101-foot obelisk was built on Crystal Point at Misery Bay on Presque Isle, Pennsylvania, in 1926 to commemorate Perry's victory in the same battle. The Pennsylvania location is both where Perry's men constructed six of his nine vessels before the Battle of Lake Erie and where they returned after battle and were quarantined for smallpox during the winter of 1813–14.

Courtesy of the National Park Service

when you come up onto Langram Road from the dock. Golf carts are available for rent just a bit farther north up Langram Road. Additional businesses in Put-in-Bay rent both bikes and golf carts.

All three Bass islands (South Bass, Middle Bass, and North Bass) airports are operated by the Put-in-Bay Township Port Authority. These airports are unattended and do not have fuel available. For more information, call Put-in-Bay Township Authority at 419-285-3371 or visit www.putinbayportauthority.com.

What to Expect

To some visitors to the village of Put-in-Bay on South Bass Island, at least after a few hours in town, the motto "Don't give up the ship," which originated on the waters surrounding the island, may seem *somehow* related to the number of bars on the main drag. But South Bass Island, despite the filled marina and aforementioned bars, can be more than a "Key West of the North." There's enough history here and some wonderful outdoor spaces to explore to keep a variety of adventurers happy.

Put-in-Bay is the name of the bay, the village, and the township on South Bass Island. Some say the name originated with the bay, when sailors would "put in" their schooners here to wait out the storms on Lake Erie. Today, come nice weather, boaters "put in" to party.

Paths to Adventure

NATURAL SITES

Scheeff East Point Nature Preserve—Dedicated in 2008 by longtime island residents, this nine-acre preserve helps to protect critical habitat for countless migratory birds, the threatened Lake Erie watersnake, and the fish that are abundant off these shores. Two dozen gourds serving as nesting sites for purple martins hang from a tall pole at the head of the preserve trail, and 16 or more nesting boxes for tree swallows are placed 25 yards apart in the preserve.

Oak Point State Park—This park, located right in town, affords a great view of Gibraltar Island and the bay. Picnic and boating facilities are available, including 20 docks for daily or overnight use. Restrooms and water are available nearby.

South Bass Island State Park—At Stone Cove on the southwest end of the island, this 33-acre park offers wooded campsites, a lakeside picnic gazebo, a public boat launch ramp, and a small (unguarded) stone beach for swimming. Kayak, fishing boat, and powerboat rentals are available nearby. Jet ski rentals are also available on the island.

Perry's Cave—Now registered as an Ohio Natural Landmark, this limestone cave is 52 feet below the island's surface and 208 feet long by 165 feet wide. Commodore Oliver Hazard Perry purportedly discovered the cave in 1813 shortly before his decisive victory on Lake Erie. The cave features stalactites, stalagmites, and "cave pearls" as well as a rare underground lake. Dress for cool temperatures (50 degrees), and wear nonskid footwear.

Note: The cave is a part of a tourist complex in the center of the island, between town and the South Bass Island State Park; this "family fun center" includes a butterfly house, miniature golf, a giant maze, rock wall climbing, a gemstone-mining attraction, an antique car museum, a snack shop, a gift shop, and a business offering island tours.

Crystal Cave—The largest geode ever found, containing the world's largest celestite crystals, is located 37 feet under Heineman's Winery, Some of the crystals have been removed ("harvested"), allowing visitors to walk right inside.

Glacial Grooves—A small set of glacial grooves is located in exposed bedrock near the group camping area in the South Bass Island State Park.

Lake Erie Islands Nature and Wildlife Center—The center's stated mission is "to promote conservation and provide education about the flora, fauna, and lands of the Lake Erie Islands ecosystem." From mid-June through mid-August the center hosts "Wild Tuesdays," focusing on a species or topic and often providing a hands-on interactive experience. For more information, see www.lakeerieislandswildlife.com/.

Natural treasures—Be on the lookout for spring wildflowers, including large-flowered trillium, bloodroot, trout lily, spring beauty, Solomon's seal, and the rare northern bog violet. The presence of migrating songbirds, migratory waterfowl, and bald eagles makes this one of best bird-watching areas in the country. And don't forget reptiles and amphibians: Lake Erie watersnake (endangered), eastern fox snake, red-eared slider, midland painted turtle, common map turtle, mudpuppy, and northern redback salamander.

HISTORY PRESERVED

The Lake Erie Islands Historical Society Historical Museum (founded in 1975)
25 Town Hall Pl.
Put-in-Bay, OH 43456
419-285-2804
www.leihs.org

Perry Victory and International Peace Memorial
93 Delaware Ave.
Put-in-Bay, OH 43456

The national park visitor center is full of exhibits, artifacts, and art related to the Battle of Lake Erie. Free admission includes a 15-minute documentary on the battle. The view from the observation deck includes the Lake Erie islands and shorelines of Ohio, Michigan, and Ontario. Open from mid-May to the end of October. Check out these special programs:

- Black Powder Demonstration—Firing demonstrations of reproduction flintlock muskets take place Friday, Saturday, and Sunday on the hour, from 11:00 to 4:00.
- Ranger Program—Interpretive talks on a variety of topics related to the Battle of Lake Erie, the War of 1812, the construction of the monument, and natural sciences are given by park rangers Monday through Thursday, on the plaza at the base of the monument, on the hour from 11:00 to 4:00.

South Bass Island Lighthouse—Climb the tower of the lighthouse, active from July 1897 to October 1962 and listed on the National Register of Historic Places. After an automated light was installed on the island, the title of the lighthouse was transferred to Ohio State University (OSU), making it the only lighthouse in the United States owned by a university. The lighthouse is used to host special events for the guests of OSU's Franz Theodore Stone Laboratory on Gibraltar Island, but the lighthouse grounds are open to the public,

Perry's Victory and International Peace Memorial, a 352-foot Doric column on South Bass Island, honors those who fought in the Battle of Lake Erie during the War of 1812, celebrates peace between Britain, Canada, and the United States, and is managed by the National Park Service.

dawn to dusk, and the tower is open to climb Mondays and Tuesdays, last week of June through mid-August, 11:00–5:00.

Crown Hill Cemetery (at Meechen and Catawba Roads, behind the South Bass Island State Park)—This cemetery is the final resting place of John Brown Jr. (eldest son of the abolitionist, 1821–95); Joseph de Rivera St. Jurgo (d. 1888), a "Spanish" merchant who left Puerto Rico at 13, poor, and eventually became a millionaire in New York City dealing in foreign trade, bought South Bass and Middle Bass islands in 1854 from the Pierpont Edwards family (the first Americans to own the islands, in 1803) as well as four other islands in the archipelago, and then set about developing them—he is remembered as the "Father of the Bass Island wine industry";[76] and Valentine Doller, born in Germany in 1834, who built the historic Doller house (aka the Doller villa), the historic Victorian Italianate mansion on the island, circa 1870, was known as a "successful tourist-industry entrepreneur,"[77] was the principal owner of the Put-in-Bay Telegraph, owned a general story, ran the only public dock, and started an ice business. He eventually became the island's first postmaster and later its third mayor.

Maple Leaf Cemetery—The newer of the two island cemeteries, it is located in the southwest area of the island, off Put-in-Bay Road (Township Rd. 260), north of the Miller Boat Line ferry dock.

Heineman's Winery—This is the oldest family-owned winery in Ohio. Take the tour and learn about harvesting the five varieties of grapes cultivated on the island (Catawba, Concord, Delaware, Ives, and Niagara), blending the varietals, bottling (the winery produces 40,000 bottles a year of wine and more of grape juice), and labeling. Sample the wares in the tasting room, and then enjoy a glass of your favorite in the wine garden.

Doller House Estate and Island Life Museum—Tour the Victorian Italianate mansion, appreciate the winery exhibit, and sample the wares of the Put-in-Bay Winery located at the estate.

Hotel Victory ruins—Once the largest hotel in the world when it opened on the bay in 1892, Hotel Victory burned in 1919. All that remains are ruins of the swimming pool in the South Bass Island State Park.

CULTURAL ATTRACTIONS

DeRivera Park and Perry Park—A lovely leafy stretch of green in the downtown of Put-in-Bay, between Bayview Avenue at the marina and Delaware Avenue's bars along the harbor. The smaller of the two parks was deeded to the island by DeRivera in 1866.

Kimberly's Carousel—Built by the Herschell Company of Tonawanda, New York, in 1917, this merry-go-round is located across from Perry Park. You have your pick of animals on which to ride, including Pete the Perch.

Ohio Division of Wildlife Historic Fish Hatchery and Aquatic Visitors Center (1 Peach Point Rd.; 419-285-3701)—An attraction with free admission where kids can go fishing and everyone can learn more about Great Lakes marine life. The historic former state fish hatchery, built in 1890 for the propagation of whitefish, now houses live fish displays, a children's playroom, and hands-on information exhibits highlighting Ohio fish species and fisheries management projects.

Goat, Soup, and Whiskey—A restaurant and tavern with an interesting story behind the name and lovely second-floor patio seating. Try the excellent perch tacos. On the first floor you'll find the Chocolate Café and the Chocolate Museum.

OTHER ISLAND THINGS TO DO

Bike the island—Bring your own on the ferry or rent one from one of the several rental businesses on the island. Mopeds are also available to rent.

Ride a golf cart—View the island up close from the comfort of a golf cart, available to rent from several rental businesses on the island.

Kayak the bay—Rent a kayak at Kayak the Bay, Ltd., Oak Point State Park.

Ferry to another island or two

- Take a passenger ferry to Gibraltar Island and take the Gibraltar Island Science and History Tour offered by Ohio State University's Stone Laboratory and see the Cooke Castle as well as glacial grooves.
- Take the *Sonny S,* a passenger ferry, to Middle Bass Island, the site of the historic Lonz Winery, which was closed after the July 1, 2000, tragedy when the terrace of

Gibraltar Island, across from Put-in-Bay, as seen from Perry's Victory and International Peace Memorial on South Bass Island. Commodore Perry used Gibraltar Island as a lookout. Today, the Stone Lab and Cooke Castle are visible.

the winery collapsed, killing one person and injuring 75.[78] In 2001, the State of Ohio purchased 124 acres including the winery and created Middle Bass Island State Park. In 2015, the Ohio DNR announced it would be investing $6 million into the property to celebrate the wine culture of the area.[79]

Treat yourself at Freshwater Retreat—Enjoy a massage, a Reiki treatment, or a life-coaching session (www.freshwatersensations.com/).

Play golf—Located adjacent to the South Bass Island State Park on Catawba Avenue, Saunders Golf Course is a public nine-hole course with a par of 30. For more information, call 419-285-3917.

Fish—A fishing pier is located near the entrance to South Bass Island State Park. A fish-cleaning house is available behind the campground. A valid Ohio fishing license is required.

Get airborne—Helicopter tours and parasailing are available on the island.

NOT FRANKENSTEIN'S CASTLE OR LAB: GIBRALTAR ISLAND

Jay Cooke bought Gibraltar Island in 1864 and built a 15-room Gothic castle on it. Ohio State University has had the Stone Lab on the island since 1929. Today, you can take a passenger ferry across from the Boardwalk in Put-in-Bay and tour the Stone Lab and the exterior of the Cooke Castle, which is undergoing restoration. You'll see lots of interesting sights—especially in the lab—but, probably, no monsters.

SPECIAL ISLAND EVENTS

Many of the special events on South Bass Island have to do with Put-in-Bay business promotions related to the town's goal of being considered the "Key West of the North." You'll know what I mean when I mention that St. Patrick's Day is also celebrated in September ("Half-Way to St. Patty's Day"). Cinco de Mayo and Mardi Gras are also big celebrations on the island, at least in the area right around the downtown area. You can find a list of all the many other island events at www.putinbay.com/calendar.htm. Here are two a bit different from the rest:

Annual Blessing of the Fleet (May)—Local clergy from the island's two churches bless the vessels that service South Bass Island, including Coast Guard watercraft and Life Flight helicopters.

Perry's Victory Triathlon and Family Races (end of June).

For More Island Information

Put-in-Bay Gazette—This island's oldest news source is published monthly, costs just 25¢ an issue, and is also available online.

Put-in-Bay Daily (pibdaily.com)—An informational and news website that covers daily news, events, and activities at Put-in-Bay.

PIBTODAY (pibtoday.com)—An information website that lists daily community events.

Ohio DNR South Bass Island and Oak Point state parks—http://parks.ohiodnr.gov/southbassisland.

Put-in-Bay Vistors and Convention Bureau—www.visitputinbay.com.

Put-in-Chamber of Commerce and Visitors Bureau—www.visitputinbay.org.

www.respecthesnake.com—Learn more about the Lake Erie watersnake, a federally protected endangered species.

Isolated Splendor: Put-in-Bay and South Bass Island, by Robert J. Dodge (Hicksville, NY: Exposition, 1975).

Island Heritage: A Guided Tour to Lake Erie's Bass Islands, by Ted Ligibel and Richard Wright (Columbus: Ohio State University Press, 1987).

Lake Erie Islands: Sketches and Stories of the First Century after the Battle of Lake Erie, edited by Michael Gora (Put-in-Bay, OH: Lake Erie Islands Historical Society, 2004).

Illustrated Port Clinton and Environs: Embracing Port Clinton, Catawba Island and Put-in-Bay (1898; repr., Put-in-Bay, OH: Lake Erie Islands Historical Society, 2003)—A retypeset and digitally enhanced reprint of the 1898 edition, which was printed in Norwalk, Ohio.

Put-in-Bay Souvenir Tour Book: Walking and Riding Tours (Put-in-Bay, OH: Lake Erie Islands Historical Society, 2010).

How You Can Support the Island

Lake Erie Islands Historical Society
25 Town Hall Pl.
Put-in-Bay, OH 43456
www.leihs.org

Parting Thoughts

I do like Key West, but I like it where it belongs, not 1,205 miles north. I have a Michigan boater friend, however, who vehemently disagrees; he lives for his summer trips down the Detroit River and straight to dock at the Put-in-Bay Marina. On South Bass Island, there's room for both types of island adventurers. It's an island; trust me, if you don't want to party, there are plenty of quiet, beautiful places here just to be.

Kelleys Island, Ohio

FROM PLUNDER TO PROTECTION

June 28, 2013

After Kim and I leave the Kelleys Island Historical Museum, we head north up Division Street to the state park turnaround and then back to Titus Road and west. Our car is the only one on the road in a tunnel of trees, and we come upon what looks like some sort of shrine a ways off in the woods on the north side of the road. We park the car and hike up to look. A wooden diamond-shaped shelter, constructed between two tree trunks, holds a large figurine of the Virgin Mary—with no baby Jesus—on the shelf that the shelter's post supports.

My first impression is of chaos—Mary is surrounded by stuff: beads and wood figurines, remembrance cards. On closer examination I see that someone's ring of tiny pearls is balanced on the Virgin's head like a crown and that a number of rosaries are strung around her neck, hanging down her full length: silver metal beads, wooden beads, turquoise glass beads, old red glass beads, pink porcelain beads, black-and-white beads. Draped among the rosaries are three crucifixes and a knot of plush fabric fashioned into a cross and hanging from a leather thong, a metal medallion of the Virgin on a chain, and at the base of the Mary statue, Mardi Gras beads, pink, purple, blue, all faded, and a silver strand with stars strung between the beads, an electric votive candle, a tiny bowling pin hanging from a chain down off the bottom of the shelter, a blue glass fish, plastic white and purple, and blue flowers and greenery, a large freshwater oyster shell like a fan, more remembrance cards, folded pieces of paper. At the base of the shrine are shells and rocks, some natural, some painted with hearts or splotches of color, bearing initials, names, or "In memory of" messages with dates. Myrtle planted at the base of the structure twines around all of the offerings.

Later, we learn from an article in the spring 2012 edition of *Kelleys Life* newspaper that the structure—referred to as a "crèche"—is a replacement for the original statue, a medieval version of Madonna and child from France, that was put in place on this private property in 1948, occupying the same crèche that is there today and overlooking a natural stone grotto. The original was vandalized sometime around 1970.

As we turn to leave, I notice the small figurine leaning against the pedestal of the sculpture of the Virgin. A smaller Mary, I think at first. But this Mary's traditional blue cloak is studded with stars, and behind her is a blaze of starshine. This is an older Queen of Heaven.

GETTING THERE: Passenger-only and car ferries; daily air service; private boat or plane
GETTING AROUND: Bring your car and/or bike and/or kayak; bicycle, canoe, and kayak rentals; tours

OVERNIGHT ACCOMMODATIONS: Hotel, motel, inns, lodges, and B&Bs; condo, cottage, and cabin rentals; vacation rentals; camping

FOOD: Restaurants; winery; brewery; groceries

DAY TRIP? Yes, but you could easily fill a week with island adventures!

STATE / PROVINCIAL / NATIONAL PARK? Kelleys Island State Park

Did pirates ever ply the Great Lakes? At least one did, according to Chris Gillcrist, executive director of the National Museum of the Great Lakes in Toledo. "Dan Seavey is the only man known to be formally charged with piracy on the Great Lakes. His most famous race [was] when he . . . [stole] the Nellie Johnson, a little schooner, and [was] chased across Lake Michigan by the U.S. Revenue Cutter Services, and is eventually caught, put in irons—that's something that's very pirate-y—and brought to justice." Gillcrist continues: "Seavey was known for putting up fake port lights so that ships coming in would crash on the rocks. Then, his people would board the ship and steal its cargo. Up until the mid-1800s, there was a Wild West mentality on the Great Lakes. Pirates stole beaver pelts, timber, and sometimes, entire ships."[80]

But such plundering in days of old didn't always happen out on the unsalted seas; some "pillaging" happened *on* Great Lakes Basin islands, sometimes by the islands' very owners. Take the Kelley brothers, Datus and Irad, for instance.

Kelleys Island—known before 1800 as Island No. 6 and later as Cunningham's Island—could well serve as a microcosm showing the progression of the "development" of the Midwest United States beginning with the advent of the "white man," the European or American settler from the East, on the scene. After the Kelley brothers arrived from Connecticut, by way of Cleveland, in 1833, they bought up all of the 13 platted lots on the two- by three-mile (three- by five-kilometer) island and then *very*—more than a few might say "too"—successfully engaged in all the popular Great Lakes area industries of the 1800s: lumbering, mining, and fishing, until in each case, and in relative succession, they'd managed to plunder the island with respect to its cedar, gypsum, and whitefish.

The only industry they engaged in that gave something back was their grape growing for the wine industry, which produced the Lake Erie wines that were becoming popular then and remain so today. The Kelley brothers also gifted the island by bringing to it something in the way of "culture." The descendants of those who benefited from this enrichment, and others who have come to the island in the last two centuries, have put a number of provisions in place to protect the island's history as well as its natural resources.

How to Get There

Kelleys Island Ferry offers a daily vehicular family-owned ferry service from the tip of the Marblehead Peninsula to Kelleys Island. Weather permitting, a ferry leaves at least every hour, with additional departures at peak times and on holiday weekends. The ride takes 20 minutes and provides views of the Marblehead Lighthouse, Put-in-Bay, Cedar Point Amusement Park, and other Lake Erie islands.

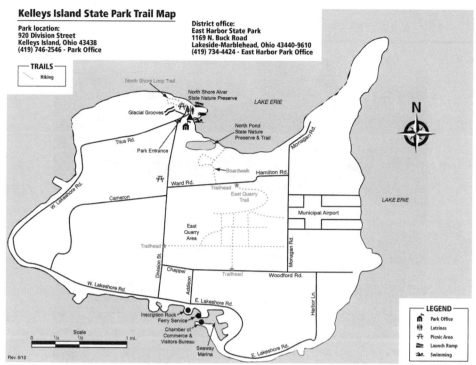

Kelleys Island State Park Trail Map

Park location:
920 Division Street
Kelleys Island, Ohio 43438
(419) 746-2546 - Park Office

District office:
East Harbor State Park
1169 N. Buck Road
Lakeside-Marblehead, Ohio 43440-9610
(419) 734-4424 - East Harbor Park Office

TRAILS
···· Hiking

North Shore Loop Trail
North Shore Alvar State Nature Preserve
LAKE ERIE
Glacial Grooves
North Pond State Nature Preserve & Trail
Titus Rd.
Park Entrance
Monagan Rd.
Boardwalk
Hamilton Rd.
Ward Rd.
Trailhead
East Quarry Trail
W. Lakeshore Rd.
Cameron
LAKE ERIE
Municipal Airport
East Quarry Area
Monagan Rd.
Trailhead
Division St.
Chappel
Addison
Trailhead
Woodford Rd.
W. Lakeshore Rd.
E. Lakeshore Rd.
Harbor Ln.
Inscription Rock
Ferry Service
Chamber of Commerce & Visitors Bureau
Seaway Marina
E. Lakeshore Rd.

Scale
0   1/4   1/2   1 mi.

Rev. 6/12

N

LEGEND
🏠 Park Office
🚻 Latrines
⛱ Picnic Area
🛥 Launch Ramp
🏊 Swimming

Courtesy of Ohio Department of Natural Resources

Kelleys Island Ferry Boat
510 S. Main St.
Lakeside Marblehead, OH 43440
419-798-9763
www.kelleysislandferry.com/

Jet Express Ferry Service offers passenger-only service to Kelleys Island from Port Clinton, Ohio, or Sandusky, Ohio, and between Put-in-Bay (South Bass Island) and Kelleys Island.

Jet Express
800-245-1JET
fast@jet-express.com

Kelleys Island Land Field Airport (K89D), on the east side of the island, is a small public airport for private planes with a terminal, single runway, and parking area. A pedestrian/bicyclist's road equipped, yes, with a stop sign crosses the runway.

What to Expect

Kelleys Island is a quieter alternative to South Bass Island. Making up for the "plunder" indulged in by its earlier Euro-American inhabitants, today approximately one-third—about 800 acres—of Kelleys Island is protected in its natural state, a habitat called Lake Erie Island. Many species thrive on this limestone-based island, including hackberry and prickly ash,

Glacial grooves on Kelleys Island were created 18,000 years ago by rocks and other debris being carried by the glacier. Some of these "tools," harder than the limestone bedrock of the island, scratched, striated, polished, and ground away at the limestone, leaving the grooves seen today at this National Natural Landmark.

which are host plants for snout butterfly and giant swallowtail caterpillars. Rock elm and the Lake Erie watersnake are other species that have found a home on this island.

Paths to Adventure

NATURAL SITES

Glacial Groove State Memorial—A National Natural Landmark, here you will find the largest exposed glacial grooves in the world, measuring 400 feet long by 35 feet wide and up to 10 feet deep. Many such glacial grooves were created 18,000 years ago by the glacial ice sheet as it moved, the debris in its path scouring grooves into the Devonian limestone bedrock, and a number of them, like these, were quarried away. Now the grooves are surrounded by a fence and quite visible from a walkway, along which a sequence of interpretive signs explains to visitors what they are seeing.

Kelleys Island State Park Beach—This 100-foot public unguarded sandy swimming beach is located in the 677-acre state park on the northern shores of the island. Two picnic areas as well as camping sites, rent-a-camp units, and yurts are also available at the park.

North Shore Loop Trail—This one-mile (1.6-kilometer) hiking trail located at the northwest end of the island is a part of the Kelley Island State Park. The entrance is west of the state park boat and trailer parking lot. Along the trail see architectural history, glacial grooves, shoreline, trees, and flowers. See www.kelleysislandnature.com/nature-preserves.html for more information.

East Quarry Trail—A grid of four miles (6.5 kilometers) of multiple-use trails for hikers and mountain bikers cuts through the East Quarry, which takes up the center of the island. The main entrance to the East Quarry Trail is on Ward Road a mile (1.6 kilometers) east of Division. The trail itself is a five-mile (eight-kilometer) moderately level trail with rocky terrain. Hikers can see trees, wildflowers, glacial markings, fossil preserves, and remnants of old fence lines. Horseshoe Lake is in the northeast corner of this area. See www.kelleysislandnature.com/nature-preserves.html for more information.

North Pond State Nature Preserve—This 30-acre sanctuary of forest, marsh, and mile-long (1.6-kilometer-long) hiking trail partially covered by boardwalk and featuring a raised observation deck is within the Kelleys Island State Park. North Pond itself is a lake embayment natural pond, a pond with a water level that rises and falls with the lake. See www.kelleysislandnature.com/nature-preserves.html for more information.

Scheele Preserve—A 28-acre preserve on the northeast side of the island, owned and managed by the Cleveland Museum of Natural History (and named in honor of museum director William Scheele in 1999). The preserve is home to a cluster of the island's only rock elm trees, a threatened species in Ohio, found only in four other locations in the state. Two members of the citrus family—wafer ash and prickly ash, Ohio's only citrus species—grow here. In addition to the relatively rare trees, you may discover butterfly weed, tufted vetch, and green milkweed and, if you're alert and looking for them, orchard orioles, eastern screech owls, and fox snakes.

Quinn Preserve—An 18.5-acre preserve, home to the only red cedar forest habitat in Ohio, Quinn is protected by the Kelleys Island Village Park District with help from the Western Reserve Land Conservancy and the Cleveland Museum of Natural History. It is a good place for hiking and bird-watching.

Huntley-Beatty Preserve—This 59-acre quarry area, formerly known as the Cut, is now protected by the Kelleys Island Village Park District with help from the Western Reserve Land Conservancy and the Cleveland Museum of Natural History. The quarry site displays a fine example of the globally imperiled Great Lakes Alvar ecosystem and is home to a dozen plant species endangered in Ohio, including the Caribbean spike-rush and Philadelphia panic grass. It's a fine place for hiking and bird-watching.

Several of the Cleveland Museum of Natural History (CMNH) preserves are accessible only with a permit from the Natural Areas Offfice at the CMNH. Researchers study birds, plants, amphibians, snakes, butterflies, and beetles on these preserves. Hunting is permitted on them during hunting season with a CMNH permit:

Sweet Valley Preserve—A 17.5-acre preserve, located on Titus Road, in a low east-west–oriented depression, the area is home to some of the island's best vineyards. It was purchased by the Cleveland Museum of Natural History with the assistance of a group of island residents in 1997 to protect it from development.

Woodford Woods—This 23-acre area on the south side of Woodford Road near the intersection with Monaghan was acquired by the Cleveland Museum of Natural History in 1955 to protect this island site with natural and archaeological significance.

The Glade—An island site, tucked in off of the Kelleys Island Bickley family's land, was purchased by the Cleveland Museum of Natural History in 1955 to preserve its natural and archaeological significance.

Coleman Tract—Also known as the Coleman Preserve; the Cleveland Museum of Natural History bought this site, which straddles Bookerman Road near the turn in the road, in 1955 to safeguard its natural and archaeological significance.

Jones Preserve—A 21-acre site inside the gate at Long Point in the island's northeast corner that serves as a vital stopover site for migratory birds crossing Lake Erie, particularly warblers, and as a key research site for a Cleveland Museum of Natural History associate who is a certified bird-bander and who, with volunteers, has mist-netted and banded over 3,825 spring migrants here. For more information, see www.kelleysislandchamber.com/events/nest-birds.

HISTORY PRESERVED

Inscription Rock State Memorial—This flat limestone slab inscribed with prehistoric Native American (probably Erie Nation) pictographs was discovered in 1833, partially buried in the south shoreline of Kelley's Island. Today, the rock is completely exposed from the ground, protected by a roof, accompanied by a relief of the pictographs made from a drawing of 1850 (before the elements wore away at the stone), and surrounded by a viewing platform at the water's edge. This historical site is owned and managed by the Ohio Historical Society.

Kelleys Island German Reformed Church (1865)—Located on Division Street, the church was vacated in 1956 and rescued by the Kelleys Island Historical Association in 1986.

Kelleys Island Historical Museum and Gift Shop—In 2010, the historical association opened a museum next to the German Reformed Church, at the location of the "haul shed" that was used for the parishioners' horses and buggies.

Addison Kelley Mansion (1867)—Datus Kelley built this three-story mansion with a widow's walk for his son. Located at 211 East Lakeshore Drive, it is being privately restored and is not open to the public, but the exterior alone is worth a stroll by.

Kelleys Island Cemetery—Also known as Village Cemetery, this old cemetery is located at the intersection of Lakeshore Drive and Division Street. Datus Kelley is buried here. At least one wild turkey favors the spot for foraging.

Monarch Winery—The ruins of the winery are on private property but visible from Division Street, across from the cemetery. This was also the site of the earlier Sweet Valley Wine Company and the original Rush Winery. The Monarch Winery, established in 1900, was closed in 1950, the last of the original island wineries to close.

Community Oven (ruins)—Built circa 1875 and located at the top of the hill leading down to the State Park Beach, this is one of two or three ovens that were used to bake bread for the over 400 primarily seasonal workers from southern and eastern Europe employed by the three quarries on the island; this oven served the North Quarry workers. Across the road from the oven are the ruins of the foundation of a quarry workers' boardinghouse.

August Schaedler's Winery Museum—Kelleys Island Historical Preservation Corporation was created in 2008 for the August Schaedler Winery Restoration Project, with the

Kelleys Mansion, a three-story house of native limestone with a widow's walk, freestanding spiral staircase, and rose-colored cut-crystal windows, was built in the 1860s for Addison Kelley, son of Datus Kelley.

purpose of preserving the history of the wine industry on Kelleys Island. Housed in the building that once was the Schaedler Winery (1866) on the southeast shore of the island, the museum is open to the public by appointment only. For a complete list of the Kelleys Island wineries of old, see www.kihpc.org.

CULTURAL ATTRACTIONS

Charles Herndon Galleries & Sculpture Garden

110 and 114 Laylin Lane

Kelleys Island, OH 43438

419-746-2249

www.charlesherndon.com

Herndon's main gallery and gallery annex as well as two studios are located on the west side of the island. Also a painter and photographer, Herndon sculpts in soapstone, alabaster, limestone, marble, and granite, the results of which you can enjoy at an outdoor exhibit in the 10-acre sculpture park and gardens even when the galleries are not open. Parking is available on Dwelle Lane.

Kelleys Island Wine Company

418 Woodford Rd.

Kelleys Island, OH 43438

419-746-2678

www.kelleysislandwine.com

A woodland scene in the Charles Herndon Sculpture Garden on Kelleys Island.

The Zettler family's winery produces seven varieties of wine using Lake Erie grapes, including vinifera wines (those derived from a European grape) as well as the sweeter Sunset Pink and Coyote White. A pizzeria and full-menu restaurant are also on-site.

Kelleys Island Brewery

504 W. Lakeshore Dr.

Kelleys Island, OH 43438

419-656-4335

kelleysislandbrewpub.com

Claiming that his brewery is "one of the smallest breweries in the world," Doug the brewmaster produces five handcrafted beers, 200 gallons at a time.

OTHER ISLAND THINGS TO DO

Rent a golf cart and tour the island.

Rent a bike and see how much of the island you can ride (a lot!).

Take a hike accompanied by a Kelleys Island trail map: www.parks.ohiodnr.gov/Portals/parks/PDFs/parks/Maps/Kelleys_Island/kelleysislandtrailmap.pdf.

Go bird-watching—Check out www.kelleysislandnature.com first for a Kelleys Island bird checklist and other information.

Go "shrooming"—So you know what you're looking at, check out www.kelleysislandnature.com/mushrooms/mushrooms.htm.

Go looking for wildflowers or fossils.

Pick up a picnic from Kelleys Island Wine Company and choose a spot on the shore, in the quarry, or at the park.

Swim at the sandy beach in the Kelleys Island State Park.

Get a dose of Key West (or Put-in-Bay atmosphere) and watch the sun set at West Bay Inn.

Visit Caddy Shack Square to shop, eat, and just generally have fun.

Rent a kayak and make the trip along 17 miles (27.5 kilometers) of the irregular island shoreline.

Arrange for a fishing charter if you have a fishing license but don't have your own boat.

Scuba dive to explore the shipwrecks and limestone ledges in the area.

Take a day trip to Put-in-Bay on the Jet Express or Goodtime island cruise ferries.

Make a day trip to Marblehead Lighthouse or Johnson's Island.

Do some island hopping using the Griffing Flying Service to Pelee Island (don't forget your passport), Put-in-Bay, or Middle Bass Island. (Even North Bass Island, not accessible by bridge or ferry, is accessible by Griffing.)

SPECIAL ISLAND EVENTS

Kelleys Island specializes in a wide variety of family-fun activities from April through November. For a full description of all upcoming island events, visit www.kelleysisland chamber.com/events.

April: Easter Egg Hunt; Early Bird Party; Blessing of the Kelleys Island Brewery; Spring Wine Fling.

May: Derby Day; Island Olympics; Free Museum Day; Nest with the Birds.

June: Perch Derby; Kelleys Island Annual 5K and 10K; Baconfest; Island-Hopping Trip; Make-a-Wish Horseshoe Tournament; Kelleys Island Music Fest.

July: Triathlon & Family Races; Island Fest; Film Fest.

August: Make-a-Wish Benefit Golf Cart Poker Run; Arts & Crafts Show; Make-a-Wish Benefit Swim; Kelly Miller Circus; Justin Horseshoe Tournament; Kelley Island Historical Association Day of Events; Homecoming; Annual Poker Run/Dice Roll.

September: Murder Mystery Weekend; Treasure Island Day; Butterfly Festival; Pig Roast; Wine Fest; Dahlia Tour; Harvest Festival; Lobster Fest; Feather and Foliage Bird Festival; Putt-Putt Pig Roast.

October: October Fest; Chili Cookoff; Wine & Art Festival; Zombie Bar Crawl; Family Hayride; Pumpkin Carving; Annual Pre-Thanksgiving Dinner; Adult Halloween.

November: Owl Festival; Annual Half Marathon; Thanksgiving Potluck Village Pump; OSU vs. Michigan Tail Gate.

For More Island Information

Kelleys Island Chamber of Commerce—www.kelleysisland.com and www.kelleysisland chamber.com.

Kelleys Island State Park—http://parks.ohiodnr.gov/kelleysisland.

Kelleys Life—The island newspaper, published monthly May through August and every two months the rest of the year. Past issues of the 25¢ newspaper can be viewed in full at www .kelleysisland.com/kelleys-life.

A History of Kelley's Island, Ohio, by Norman E. Hills, repr. ed. (Kelleys Island, OH: The Kelleys Island Historical Association, 1987).

A History and Some Tales of Kelleys Island, Ohio, by Jessie A. Martin (Minneapolis: T. S. Denison, 1975).

Kelleys Island, by Jessie A. Martin (Detroit: Harlo, 1988).

Kelleys Island: An Island for All Seasons, by Becky Linhardt (Kelleys Island, OH: Kelleys Cove, 1995).

Kelleys Island: An Island Story, by Claudia M. Brown (Kelleys Island, OH: Kelleys Cove, 2007).

Kelleys Island, by John T. Sabol (Charleston, SC: Arcadia, 2013).

Kelleys Island, 1810–1861: The Courageous, Poignant & Often Quirky Lives of Island Pioneers, by Leslie Korenko and Amy Amoroso (Enumclaw, WA: WinePress, 2009).

Kelleys Island 1862–1865: Civil War, the Island Soldiers, & the Island Queen, by Leslie Korenko (Enumclaw, WA: WinePress, 2010).

Kelley's Island, 1866–1871: The Lodge, Suffrage & Baseball, by Leslie Korenko (Amazon Digital Services, 2015).

Kelleys Island, 1872–1876: The Hotels, the Telegraph & the Lime Company, by Leslie Korenko (Enumclaw, WA: WinePress, 2013).

Kelleys Island, 1877–1884: The Fire, the Great Grooves and a Mysterious Disappearance, by Leslie Korenko (Enumclaw, WA: WinePress, 2015).

How You Can Support the Island

Kelleys Island Historical Association
PO Box 328
Kelleys Island, OH 43438
419-746-2399
www.KelleysIslandHistorical.org

Benefits of membership include free admission to the museum, a quarterly newsletter, and a 10 percent discount on museum gift shop items.

Parting Thoughts

June 29, 2013

Yesterday, back at The Inn on Kelleys Island, looking at the shot on my camera of the shrine of the Virgin Mary in the woods, I notice a very healthy stalk of poison ivy shooting up alongside the shrine, as tall as its base, just brushing the bottom of the diamond structure, the leaves still wet from the earlier rain. Our Lady of the Woods, of course, belongs to an even more ancient time than Mary or the Queen of Heaven.

This was an intriguing introduction to a number of places on the island that feel as if they possess doors that open into other, earlier times, but not all the same earlier time. Or maybe it's that I feel out of time here, deliciously untethered from the everyday, but grounded in something else. Someone could sell this type of experience, the ultimate vacation; slip into a time in another century.

Or maybe it's the preponderance of stone that draws this island visitor to other times here. The big rock on the island's shore: what history were the members of the Erie tribe recording before they were wiped off the face of this earth? On that summer evening front porch of Kelley's Island Wine Company I kept thinking I heard the faint laughter of more people coming on foot up a stone road—I could hear their soles striking stone—but they never arrived. Tucked up in the Crow's Nest at the Inn, I saw the filmy flash of a sheer curtain—on what was in the morning only a bare shuttered window—and could almost just put my finger on some long ago evening. The circumstances were on the tip of my tongue; the story I could not articulate, nonetheless, stirred some emotions attached to nothing in this lifetime of mine. Under that window, I woke up from a dream holding onto an image of rocks and fossils from the beach lined up on the empty windowsill.

The turkey in the cemetery, a Fourth of July outing amid stone memories of 100 years ago, the lichen and cobwebs on the stone cross there.

What did the quarrymen think as they mined away pieces of those sinuous glacial grooves that stretched on and on? Did they take that Devonian limestone full of a record, a history, for granted? Were their thoughts on their lunch buckets? The air around the ruins of the brick community bread oven was thick with talk. Or heavy with silence.

The balanced grandeur of Addison Kelley's limestone mansion. The simple sweeping beauty of the limestone German Reformed church. The broken limestone walls of the roofless winery glimpsed through the trees. Each place anchored in stone. Each place full of doors to other times. Each place a chance to step into the ether of the almost forgotten, the almost unreachable. But not quite.

All the carved and polished stone in Charles Herndon's sculpture garden. No people on this lawn today except for people of stone. The daylilies crane, their antennas tuning in the breeze off the lake to pick out the biographies from the gathering dusk. The roosters scratch and peck out their own story. Their story is the day.

Johnson's Island, Ohio

A DIXIE MEMORIAL IN THE NORTH

May 26, 2013, 10:55 a.m.

Imagine Susan's and my surprise, upon crossing the Johnson's Island Causeway, to pull into the cemetery parking lot and find ourselves surrounded by people dressed in Civil War–period costumes. I vaguely remember something about Memorial Day originating after the Civil War under the name of Decoration Day, but wait, this isn't the last Monday of May; it's Sunday.

By asking one of the men dressed in what he informs us is "Freemason attire," including apron and amulet, we learn that the Masonic Lodge Oliver H. Perry 341 of Port Clinton, Free and Accepted Masons of Ohio, annually holds a Masonic Memorial Service on the Sunday of Memorial Day weekend in honor of the Masons who died at the Depot of Prisoners of War on Johnson's Island while imprisoned there during the Civil War.

Just to be clear, these are descendants of Northerners holding services for the Southern dead—but Masons all.

GETTING THERE: Automated toll bridge

GETTING AROUND: Vehicles of nonresidents are allowed only on the causeway and in the area of the Confederate cemetery

OVERNIGHT ACCOMMODATIONS: None

FOOD: None; no suitable picnic areas

DAY TRIP? Yes, only option

STATE / PROVINCIAL / NATIONAL PARK? Johnson Island Confederate Stockade Cemetery is U.S. government property and the prison site has been designated as a National Historic Landmark by the U.S. National Park Service; it is also an Ohio Historic Site

During the Civil War, this 300-acre island served as what is known as the Depot of Prisoners of War for commissioned Confederate officers. In total, 65 prisoner-of-war camps were in operation during the Civil War. No prison in the North—except this one on Johnson's Island—imprisoned only commissioned Confederate officers. Between April 1862 and September 1865, more than 9,000 prisoners, as many as 3,000 at a time, were confined on Johnson's Island in the Sandusky Bay, today just a causeway away from Ohio's Marblehead Peninsula, which juts into the Western Basin of Lake Erie. The prison's island site was

Johnson's Island Confederate Stockade Cemetery contains the graves of 206 men who died while incarcerated in the island prisoner-of-war camp during the Civil War. In 1890, the original wooden grave markers were replaced with headstones of Georgian marble.

apparently effective; only 12 successful escapes from the prison—all of which involved crossings on ice—were documented.

Prisoners—206 men—who died as a result of disease, wounds, or execution were buried in a cemetery created for the purpose. You can learn what is known about the men buried from historian Roger Long's research at the website of the Hayes Presidential Center: www.rbhayes.org/hayes/civilwar/display.asp?id=759&subj=civilwar. In 1865, the remaining prisoners were released, many to walk to their homes in the South, and the prison was disbanded by Union soldiers.

In 1887, Congress appropriated $2,000 to enclose the prison's cemetery with an iron fence. In September 1889, a "sightseeing" group from the South (identified in some sources as "a delegation of Georgia newspapermen and farmers") saw the deteriorating condition of the cemetery and took action, raising money from donations to replace the wooden cemetery markers with headstones of Georgian marble. Multiple railroad companies absorbed the

FROM MILITARY PRISON TO PLEASURE RESORT

Why did Leonard B. Johnson bring a case against the United States? It may have had everything to do with developing the island for suburban residences, as the island ultimately was, but possibly Johnson had other development interests. In 1894, the first Johnson's Island Pleasure Resort Company leased 10 acres of land north of the Confederate cemetery from Johnson—that's less than one-tenth the size of the island, which is, after all, 300 acres. However, the north fence line of the cemetery was the star of the park's boundary line. One of the very first things park-goers would see on their arrival to the island was the cemetery. Only 30 years after the war's end, would the sight of a Civil War cemetery have had the power to dampen the spirits of gaiety with which pleasure seekers arrived on the island?

Some would say no: "The island had historical significance as it was a Prisoner of War Depot during the War Between the States. Walking paths led to areas where visitors could enjoy a picnic lunch near what remained of the Union Officers Quarters and the two Civil War forts. Much of the resort area was wooded, offering shade from the hot summer sun."*

Regardless of how park-goers might have felt about the park's proximity to the cemetery, park management from the beginning had purportedly been concerned about competing with the very successful Cedar Point Pleasure Resort Company in Sandusky, which had initiated park operations in 1870 and opened its first amusement ride, a water toboggan, in 1890. The first company discontinued park operations in 1897 after a tragic accidental shooting, a subsequent lawsuit, and a fire that destroyed the main pavilion. "In June of 1899, most of Johnson's Island, owned by the estate of Leonard B. Johnson, was sold at a sheriff's sale" to a new group under the same name, the Johnson's Island Pleasure Resort, which ran the park until it was sold in 1908, this time to the competition, the Cedar Point Pleasure Resort Company.** That was the end of pleasure resorts on Johnson's Island.

Instead, the island land was used for farming and rock quarrying. Most of the Civil War sites, other than the cemetery, were razed and built over. Today, there are two subdivisions that cover much of the rest of the island.

* "Island History: Pleasure Resort Era," in *Depot of Prisoners of War on Johnson's Island, Ohio* (Marblehead, OH: Johnson's Island Preservation Society, 2002), http://johnsonsisland.org/history-pows/pleasure-resort-era.
** Ibid.

---

cost of transporting the headstones to Sandusky. Leonard B. Johnson, owner of the island both before and after the Civil War, supplied teams of horses to use for the project once the headstones arrived on the island. The headstone installation was complete in May 1890.

Several years later, however, Johnson sued the United States, claiming that officers of the U.S. Army had established the cemetery on a part of the island that was not leased to the army and that "the cemetery occupies an important point on the island and prevents the sale of lots for suburban residences."[81] The case was dismissed on April 6, 1896.

In 1905, the Robert Patton Chapter of the United Daughters of the Confederacy purchased a 100- by 485-foot site on the island for $1,200; the parcel included the 100- by 209.5-foot cemetery.

On June 8, 1910, the bronze memorial of a Confederate soldier standing watch, created by American sculptor Sir Moses Ezekiel—who himself had been a Confederate sergeant—was unveiled. This monument was the first on Northern soil honoring the Civil War's Confederate dead. "According to stories published in the June 8, 1910, editions of the *Sandusky Daily Register* and *Sandusky Star Journal*, the original dedication drew visitors from across the East Coast, including former Johnson's Island prisoners who had not set foot on Northern soil since they were released 45 years earlier. Later that day, the *Star Journal* reported, 'The United States flag and that of the Confederate states were carried side by side as if all the old

A statue of a Confederate soldier standing watch by American sculptor and Confederate sergeant Sir Moses Ezekiel was unveiled in 1910. It was the first monument on Northern soil honoring the Civil War's Confederate dead.

bitterness were forgotten. . . .' [I]n many ways it was one of the most remarkable gatherings ever held on Northern soil."[82]

On June 8, 2010, a century later, the remaining Ohio chapters of the United Daughters of the Confederacy rededicated the monument, re-creating much of the original dedication ceremony, including the performance of popular Civil War "golden oldies": "Listen to the Mocking Bird" (1855), "Maryland, My Maryland," (1861), "Old Folks at Home" (aka "Swanee River," 1851), and "Dixie" (1859).

How to Get There

You can get to Johnson's Island by a toll bridge on the Johnson's Island Causeway.

From Sandusky, Ohio—it's about a 30-minute drive to the causeway—take Highway 2 across the Sandusky Bay Bridge, exiting at the Ohio State Route SR 269 ramp and heading south (turning right) on SR 269. Turn left (east) at the first intersection onto East Bayshore Road (County Highway 135) and travel 5.9 miles (9.5 kilometers), remaining on East Bayshore Road (which curves to the right) when Hartshorn Road splits off (to the north), to Gaydos Drive (not South Gaydos Road, which intersects East Bayshore Road first). (Directions from here are continued below.)

From Port Clinton (about a 30-minute drive), take OH-163E (East Perry Street in town) east. Follow South Quarry Road and continue south when it becomes Hartshorn Road to County Road 135/East Bayshore Road, turning left to head east to Gaydos Drive (not Gaydos Road, which intersects East Bayshore Road first).

At Gaydos Drive—coming either from Port Clinton or Sandusky—turn right (south), drive to the tollgate (come prepared with quarters or $1 bills for the unstaffed tollbooth; at the time of writing, the toll was $2) and cross the Johnson's Island Causeway to the island. At the four-way intersection, cross Memorial Shoreway Drive to proceed straight ahead to the cemetery, which is on your left on the east side of the causeway road, which becomes Confederate Drive.

There is no public dock or airport on the island.

What to Expect

Self-guided tours of the cemetery are free.

No public picnic areas, restrooms, or concessions are available on the island. The village of Marblehead, at the tip of the Marblehead Peninsula, does have a number of businesses, including restaurants and a market.

Paths to Adventure

The island's only attraction open to the public is the Confederate cemetery. The rest of the property on the island, one mile long by .5 mile wide (1.6 kilometers long by .8 kilometer wide), is privately owned.

HISTORY PRESERVED

Johnson's Island Confederate Stockade Cemetery

Johnson's Island Causeway just south of Memorial Shoreway Dr.
Johnson's Island
Danbury, OH 43440
www.johnsonsisland.org
Open daily, from dawn to dusk.

NEARBY THINGS TO DO

There are several other interesting sites near Johnson's Island:

Marblehead Lighthouse State Park—Located at the tip of the Marblehead Peninsula (3.3 miles/5.3 kilometers northeast of Johnson's Island), this pleasant lakeside picnic spot is the site of the Marblehead Lighthouse and Museum. Built by William Kelley, completed in 1821, and commissioned in 1835, Marblehead Lighthouse (5681 E. Harbor Rd.,

Unknown soldiers: 52 of the Confederate officers buried in the cemetery on Johnson's Island are listed as unknown.

Marblehead, OH) is the oldest continuously operating lighthouse on all of the Great Lakes. When it is open, you can climb the 77 steps to view the lake from the top. For more information, see www.marbleheadlighthouseohio.org.

The Keeper's House (aka Wolcott House) (9999 Bayshore Rd.)—On the National Register of Historic Places, this was the home of the first three lighthouse keepers of the Marblehead Lighthouse. The first, Benajah Wolcott, who served from 1822 to 1832, was succeeded when he died by his wife, Rebecca, the first female lighthouse keeper on the Great Lakes. Located 1.8 miles (2.9 kilometers) northwest of Johnson's Island, the Keeper's House is open weekdays 1:00–5:00. For more information, visit www.keepers.house.

Lakeside Daisy State Nature Preserve—This unusual nature preserve, located on the Marblehead Peninsula just across the causeway from Johnson's Island, is home to the only natural population of Ohio's rarest plant. Here flourishes the lakeside daisy (*Hymenoxys herbacea*). On the federal list of endangered species, this bright yellow flower, which blooms from early to mid-May, grows on the ledges of the 19-acre abandoned LaFarge limestone quarry.

One of the Great Lakes region's rarest plants, "it is known only from the Marblehead Peninsula area in northern Ohio, three restored populations in northern Illinois (where it was known historically from two sites), and a single, extremely small colony in Michigan's Upper Peninsula. In Ontario, Canada, where lakeside daisy is most abundant, it occurs along much of the southern coast of Manitoulin Island and in several restricted areas near the tip of the Bruce Peninsula."[83]

The Marblehead Peninsula site, on the east side of Alexander Pike (Township Road 142), .5 mile (.8 kilometer) south of SR 163, 2.4 miles (3.9 kilometers) northeast of Johnson's Island, is open only in May. You will find more information at http://nature preserves.ohiodnr.gov/lakesidedaisy.

Maritime Museum of Sandusky

125 Meigs St.

Sandusky, OH

419-624-0274

www.sanduskymaritime.org

Dedicated to helping visitors discover the rich maritime history of the Sandusky Bay area, this museum's interactive exhibits and educational programs will help you learn about boatbuilding, ice harvesting, commercial fishing, shipwrecks, wetlands, Sandusky's role in the Underground Railroad, recreational boating, commercial shipping, passenger boats, and more.

Cedar Point Amusement Park—Directly across Sandusky Bay from Marblehead Peninsula is what bills itself as the "World's Best Amusement Park!" It's the site of over 70 rides, including 16 roller coasters, four children's areas, live shows, and a beachfront hotel.

SPECIAL ISLAND EVENTS

Masonic Memorial Service (Memorial Day weekend)—On the Sunday morning of every Memorial Day weekend, the Masonic Lodge Oliver H. Perry 341 of Port Clinton, Free and Accepted Masons of Ohio performs a service in honor of the Masons who died at Johnson's Island federal prison during the Civil War. More information about the event and about the connection between the Johnson's Island cemetery and the Masons can be found at www.ohperry341.com/JohnsonsIsland.html.

For More Island Information

If you are interested in learning more about the Johnson's Island Depot of Prisoners of War, include a visit to the Johnson's Island Preservation Society Museum in Sandusky, just 20 miles (32 kilometers) away from the cemetery. Opened in the summer of 2001, the museum is dedicated to preserving the prison camp's history and the heritage of Johnson's Island. Exhibits include Civil War artifacts; models of the camp; prisoners' photographs, letters, and diaries; and island archaeological finds.

Johnson's Island Preservation Society & Museum

Ohio Veteran's Home

I.F. Mack Bldg.

3416 Columbus Ave.

Sandusky, OH 44870

419-625-2454

www.johnsonsisland.org
Hours: 1:00–4:00 p.m. weekend days, Memorial Day to October 1, or by appointment.
www.johnsonsisland.com.

The Johnson's Island Civil War military prison website is maintained by the Center for Historic and Military Archaeology at Heidelberg University (a private college located in Tiffin, Ohio) for "Friends and Descendants of Johnson's Island Civil War Prison." The items below are available to purchase at the website's "Sutler's Shop" feature (www .johnsonsisland.com):

I Fear I Shall Never Leave This Island: Life in a Civil War Prison, by David R. Bush (Gaines-ville: University Press of Florida, 2011).
Guide Map to the Confederate Cemetery on Johnson's Island.
1864 Edward Gould print of the Johnson's Island prison.
Rebels on Lake Erie, by Charles E. Frohman (Fremont, OH: Rutherford B. Hayes Presiden-tial Center, 1997).
I Had Rather Lose a Limb & Be Free: The Johnson's Island Experiences of Lt. John Taylor, 7th SC Cavalry, edited by Frances Taylor Meissner and Charles William Meissner Jr. (Sea-ford, VA: Frances Taylor Meissner and Charles William Meissner Jr., 2005).
Far from Home: The Diary of Lt. William H. Peel, 1863–1865, edited by Ellen Sheffield Wilds—The diary, in the care of Mississippi Archives, was transcribed by a Peel descen-dant and self-published via Authorhouse in 2009.
Rebel Fire/Yankee Ice: The Johnson's Island Story (1995; DVD).
Echoes of Grey: Voices from Johnson's Island (1997; DVD).
"Johnson's Island Prison," by Roger Long, *Blue and Gray Magazine,* February–March 1987, 6–31, 45–63.
"They Were Masons: The Rebels on Johnson's Island," by Roger Long, *Scottish Rite Journal,* September 1991, 31–36.

How You Can Support the Island

Johnson's Island Preservation Society & Museum
PO Box 1865
Marblehead, OH 43440
www.johnsonsisland.org
According to the website, the organization is "committed to preserving and document-ing the history of Ohio's most significant Civil War site and . . . [continuing to make] that information available to the public."

The Friends and Descendants of Johnson's Island Civil War Prison (FDJI)
3510 Confederate Dr.
Johnson's Island, OH 43440
www.johnsonsisland.heidelberg.edu/
According to its website, the organization is "dedicated to the preservation of the John-son's Island Prisoner of War Depot located in Sandusky Bay, Lake Erie, Ottawa County, Ohio. Our mission is to preserve and maintain this National Historic Landmark for present and future research, education and interpretive uses."

Parting Thoughts

Such a small island to raise so many historical questions! Here are just two of many other inter-esting historical tidbits we learned about Johnson's Island. Among the prisoners on Johnson's Island was Sergeant Major Horace H. Lurton, who was paroled by President Lincoln after Lur-ton's mother personally pleaded for mercy when she learned her son had been six months in the prison hospital with tuberculosis. Later in life, Lurton was appointed to the U.S. Supreme Court by President Taft.

One of the Confederate officers buried here, Captain Simeon Hamilton, was also a member of the Choctaw Nation, the only Native American to die at Johnson's Island and possibly the only Native American to be imprisoned there. He was also a writer; to read a poem Hamilton wrote while imprisoned on Johnson's Island, visit http://GreatLakesIslandEscapes.com.

For all you history buffs who may not want to stop imagining history after visiting this his-toric island, here are some questions—a veritable Johnson's Island historical scavenger hunt—the answers to which may allow a few glints of history to shed light on how the Great Lakes Basin region was shaped, in part, by what was happening on its islands:

- What are "the Firelands," and how are they connected to the history of Johnson's Island?
- What was the name of the island during the War of 1812, and how was the island used then?
- What gave President Lincoln the occasion to mention Johnson's Island in a letter dated October 2, 1864?
- What part did female spy Anna Davis and Johnson's Island play in the botched Confederate plot known as the "Lake Erie Conspiracy"?
- What did it mean to prisoners on Johnson's Island to "swallow the eagle"?
- What is the Freemason connection to the Confederate Civil War cemetery?
- What was one type of produce grown on the island after the Civil War that the Great Lakes region is still known for producing?
- What destroyed the first (1895–97) of the two Johnson's Island "pleasure resorts," and what well-known attraction of today helped destroy the second (1904–7)?
- What is the ghost story connected to the Breakwater Company's quarry operations (1908–13)?
- When did development of Johnson's Island as a vacation site—with Bay Haven Estates—begin, and what is unusual about the second property development—Baycliffs Subdivi-sion—on the island?

(Answers to the above questions can be found at http://GreatLakesIslandEscapes.com.)

Presque Isle, Pennsylvania

BY SMACK OF STORM . . . OR TAIL

August 15, 2014

Must have just been meant to be. After all, my older daughter, Meagan, and I were already five minutes late when we arrived at the Sunset Pontoon Boat Tours, without the recommended reservations. Only one seat was available for this single sunset tour until Allen, a fourth-time passenger, offered to give up his seat so Meagan and I could share the experience. We gratefully got in line to board with two park rangers and 14 other passengers, most with kids and cameras.

The boat's captain is making her maiden voyage tonight. As we weave through the lagoon system, the other ranger on board directs our attention to the dense colonies of smartweed on the lake, the herb's thousands of pink flowers scattered on its raised carpet of green above the water, a dead ash tree filled with hundreds of purple martins; a family of Canada geese hanging out under an overpass, their half dozen ducklings all adolescents now; two blue herons; and a very large beaver lodge made with a number of larger-than-expected sticks.

GETTING THERE: Causeway; private boat

GETTING AROUND: Bring your car or bike, kayak or canoe; bicycle, surrey (four-wheeled, pedal-driven cart), canoe, rowboat, kayak, motorboat, and pontoon rentals

OVERNIGHT ACCOMMODATIONS: Camping only on the peninsula; hotels and motels in close proximity on the mainland

FOOD: Bring your own (picnic opportunities abound!); concession stands; restaurants and groceries available on the mainland

DAY TRIP? Yes, recommended

STATE / PROVINCIAL / NATIONAL PARK? The entire peninsula constitutes Presque Isle State Park

Pennsylvania calls 51 miles (82 kilometers) of Lake Erie shoreline its own, and Presque Isle can be considered Pennsylvania's one "wannabe"—and only candidate for—Great Lakes Basin island. *Presque Isle* translates to "Almost Island" from the French. While this island has been attached to the mainland consistently for more than 150 years now, it has kept its status as a peninsula thanks only to the persistence of the Army Corp of Engineers.

The Army Corps of Engineers was first charged to secure Presque Isle to protect Erie Harbor, which provided safety for American ships in the War of 1812. The task became harder

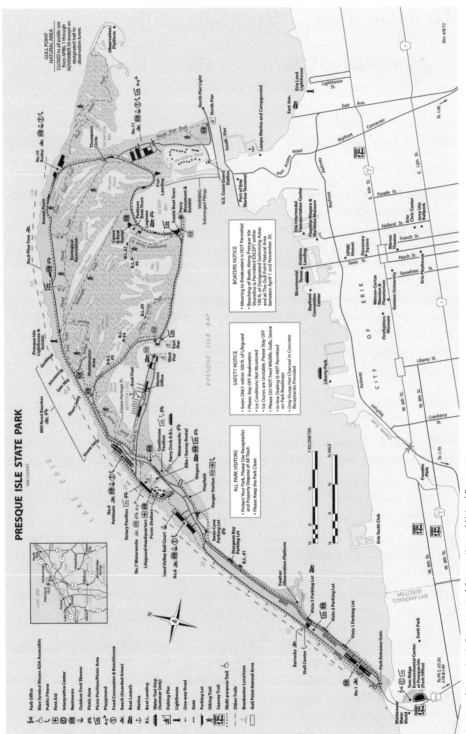

PRESQUE ISLE STATE PARK

Courtesy of Pennsylvania Department of Conservation and Natural Resources

when the winter of 1828–29 saw the first recorded instance of the long neck of the peninsula being breached in a storm. Then, "in 1833, a massive storm opened [a] major break from the mainland which in less than two years expanded to over a mile [1.6 kilometers] wide, making Presque Isle a true island, [and it] . . . remained an island for 32 years until 1864 when the natural sand flow down Lake Erie closed the gap."[84]

This "almost island" has been a Pennsylvania state park since 1921, and in 1937 it was named Presque Isle State Park. In 1967, Presque Isle was designated a National Natural Landmark, a place where geology and history have converged. Given the emphasis on environmental education here and the helpful interpretation visitors are offered while they're having fun exploring the park's attractions, Presque Isle feels like it fits the profile of a Great Lakes Basin island very closely.

How to Get There

Head for Erie, Pennsylvania. The Presque Isle peninsula is accessible by bridge or ferry.

If you plan to arrive by "bridge," that is, the long causeway at the neck of Presque Isle peninsula, you can take either PA Route 55 or U.S. Route 20, coming from east or west, which will intersect PA 832 (aka Sterrettania Road), which becomes Peninsula Drive, the main road in Presque Isle State Park.

You can also arrive by the Presque Isle Water Taxi, sometimes referred to as the Aquabus and operated by the Erie–Western Pennsylvania Port Authority (www.porterie.org). The passenger ferry departs, on the hour, from Dobbins Landing at the end of State Street in downtown Erie. With a stopover at the mainland Liberty Park, the trip is 50 minutes. Passengers disembark at Waterworks Park, which is across from the bike/surrey rental in Presque Isle State Park.

What to Expect

The Tom Ridge Environmental Center, built in 2006, appears just before you drive onto the long causeway neck of the peninsula. On the north side of the 3,200-acre sandy peninsula, you'll find beaches, many beaches, with lifeguards and concession stands. You can rent bikes (single, tandem, and four-seater "surreys"), kayaks, canoes, or pontoons or charter a fishing trip. The south side offers many places to fish.

If you arrive in mid-August, you should expect goldenrod blooming and purple martins congregating. All year, you can expect beautiful beaches, a system of lagoons and trails to explore, two lighthouses that present wonderful photographic opportunities, and then some. And if you're lucky, you just might see the largest native rodent on the continent, a North American beaver.

Paths to Adventure

NATURAL SITES

Presque Isle is an ecological preserve, described as "fragile," composed of woods, wetlands, and the six sand ridges that are the highest points on the peninsula.

The Tom Ridge Environmental Center (TREC) at Presque Isle State Park introduces visitors to the 3,200-acre peninsula and the life that lives on it.

Tom Ridge Environmental Center (TREC) at Presque Isle State Park—This is the best place to begin your visit to this unique "island." Here you will find great interpretive exhibits that explain what you're about to see on the peninsula: What has caused this recurving sand spit? What influenced its transformation through a series of natural successions? What flora and fauna call it home? Take in the nature displays (note their beautiful and unusual use of watercolor) and the art, and catch a film on the "Big Green Screen" (four stories high and 45 feet wide). You'll find all things beach and many resources specifically related to Presque Isle at the Nature Shop located in TREC (www.facebook.com/The-Nature-Shop-114636031907888/timeline).

Beaches—Enjoy one or more of the park's 10 beaches, open daily from 10 a.m. to 7:30 p.m., Memorial Day weekend to Labor Day, unless otherwise posted. (Free loaner beach wheelchairs are available at the Yellow Bike Shop.)

Trails—Hike one or more of the 15 trails in the park: there are approximately 11 miles (18 kilometers) of trails here, from the B Trail at .3 miles (.4 kilometers) to Gull Point Trail, 3.5 miles (5.6 kilometers) in distance. For descriptions of them all, consult the interactive trail map on the Presque Isle website at www.presqueisle.org/things-to-do/trails; Eugene H. Ware's book *A Walk on the Park,* available in the TREC Nature Shop; or the Pennsylvania Department of Conservation and Natural Resources website at www.dcnr.state.pa.us/stateparks/findapark/presqueisle/.

Gull Point Trail—If you plan on biking around the entire peninsula, the trailhead of Gull Point Trail comes at a convenient point, approximately at the halfway mark in the loop. If you are driving the loop, you'll find parking at the trailhead. The trail starts at the southeast end of the parking area just to the east of Budny Beach (Beach 10), and there is an information kiosk located at the trailhead. This is the longest trail in the park (3.5

miles/5.6 kilometers round trip). This open walk (with limited tree cover) winds through Gull Point Natural Area (GPNA, a closed bird sanctuary), bisecting the point on a sand plain, crossing through all the phases of natural succession seen in the park, and encountering ponds, ridges, dunes, and swales, all formed by Lake Erie's wave action (and all of which you can learn more about at the Tom Ridge Environmental Center). Much of the trail is sandy, but you may encounter mud or water depending on lake level and conditions. In addition to diverse bird species, some of the beach and dune plants here are not found anywhere else in Pennsylvania. Gull Point provides a safe haven for migrating birds to feed and rest on their migration across Lake Erie. Between April 1 and November 30, visitor access through the GPNA is only on the trail surface to and from the observation platform, which is located at the Thompson Bay area and the shore of Lake Erie. From the observation platform, you will be able to see wide vistas of Lake Erie and beach, the entrance channel to Erie Harbor at North Pier, and the North Pier Light. You may also be able to observe research being carried out in the sanctuary in the distance. Bring water to drink and a camera to shoot both nature up close and the wider view. Allow about two hours; the park classifies this trail as a "moderate to difficult" hike due to the deep sand in places. Although we did experience some deep sand, we enjoyed a greater challenge in the amount of water we came across on portions of the trail. A great hike!

HISTORY PRESERVED

Presque Isle Lighthouse—Regardless of when you come by during park hours, you can view this 1873 lighthouse, the second oldest on Lake Erie's shore, from Lighthouse Beach as well as take in the exhibit between the road and the lighthouse. You can also tour the lighthouse on the half hour between 10 a.m. and 4:00 p.m. every Saturday and Sunday from Memorial Day to Labor Day (as well as on some summer holiday Mondays). Tickets can be purchased at the lighthouse ($5 in 2015), and a gift shop is on the premises.

North Pier Light—Walk North Pier to this lighthouse (originally built in 1828), whose current structure and location were established in 1940.

Waterworks Park—In searching for a cleaner water source, the City of Erie developed a system on Presque Isle. In 1908, a pipe was installed from the lake to settling basins on the peninsula. In 1917, a pump house containing a steam boiler and engine was built. Water was drawn from the lake to the first settling basin, pumped to a second settling basin, and then pumped across the bay to the city. This water system was in operation until 1949. Today the pump house is used to help control zebra mussels in Erie's water supply. The park is a popular picnic area.

Perry Monument (1926)—170 miles (274 kilometers) west of the site of Commodore Perry's 1813 victory in the Battle of Lake Erie, the Presque Isle monument is located at Crystal Point on Misery Bay, where Perry and his men spent the winters before and after the decisive battle that turned the tide in the War of 1812. Six of his nine vessels—including the two brigs the *Lawrence* and the *Niagara*—were built here, most likely from lumber harvested from the peninsula, in the winter of 1812–13; the bay, then known as Little Bay, afforded him protection. After the September 10 battle Perry and his men returned to the bay, where they ultimately were quarantined, as many of them had contracted smallpox. Many died from the disease and were buried at the nearby pond, now known as Graveyard Pond. Misery Bay's name came from the misery Perry and his men suffered there that winter. The hulls of the two brigs were sunk in the bay to protect them from the weather. (They were both later raised; the U.S. brig *Niagara,* recovered in 1913, was rebuilt and is now docked at the Erie Maritime Museum at 150 E. Front St. #100, Erie, PA).

The Perry Monument, a 101-foot obelisk at Crystal Point on Presque Isle, was built in 1926 to honor War of 1812 naval hero Commodore Oliver Hazard Perry.

CULTURAL ATTRACTIONS

Horseshoe Pond houseboats—Don't miss seeing—by land or boat—the gently bobbing and eclectic group of 24 houseboats anchored in this pond off Misery Bay in the east end of the park. At one time, houseboats were anchored all over Presque Isle Bay—referred to as the "poor man's vacation home"—and a plan was developed to get rid of all of them. Instead, the houseboats were collected and moved to Horseshoe Pond in the 1960s. The private owners of the houseboats pay rent to the state for the docking space.[85]

Waldameer Park and Water World—This amusement and water park is located at the base of the Presque Isle peninsula. "Rides, slides, and attractions" is how it's billed, and one of those attractions is the Ravine Flyer II, a wooden roller coaster ranked sixth best in the world. Waldameer is the fourth-oldest amusement park in Pennsylvania and the tenth oldest in the United States.

OTHER ISLAND THINGS TO DO

Rent a surrey, bicycle, tricycle, paddleboat, or rollerblades—All are available from the Yellow Bike Rental Company in the park, giving you a choice of means by which to make the entire circuit of the peninsula. We spent an entire—very full and fun—day riding around on bikes, exploring every little thing. In fact, I would drive to Erie, Pennsylvania, just to spend another day like this!

Take a Segway tour—Presque Isle Touring Company offers Segway rentals and is located at the Yellow Bike Rental Company.

Kayak or canoe the lagoons—Rentals are available in the park.

Make reservations for the Sunset Pontoon Boat Tour—Park rangers serve as interpretive guides.

Take a scenic boat tour—The *Lady Kate* and other vessels await you.

Go bird-watching—Presque Isle is located on the Atlantic Flyway and has been rated by *Birder's World* magazine as one of the top birding spots in the country. Over 300 species of birds have been recorded here. You can get a checklist of birds at the TREC or online at www.presqueisleaudubon.org/uploads/2/5/0/0/25009090/_eriecountypabird checklist2014.pdf.

Hike a part of the Great Lakes Seaway Trail (aka Seaway Trail)—This 518-mile (834-kilometer) "National Scenic Byway," located in Pennsylvania and New York, follows the shoreline of Lake Erie, the Niagara River, Lake Ontario, and the St. Lawrence River.

SPECIAL ISLAND EVENTS

Joe Root's Frostbite Open (a Sunday in February)—An annual Presque Isle Partnership fund-raiser that pays tribute to Presque Isle's legendary Joe Root with nine holes of golf on Presque Isle Bay and dinner at Joe Roots Grill.

Festival of Birds (second Saturday in May)—Celebrate International Migratory Bird Day at Presque Isle.

Three Mile Isle Obstacle Course Challenge (June)—Featuring 11 obstacles over three miles (5 kilometers) through Beaches 10 and 11.

Bayswim (June)—One-mile (1.6-kilometer) swim across Presque Isle Bay from Presque Isle State Park to Erie Yacht Club.

Pushing off for an evening "Lagoons by Pontoon" boat tour on Presque Isle. In addition to many park attractions, what was seen: a family of Canada geese; hundreds of purple martins using a dead tree as a staging site, lifting into synchronous circles of flight and returning to settle, silhouetted on the bare branches; thousands of smartweed's pink spikes rising above the water; and, just as the sun was setting, a beaver out in front of the boat, swimming across the lagoon.

Sunset Music Series (June and July)—Every Wednesday night for six weeks, Beach 1 becomes a free open-air concert venue. Bring a chair and/or blanket.

Discover Presque Isle (last full weekend in July)—This annual event offers numerous activities—nature programs, craft displays, children's activities, various competitions, food vendors, live music, bonfires, and more. Check out www.discoverpi.com for more event details.

Annual Presque Isle Triathlon (August).

Peninsula Polar Fest (December).

Races and walks—Erie Runner's Club hosts several races and walks throughout the year. For more information, visit www.erie-runnersclub.org.

For More Island Information

Presque Isle State Park—www.presqueisle.org.

Presque Isle Naturally: A Field Guide, by Robert K. Grubbs (Baltimore: American Literary Press, 2006).

A Field Guide to the Birds of Presque Isle, by Robert K. Grubbs. (Erie, PA: n.p., 2011).

Whispers across the Pond, by Eugene H. Ware (Bloomington, IN: Xlibris, 2009).

A Walk on the Park: Twenty Self-Guided Walking Tours on Presque Isle State Park, by Eugene H. Ware (Erie, PA: Eugene H. Ware, 2006).

A History of Presque Isle: As Told through Conversation with the Park's Legendary Hermit, Joe Root, by Eugene H. Ware (Bloomington, IN: iUniverse, 2013).

Presque Isle State Park, by Eugene H. Ware (Charleston, SC: Arcadia, 2011).

The Moods of Presque Isle: A Chronicle of Presque Isle State Park, Erie, Pennsylvania Presented in Photographs, Prose, Poetry, and Personal Reflections, by Eugene H. Ware (Bloomington, IN: Xlibris, 2004).

How You Can Support the Island

Presque Isle Partnership (PIP)

The PIP website states the organization's mission as being to work "to improve the environment and educate the public on the value of the park's ecosystem."

Become a member at https://app.etapestry.com/onlineforms/PresqueIslePartnership Inc/PImembership.html.

To volunteer, e-mail a PIP event coordinator or call 814-838-5144.

Parting Thoughts

The sun is a fiery ball sinking fast and the air has an edge of chill to it as the pontoon turns to thread its way back through the kayakers in the lagoon, gradually leaving them behind. When we turn to look forward at the serene water in front of the boat, lapping pink to indigo, a long narrow wake has appeared. At the apex of the V, there's a dark knob just above the water. As our eyes adjust to looking into the low sun, we can see it's a head out of the water, something swimming. Beaver! Very cute ears, but as we draw closer, I see the shadowy underwater bulk of an animal bigger than I expected. Maybe the resident of that large lodge? I lean over the rail with my camera . . .

Smack! A big splash. Smack! A sudden second slap of tail on the water's surface. A clear message that this is his neighborhood, after all, and we're the guests who need a reminder—maybe two—to mind our manners.

Niagara River Islands

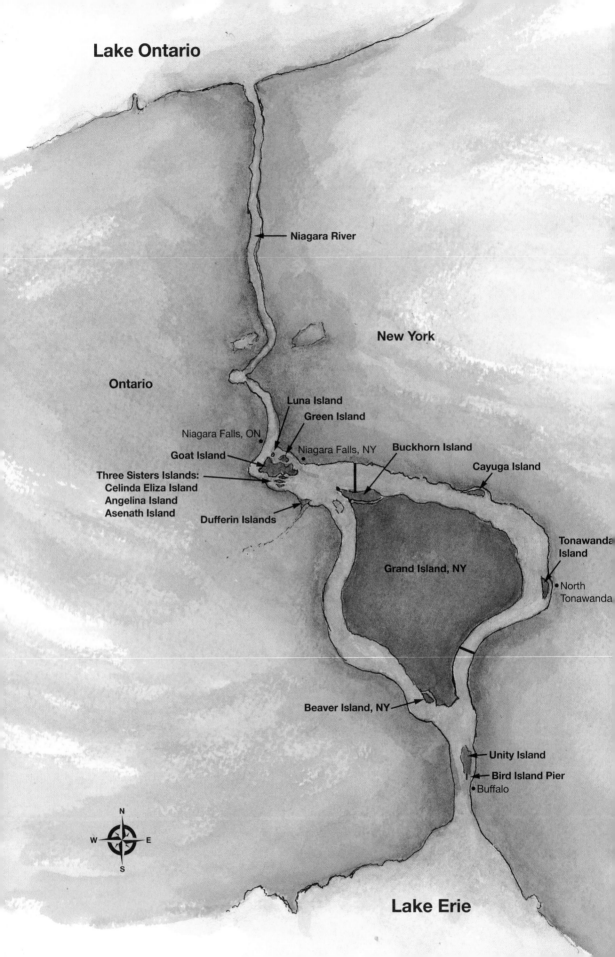

An Introduction to the Niagara River

The Niagara River flows northward from Lake Erie to Lake Ontario with a drop of 326 feet in elevation during its 36-mile (58-kilometer) course. The river creates the U.S.-Canadian border between the province of Ontario on its western banks and the state of New York on its eastern banks, with Fort Erie, Ontario, and Buffalo, New York, at its (southern) source and Niagara-on-the-Lake, Ontario, and Youngstown, New York—with Old Fort Niagara—at its (northern) mouth.

On the Ontario side of the Niagara River, the bridge of land with Lake Erie to the south and Lake Ontario to the north is known as the Niagara Peninsula. Across the river in New York, the American side of this bridge of land is known as part of the Niagara Frontier.

Of course, the Niagara River's most interesting natural feature—which accounts for much of the river's decreasing elevation—are the three magnificent waterfalls located in the "elbow" bend of the river about halfway downstream, between Niagara Falls, Ontario, and Niagara Falls, New York. The American Falls are 176 feet above the Niagara Gorge with a 1,100-foot-wide brink. The Bridal Veil Falls (also belonging to the United States), the smallest of the three, are named for their resemblance to the train of a bridal veil. The Horseshoe Falls, located in Canada, are 167 feet high, with a brink that is 2,500 feet wide.

The Niagara Falls State Park, the oldest state park in the country, is located in Niagara Falls, New York. The Niagara appropriations bill was signed into law in 1885, creating the "Niagara Reservation," which was declared a U.S. National Historic Landmark in 1963.

In addition to the three world-renowned waterfalls, there are 19 islands in the Niagara River between Lake Erie and the Niagara Falls. Most of them are on the U.S. side of the border, and the majority of them are accessible by bridge.

How You Can Support the Niagara River

Buffalo Niagara Riverkeeper
721 Main St.
Buffalo, NY 14203
http://bnriverkeeper.org/get-involved/volunteer/

Islands of the Upper Niagara River, New York and Ontario

BEFORE THE FALLS

August 17, 2013, 7:45 p.m.
Dick & Jenny's
Grand Island

Nancy and I are having dinner at Dick & Jenny's on Grand Island tonight. The owners' first restaurant was in New Orleans until Hurricane Katrina, and here in New York—although Grand Island is like no "New York," as in the city or upstate, I've ever experienced—the New Orleans flavor shows in their menu, the music, and the ambiance. This is the perfect place to relax and consider our time together islanding on the Niagara River.

Who'd have thought how many adventures are to be had upstream from Niagara Falls? I am realizing, after the hiking we did yesterday on Beaver Island and today on Buckhorn Island and our wonderful summertime stroll down Bird Island Pier, with Black Rock Canal on one side and the Niagara coursing on the other, that New York has a Great Lakes character, too. There is definitely turning out to be much more to the Niagara River than just the falls, a big part of which is the "nonwater" part of the river, its islands.

GETTING THERE: Bridge

GETTING AROUND: Bring your car and/or bike; other than Grand Island proper, all islands provide good opportunities for exploration by foot

OVERNIGHT ACCOMMODATIONS: Grand Island: A variety of overnight accommodations and three campgrounds

    Beaver Island State Park and Buckhorn Island State Park: None

    Unity Island, Tonawanda Island, Cayuga Island: None

FOOD: Grand Island: Restaurants; groceries

    Tonawanda Island: The Shores Waterfront Restaurant

    Bring your own! Unity Island, Beaver Island, and Buckhorn Island in particular provide good picnicking opportunities

DAY TRIP? Yes, the only option except for Grand Island

STATE / PROVINCIAL / NATIONAL PARK? Beaver Island State Park and Buckhorn Island State Park

Before the water in the Great Lakes Basin reaches the Niagara Falls, it flows around six easily accessible American islands, all of which offer the beautiful scenery of the Niagara River and a number of island paths to adventure.

How to Get There

The six American islands described below are all accessible by bridge from the New York side of the river and are located between the cities of Buffalo and Niagara Falls, New York, between the Peace Bridge (an international bridge) and the North Grand Island Bridge (a toll bridge), which carries interstate highway I-90. Besides I-90, U.S. Route 62 may be helpful in traveling to these islands.

What to Expect

These six Niagara River New York islands are different from one another and have a variety of paths to take to adventure listed within the island descriptions below.

UNITY ISLAND

This beautiful 60-acre island in the area that has become Buffalo's Black Rock neighborhood was first named De-dyo-we-no-guh-doh, meaning "Divided Island," by the Seneca; the "divided" refers to the island being divided by a marshy creek that, at a later time, came to be known as Smuggler's Run. The island was renamed Squaw Island by La Salle's expedition in 1679, and so it remained until two women of Native American heritage petitioned the Buffalo Common Council to change the name of the island. They were later joined by the president of the Seneca Nation of Indians. The original Native name was proposed, but ultimately the council voted to change the island's name to Unity Island on July 6, 2015. The island has seen much more action than just a name change. This is where the British warship HMS *Detroit* was beached, burned, and sunk in the War of 1812, and the island was a significant site in the Underground Railroad. At one time used as a municipal garbage dump, the island is now home to Broderick Park, Unity Island Park, and a waste-treatment facility. Unity Island also provides access to Bird Island Pier (www.buffaloah. com/a/water/bird/1/).

Bird Island Pier—Unity Island's lovely waterfront walk leads to Bird Island Pier, aka Nowak Pier, 16 feet in height and 18 feet wide, which extends approximately two miles (three

MOVING FORWARD WITH UNITY

Jodi Lynn Maracle, a Tyendinaga Mohawk scholar-activist, and Agnes Williams, a Seneca Nation member, worked with the Buffalo City Common Council to change the racist and misogynist name of Squaw Island. The origins of the word *squaw* are unclear—it may have come from the Iroquoian word for female genitalia—but many consider the term demeaning to Native women and believe it implies promiscuity. Six states have passed legislation to eradicate the term *squaw* in place-names. New York is not one of these states, not yet, but one of its cities, Buffalo, is clearly on the side of the forward-looking.

Bird Island Pier (aka Nowak Pier), New York, extending into the Niagara River from Unity Island and going under the international Peace Bridge.

kilometers), goes under the international Peace Bridge, and was connected to Unity Island in 1822 as a part of improvements made to Black Rock Harbor. Bird Island Pier remained for some time a place for boarding the pleasure steamers en route to the resorts on Grand Island. Bird Island itself was demolished and used to build the Bird Island Pier walkway. A walk on Bird Island Pier, with the rushing Niagara River on one side and the calm waters of the Black Rock Channel on the other, allows you to see what you could usually experience only from a boat.

TONAWANDA ISLAND

Located between Niagara Falls, New York, and Buffalo, the island is accessible by a vehicular bridge from North Tonawanda, New York. Tonawanda Island would be an interesting location to work, and most of the island is light industrial, except for Placid Harbor Marina (the warehouse of which was destroyed in April 2015 by a massive fire; there are plans to rebuild) and the Shores Waterfront Restaurant (www.shoreswaterfront.com), the clientele of which arrives by private boat, car, or foot. Visiting there, it is easy to pretend you're on a "northern

Key" as you sip a margarita and munch coconut shrimp under a thatched umbrella while the sun sparkles on the water and the river flows quickly by.

CAYUGA ISLAND

Cayuga is an attractive island neighborhood of the city of Niagara Falls, New York, consisting of eight streets of homes and a park on the river, which flows around the island (www.facebook.com/pages/Cayuga-Island-Niagara-Falls-New-York/121797127875568). This island is not far from the infamous Lasalle neighborhood, the site of the Love Canal hazardous waste tragedy caused by Hooker Chemical Company, first brought to the public's attention in 1978. To get to the island from the falls, take Robert Moses Parkway to 66th Street to Buffalo Avenue (384) to 86th Street. Cross the South 86th Street bridge to the island. Across from the island is Griffon Park, so named for the first sailing vessel on the Great Lakes, *Le Griffon*, built in 1679 at the nearby Cayuga Creek on the Niagara River and launched by Robert de La Salle.

BUCKHORN ISLAND

Located on the north end of and separated from Grand Island, New York, by Burnt Ship Creek, this island is home to the Buckhorn Island State Park and Nature Preserve (http://nysparks.com/parks/174/details.aspx). The park contains 895 acres of marsh, meadow, and woods and is primarily an example of Niagara River wetlands. Visitors are welcome to walk the nature trails, hike or bike, kayak or canoe, or to fish or cross-country ski in season. The park's restoration plan includes more nonintrusive trails, overlooks, and bird-watching blinds. (Note: There are no public restrooms available at this park.)

The Shores Waterfront Island Restaurant and Marina at the southern tip of Tonawanda Island, New York. Despite the grass umbrellas and the coconut shrimp served beneath them, the waterfront belongs to the mighty Niagara River.

GRAND ISLAND

Originally called Ga-We-Not (Great Island) by the Senecas, Grand Island is the largest island in the Niagara River, some eight miles (13 kilometers) long and six miles (10 kilometers) wide at its widest point. The I-90 expressway runs from Niagara Falls, New York, across Grand Island to Tonawanda, New York. The island is mostly residential and industrial, but at both the north and south tips are other islands: Buckhorn Island and Beaver Island, both of which are state parks with trails and plenty of opportunities to kayak or canoe.

Paddles Up Niagara Trail—An up-to-25-mile (40-kilometer) paddlesports adventure around Grand Island with the opportunity to paddle through two New York State Parks (www .niagaragreenway.org).

Martin's Fantasy Island—Since 1961, this amusement park has been adding attractions: rides for all ages; Kiddie Land; water slides, including the Dragster Drench and the Cannon Bowl; a wave pool; live shows; restaurants; and shops.

For More Grand Island Information

Grand Island—www.grand-island.ny.us.

Cinderella Island: Grand Island, by Rob Roy Macleod (Grand Island, NY: self-published, 1950).

Grand Island, by Gerald Carpenter and June Justice Crawford (Mount Pleasant, SC: Arcadia, 2015).

How You Can Support Grand Island

Grand Island Historical Society
PO Box 135
Grand Island, NY 14072
www.isledegrande.com/historicalsociety

BEAVER ISLAND

Also known as Little Beaver Island, Beaver Island is located on the south end of Grand Island, New York, 14 miles (23 kilometers) up the Niagara River from the falls. The island is a part of the Beaver Island State Park and Beach (www.nysparks.com/parks/56/details.aspx), a 950-acre park featuring:

A .5-mile (.8-kilometer) sandy swimming beach

An 80-slip marina and boat launch

Canoe/kayak launches

Fishing access

Bike trail, nature trail, and three hiking trails: East River Trail, Lagoon Walk, and Spaulding Trail

Bird-watching

Playgrounds, picnic areas, and horseshoe pits

An 18-hole championship disc golf course and an 18-hole championship golf course

Snowmobiling (by permit), **cross-country skiing, snowshoeing, sledding, and ice fishing**

Waterfowl hunting (in season for permit holders)

Beaver Island Nature Center—Open July and August on weekend afternoons; check for current hours online, or for more information call 716-282-5154. Interpretive programs are offered at the park.

The Villa at River Lea—Lewis Allen bought 600 acres on the south side of Grand Island, which became Allenton Farm. His son later built a villa called River Lea on the land. The State of New York intended to demolish the house in the 1960s after buying the property to enlarge Beaver Island State Park. "The Grand Island Historical Society convinced the state to restore the house instead because William Cleveland Allen's cousin—President Grover Cleveland—had visited it several times."[86] The Villa at River Lea is currently home to the Grand Island Historical Society and its museum.

Nearby Mainland Paths to Adventure

Buffalo Botanical Gardens (2655 South Park Ave., Buffalo, NY; www.buffalogardens.com/).

Buffalo Naval Park (1 Naval Park Cove, Buffalo, NY; www.buffalonavalpark.org).

Buffalo Niagara Heritage Village (3755 Tonawanda Creek Rd., Amherst, NY; www.bnhv.org).

Buffalo Zoo (300 Parkside Ave., Buffalo, NY; www.buaffalozoo.org).

Erie Canal Discovery Center (24 Church St., Lockport, NY; www.NiagaraHistory.org)—The Erie Canal was built in 1825 and now is a 36-mile linear recreational park that includes Victorian villages, working farms, two locks, and Buffalo's historic Canalside district.

Lockport Locks and Erie Canal Cruises (210 Market St., Lockport, NY; www.lockportlocks.com).

A number of buildings designed by Frank Lloyd Wright are in the Niagara River–Buffalo area.

- Fontana Boathouse—Located at the foot of Porter Avenue next to the West Side Rowing Club in Buffalo. The design for this—Wright's only boathouse—was originally conceived in 1905 for a boathouse for the University of Wisconsin Boat Club. The design was finally manifested in 2007 in Buffalo along the shore of the Black Rock Channel. It is currently used as a rowing facility. (Note: 48-hour advance reservation is required.)

- Martin House Complex (125 Jewett Pkwy., Buffalo)—These five interconnected buildings were built between 1903 and 1905 for a wealthy Buffalo businessman. The complex recently underwent a $50 million restoration. Reservations are recommended. For further information, see www.darwinmartinhouse.org.

- Graycliff Estate (6472 Old Lake Shore Rd., Denby, NY)—Built as a summer home between 1926 and 1929, the estate has views of Lake Erie. Reservations are required. Visit www.GraycliffEstate.org.

- Blue Sky Mausoleum at Forest Lawn (1411 Delaware Ave., Buffalo)—Built in 2008 to a Wright design.

- William R. Heath House (76 Soldiers Pl., Buffalo)—Wright's first residential commission in Buffalo, built 1903–5. The private residence is not open to the public.

- Walter V. Davidson House (57 Tillinghost Pl., Buffalo)—Built in 1908, this private residence is not open to the public.

Visit a Frederick Law Olmsted park in the area—For more information, consult *Olmsted in Buffalo and Niagara,* by Lynda Schneekloth, Robert Shibley, and Thomas Yots (Buffalo, NY: Urban Design Project, School of Architecture and Planning, University at Buffalo, 2011).

OTHER THINGS TO DO

Go fish—The Niagara has a reputation as one of North America's finest fisheries, affording the opportunity to catch smallmouth bass, muskellunge, chinook salmon, rainbow and steelhead trout, and walleye.

Niagara Wine Trail—Listed in the Weather Channel Travel Top Ten Picks as "one of the top-ten wine regions in the world" and lauded by the *New York Post* as "New York's most cutting-edge wine region,"[87] the Niagara Wine Trail strings together towns, restaurants, farm markets, and antique shops as well as more than a dozen and a half wineries between the Niagara Escarpment and Lake Ontario in Niagara County. For more information, visit www.NiagaraWineTrail.org.

Parting Thoughts

Nancy and I have been walking and talking and walking some more these last few days. It turned out to be an adventure just to find some of the islands upstream from the falls, and while we were searching for them, we had additional adventures along the way. How many people come to visit the Niagara Falls and have no idea what is just around the corner? We both had been clueless about these island opportunities on earlier visits. Sure, spend a day or two with the tourists at the falls—we also learned that walking the trails on Goat Island made that entire experience much more fun and relaxing—but keep in mind that just minutes away are places of quiet seclusion that feel like they're miles away and that allow for exploration and discovery. Taking those less traveled paths to adventure allowed us to get much closer to and appreciate the Niagara, the river itself, in a whole different way.

Islands at the Falls, New York

THE CLOSEST PROSPECT

August 15, 2013, 4:45 p.m.
Goat Island

Sure, the falls are stupendous. But what I'm finding myself drawn to on this visit are the rapids leading up to the falls. In this river, here, they've been left, by both the Americans and Canadians, for the most part, to sweep and tumble and rush. To a large degree, this would have been because here a canal or a lock, unlike in other spots in the Great Lakes Basin where rapids roiled—the St. Marys Rapids and the Long Sault Rapids come immediately to mind—was not going to help commerce move up or down past this invigorating spot in the river. It took the Canadian Welland Canal with its eight locks to connect Lake Erie to Lake Ontario, allowing sailors to avoid the Niagara Falls.

It's really the islands at the falls that let us get up close and feel the power in the water here. There are two interesting statues in the Niagara Falls State Park commemorating the inventor and futurist (in his time apparently regarded as more than a bit of a "mad scientist) Nikola Tesla (the original "AC/DC man"). Fascinating to consider who the falls draw to their energy and why: Tesla, the hermit of Hermit's Cascade (see below); artists, writers, photographers; lovers, brides, suicides.

What must this thundering place have been like before all the tourists came? What did the Anishinaabe see here at this, their second stop on their migration west?

GETTING THERE: Pedestrian bridges; the American Rapids Bridge, which connects the mainland to Goat Island, also carries motor vehicles

GETTING AROUND: No cars allowed, except on Goat Island; tour bus; easy walking paths

OVERNIGHT ACCOMMODATIONS: None; the park closes at 8:00 p.m. (in the summer) or earlier

FOOD: Top of the Falls Restaurant (Goat Island); Cave of the Winds Snack Bar, Prospect Point Café, and concession stands; bring your own picnic food (groceries are available on the mainland)

DAY TRIP? Yes, the only option

STATE / PROVINCIAL / NATIONAL PARK? Niagara Falls State Park

Visitors to the Niagara Falls State Park can access six Niagara River islands situated above—immediately upstream from—the falls on foot and one of these, Goat Island, by vehicle as well.

How to Get There

If you are coming to Niagara Falls through Canada, follow Ontario Highway 401 (east or west, depending on your departure point) to Ontario Highway 403 to Queen Elizabeth Way, which intersects the Niagara Parkway on the Canadian side of the Niagara River. If you want to cross to the American side of the river, you can do so by following Queen Elizabeth Way to Ontario Highway 405 and onto Lewiston-Queenston Bridge to the United States, whereupon it becomes Interstate 190 S and intersects the Robert Moses Parkway on the American side of the river. Or you can follow the Niagara Parkway (and the river) south to the Niagara Falls International Rainbow Bridge.

If you are heading to Niagara Falls through the United States, follow Interstate 90 (I-90 E or I-90 W, depending on your departure point) to Interstate 190 to U.S. Route 62, which leads to the Niagara Falls International Rainbow Bridge.

The International Rainbow Bridge connects Ontario King's Highway 420 and New York State Route 384, the two cities (of Niagara Falls), and crosses the international border. North of the Rainbow Bridge is the aforementioned Lewiston-Queenston Bridge, and between the two is the Niagara Falls Whirlpool Bridge (which allows access only to NEXUS card holders). South of the Rainbow Bridge is the Buffalo and Fort Erie Public Bridge, also known as the Peace Bridge.

When you are planning your trip to the Niagara River, consider the fact that even though you may, say, be heading from the Detroit area to Niagara Falls, New York, the fastest route may be through Ontario because it is a more direct route by which you can avoid having to circumnavigate the entire south shore of Lake Erie.

Pedestrian bridge from the New York mainland, over the American Rapids, to Green Island.

What to Expect

Expect other tourists. Expect a certain level of commercialism that comes with being the oldest state park in the country. Expect a great deal of thunderous majesty of waterfall! And also, if you're looking for it, expect plenty of a quieter sort of scenic beauty, often discovered by using walking as a way to savor the islands.

The six islands at the falls provide unique views of the waterfalls, which are just below them, and the rapids, which surround them. These islands have a variety of paths to take to adventure—and most of them involve actual walking paths—listed within the island descriptions below.

GREEN ISLAND

This New York island of 1.5 acres, located in the American Goat Island Channel just upstream from the American Falls, was purchased together with Goat Island in 1816 from the State of New York by Judge Augustus Porter, "the first white settler of what is now the city of Niagara Falls, . . . a pathfinder and pioneer in the promotion of the development of the power of the Niagara river . . . an engineer, a lawyer and a business man, as well as a statesman."[88] In the 1800s, the island was known as Bath Island because of the bathhouses, said to contain both warm and cold, as well as "showering" baths, at the western end visited by tourists. Bath Island was also the site of a toll gatehouse, built in 1821, where tourists paid to cross a bridge to Goat Island.

Although small, Bath Island had quite a bit of manufacturing going on beginning in the 1820s—a woolen factory, forge rolling mill, nail factory, and paper mill all operated here before the island became a part of the park in 1885.

The island received its present name in 1898 in honor of Andrew Haswell Green, one of the first, and the longest-serving, Niagara Reservation commissioners.

Two bridges built in the 1900s connect Green Island: one to the mainland, the other to Goat Island.

GOAT ISLAND

This New York island was named by its owner (who also owned Green Island, but himself lived on the mainland), John Stedman (also spelled Steadman), who was appointed Master of the Portage by the British as early as 1764 and had a sawmill on the island. Although Porter, according to the story that has come down to us (or an "early proprietor," according to earlier histories) attempted to change the name to Iris Island (after the Greek goddess of the rainbow), local residents were apparently as stubborn with respect to the name Goat as is the animal the island was named after.

Although Britain accepted the Great Lakes as the northern boundary of the United States under the treaty of 1783, the land around the falls, including the island, was not surrendered until 1796, after the ratification of Jay's Treaty in 1794. A tenant of Stedman's was legally removed from the island in 1806, and finally, in 1825, a circuit court case (*Jackson v. Porter*) was heard, involving a "lost"—and ruled false—conveyance of deed by the Seneca to Stedman. Stedman lost.

Located at the brink of the Horseshoe Falls, Goat Island divides the Horseshoe Falls from both of the American waterfalls, most immediately the Bridal Veil Falls (situated in the middle of the two larger waterfalls). Goat Island is accessible by pedestrian bridge from Green Island or by the vehicular American Rapids Bridge (parking is available on the island).

A number of falls attractions are located on Goat Island.

OF WOLVES AND BEARS AND GOATS

Legend has it that the island was named in honor of a tough old billy goat Stedman had, the only survivor of a winter too rough for Stedman to cross to the island to feed the goats he had pastured there (supposedly to keep them safe from the wolves, although other sources claim there were wolves—and bears—on the island at that time). This account from a descendant of Augustus Porter is perhaps more likely, although it lacks a happy ending: Stedman "cleared about ten acres of the upper end of Goat Island, and put a number of goats there, from which fact the island derived its name. These goats all perished in the winter of 1780, memorable for its severity."*

* A. H. Porter, *Historical Sketch of Niagara from 1678 to 1876* (N.p.,1876), 26.

Terrapin Point—This is the ideal place from which to watch the water flow over the brink of the Horseshoe Falls.

Cave of the Winds—Ride an elevator 175 feet down to the base of the Bridal Veil Falls for a guided walking tour beneath the American Falls and experience their power just feet from them—wearing a supplied rain poncho—on the Hurricane Deck.

Top of the Falls Restaurant—Enjoy a meal or a drink at this establishment overlooking the Horseshoe Falls. This restaurant serves locally grown sustainable products and seafood approved by the Monterey Bay Aquarium Sustainable Seafood Program.

Hermit's Cascade—This small cascade that flows between Goat Island and what is now called Asenath Island was named after writer and artist Francis Abbott. He wanted to build a cottage on Asenath Island, the first of the Three Sisters Islands, then known as the Moss Islands, but could not obtain permission from the Porters to do so. So instead he lived for two years in the area of the falls, first on Goat Island and then north of Prospect Point. Year-round, "the hermit" bathed in the cascade. He drowned swimming in the river below the falls two years after moving to the area.

Cross more bridges from Goat Island to access Luna Island and the Three Sisters Islands.

LUNA ISLAND

Accessible from Goat Island, this small island, which divides the American Falls and the Bridal Veil Falls, was originally called Prospect Island because it provides a wonderful "prospect"—or view—of the falls. Its name was changed in the nineteenth century to bring attention to the fact that on a moonlit night—before artificial lighting—the misty spray from the falls created "lunar bows" dancing in the air around the island.

THE THREE SISTERS ISLANDS

Accessible from Goat Island, these three islands were formerly known as Moss Islands because of the moss covering the rocks on their banks. East of the Horseshoe Falls, these islands provide an ideal spot from which to view the upper Horseshoe Rapids.

The islands were renamed in 1843 for the three daughters of U.S. Army general Parkhurst Whitney, a commander in the War of 1812 and a local businessman. Their proud papa wanted to immortalize his daughters' names in honor of their intrepidity: pedestrian bridges, first built in 1868, now connect the Three Sisters Islands, but before that, because of the dangers of the rapids, the third island could be accessed only by crossing ice jams in the winter, a challenge that the sisters accomplished. Thus, with the concurrence of the islands' owners,

Luna Island, the tiny island (130 feet wide by 350 feet long) between the American Falls and the Bridal Veil Falls, as seen from Goat Island. The Niagara Falls International Rainbow Bridge is in the background.

IN CANADA AND BY CAR

You will find the Dufferin Islands on the Canadian (Ontario) side of the river. Part of the Niagara Parkway, the islands—four natural and a number of man-made ones—serve as lovely parkland. The number of islands in this grouping is dependent on who's doing the counting, but there are at least 10 small green islands with walking paths and shady sitting spots set among lagoons. On the Niagara Parkway, this is a perfect place to picnic and relax, away from the excitement of other Niagara tourist attractions.

The Niagara Parkway is a 35-mile (56-kilometer) road in Ontario, formerly known as Niagara Boulevard and historically as the Niagara Road, that runs along the Niagara River from Niagara-on-the-Lake to Fort Erie. It was started with the creation of the park near the Niagara Falls in 1878, and when it opened in 1888, it covered 154 acres. Today the Niagara Parkway covers more than 3,000 acres. In 1943, Sir Winston Churchill proclaimed the Niagara Parkway "the prettiest Sunday afternoon drive in the world."

Bridge to the Three Sisters Islands from Goat Island. All four islands are in New York, although the Three Sisters Islands are at the edge of the Canadian Horseshoe Rapids.

the Porter brothers, they became Asenath Island (the first of the series), Angeline Island (the middle and largest of the three, known at one time as Deer Island by local residents), and Celinda Eliza Island (the third of the islands, farthest out into the Horseshoe Rapids). A fourth island, Little Brother Island (aka Solon Island), named after the Whitney sisters' baby brother, has never been accessible.

Nearby Paths to Adventure

Note: The Niagara Falls USA Discovery Pass will save you up to 36 percent, depending on when during the tourist season you visit, on the cost of five popular attractions in Niagara Falls State Park: the Niagara Adventure Theater, the Cave of the Winds trip, the *Maid of the Mist* boat tour, the Niagara Gorge Discovery Center, and the Aquarium of Niagara. The pass also gives you free unlimited transportation aboard the Niagara Scenic Trolley for one day.

Niagara Falls Visitor Center (aka the Orin Lehman Visitor Center)—Stop here first to get oriented for your visit to the Niagara Falls. Admission is free with entrance to Niagara Falls State Park, of which this center is a part.

Niagara Adventure Theater—Located on the lower level of the visitor center, here you can see *Niagara: Legends of Adventure*, a film advertised to take you "from the historic to the heroic in a spectacular recreation of legends and real life." Admission is charged.

Prospect Point Park Observation Tower—Ride an elevator to the 230-foot overlook, the only U.S. location from which to photograph both the American Falls and the Horseshoe Falls. This handicapped-accessible observation deck extends out over the Niagara Gorge and gives you the bird's-eye view shared with the peregrine falcons, hawks, and gulls that soar above the gorge and that you may spot, too. Admission is charged.

Maid of the Mist—Get sprayed aboard the *Maid of the Mist;* the boat tour leaves from the base of the Prospect Point Park Observation Tower for an exciting trip into the frothing water below the American Falls and the Horseshoe Falls. Rain ponchos are supplied. Admission is charged.

Niagara Gorge Discovery Center (200 Robert Moses Pwy. North, Niagara Falls, NY; www .niagarafallsstatepark.com/discovery-center)—Also known as the Schoellkopf Geological Museum, the center is located where the Schoellkopf Power Station, one of the first hydroelectric plants in the United States, built in 1881, stood before it was destroyed by a rockfall in 1956. The power station was named after Jacob Schoellkopf, the founder of the Niagara Falls Hydroelectric Power and Manufacturing Company. The Niagara Gorge

Dufferin Islands Nature Area, Ontario, a secluded 10-acre park consisting of a series of four natural and six or so man-made islands connected by small bridges, located about a mile (1.6 kilometers) upstream from Horseshoe Falls, accessible by foot along the banks of the Niagara River.

Discovery Center features interactive displays, an 180-degree multiscreen theater showing 12,000 years of the history of the Niagara River to help visitors learn about the natural history of the falls and the Niagara Gorge, and and a 26-foot rock-climbing wall. Admission is charged.

Niagara Scenic Trolley—Enjoy a half-hour overview of the park with a guide on the three-mile (five-kilometer) route, or get off at each of the six stops and explore the Niagara Falls attractions. Admission is charged.

Aquarium of Niagara (701 Whirlpool St., Niagara Falls, NY; ww.aquariumofniagara.org)—More than 1,500 aquatic animals are on display here, and your visit may include sea lion performances, shark feedings, and extra time spent at the penguin display. Admission is charged.

Historic Walking Tour—Stop by the Niagara USA Official Visitor Center (10 Rainbow Blvd., at First St., Niagara Falls, NY)—sponsored by the Niagara Tourism and Convention Corporation—just outside the Niagara Falls State Park, and pick up the brochure *The Historic Walking Tour of the Niagara Reservation*, which includes a map and history of 16 Niagara Falls landmarks. This is a great way to explore the falls on your own.

Niagara Gorge Trailhead Building—Stop by here for information about and maps of popular hiking trails in the Niagara Falls area:

- Great Gorge Scenic Overlook—This easy one-hour hike begins from the Niagara Gorge Discovery Center.
- Upper Great Gorge—This easy two-hour hike follows the Great Gorge Railway Trail, which begins from the Niagara Gorge Discovery Center.
- Devil's Hole Rapids and Giant Rock—This moderate 2.5-hour hike begins at Devil's Hole State Park.
- Whirlpool Rapids Trail—Beginning at Whirlpool State Park, this difficult, three-hour hike includes some "boulder-hopping."

  Note that the last two trails on the list above are only open to hikers eight and older. Guided Niagara Falls hiking tours are offered in the summer.

ONTARIO ATTRACTIONS

Niagara Botanical Gardens—Take some time to smell the roses. Located on the scenic Niagara Parkway and the Great Gorge just 10 minutes north of the falls. Established in 1936, these 99 acres of gardens include perennials, rhododendrons, azaleas; shade, herb, and vegetable plantings; a parterre (formal garden); and a rose garden featuring over 2,400 roses. The gardens are open from daily from dawn until dusk. Admission is free with paid on-site parking.

Butterfly Conservatory—Home to more than 2,000 butterflies of up to 45 different species, the conservatory is located on the grounds of the Niagara Botannical Gardens. Admission is charged.

Niagara River Recreation Trail—Hike or bike this trail on the Canadian Niagara River shore. Constructed in 1986, this is a paved trail for nonmotorized traffic—bicyclists, joggers, walkers—stretching from Anger Street in the north end of the town of Fort Erie north 35 miles (56 kilometers) all the way to Fort George in Niagara-on-the-Lake—the entire length of the entire Niagara peninsula—along the Canadian side of the Niagara River. The trail passes through the urban areas of the village of Queenston and the city of Niagara Falls, Ontario. More than 100 monuments and plaques mark historic waypoints along the trail.

OTHER AREA ATTRACTIONS

Splurge on an aerial tour of the falls—Three helicopter services—Niagara Helicopters, Rainbow Air Helicopter, and National Helicopter Tours—provide, respectively, nine, 10, and 20 minutes of viewing the falls from the air.

Old Fort Niagara (Fort Niagara Historic Site, Youngstown, NY; www.oldfortniagara.org)—Located downstream from Niagara Falls, this is the oldest continuously occupied site in North America. Opened as a historic site and museum in 1934, the fort includes buildings where Native American, French, British, and American soldiers lived and worked from the eighteenth to the twentieth centuries. A visitor center provides orientation in the way of original artifacts, educational exhibits, and an award-winning 16-minute film. Admission is charged.

"Ride the Falls"—A number of theater and simulation amusement rides are available in the area.

Visit a waterpark—If all the water around you has you yearning to submerge yourself in some, there are several waterparks in the vicinity of the falls.

Golf—If, on the other hand, you'd like less water and more greens, there are several "Legends on the Niagara" golf courses as well as a couple others in the area.

SPECIAL EVENTS

Illumination of Niagara Falls—Every evening at dusk since 1925, the falls have been illuminated by the Niagara Falls Illumination Board in partnership with Niagara Parks. The falls are often lit in special colors for a registered charity or not-for-profit organization.

Niagara Falls events, shows, and festivals—For an up-to-date listing of other special events involving the Falls, visit www.niagarfallstourism.com.

For More Information

Niagara Falls State Park—www.niagarafallsstatepark.com.

Berketa's "History of the Niagara River Islands" at www.niagarafrontier.com/islands.html—After retiring in 2008 after 36 years as an officer with the Niagara Regional Police, Detective Sergeant Rick Berketa, now appreciated as a "Niagara Falls Internet historian," hosts a nonprofit private website, Niagara Falls Thunder Alley. This is a good place to find up-to-date information about many Niagara Falls attractions. It includes pricing information and hyperlinks to the individual attractions: www.niagarafrontier.com (click on the "Attraction Prices" button).

There have been many books written about Niagara Falls, and most of them fall into one of three categories: travel guides, children's books, and books that involve barrels. A number of books are for sale at the Niagara Falls Visitor Center gift shop. Here are three available there that cover the islands, the falls, and more than a few barrels, respectively:

Goat Island: Niagara's Scenic Retreat, by Paul Gromosiak (Buffalo, NY: Western New York Wares, 2003)—This book includes information about all the islands at the falls.

Niagara Falls Q & A: Answers to the 100 Most Common Questions about Niagara Falls, by Paul Gromosiak (Buffalo, NY: Meyer Enterprises/Western New York Wares, 1989).

Niagara and the Daredevils: The Story of the Niagara River and the Men and Women Who Defied It, by Philip Mason (Niagara Falls, ON: Travelpic, 1995)—The stories of 38 people who hatched plans involving fame, fortune, and the falls: "[S]ome lost their lives. Almost all went away empty-handed."

Parting Thoughts

There is *absolutely* so much more to the Niagara River than just the falls, and its islands are a very big part of that "more."

Lake Ontario Islands

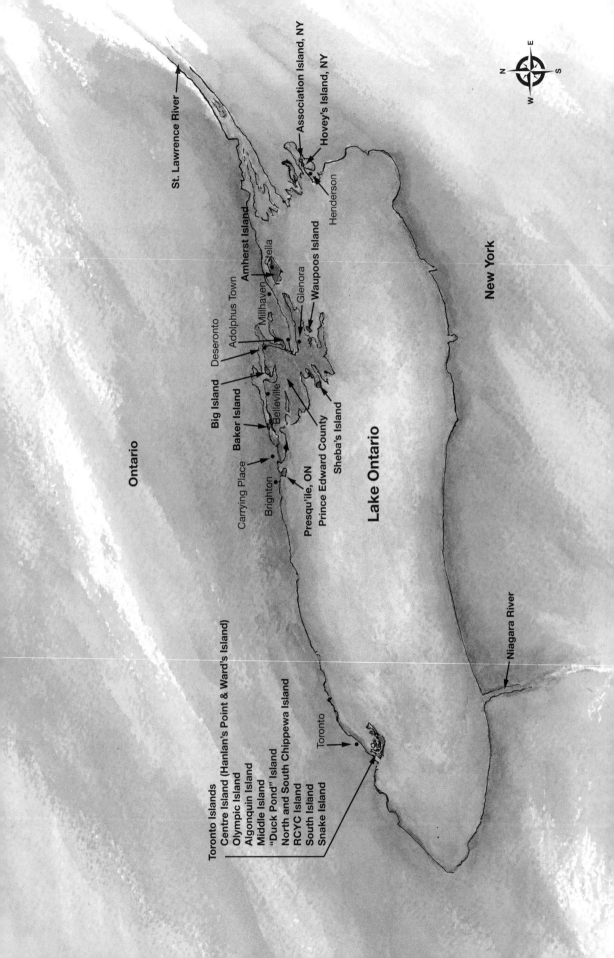

An Introduction to Lake Ontario

Lake Ontario's proglacial lake version is known as Lake Iroquois. Lake Iroquois was a larger and higher version of the current lake due to the St. Lawrence River being blocked by the glacial ice sheet near the current Thousand Islands. Instead of draining to the ocean via the St. Lawrence River, this lake, geologists speculate, drained out through a channel running toward New York's present Oneida Lake, on to the Mohawk River, then to the Hudson River, and finally out to the Atlantic.

In today's Great Lakes Basin, the Niagara River drains into Lake Ontario and Lake Ontario drains into the St. Lawrence River. Similar in both shape and size to the lake that precedes it upstream in the Great Lakes Basin, Lake Erie, Lake Ontario is just a bit smaller: 193 miles (311 kilometers) from west to east (compared to Lake Erie's 241 miles/388 kilometers) and 53 miles (85 kilometers) from south to north (compared to Lake Erie's 57 miles/92 kilometers).

However, Lake Ontario is much deeper than Lake Erie. Lake Ontario's average depth is 283 feet (compared to Lake Erie's 62 feet), with the result that Lake Ontario holds almost four times the volume of water than does Lake Erie.

Being downstream from the Niagara Falls, Lake Ontario's surface elevation of 243 feet is significantly lower than Lake Erie's 571 feet.

Lake Ontario's entire west and north shores are within Ontario and include some major urban and industrial centers, such as Hamilton, Mississauga, and Toronto. Much but not all of its southern shore is in the state of New York in an area where, relatively speaking, neither significant industrial development (Rochester would be the one exception) nor extensive farming has been centered.

For more information on Lake Ontario, visit www.great-lakes.net/ontario.html and consider looking for a used or library copy of the American Lake Series volume *Lake Ontario,* by Arthur Pound (Indianapolis: Bobbs-Merrill, 1945).

Lake Ontario has relatively few islands, but most are accessible by ferry or bridge, except for a scattering of New York islands at the western end of the lake.

The Toronto Islands are accessible by ferry from the Jack Layton Ferry Terminal, where ferries head for three different locations on the chain of islands. Once on the islands, pedestrian bridges connect the dozen or so (depending on who's counting and how) islands:

Centre Island (aka Toronto Island)—The island is called Ward's Island at the east end and Hanlan's Point at the west end.

Olympic Island

Algonquin Island

Middle Island

The "Duck Pond" island

Snake Island
South Chippewa Island
North Chippewa Island
RCYC Island
South Island

Accessible by bridge at the east end or by ferry at the west, **Prince Edward County** is not to be confused with Prince Edward Island proper. This large peninsula became an island with the construction of the Trent-Severn Waterway and has several other islands associated with it:

Big Island—An agricultural island with a historical cemetery accessible by causeway through wetlands from the main island.
Huffs Island—An island you'll never know you've crossed to.
Sheba Island—A small island of cottage and rentals on West Lake, which is contained by the Sandbanks Provincial Park peninsula and accessible by causeway.
Waupoos Island—Accessible by water taxi, this island of sheep has the Harinui Farm with a lodge and half a dozen cottages available as vacation rentals.

Amherst Island is accessible by the Amherst Island Ferry Service from Millhaven, Ontario; the 15-minute ride (less than two miles/three kilometers) takes you to the island community of Stella. This 27-square-mile (70-square-kilometer) island is part of Loyalist Township.

THE TRENT-SEVERN WATERWAY

A National Historic Site of Canada administered by Parks Canada and originally constructed to serve industry's shipping purposes, the waterway was begun in 1833 but not completed until 1907. By the time it was open, the increased size of commercial ships had made it obsolete. It is now used for recreational watercraft.

The Toronto Islands, Ontario

AN INVITATION TO STEP INTO A SPELL

July 13, 2013

At the foot of the very first long arching wooden bridge of our island day, Judy and I stop at a telephone pole, bearing many staples and corners of announcements of events now past. It has one full-color, larger-than-life tarot card tacked to it, titled "The Reader." The card shows a woman wearing a long flowing dress and a blue cape. A black cat peers around one side of her, a sickle moon lies at her feet, and a book, *Potions, Lotions, Spells*, is behind her. In the background: the Island Café—where we've just had lunch after getting off the ferry—a sailboat on the lake, an owl on a tree branch, and a house with a covered bridge leading to it. In her right hand, the woman holds a deck of tarot cards. The single tarot card she holds in her left hand shows a traveler carrying a bandana bundle at the end of a stick and stepping off a bridge into the sun.

We are about to learn what a perfect invitation this is to this chain of islands: this magical mosaic of bridges arching over reflective canals; lush gardens filled with lusty dahlias, hydrangeas on steroids, and quirky outdoor art; leafy, leafy lanes leading everywhere; sandy beaches with more sailboats on the horizon than seem probable; and a 1.5-mile boardwalk on the very edge of Lake Ontario. The perfect invitation—in more ways than we could possibly understand until we'd experienced the Toronto Islands for ourselves.

GETTING THERE: Passenger-only ferry; private boat or plane; water taxi

GETTING AROUND: No cars allowed; bring your own bike; bicycle, tandem, and quadracycle rentals (cash only); kayak, canoe, and paddleboard rentals

OVERNIGHT ACCOMMODATIONS: Limited options: B&Bs; vacation rentals; no camping

FOOD: Restaurants; concession stands; no grocery stores

DAY TRIP? Yes, recommended—given limited overnight accommodations—but a wonderful place to find oneself after the last ferry back to the city has left . . .

STATE / PROVINCIAL / NATIONAL PARK? No, but other than the two residential areas, the Toronto Islands are the largest park managed by the City of Toronto Parks, Forestry and Recreation Department

The Toronto Islands were once a peninsula, formed from a long series of moving sandbars created from the material Lake Ontario eroded from the Scarborough Bluffs, east of the islands on the lake. The sandbars were known to the Native people as a place of leisure, and

Toronto Island Park

Parks, Forestry & Recreation

LEGEND

🍴 Snack Bar   ▮ Historic Plaque   🚻 Washrooms

1. Island Paradise Restaurant
2. Lockers
3. Toronto Hong Kong Lions Club Pavillion
4. Island Information Booth
5. Island Outfitters Kiosk
6. First Aid/Lost Children/Lost Parent Station
7. Police Station
8. Lagoon Theatre
9. Centreville Amusement Park
10. Carousel Café
11. Far Enough Farm
12. Island Tram Tour Departure
13. Harbour Tours Kiosk
14. Amazing Maze
15. The Boat House – Boat Rentals
16. Island Bicycle Rental
17. Pier
18. Changerooms/Lockers
19. Wading Pool/Saturn Playground
20. Franklin Children's Garden
21. Island Public and Natural Science School
22. Island Filtration Plant
23. T.I.R. Ropes Challenge Course
24. Gibralter Point Centre for the Arts
25. Gibralter Point Lighthouse
26. Island Yacht Club
27. Babe Ruth's First Professional Home Run Plaque
28. Ned Hanlan Statue
29. Toronto Island Marina
30. St. Andrews by the Lake Church
31. Disc Golf Course
32. Fire Station
33. Shaw House Seniors Co-op
34. The Rectory Cafe and Island Information
35. Island Canoe Club
36. Ward Island Association Clubhouse
37. Queen City Yacht Club
38. Algonquin Island Association Clubhouse
39. Royal Canadian Yacht Club
40. Toronto Island Information Booth @ Pier 6

ISLAND INFORMATION: 416•397•BOAT (2628)   VISIT ON-LINE: www.toronto.ca/parks

Courtesy of the City of Toronto

at one point during European encroachment, the peninsula became known as the Island of Hiawatha.

The natural harbor formed by the hook of the peninsula drew the interest of the British navy, which was looking for a defendable capital, which they originally called York. That capital became Toronto, whose large natural harbor eventually became accessible from the southwest as well as the northeast side. Strong storms and the subsequent wave action pulled the peninsula apart over the years, sometimes entailing repair. In 1858, a storm thrashed a channel through the isthmus, cutting the hook of the peninsula off from the mainland.

In the 1800s, many of Toronto's wealthiest families built Victorian summer homes along Lake Shore Avenue on Centre Island. Ward's Island community started as a tent community. Hanlan's Point, then known as West Point, became the first summer cottage community—it's been referred to as the "Coney Island of Canada." Hotels, an amusement park, and a 10,000-spectator baseball stadium sprang up at the end of the nineteenth and beginning of the twentieth centuries. The baseball stadium was built in 1897 for the minor league team the Toronto Maple Leafs (which predated the NHL team of the same name). Babe Ruth hit his first professional home run there on September 5, 1914. The field remained in use until 1937 when the Toronto Island Airport was built and the land around it became parkland.

Rising lake levels continually damaged island properties in the first half of the twentieth century, and on January 1, 1956, the City of Toronto transferred responsibility for the Toronto Island to the Municipality of Metropolitan Toronto to be developed as a regional park, which eventually became one of Toronto's major recreational areas.

Residents willing to leave the islands had moved by 1963. Those who wanted to stay fought for decades until, in 1993, islanders in two neighborhood communities were allowed to purchase 99-year land leases from a land trust.

How to Get There

Find your way to Toronto, and then head for the lake. Toronto Parks, Forestry and Recreation operates passenger ferries to the Toronto Islands year-round. All the ferries depart the mainland from Toronto's Jack Layton Ferry Terminal, located at 9 Queen's Quay West, south of Queen's Quay, between Yonge Street and Bay Street. Plenty of pay parking is available in the area of the ferry terminal, which is also only a 10-minute walk from Union Station.

The current ferry schedule is available at www.toronto.ca/parks/island or by calling 416-392-8193. In the summer, ferries run to three different docks on the Toronto Islands—Ward's Island, Centre Island, and Hanlan's Point. You can count on just about a 15-minute ferry ride, regardless of your destination on the islands. Passengers may bring their bicycles on the ferry with them; however, rental bicycles (standard, tandem, quad-cycles) are available from Toronto Island Bicycle Rental on Centre Island.

When you arrive at the ferry terminal (named after a Toronto politician who was a beloved contributor to the island community), don't miss *Shore Stories,* the beautiful 80-foot outdoor mosaic mural created in 2012 by 18 young artists and one professional mosaic artist through the Arts for Children and Youth program. The permanent outdoor mural, installed on a retaining wall, highlights histories and myths of both the islands and the harbor and is composed of tile, glass, pebbles, and mirror. You can learn more about how this extraordinary piece of art was made at www.afcy.ca/revitalization-of-torontos-jack-layton-ferry-terminal/.

The Toronto Islands are just a short ferry ride away from downtown Toronto—waiting to buy tickets takes longer than the crossing itself. However, from the end of a shady lane on one of the Toronto Islands' residential communities, Algonquin Island, the city seems very far away.

The Billy Bishop Toronto City Airport, also known as the Toronto Island Airport, is located on the western area of the islands, just south of the Western Channel. Although small, it is Canada's ninth-busiest airport and was recognized in 2013 by Skytrax as one of the world's best small airports.

What to Expect

Expect a little bit of confusion regarding island names. On the map, the Toronto Islands consist of 12 islands: some attached by bridge, some accessible only by boat. Some so-called islands are in fact actually just a part of a larger island. People call Hanlan's Point—the "elbow" of Centre Island (the main island)—"Hanlan's Island." There is a small inaccessible island named Hanlan's Island in Hanlan's Bay, but Hanlan's Point is not an island; it is a part of Centre Island. Ward's Island is also a part of Centre Island. All three of these islands are sometimes misnamed or misrepresented on popular maps. The Centreville Amusement Park is not on Centre Island; it is on Middle Island and Olympic Island. The Toronto Island Park is not on Centre Island, but Centre Island is sometimes called Toronto Island (singular).

You can also expect no cars and many bicycles. There are 262 small houses in two communities covering 40 acres total, on Ward's Island and Algonquin Island (after World War II, the Canadian government gave veterans lots on Algonquin). The Toronto Island Park, which takes up 820 acres, offers beaches, lagoons to paddle on, amusement rides, and picnic spots galore.

Paths to Adventure

NATURAL SITES

Lake Ontario beaches—Relax on one of several: Ward's Island Beach, Centre Island Beach (aka Manitou Beach), Gibraltar Point Beach, or Hanlan's Point. For a "natural site" of the *au natural* variety, visit the "clothing-optional" beach on western Hanlan's Point.

Canadian tree tours: Toronto Island—Print the maptree identification plaque numbers, and information on 58 tree specimens on a route of three miles (five kilometers), from one end of Toronto Island to the other before you go at www.canadiantreetours.org/maps/torontoisland.html or get the phone app to take the tour information along with you.

HISTORY PRESERVED

Gibraltar Point Lighthouse—Built in 1808, this is the oldest stone building in Toronto, Canada's second-oldest lighthouse, and the Great Lakes' oldest standing lighthouse.

St. Andrew-by-the-Lake Anglican Church—At the corner of Cherokee and Lakeshore Avenues, this early English Gothic-style frame church was designed by architect Arthur R. Denison and opened in 1884. Sunday morning church services are open to the public, and the congregation is most welcoming.

Monument to Edward Hanlan—"The most renowned oarsman of any age" and victor in 300 consecutive rowing races, beginning with the Centennial Regatta in 1876, Hanlan was born and died in Toronto (1855–1908). He took up rowing when his family settled on the islands in the area of what is now known as Hanlan's Point. He also was elected an alderman for the area in 1898 and 1899.

CULTURAL ATTRACTIONS

Centreville Amusement Park—An old-fashioned theme park with over 30 rides and attractions including a re-created turn-of-the-twentieth-century village featuring Main Street shops; a firehouse; antique cars and trains; an 1890 carousel, a "windmill" Ferris wheel, and other "kiddie" rides; the Lumber Mill Log Flume water slide; a miniature golf course; train rides; and picnic spots. A nearby restaurant (Carousel Café) is on an island—unnamed as far as I know—in a lake (okay, a duck pond) on an island (Centre) in a lake (Ontario); after we had a relaxing lunch there, I decided to include it in my island count.

Far Enough Farm—This year-round petting zoo established in 1959 in Centreville Amusement Park features sheep, cows, goats, pigs, horses and donkeys, llamas and alpacas, chickens, ducks, farm geese, pheasants, turkeys, guinea fowl, quails, emus, pigeons, black swans, and peafowl.

The Toronto Islands have a number of attractions for families with young children: Centreville Amusement Park (shown here), Far Enough Farm, and Franklin Children's Garden are clustered within easy walking distance on Middle Island, Olympic Island, and Centre Island, and families can take a break from a fun-filled day at the restaurant on yet another island in the middle of Toronto Island Park's duck pond.

Franklin Children's Garden—Inspired by Franklin the Turtle, the character from the children's book series, this garden is designed with young children in mind and includes interactive exhibits and play structures. It also serves as a venue for special storytelling and performing arts events.

Artscape Gibraltar Point Centre for the Arts (443 Lakeshore Ave., Toronto Island)—A year-round event venue that offers short- and long-term studio rental to artists of all sorts. For more information, visit www.torontoartscape.org/artscape-gibraltar-point.

Island Public and Natural Science School (30 Centre Island Park)—The school serves junior kindergarten through grade 6. A nursery school and day program service the island and the Harbourfront community, and a residential science program accommodates 68 students in grades 5 and 6 for half-week periods to study natural science and outdoor education.

OTHER ISLAND THINGS TO DO

Walk or bike the trails—Choose from three: 1.54 miles (2.48 kilometers) from Hanlan's Point's ferry dock to the island filtration plant, .69 miles (1.11 kilometers) from the Boardwalk to the Ward's Island ferry dock, or .47 miles (0.76 kilometers) from Centre Island's ferry dock to Lookout Pier.

Take a historic tram tour (June–September).

Kayak or canoe—Rentals are available at the Boat House, not far from Centre Island docks.

Play disc golf (PDGA-approved).

Wade in one of the wading pools.

Swim on one of islands' five Blue Flag[89] beaches including Toronto's only "clothing-optional" beach at Hanlan's Point, one of a handful of legal nudist beaches in Canada.

Play softball or volleyball.

Dine at one of the islands' restaurants and concessions.

Cross-country ski—The largest urban car-free community in North America, the island offers 5.6 miles (9 kilometers) of pathways and trails ideal for cross-country skiing.

Ice-skate—The harbor offers designated safe areas for ice-skating.

Ice surf, ice sail, ice para-ski—Or enjoy watching those who do!

Take a "shutterbug" field trip—Four seasons of the year, capture Toronto Islands' architecture, gardens, art, and the best land view of Toronto's skyline.

SPECIAL ISLAND EVENTS

Toronto Island Challenge Course (TICC) (April–May).

Island Natural Science School Camp (July)—For more information, see http://toes.tdsb.on .ca/residential/island/summer_camp/.

Several Blue Flag–certified Lake Ontario beaches stretch along the outer rim of the Toronto Islands: Centre Island Beach (aka Manitou Beach), shown here, Ward's Island Beach, Gibraltar Point Beach, and Hanlan's Point Beach, which includes a section that is Ontario's only officially designated "clothing-optional" beach.

Longboat Toronto Island Run (September)—Toronto's oldest 10K run. For more information, see torontoislandrun.com.

Toronto Island camps—Each eco-camp includes nature and environmental studies, crafts, tram rides, the high ropes course, fishing, and swimming on the island. For more information, see www1.toronto.ca and click on "Parks, Forestry & Recreation"; camps are detailed under "Recreation Programs & Registration."

- Franklin's Junior Sprouts Camp—Spend a morning with your child at Franklin Children's Garden and a Franklin garden expert. Activities include storytelling, bug identification, organic gardening, eco and nature studies, and crafts.
- Island Explorer Camp.
- Island Voyageur Camp.
- Voyageur Camp.

For More Island Information

Friends of Toronto Island—www.torontoisland.org.
Toronto Island Park—www1.toronto.ca (click on "Parks, Forestry & Recreation," then "Toronto Islands & Ferries").

Several excellent sources of information are available online or once you are on the islands.

Toronto Islands: Toronto Island Park—A brochure and map listing island attractions produced by Toronto Parks, Forestry and Recreation. You can access the map from the main Toronto website; click on "Toronto Islands & Ferries" and look for "Toronto Island Maps."

Discover Toronto Island: 27 Facts about Its History, Environment and Community—A brochure about and map of the islands produced by the Toronto Island Grannies in Spirit 2013. The map is $2.00; to order multiple copies, e-mail granniesinspirit@gmail.com. To see the map, visit www.facebook.com/144426492350455/photos/a.356785204447915 .1073741825.144426492350455/356785207781248.

Nature on the Toronto Islands: An Explorer's Guide—A 20-page nature guide by Joanna Kidd produced by Toronto Parks & Recreation and available at www1.toronto.ca/city_of_toronto/parks_forestry__recreation/island/files/pdf/explorers_guide.pdf (or via a link from the ferry website).

A Magical Place: Toronto Island and Its People, by Bill Freeman (Toronto: James Lorimer, 1999).

More Than an Island: A History of the Toronto Island, by Sally Gibson (Toronto: Irwin, 1984).

A History of the Toronto Islands, by Students of the Toronto Island Public School (Toronto: Coach House, 1972).

How You Can Support the Island

Friends of Toronto Islands (FOTI)
www.torontoislands.org
FOTI's mission, according to its website:

To promote usage of the Toronto Islands Park through social and recreational activities.

To be a source of information about the Toronto Islands Park.

To enhance what the Toronto Islands Park offers.

To promote community spirit around the Harbourfront district of Toronto.

Parting Thoughts

From the envelope stapled below the advertisement for "The Reader," I take a business card–sized tarot card, which shows the reader seated with cards spread before her and a pot of tea on the front and advertises "Tea & Tarot" with "M," a "certified Tarot practitioner" on the back, and tuck it into my pocket. Then Judy and I step out from the leafy lane into the sun, onto the arching bridge, and into the spell of the Toronto Islands.

Prince Edward County, Ontario

WATER AND SAND, WINE AND ART

June 23, 2013

Not a minute after I pass the "Turtle Crossing Area" sign, Marsh Road—on the map, a "short-cut" to Huffs Island—transforms itself into a huge puddle, a small lake spanning the gravel road from shoulder to shoulder. That probably explains the road's name. And what appears to be an endless expanse of cattails. So back to King's Highway 62 and Huffs Island Road. When I arrive at the other end of Marsh Road on Huffs Island Road and look down it, it is dry as a bone, but now I've arrived at a "No Exit" sign.

Once I stop and pull out a map, I realize that if there were such a thing as "Huffs Island," I'd surely have crossed onto it by the time I'd crossed Marsh Road, but I'm not sure; I don't feel like I'm on an island. Beyond the "No Exit" sign is a strawberry farm about to reopen for picking, gorgeous brick Victorian farmhouses, and birdsong. The road narrows. And then, behind the dry fields of last year's corn: Big Bay.

Although there's a peninsula labeled "Huffs Island" on the map, it doesn't appear to be cut off from the mainland island of Prince Edward County by water on all sides.

I backtrack and stop at Shroedter's Farm Market Café and Bakery. Which I find out from Suzanne, who is managing the business this morning, used to be "Huff's Grocery" at the intersection referred to as "Huff's Corners," still referred to as a settlement. Apparently, "Huffs Island Road" was the road on the island that the Huffs, and others, used coming to and from Huffs Corners, as opposed to a road to Huffs Island. Or at least, that is the best anyone in the market can figure. "Huffs, you know, were Loyalists," she adds.

I knew Loyalists were American colonists who had remained loyal to the British Crown during the American Revolution. I'd read somewhere and noted that Prince Edward County (PEC) was a "gift of goodwill from the Crown to the British Loyalists following the American Revolution" and that PEC was famous as a part of the United Empire Loyalist settlement.

But there are still Huffs around, Suzanne assures me. Having arrived on Prince Edward County in 1825, by now, 12 generations later, the Huff family tree has many branches, and one of them apparently has grown to vines: in 2004, Lanny Huff started the Huff Estates Winery, within walking distance of the old Huffs Corners.

If I couldn't spend the afternoon exploring my mythical Huffs Island, yet another island off the island of Prince Edward County, I could certainly walk over and sample Huff's wine.

GETTING THERE: Bridges; car ferry; private boat or plane

GETTING AROUND: Bring your car; bicycle, canoe, and kayak rentals

OVERNIGHT ACCOMMODATIONS: Motels, hotels, inns, resorts, lodges, spa, B&Bs; vacation rentals; campgrounds

FOOD: Restaurants; wineries; groceries

DAY TRIP? Yes, but you could fill more than a lifetime with island adventures on the County!

STATE / PROVINCIAL / NATIONAL PARK? Sandbanks Provincial Park, North Beach Provincial Park, and Lake on the Mountain Provincial Park as well as 14 conservation areas

"The County"—what are we talking about? Prince Edward County—not to be confused with Prince Edward Island in the Gulf of St. Lawrence—*was* a piece of the Ontario mainland, a massive peninsula jutting into Lake Ontario, until 1889, when the five-mile-long (eight-kilometer-long) Murray Canal, connecting the Bay of Quinte and the Presqu'ile Bay on Lake Ontario, was completed, cutting across the narrow isthmus that connected it to the mainland. The Murray Canal is now a part of the historic Trent-Severn Waterway, a canal route administered by Parks Canada that crosses southern Ontario's cottage country.

And two centuries later, Prince Edward County is known to artists and "foodies" alike as well as to history buffs, nature lovers, and photographers, but most recently it is also being recognized for the quality of its wines. Canada's weekly news magazine *Maclean's* selected Prince Edward County in 2014 as one of "10 Places You've Got to See." There are galleries and wineries galore, and at least at one of them, you now can have your art and drink it, too.

How to Get There

You'll find yourself on the County by taking the free 15-minute (vehicle) Glenora Ferry, which runs from the Loyalist Parkway (Ontario Highway 33) west of Kingston every half hour year-round and more often during peak times in the summer.

Or you can get there using a bridge:

Cross the Murray Canal (part of the Trent-Severn Waterway) on a swing bridge at either County Road 64 or Ontario Highway 33.
Cross the Bay of Quinte on the Bay Bridge on King's Highway 62 in Belleville, Ontario.
Cross the Bay of Quinte on the Skyway Bridge on King's Highway 49, in Tyendinaga Mohawk Territory just east of Deseronto.

"THE COUNTY" AND ITS GRAPES

" 'The County' as it's called, is Ontario's most northern VQA [Vintners Quality Alliance, a regulatory system that assures quality and authenticates the origin of the vintage] appellation, and lies at a latitude of 44 degrees, well within the 30-50 [degrees north of the equator] band where grapes thrive. In fact, this is the same latitude of Bordeaux and within a mere stone's throw of the 44-degree line lies Tuscany. . . . Burgundy is home to both pinot noir and chardonnay and its soils are uncannily similar to those of the County."*

* Sara d'Amato, "Prince Edward County's New Releases Kicked off at County in the City," *Ontario Wine Report*, Wine Align www.winealign.com/articles/2014/06/24/prince-edward-countys-new-releases-kicked-off-at-county-in-the-city.

Prince Edward County is wine and art. Among the many wineries and art galleries, Huff Estates Winery and Oeno Gallery, which share the same piece of real estate, provide both. The former features vineyards and a tasting bar, and the latter a four-acre sculpture garden as well as fine-art exhibitions.

What to Expect

Expect 270 square miles (700 square kilometers) of low-lying fertile fields, wineries, art galleries, water, and sand.

Paths to Adventure

NATURAL SITES

Color brochures and maps are available online for most of the parks and conservation areas listed below.

Sandbanks Provincial Park—Located near Picton on Lake Ontario, the park has the world's largest baymouth bar dune formation[90] on a freshwater lake, expansive sandy beaches, and sand dunes as high as 197 feet (60 meters). Family camping with sites close to the beach is available. The park offers Jacques Cottage and the Maple Rest Heritage House for year-round accommodations.

Lake on the Mountain Provincial Park—The lake is a natural curiosity, with a constant flow of clean, fresh water with no apparent source. Situated approximately 200 feet (60 meters) above Lake Ontario, the site provides views of the Bay of Quinte, the Glenora Ferry and the north shore. This is a day-use park; no camping is permitted.

North Beach Provincial Park—A quiet and smaller version of the sandy Sandbanks Provincial Park, this park is for day use only, a good place to boat, fish, bird, and picnic.

Little Bluff Conservation Area—This preserve features a 66-foot-high (20-meter-high) limestone bluff, waterfowl in the nearby marsh, swimming (unguarded) on a cobblestone beach, trails, biking, and a panoramic view of Prince Edward Bay.

Massassauga Point Conservation Area—This is a well-wooded and magnificent stretch of Bay of Quinte shoreline. Here you'll find 8.7 miles (14 kilometers) of hiking trails and a boat launch ramp. Other features of the area include a small, globally rare burr oak savanna, remains of a wharf, and an abandoned limestone quarry.

Prince Edward County is water and sand. Sandbanks Provincial Park is a fine place to explore and enjoy both, even on a gray day.

H. J. McFarland Conservation Area—This seven-acre site has a boat launch and docking facilities, a picnic shelter, and restrooms. You'll get a good view of the Bay of Quinte from here.

Harry Smith Conservation Area—Here you'll find a small pond and a picnic area but no trails.

Macaulay Mountain Conservation Area—This site features Birdhouse City (over 100 birdhouses that are miniature reproductions of local buildings), 440 acres with 12.5 miles (20 kilometers) of trails (ranging from gravel paths to easy lowland trails to more rugged escarpment trails), and cross-country skiing and tobogganing in winter.

Beaver Meadow Wildlife Management Area—This 220-acre preserve offers a great blue heron rookery, osprey, and wood ducks. Two short trails end at a scenic observation platform overlooking a large wetland.

Rutherford Stevens Lookout—This small conservation area has a large viewing deck from which to view Smith's Bay and Waupoos Island as well as Prince Edward Bay and Prince Edward Point.

Demorestville Dam Conservation Area—In the area's 65 acres, you can enjoy Demorestville Creek, an almost two-mile (three-kilometer) hiking trail through red cedars on a limestone plain, and bird-watching.

Whiney Memorial Dam Conservation Area—There is a recreation area here around the dam.

Consecon Mill Dam Conservation Area—Enjoy swimming (unguarded), picnic areas, fishing, and boat ramps.

Bloomfield Mill Pond Conservation—The restored pond features fishing and picnic areas.

Milford Mill Pond Conservation Area—The 30-acre picnic area borders the pond at the site of historic Scott's Mill (now closed).

The dock at Happiness Haven B&B in Waupoos, on the "mainland island" of Prince Edward County, looking out on Lake Ontario's Smith's Bay with Waupoos Island in the distance.

Prince Edward Point Bird Observatory (www.peptbo.ca)—A migration research station on the eastern tip of PEC in operation from April 15 to May 31 and August 15 to October 15, with trails open year-round.

HISTORY PRESERVED

Ameliasburgh Historical Museum and Pioneer Village
517 County Rd. 19
Ameliasburgh, ON K0K 1A0
613-476-2148
www.ameliasburgh.com/pioneer-village/
www.pecounty.on.ca/government/community_development/museums/ameliasburgh.php

Macauley Heritage Park
35 Church St. (at Union St.)
Picton, ON K0K 2T0
613-476-3833
www.pecounty.on.ca/government/community_development/museums/macaulay.php

Mariners Park Museum
2065 County Rd. 13
South Bay, ON K0K 2P0
613-476-8392
www.pecounty.on.ca/government/community_development/museums/mariners.php

Rose House Museum
3333 County Rd. 8
Waupoos, ON K0K 2T0
613-476-5439
www.pecounty.on.ca/government/community_development/museums/rose_house.php

Wellington Heritage Museum
290 Main St. (Hwy 33)
Wellington, ON K0K 2T0
613-399-5015
www.pecounty.on.ca/government/community_development/museums/wellington.php

Naval Marine Archive—The Canadian Collection
205 Main St.
Picton, ON K0K 2T0
613-476-1177
navalmarinearchive.com
   A nonprofit organization dedicated to marine history and conservation, maritime research, and nautical education, the organization has a reference library of more than 200,000 documents, includes a gallery of marine art, and is home to the classic boat forum.

Point Petre Lighthouse—A 19-meter (62-foot) red-and-white striped tower was erected in 1967 to replace the 1833 tower, located at the very southern tip of PEC. There is also a lightkeeper's cottage, circa 1962.

Prince Edward Point Lighthouse—Circa 1881, this is located at Long Point in Prince Edward Point National Wildlife Area on the southeastern peninsula of PEC.

Salmon Point Lighthouse (aka Wicked Point)—This privately owned lighthouse is located in the campground in Salmon Point Campground (aka Quinte's Isle Campark) on the tip of PEC's western peninsula.

Scotch Bonnet Lighthouse—Scotch Bonnet Island is off the west coast of PEC, on a very low and small rock of an island. All that is on it other than cormorants are the remains of the lighthouse, which became operational in 1856. A private boat is required to come within view of it.

False Ducks Island Lighthouse—False Ducks Islands are a pair of islands off the southeast tip of PEC; the easternmost one, on which the lighthouse is located, is also known as Swetman Island (the western one of the pair is also called Timber Island). The lighthouse, built in 1828, was replaced by a hexagonal tower in 1965. A private boat is required to come within view of it.

Main Duck Island (aka Real Duck Island or Real Ducks) Lighthouse—The structure was built in 1914 with two lightkeepers' cottages. The area is part of St. Lawrence Islands National Park, beyond False Ducks Island and almost to the U.S.-Canadian border in Lake Ontario. A private boat is required to come within view of it.

Gallows & Graveyards Walking Tours—Tour the grounds and graveyards at Macaulay Heritage Park and the adjacent County Gaol & Gallows (the site of a notorious double hanging in 1884) in Picton on a Friday night in July or August. Tours are booked through Regent Theatre in Picton.

CULTURAL ATTRACTIONS

On Prince Edward County, you'll find over 35 wineries (www.princeedwardcountywine.ca/) and almost 20 art galleries and studios (http://artstrail.ca/). And here's a place where you'll find both as well as a four-acre sculpture garden and inn:

Huff Estates Winery and Oeno Gallery
2274 County Rd. 1
Bloomfield, ON K0K 1G0
616-393-2216
www.oenogallery.com

A number of annual special events on Prince Edward County celebrate the wine- and art-making that transpires there.

***Terroir* Wine and Farmers Market** (May)—This is PEC's spring market featuring local food, handcrafted wine, artisan bread, preserves, and other one-of-a-kind products from local farmers. "'Terroir' is the complete natural environment in which a particular wine is produced, including factors such as the soil, topography, and climate. [It can also mean] the characteristic taste and flavor imparted to a wine by the environment in which it is produced."[91]

Art in the County (end of June–mid-July)—County artists and artisans show original works of paintings, photographs, jewelry, sculpture, fiber arts, and glass at this annual juried exhibition hosted by PEC Arts Council. Free admission.

Rotary Wine Celebration (August)—In this celebration of County wine and food, a dinner is paired with a selection of 100 percent County-grown and County-produced wines, featuring PEC's newest wine releases.

Rednersville Road Art Tour (September).

Red White & Blues (mid-September)—A weekend celebration of innovative local wine, food, and music set among four PEC winery estates.

PEC Studio & Gallery Tour (mid-September)—Special three-day weekend when artists demonstrate and discuss their work.

TASTE! Community Grown (end of September)—Showcases the finest artisanal products, wines, beers, cider, and cuisine that Ontario's "Gastronomical Capital," PEC, has to offer.

The Maker's Hand (early November)—Show and sale of works by eastern Ontario's finest artists and artisans.

Slow & Sinful Gala (November)—From Slow Food (the County website promoting the event for 2014) comes "[s]infully delicious offerings, both savory and sweet from some of the best chefs working in the County today. Each culinary item is matched to a local champagne-style wine from our very own terroir."

Wassail (three weekends at the end of November and beginning of December)—Visit five wineries for tastes while paying tribute to the age-old tradition of celebrating the harvest before winter arrives.

Prince Edward County Wine Tours—The PEC Wine Tours' website offers customers an opportunity to experience "the full 'County' experience, including history and art as well as the chance to indulge in local cuisine prepared by world-class chefs and national and international award-winning wines."

OTHER ISLAND THINGS TO DO

Water activities—Indulge in all things aquatic: surf, windsurf, waterski, jet ski.

Regent Theatre—Take in a show—on-screen, onstage, or via satellite—at this historic theater on Main Street in Picton.

Barley Days Brewery—Visit this Picton brewery and sample craft beers like Loyalist Lager and the County IPA as well as seasonal brews like Sugar Shack Ale (brewed during maple-sugaring season) and Yuletide Cherry Porter (during the winter holidays). The name of the brewery harkens back to a point in the history of the county when the region grew and shipped barley to the United States.

Golf—Get to the greens at Wellington on the Lake Golf Course or Picton Golf and Country Club.

Farm Cooking School—Offers farm-to-table cooking classes held in a 1830s heritage farmhouse cooking school in Prince Edward County. For more information, see www.fromthefarm.ca/.

SPECIAL ISLAND EVENTS

Links for PEC events below can be found at www.prince-edward-county.com/events/calendar-events.

Maple in the County (end of March)

Waterfall tours (early April)

Author's Festival (mid-April)

Walleye World Fishing Tournament (May)

***Terroir* Run** (May)—A 10k run along winery back roads.

County Antique Show & Sale (mid-May)

Spring Birding Festival (latter half of May)

Quinte's Isle Bluegrass Celebration (end of May)

Festival Players (June, July, August)—Annual festival of professional theater throughout the County.

Great Canadian Cheese Festival—Picton (June)

Chapel Service at the White Chapel (June)—Annual service held in an over 200-year-old chapel.

Canada Day Celebrations at Wellington and Picton (July 1)

Lavender Festival (early July)—Held at the Prince Edward County Lavendar Farm in Hillier wine country.

Prince Edward County Quilters Guild Quilt Show in Picton (even years in July)—Juried competition, a featured artist, a quilt raffle, a silent auction, and scissor sharpening.

Annual Fish Fry at Mariners Park Museum (July)—Fish fry, music, silent auction.

Music at Port Milford (July–August)—Chamber music festival.

Annual Mariners Service (second Sunday of August)—Held at Mariners Park Museum.

PEC Jazz Festival (August 11–16)

Heritage Activity Day (early September)

Picton Fair (September)

PEC Music Festival (mid-September)

Milford Fair (September)

County Antique Show & Sale (September)

Model Train Show (September)

Ameliasburgh Country Fair (end of September)

County Marathon (early October)

Pumpkinfest (mid-October)

Bloomfield Festival of Lights (end of November)—Annual nighttime holiday parade.

Festival of Trees (end of November)

Picton Santa Claus Parade (end of November)

For More Island Information

Prince Edward County—www.prince-edward-county.com.

Prince Edward County Chamber of Tourism—www.pecchamber.com.

County Magazine—A quarterly feature magazine about the people, places, and history of Prince Edward County (PO Box 30, Bloomfield, ON K0K 1G0).

Prince Edward County: An Illustrated History, by Steve Campbell, Janet Davies, and Ian Robertson (Bloomfield, ON: County Magazine Books, 2009).

The County Handbook, by Steve Campbell (Bloomfield, ON: County Magazine Books, 2005).

Camp Picton: Wartime to Peacetime, by Ian S. Robertson (Bloomfield, ON: County Magazine Books, 2013).

The Settlement of Prince Edward County, by Nick Mika and Helma Mika (Belleville, ON: Mika, 1984).

Prince Edward County Heritage, by Nick Mika and Helma Mika (Belleville, ON: Mika, 1980).

Impressions of Prince Edward County: The Island County of Ontario, by Sue Cory (Picton, ON: Cory Cards and Photographs, 1990).

Farm to Table: Breakfast, by Elizabeth Pulker (Waupoos, ON: Waupoos Publications, 2012).

The Lazier Murder: Prince Edward County, 1884, by Robert J. Sharpe, Osgoode Society for Canadian Legal History (Toronto: University of Toronto Press, 2012).

How You Can Support the Island

This island is like a small country unto itself containing a number of regions—Picton and Bloomfield, Huff's Corner and Waupoos, for instance. Supporting one or more of the numerous conservation efforts available throughout Prince Edward County would surely support the island, as would buying wine and art!

Parting Thoughts

The call of more islands brought me to Prince Edward County. And then I discovered that "the County" itself was an island, a small continent of art and wine, beaches and sun.

Other islands in the vicinity of PEC Bronwen and I explored:

- **Presqu'ile, Ontario**—A tombolo, or "tied island," in Lake Ontario, accessible from the mainland west of PEC, this is the site of Presqu'ile Provincial Park.
- **Baker Island**—Between PEC and mainland Ontario in the Bay of Quinte, this island is part of Canada's largest military base: 8 Wing/CFB Trenton. The island is attached by a causeway, Hurricane Drive, and contains only a circular gravel drive and the Baker Island Community Centre, set atop a small hill overlooking the Bay of Quinte, used for weddings, conferences, and other gatherings.
- **Sheba's Island**—A small residential island attached by a causeway near Sandbanks Provincial Park.
- **Big Island**—A rural island accessible by bridge from PEC in the Bay of Quinte, this is the site of an old Loyalist cemetery.
- **Waupoos Island**—A private island in Lake Ontario with one public accommodation on it—Harinui Farm. Waupoos Island is just across Smith Bay from the hamlet of Waupoos in Prince Edward County and is accessible by water taxi from Waupoos Marina.
- And then, of course, there is **"Huffs Island"** . . .

Amherst Island, Ontario

LITTLE LAMBS AND IRISH STONE WALLS

June 10, 2013

Bronwen and I have arrived on Amherst Island after quite a number of adventures in a relatively short period of time. We came from the west by way of the 401; an overnight at McEwan's Gold B&B, across the causeway within Presqu'ile Provincial Park; the Canadian Forces Base (CFB) Trenton, the public part of which includes hard-to-find Baker's Island, where Baker Island Community Centre is located and not much more; pastoral Big Island off Prince Edward County in the Bay of Quinte—with egg-laying common snapping turtles on the shoulder of the gravel roads and an old pioneer Loyalist cemetery; an attempt (foiled by it being private property) to access Huffman's Island (the elusive Huffs Island was what we should have been looking for, but that story belongs to another trip); and through the mainland Tyendinaga Mohawk Territory, also on the Bay of Quinte, home of L'il Crow Native Arts Centre Café with offerings of incredible food by Kimberly Maracle and the art, wooden flutes, and music of David Maracle. And finally, by way of the *Quinte Loyalist* ferry from Millhaven, Ontario, crossing the north channel of Lake Ontario in a rainstorm, we have reached the hamlet of Stella on Amherst Island.

GETTING THERE: Car ferry

GETTING AROUND: Bring your car; bring your own bike

OVERNIGHT ACCOMMODATIONS: Limited options: one lodge, two B&Bs; cottage rentals; limited camping

FOOD: One restaurant; groceries

DAY TRIP? Yes, recommended

STATE / PROVINCIAL / NATIONAL PARK? No

Is Amherst Island the *first* of "the Thousand Islands"? In some quarters, Amherst is heralded as exactly that. Other sources point out, some with more than a bit of attitude, that Amherst Island is located in Lake Ontario, not the St. Lawrence River, so it cannot be counted as a part of that river's archipelago.

Before we consider the question, you should know that 1,864 islands actually comprise the archipelago, not merely 1,000, so the question is if the island is number one of 1,864 or 1,865 islands. On a blustery day, as we watch low banks of dark clouds over the Lake Ontario's North Channel, Ian, of the island's Topsy Farms, points out that North Channel, with its

This dry stone wall is on Back Beach Road on Amherst Island. Some of the island's historic stone walls are nearly 200 years old and harken back to early Irish settlement in Canada. In this century, islanders have undergone extensive training to be able to repair and maintain the walls. The 2015 Dry Stone Festival took place on the island, with guest wallers coming from Ireland.

current, is the start of the St. Lawrence River and at the island's south shore is Lake Ontario, which I suppose would make Amherst the first *half* of an island of 1,863.5 or 1,864.5. But as Ian adds, "It's not an argument, but for stupid people."

One thing you can't argue with, regardless of where the island falls downstream in the Great Lakes Basin, is the feeling of stepping—and being welcomed—into community when you get off the Amherst Island ferry at the village of Stella. According to *Harrowsmith Country Life* (as is proudly quoted on the island's website), Stella is "one of the prettiest towns in Canada." I am a bit biased when it comes to the Irish, but I suspect the entire island's prettiness may be due to the influence of its Irish immigrants, who farmed the island and the population of which peaked at 2,000 in 1842. Many islanders today are descendants of that wave and have created a community of art and music, nature conservation and historic preservation, to say nothing of stone houses and stone walls and hives of bees and fields of lambs—all of which await your discovering on this 27-square-mile (70-square-kilometer) island. Do not leave home without your camera when you head for this island!

So what about Amherst Island's lambs and stone walls? Topsy Farms, which had its beginnings in 1971 with the purchase of a farm on the island by the commune Headlands Community, and whose first 50 sheep came from another Great Lakes island, Manitoulin Island, in 1974, is here with a flock of 2,300 sheep and lambs and wool products for sale. The island has a number of stone walls running between grazing fields of green. The Dry Stone Walling Association of Canada chose to hold the Irish-Canadian International Dry Stone Festival in September 2015 on the island. This three-day festival included a two-day Irish Dry Stone

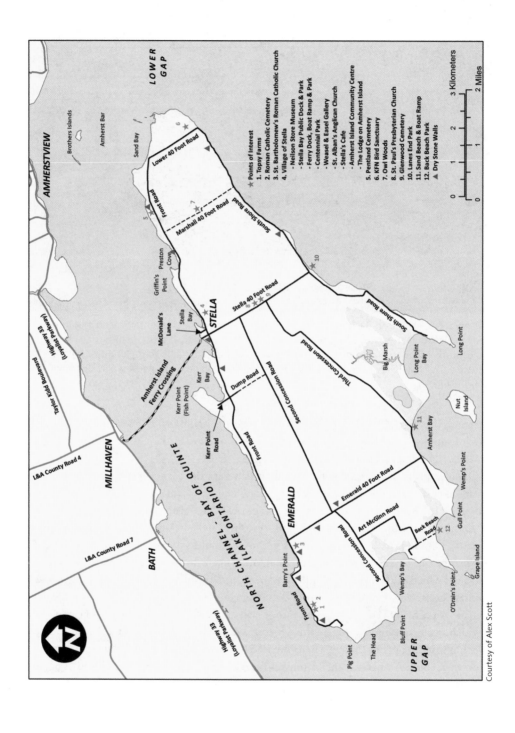

Points of Interest
1. Topsy Farms
2. Roman Catholic Cemetery
3. St. Bartholomew's Roman Catholic Church
4. Village of Stella
   - Neilson Store Museum
   - Stella Bay Public Dock & Park
   - Ferry Dock, Boat Ramp & Park
   - Centennial Park
   - Weasel & Easel Gallery
   - St. Alban's Anglican Church
   - Stella's Cafe
   - Amherst Island Community Centre
   - The Lodge on Amherst Island
5. Pentland Cemetery
6. KFN Bird Sanctuary
7. Owl Woods
8. St. Paul's Presbyterian Church
9. Glenwood Cemetery
10. Lanes End Park
11. Sand Beach & Boat Ramp
12. Back Beach Park
▲ Dry Stone Walls

0   1   2   3 Kilometers
0   1   2 Miles

AMHERSTVIEW

LOWER GAP

Brothers Islands

Amherst Bar

Sand Bay

Lower 40 Foot Road

Front Road

Marshall 40 Foot Road

South Shore Road

Preston Cove

Griffin's Point

Taylor Kidd Boulevard

Highway 33 (Loyalist Parkway)

McDonald's Lane

Stella Bay

STELLA

Stella 40 Foot Road

Amherst Island Ferry Crossing

Kerr Point (Fish Point)

Kerr Bay

Kerr Point Road

Dump Road

Front Road

Second Concession Road

Third Concession Road

South Shore Road

Big Marsh

Long Point

Long Point Bay

Long Point

Nut Island

Amherst Bay

MILLHAVEN

L&A County Road 4

BATH

L&A County Road 7

Highway 33 (Loyalist Parkway)

NORTH CHANNEL - BAY OF QUINTE
(LAKE ONTARIO)

Barry's Point

Front Road

Second Concession Road

EMERALD

Art McGinn Road

Emerald 40 Foot Road

Back Beach Road

Wemp's Bay

Wemp's Point

Gull Point

Grape Island

O'Drain's Point

Pig Point

The Head

Bluff Point

UPPER GAP

Courtesy of Alex Scott

Amherst Island Public Radio is broadcast from a dairy barn in Stella. CJAI 92.1 FM touts itself as the smallest radio station in Canada.

Workshop as well as appearances by Dr. Ray Bassett, the Irish ambassador to Canada; author Jane Urquhart (*The Stone Carvers*); world-renowned Irish wallers, including "the Queen's waller for Balmoral Estates"; and 25 other eminent wallers and stone carvers. The festivities were enlivened by Irish musicians and dancers (see www.drystonecanada.com).

But Amherst Island is much more than a farming community. A long, hand-printed notice posted in the Neilson Store and Museum window lists "Island Attractions" as including Amherst Island's Saturday-Morning Market, the Lodge, Amherst Island General Store, several art galleries, and the Waterside Summer Series of world-class musical concerts. Another list follows: "Bed & Breakfasts, Bird Watching, Flat Road Cycling, Thousands of Sheep, Hundreds of Deer, 400 Friendly Islanders." And finally, "For more information about Amherst Island, please visit our website, www.amherstisland.on.ca or listen to CJAI 92.1 FM Amherst Island Public Radio." That's right, the island has its own public radio station.

And where else do you know where you can go to cuddle a lamb?

How to Get There

From the village of Millhaven, Ontario, the Amherst Island Ferry Service picks up passengers hourly (except for five hours of the early morning) on the half hour for the 15-minute ride, less than two miles (three kilometers) to Stella, the larger of the two communities on Amherst Island.

Millhaven is 14 miles (22 kilometers) west of the city of Kingston via Highway 33, which is also known as the scenic Loyalist Parkway. Millhaven also has a direct connection with

Highway 401 (Interchange #593), six miles (10 kilometers) north of the ferry. Millhaven is two and a half hours east of Toronto, three hours west of Montreal, and two and a half hours south of Ottawa (via 416).

Amherst Island Ferry Service
5555 Front Rd.
Stella, ON K0H 2S0
613-389-3393
www.amherstisland.on.ca/ferry.htm

What to Expect

The island is over 12 miles (20 kilometers) long by over four miles (seven kilometers) wide and currently has a year-round population of about 450.

Islands of Life, a report published in 2010 by the Nature Conservancy of Canada, ranks Amherst Island second in biodiversity significance among the islands of northeast Lake Ontario (exceeded only by its larger neighbor, Wolfe Island).

Finally, expect an evocation of Ireland. The geography and landscape contribute, certainly, as does the history. Amherst Island is a part of the Loyalist Township, in their own way, like the Irish, a people set apart.

Paths to Adventure

NATURAL SITES

Owl Woods Nature Reserve—This is private land on which the public is welcome. Short-eared, long-eared, and great horned owls are among the resident bird population. Late-fall and winter visitors from the far and near north include snowy owls, saw-whet owls, and the rare boreal owl. Rumor has it chickadees will eat from your hand here.

Kingston Field Naturalists Bird Sanctuary—According to the Kingston Field Naturalists' "Birding Hot Spots of the Kingston Region," "Amherst Island is one of the best-known

JUST WHAT IS AN EASTERN COYOTE?

When asked about the nature of the predators attracted to Topsy Farms, sheep farmer and blogger Sally Bowen responded, "Wolves have cross-mated with coyotes to produce a hybrid officially called the eastern coyote." In 2011, a *National Geographic* headline read: "Coyote-Wolf Hybrids Have Spread across U.S. East: Predators Bred with Great Lakes Wolves, Then Moved South, DNA Shows."* Sally confirmed, "As soon as the ice across the North Channel to the mainland is solid, we see them crossing toward the island, so they repopulate nicely." She noted that a DNA study similar to the one mentioned above was conducted on Amherst Island. For more information, Sally recommends Gerry Parker's book *Eastern Coyote: The Story of Its Success.*** She added, "In other areas, packs of dogs can be vicious predators, but we don't experience that problem here." Nope, they have their wonderful guard dogs!

* http://news.nationalgeographic.com/news/2011/11/111107-hybrids-coyotes-wolf-virginia-dna-animals-science/.
** Gerry Parker, *Eastern Coyote: The Story of Its Success* (Halifax, NS: Nimbus, 1995).

Topsy Farms on Amherst Island is concerned with "all things lamb." A fun place to visit lambs, see whole flocks of sheep, and watch guard dogs do their job—although in this photo of Rosie with the flock, it's hard to tell who is guarding whom! (Courtesy of Don Tubb, Topsy Farms)

spots in Ontario for winter birding because the island regularly supports large populations of hawks, harriers, owls, shrikes, and waterfowl. In spring and autumn, Amherst Island can be a great place to see migrating waterfowl, shorebirds, and passerines. During the summer months, the island is home to a few notable breeding species like Wilson's Phalarope. . . . You must be a member of the Kingston Field Naturalists Club (or be accompanied by a member) to access this property. Virtually all of the land on Amherst Island is privately owned, so most birding is done from the roadside." However, a few landowners allow public access to theirs.

To see a list of some of the best birding spots on the island, visit http://kingstonfield naturalists.org/birding/amherst_island.pdf.

HISTORY PRESERVED

Amherst Island Museum
5220 Front Rd.
Stella, ON K0H 2S0
616-634-9512
Located in the Neilson Store with the Weasel & Easel Art Gallery.

CULTURAL ATTRACTIONS

Weasel & Easel—A fine-art and handcrafts gallery that displays and sells the work of local artists and craftspeople. Open during the summer season.

Topsy Farms and the Wool Shed—Here's an opportunity to see a farm that has been in operation for over 35 years. Over 1,200 sheep, protected from coyotes by large guard dogs, graze on pesticide-free land. All-natural pasture-fed lamb is available from this family farm, as are sheepskins and products from sustainably produced natural wool (blankets, throws, yarn, and hand-crafted products). For more information, visit www .topsyfarms.com.

OTHER ISLAND THINGS TO DO

Bike the island—Bring your own; no rentals are available.

Fish offshore—You'll need your own boat; no rentals are available.

Watch the birds—Pack your binoculars and bird guide.

Dive the wrecks—A number of interesting shipwrecks ring Amherst Island. The *Comet* sank off the northeastern tip of the island near the Brothers Islands, and an area south of the island is known as the Amherst Island Graveyard for its many shipwrecks.

SPECIAL ISLAND EVENTS

Waterside Summer Series (July and August)—Features concerts performed by top-caliber classical musicians in the beautiful setting of St. Paul's Presbyterian Church, just south of Stella, 1.25 miles (two kilometers) straight south from the ferry dock on the island. For more information, visit www.watersidemusic.ca.

Emerald Music Festival (August)—An impressive lineup of bluegrass, country, and Celtic musicians perform over three days on a farm site on the waterfront with informal camping facilities. For more information, visit www.emeraldmusicfestival.com.

Wooly Bully Run (Sunday morning in August)—5K or 10K run along the waterfront. Proceeds go to the Amherst Island Public School to support extracurricular activities. For more information, visit www.amherstisland.on.ca/WoolyBully/.

Biennial Open Studio Art Tour—As many as 11 artist studios have been included on this every-other-year tour featuring oil, acrylic, and watercolor paintings; photography; pottery; bookbinding; and more.

For More Island Information

www.amherstisland.on.ca—The Amherst Island website has information about the ferry service, accommodations, and island businesses; island geography, history, and genealogy; island activities and special events; and island maps, weather, and photos.

Amherst Island Beacon—Currently published monthly, this island newsletter has been in existence for over 40 years, is supported by paid subscription, and is archived at the island website (see above).

Tales of Amherst Island, by H. C. Burleigh (Kingston, ON: self-published, 1980)—This book is available to read online at www.ourroots.ca/e/page.aspx?id=1020422.

How You Can Support the Island

Association to Protect Amherst Island
PO Box 6
5695 Front Rd.
Stella, ON K0H 2S0
protectai@kos.net

This is an organization of birders and naturalists who have come together to oppose the placement of wind turbines on Amherst Island. Amherst Island has been named one of the "Top Ten Endangered Places" in Canada by the Heritage Canada Foundation (now known as Heritage Canada The National Trust) due to the threat of the turbines to its rich cultural and natural heritage.

Amherst Island in its entirety is an Important Bird Area (IBA) of global significance on the Atlantic migratory flyway and is home to 34 species at risk, including Blanding's turtle. With the introduction of wind turbines, habitat will be fragmented and lost.

The island is internationally recognized for concentrations of wintering hawks and owls, with birders traveling from around the world to visit Owl Woods, where it is possible to see up to 11 species of owls.

Amherst Island was ranked second in biodiversity significance (Lake Ontario Islands–Northeast) and includes 400 hectares of provincially significant coastal wetland.

Parting Thoughts

What that hand-printed notice posted in the Neilson Store window doesn't tell you is that Amherst Island Radio is the smallest radio station in all of Canada and that not only was it "born in a barn" in 2006, today it is still broadcast from the milk house of the old dairy barn and is serviced entirely by volunteers. The title of their morning show? The *Udder Morning Show.* To listen live to Island Radio from your computer (www.cjai.ca/playing.html?buster=0.8637193278409541), click on the close-up of the cow with its tongue out.

As I type, I'm listening to the Chet Doxas Quartet's "Nouveau Brit," currently on *Jazz Jim's Vault* and wondering: How it is I can listen to good jazz being broadcast from a Loyalist island half in Lake Ontario and half in the North Channel more easily than I can in the Detroit area?

St. Lawrence River Islands

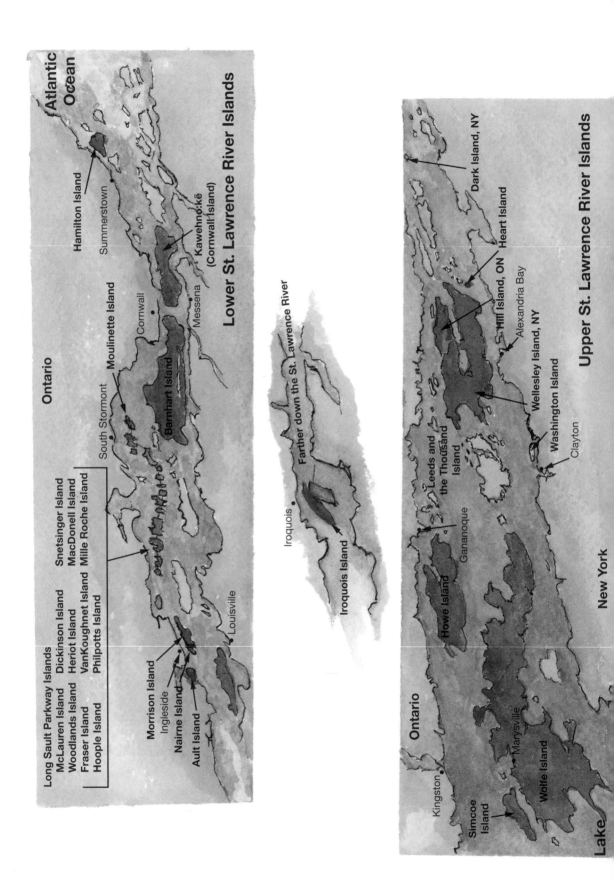

Lower St. Lawrence River Islands

Atlantic Ocean

Ontario

Hamilton Island

Summerstown

Kawehnó:ke (Cornwall Island)

Messena

Moulinette Island

South Stormont

Cornwall

Barnhart Island

Long Sault Parkway Islands
McLauren Island   Dickinson Island   Snetsinger Island
Woodlands Island   Heriot Island   MacDonell Island
Fraser Island   VanKoughnet Island   Mille Roche Island
Hoople Island   Philpotts Island

Morrison Island

Ingleside

Nairne Island

Ault Island

Louisville

Farther down the St. Lawrence River

Iroquois

Iroquois Island

Upper St. Lawrence River Islands

Dark Island, NY

Heart Island

Hill Island, ON

Alexandria Bay

Wellesley Island, NY

Washington Island

Clayton

Leeds and the Thousand Island

Gananoque

Howe Island

Ontario

Kingston

Marysville

Simcoe Island

Wolfe Island

New York

Lake

An Introduction to the St. Lawrence River

The body of water farthest downstream in the Great Lakes Basin, the St. Lawrence River connects Lake Ontario with the Atlantic Ocean, flowing into and through what is the St. Lawrence Basin on its way. The St. Lawrence River is about 745 miles (1,200 kilometers) long and drops 226 feet between Lake Ontario and Montreal, Quebec, where a new basin, the St. Lawrence Basin, begins.

Without being a hydrologist, geologist, or Great Lakes historian, it would be difficult to say what the "natural," pre-1954 width of the river at any one point would have been. Between 1954 and 1959, the St. Lawrence Seaway was built. The building of the seaway was a monumental joint project between the United States and Canada to increase the ease of shipping for industry by opening the Great Lakes to oceangoing vessels. This five-year project involved dredging channels; building canals; creating new bodies of water; constructing locks; displacing 6,500 people; moving a number of buildings; destroying some buildings, farms, and entire settlements; and changing several natural habitats that supported a variety of wildlife in the water, on land, and in the air. The end result was that Duluth, Minnesota, 2,340 miles (3,766 kilometers) away in the very farthest western point of the Great Lakes Basin, was connected to the Atlantic Ocean—and not just by the flow of water between the two points but by the flow of commerce represented by ship traffic.

In the Great Lakes Basin, the St. Lawrence River flows in a northeasterly direction from Lake Ontario between Ontario on its eastern banks and the state of New York on its western banks. When the river reaches the point where the province of Quebec is on both riverbanks, this signals that it has left the Great Lakes Basin (95,000 square miles/245,759 square kilometers) and entered the St. Lawrence Basin (519,000 square miles/1,344,200 square kilometers). While Quebec is not a part of the Great Lakes Basin, the city's position along the St. Lawrence Seaway makes it a partner in water resource management with the province of Ontario and the eight "Great Lakes states," Illinois, Indiana, Michigan, Minnesota, New York, Ohio, Pennsylvania, and Wisconsin. Just north of Quebec City, at the eastern tip of the island Île d'Orléans, the freshwater river becomes an estuary.

The St. Lawrence River is all about islands. Four archipelagoes dot the river, and it is perhaps best known for the one located in the Great Lakes Basin, the Thousand Islands. The actual number of islands in this archipelago is almost double that of its name—1,864 islands are visible above the approximately 50-mile (81-kilometer) stretch of river between Lake Ontario and the "Brockville Narrows" in between Brockville, Ontario, and Morristown, New York. At the Brockville Narrows, the St. Lawrence River is only 1,531 *yards* (1.4 kilometers) wide, and its width contains 70 islands and 60 shoals.

A number of St. Lawrence River Great Lakes Basin islands—both in the Thousand Island archipelago and those, either in the United States or Canada, related in some way to the

THE THOUSAND ISLAND DEFINITION OF "ISLAND"

What constitutes an island in this part of the Great Lakes Basin does not appear to be necessarily uniformly defined. Here are just two examples found floating on the Web; see if you can identify the points on which they differ:

"Any island must be above water level all year round, have an area greater than 1 square foot, and support at least one living tree."[*]

"To count as one of the Thousand Islands, emergent land within the river channel must have at least one square foot (0.093 m²) of land above water level year-round, and support at least two living trees."[**]

[*] "Thousand Island Facts: Ganannoque & the 1000 Islands," http://www.gananoque.com/tifacts_07.htm.
[**] http://en.wikipedia.org/wiki/Thousand_Islands.

construction of the St. Lawrence Seaway—are accessible by ferry or bridge. And many of them far exceed the definition of a Thousand Island island in terms of tree count and otherwise.

The three largest of the Frontenac Islands are accessible by ferry:

- Wolfe Island, Ontario—Take the *Wolfe Islander III* ferry from Kingston, Ontario, or the *Horne's Ferry* from Cape Vincent, New York, to the very largest of the Thousand Islands.
- Simcoe Island, Ontario—Take the *Simcoe Islander* from Wolf Island to this rural island, three to four miles (five to 6.5-kilometers) long, also the site of the Nine Mile Point Lighthouse (to which there is no public access).
- Howe Island, Ontario—It's just a 10-minute ride and under $10 for a round-trip ride, on either the county-operated, cable-driven, 15-vehicle *Frontenac Howe-Islander* ferry with a dock in the community of Pitts Ferry, a part of Kingston, or on the township-operated Howe Island "Foot Ferry" from west of Gananoque to this 12-square-mile (31-square-kilometer) island.

Islands at the Thousand Islands Bridge—Pay the toll and take the bridge from Leeds and the Thousand Islands, Ontario, or Collins Landing, New York, to:

- Hill Island, Ontario.
- Wellesley Island, New York.

Two "Castle Islands" are accessible by passenger ferry:

- Heart Island, Alexandria Bay, New York—Site of the Boldt Castle. Take a passenger ferry from Alexandria Bay or Clayton, New York, or Gananoque, Rockport, or Mallorytown, Ontario.
- Dark Island, Chippewa Bay, New York—Site of the Singer Castle. Take a passenger ferry from Alexandria Bay or Hammond, New York, or Rockport or Brockville, Ontario.

The islands most closely connected to the St. Lawrence Seaway Project (from southwest to northeast, on both sides of the international border) are all accessible by bridges or causeways. But before we look at the islands in this part of the Great Lakes Basin, it is helpful to understand a little bit about how the St. Lawrence Seaway shaped them.

The Great Lakes St. Lawrence Seaway System, 2,342 miles (3,769 kilometers) long, is the world's longest inland waterway. Inaugurated by Queen Elizabeth II and President Dwight D. Eisenhower, the seaway flows through two Canadian provinces and eight

American states. The construction began in 1954, and the seaway opened on June 26, 1959. The project had two objectives: water-level control and the generation of hydroelectric power. The system, which supports 15 major international ports and more than 50 regional ports, includes five connecting canals and 15 locks, which makes it possible for human beings to regulate the water level of the huge bodies of water making up the Great Lakes Basin. And the human beings do it through the International Joint Commission (IJC). "In 1909, as part of the Boundary Waters Treaty, the International Joint Commission was established to help manage the shared waters along the Canadian-U.S. border. During the 1950's, the IJC approved the construction and operation of a hydropower project in the international section of the St. Lawrence River for the purpose of producing hydroelectricity, enabling seaway navigation, and providing some flood protection to Lake Ontario and the St. Lawrence River. . . . Under the treaty, the IJC is tasked with ensuring that all affected interests are considered in decisions that change the levels and flows of boundary waters."[92]

A series of locks in six canals (South Shore, Beauharnois, Wiley-Dondero, Iroquois, Welland, and St. Mary's) raise an upbound ship from the Gulf of the St. Lawrence—the mouth of the St. Lawrence River at the Atlantic Ocean—601 feet (183 meters) by the time it has sailed the 1,499 miles (2,412 kilometers) to Duluth, Minnesota, in Lake Superior. The locks? Between Montreal (just on the other side of the Great Lakes Basin in the St. Lawrence Basin) to Lake Ontario: four Canadian—St. Lambert, Cote Ste. Catherine, Upper Beauharnois, Lower Beauharnois—and two American—Snell and Eisenhower, and then a fifth Canadian: Iroquois. Then the eight Canadian locks that make up the Welland Canal between Lake Ontario and Lake Erie, across the Niagara Peninsula. And finally, the Soo Locks in the St. Mary's River, between Lake Huron and Lake Superior, four (parallel) American locks—Sabin, Davis, Poe, and McArthur—and the Canadian lock, now used for recreational watercraft only.

What about the dams? To see photographs following a narration of the construction of the St. Lawrence Seaway, visit http://stlawrencepiks.com/seawayhistory/Seaway Construction/CornwallMassena/index.html.

Ports on the seaway include Thunder Bay, Ontario, and Duluth, Minnesota, on Lake Superior; Milwaukee, Wisconsin, Chicago, Illinois, and Gary, Indiana, on Lake Michigan; Port Huron, Michigan, on Lake Huron; Detroit, Michigan, and Windsor, Ontario, on the Detroit River; Toledo, Ohio, Cleveland, Ohio, Erie, Pennsylvania, and Buffalo, New York, on Lake Erie; Hamilton, Ontario, and Toronto, Ontario, on Lake Ontario; and Montreal, Quebec, and Quebec City, Quebec, on the St. Lawrence River (these last two are north of the Great Lakes Basin in the St. Lawrence Basin).

The bridge- or causeway-accessible islands that were impacted—or in some cases *created*—by the construction of St. Lawrence Seaway include:

Iroquois Island, Ontario—The site of the Iroquois lock and two cemeteries.

Wilson Hill Island, New York—Created by the flooding of the seaway, this island was designated as a relocation area for New York State residents displaced as a result of the flooding. Over half of the island consists of the Wilson Hill State Fish and Game Wildlife Management Area, which also connects to Bradford Island (restricted access other than for permit hunting) by causeway.

Ault Island, Ontario—The northern part of the island is a part of the Upper Canada Migratory Bird Sanctuary, and the southern part is the residential community of South Stormont. Located near the historic Upper Canada Village, this is the largest of the Canadian islands created when flooding for the seaway.

Nairne Island, Ontario—This is also a part of the Upper Canada Migratory Bird Sanctuary.

Morrison Island, Ontario—Accessed from Nairne Island, the island is another part of the Upper Canada Migratory Bird Sanctuary.

Long Sault Parkway islands—The 11 islands of the Long Sault Parkway, one of the Parks of the St. Lawrence, are connected by the parkway, a road that crosses and connects these islands, which at one time were the highest elevation of the some of the family farms and communities of the Canadian mainland that were flooded in 1958 for the seaway.

Moulinette Island—Accessible by bridge from Mille Roches, one of the Long Sault Parkway islands, the twelfth island in this group of "hilltops" is not a part of the park and has seasonal cottages on it.

Barnhart Island, New York—Accessible by underwater tunnel below the Eisenhower Lock, this island is a continuation of the mainland Robert Moses State Park and the site of the St. Lawrence State Park.

Kawehno:kë (aka Cornwall Island)—Mohawk First Nation land accessible by the Seaway International Bridge, this island is a part of the Akwesasne Mohawk Reserve that straddles the Canadian-U.S. border. The island is considered to be located in Canada.

For More Information on the St. Lawrence River

www.visit1000islands.com

Great Lakes Information Center—www.great-lakes.net.

Fools' Paradise; Remembering the Thousands Islands, by Paul Malo (n.p.: Laurentian, 2003).

A Floating World: More People, Place and Pastimes of the Thousand Islands, by Paul Malo (n.p.: Laurentian, 2004).

"Island Names," by Ross D. Pollack, *Thousand Islands Life.com,* www.thousandislandslife .com/BackIssues/Archive/tabid/393/articleType/ArticleView/articleId/227/Island -Names-Updated-May-2009.aspx.

Pilot and photographer's Ian Coristine's series of seven volumes showcasing 20 years of aerial and landscape photographs of the Thousand Islands. For more information, see www.1000islandsphotoart.com/Home.aspx.

Wolfe Island, Ontario

TILTING TOWARD WINDMILLS

June 19, 2014, 5:20 p.m.
Wolfe Island Ferry Dock
Kingston

I saw the ferry arriving, going by the foot of Queen Street just as I was turning onto the street. I did arrive in time for the 5:00 Wolfe Island ferry from Kingston, after all . . . but I was the 57th car in line and the ferry holds only 55 cars (300 passengers), so now I'm waiting for the 6:00. Lucinda is already waiting for me to pick her up with her bike on the east side of Wolfe Island; she ferried over from Cape Vincent.

Finally I drive onto the *Wolfe Islander III* for the free(!) ride, car included, to the Marysville dock on Wolfe Island. We head out past the green trunnion bascule lift bridge, completed in 1916 and designed by Joe Strauss, an American engineer and pioneer of lift-bridge design.

On this Friday, approaching the first day of summer, we're cutting through a regatta of sailboats and heading toward a "regatta" of "windmills," all in full sail.

GETTING THERE: Car ferry; private boat

GETTING AROUND: Bring your car (free to transport on ferry) and/or bike; bicycle rentals

OVERNIGHT ACCOMMODATIONS: Limited on island (but Kingston is just a short, free ferry ride away): one hotel, one inn, B&Bs, vacation rentals; no camping

FOOD: Restaurants; a wonderful bakery; groceries

DAY TRIP? Yes, recommended

STATE / PROVINCIAL / NATIONAL PARK? No, but Big Sandy Bay Conservation Area, managed by the Township of Frontenac Islands, is in the southwest corner of the island

Water, sun, wind: the Great Lakes area, and Great Lakes islands in particular, with their relatively small energy-grid requirements, are naturals when it comes to considering renewable energy resources. (For more information, see Great Lakes Renewable Energy Association www.glrea.org/.) Located where Lake Ontario ends and the St. Lawrence River begins, Wolfe Island is the largest of the Thousand Islands, just under 48 square miles (124 square kilometers).

Frontenac Islands is the name of a township in Frontenac County, Ontario, that includes Wolfe Island and four other islands as well as a few smaller islands often overlooked. The

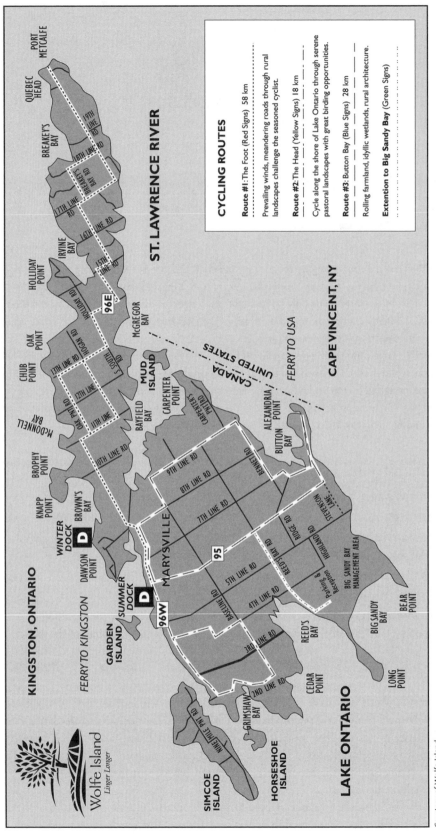

CYCLING ROUTES

Route #1: The Foot (Red Signs) 58 km

Prevailing winds, meandering roads through rural landscapes challenge the seasoned cyclist.

Route #2: The Head (Yellow Signs) 18 km

Cycle along the shore of Lake Ontario through serene pastoral landscapes with great birding opportunities.

Route #3: Button Bay (Blue Signs) 28 km

Rolling farmland, idyllic wetlands, rural architecture.

Extention to Big Sandy Bay (Green Signs)

Courtesy of Wolfe Island

Wolfe Island has embraced the wind: 86 wind turbines have been "planted" on the island, making Wolfe Island Wind Farm the second-largest wind plant in Canada.

archipelago, township, and county were named after Louis de Buade, Comte de Frontenac et de Palluau (1622–1698), a French soldier, courtier, and governor general of New France. On June 28, 1672, over 340 years ago, Frontenac sailed from La Rochelle, located on the southwest coast of France, for New France—the area colonized in North America by France between the exploration of the St. Lawrence River by Jacques Cartier (1534) and the end of New France (brought about by Great Britain and Spain in 1763). Frontenac would most likely have been familiar with windmills and their power to mill grain or pump water from a well, but he surely never could have imagined this scene of wind turbines or understand their process of generating electricity—something yet to be discovered—to power all of our electrical machinery, appliances, and devices, yet to be invented.

The 197.8-megawatt Wolfe Island Wind Facility, made up of 86 Siemens 2.3-megawatt turbines, had already been operational for almost exactly five years when I visited Wolfe Island. When I stopped at a Saturday morning garage sale on the front porch of a house on Main Street, a discussion started up about the island's wind turbines. Other garage sale browsers chimed in. It has been said that "energy facilities ... generate more than electricity; they ... also generate conflict,"[93] and islanders have not been of one mind about this project. From the time the wind farm project was first considered, Wolfe Island residents had been split over the issue—sometimes family members and neighbors found themselves holding opposite opinions. Some islanders were interested in the $25 million that went directly to the community during construction and the ongoing economic benefits of municipal tax revenues and land lease agreements amounting to $3 million a year;[94] participating land-owners receive supplementary income by agreeing to have wind turbines installed on their land. Many also appreciated the tourists the project brought to the island as "2000 people ... toured the facility during its the first summer of operation."[95]

Other islanders were concerned that the negative effects often attributed to industrial wind turbines outweighed any financial gain. Primary concerns include noise annoyance, which can cause "stress, sleep disturbance, headache, difficulty concentrating, irritability, fatigue, dizziness or vertigo, tinnitus, anxiety, heart ailments, and palpitations."[96] Visual disturbances include shadow flicker as well as the burden of altered landscape aesthetics. These audio and visual effects are believed to contribute to a decreased quality of life. There are also damaging effects on wildlife, particularly birds and bats; an impact on the radar for weather-reporting services; and a detrimental influence on the resale value of homes.

After considering the evidence and testimony presented by 26 witnesses, a 2011 Ontario environmental review tribunal acknowledged that industrial wind turbines can harm human health, although to what extent remains unclear: "This case has successfully shown that the debate should not be simplified to one about whether wind turbines can cause harm to humans. The evidence presented to the Tribunal demonstrates that they can, if facilities are placed too close to residents. The debate has now evolved to one of degree."[97]

The general consensus, here at this spot on Main Street on this day between these neighbors, is that healing is beginning between members of the two factions, above whom—for or against—the blades turn.

How to Get There

Take the *free* 20-minute ferry ride aboard the 55-vehicle *Wolfe Islander III*.

Ontario Ministry of Transportation
295 Ontario St. (at Ontario and Barrack Streets)
Kingston, ON K7K 2X7
613-548-7227
www.wolfeisland.com/ferry.php#wolfe

Or take the low-cost, 10-minute ride on the smaller (10–12 vehicle) Horne's Ferry from Cape Vincent, New York, across the international border (the only international car/passenger ferry on the St. Lawrence River).

Horne's Ferry Transportation
319 Club St.
Cape Vincent, NY
315-783-0638 (in the United States); 613-385-2404 (in Canada)
www.facebook.com/hornesferry and www.wolfeisland.com/ferry.php#hornes

Wolfe Islander III—the only free public ferry in the Great Lakes Basin—makes hourly 20-minute trips from Kingston, Ontario, to the town of Marysville on Wolfe Island and back.

What to Expect

Wind turbines! And a bit of what makes all 86 of them work so well on the island: wind! Although it's not so windy that you notice it particularly, at least not on a sunny day in mid-June—except maybe when you're riding a bike.

And bikes (they are available to rent) are an excellent way to see the island. Three routes are suggested: the Foot, the Head, and Button Bay. We rode to Big Sandy Bay and did the wind farm tour by bike, too. You can get a cycling route map here: www.wolfeisland.com/downloads/WI-bicycle-map-final2.pdf.

If you stay in town, you can expect to get your bearings at the Old House Museum (be sure to pick up a copy of the Wolfe Island Historical Society's *Marysville Walking Tour* pamphlet here, too—or, if they're not open, head for the Tourist Information Centre by the Township Hall, 1195 County Road 96 in Marysville). You can get some "good bean" at Café Tenango, see some (really) good local art at the Stone Heron Gallery, and discover plenty of other interesting facets in Marysville if you let the walking tour pamphlet be your guide (one thing you may not expect is the wonderful historic mural series).

Expect congenial island folks, long lazy days of exploring, cool breezy nights.

Paths to Adventure

NATURAL SITES

Big Sandy Bay Conservation Area—Jointly owned by the Canadian Ministry of Natural Resources, Duck Unlimited Canada, the Nature Conservancy of Canada, and the

Canadian Wildlife Service and operated by the Township of the Frontenac Islands. A .8-mile (1.3-kilometer) walking trail traverses wetlands, grasslands, and woodlands to get visitors to the 1.8-mile (3-kilometer) stretch of white sandy beach. Along the trail, some trees are identified and benches are available for resting. On the beach, a wildlife observation platform atop a sand dune allows you to see Black Lake and a number of wind turbines. There's a carry in, carry out garbage policy in effect, and no camping is allowed.

HISTORY PRESERVED

Old House Museum—Wolfe Island's historical museum, run by Wolfe Island Historical Society volunteers and donations, was established in 2009 in the oldest house on the island. Known as the Tiner LaRush House, it was built in the early 1800s and may once have housed the sole island school. It is located in the island village of Marysville at 5 Leander Street, not far from the ferry landing.

Trinity Anglican Church—First church built on the island (begun in 1845 and finished in 1851), located in Marysville, and still in use. Three other churches are on the island: Christ Church (Anglican), Sacred Heart of Mary Catholic Church, and Wolfe Island United Church.

Trinity Anglican Cemetery—Located behind the Trinity Anglican Church. Five other cemeteries are located on the island: Christ Church Cemetery, Sacred Heart New Roman Catholic Cemetery, Sacred Heart Old Roman Catholic Cemetery (near the Trinity Anglican Cemetery), St. Lawrence Cemetery, and Wolfe Island United Church Cemetery (aka Horne Cemetery and Point Alexandria United Church Cemetery). (Note: Two of the island churches have cemetery grounds in two locations.)

Wolfe Island Lighthouse—Built in 1861 on the eastern end of the island on what is currently called Quebec Point or Quebec Head (in the past known as East Point or Hemlock

Lake Ontario sparkles in Big Sandy Bay at the southwest end of this St. Lawrence River island. Big Sandy Bay Conservation Area, a 1,000-acre day-use area on Wolfe Island, has a coastal ecology that is rare in Ontario, including, according to the Friends of Big Sandy Bay, "provincially and regionally significant birds, provincially rare trees and other rare plant species."

Point), this wooden lighthouse is on a small plot of land owned by the Canadian Coast Guard. The lighthouse, 33 feet in height above the water, has no top lantern housing or lantern—just a bare light. While the lighthouse continues to aid navigation on the river, it has lost the top of the tower that housed the lantern. Its white-wood-shingled, red-trimmed, square tower with sloping sides is completely dwarfed by a private residence next to it, which is an accurate replica of a historic Chesapeake Bay lighthouse.[98]

Knapp Point Lighthouse (aka Brown's Point Light)—Built in 1874 on the northern shore of the island, northeast of Marysville, on a peninsula that has been known as Brown's Point, Brophy's Point, and Knapp's Point over the years, this lighthouse was automated in 1947 and deactivated in 2000. It is the most westerly of all of the Canadian lighthouses in the Thousand Islands. The adjacent keeper's house is privately owned and used as a cottage.

CULTURAL ATTRACTIONS

Historic Mural Series—At the time of my first visit, three historic murals graced downtown Marysville, *Wolfe Island 1907* (2005), *Scene of the Crime* (2006), and *Underwater Bubble System* (2007), and a fourth was in the process of being painted, depicting Elwyn Hinckley "Buck" Mullin (1922–96) and his boat *Rebola,* named after his mother Ola Mullin and his sister Reba. *Rebola* served as the water taxi used by many islanders to get to the mainland in emergencies or when the regular ferry wasn't available. The four murals are painted in shades of ochre, umber, and sienna, reminiscent of sepia-toned photographs, by Wolfe Island artists Patricia Sanford, Linda Sutherland, and Kim Woodman.

Wolfe Island Wind Farm—Beginning operation in 2009, by 2014 this wind facility included 86 wind turbines and was the second-largest wind farm in Canada. Get your free six-page self-guided walking tour guide, which includes the ferry schedule, at http://sites.sitemajic .com/-1522/SelfGuidedWolfeIslandWalkingTour.pdf.

Stone Heron Gallery—Open from Canada Day to Labor Day, the gallery is filled with the work of 20 or more local artists and craftspeople (www.wolfeislandart.net).

Wolfe Island Community Garden—The motto of the garden is "Growing Strong Roots." In 2014, there was a raised bed labeled "Stone Soup." Can you guess what—not stones—was planted here?

Shanti Retreat—A century-old inn and waterside cabins provide accommodations for yoga and meditation retreats. For more information, visit www.shantiretreat.ca/.

OTHER ISLAND THINGS TO DO

Take the Marysville Walking Tour—The Wolfe Island Historical Society's pamphlet is available from the Old House Museum and the Tourist Information Centre near the town hall.

Take the Wind Farm Tour—For a copy of the *Wolfe Island Wind Farm Free Self-Guided Tour,* visit http://sites.sitemajic.com/-1522/SelfGuidedWolfeIslandWalkingTour.pdf.

Bicycle the island—Bikes are available for rent at Cycle Wolfe Island (http://cyclewolfe island.blogspot.com).

Bird-watch.

Fish the waters—Try for walleye, smallmouth bass, great northern pike, muskellunge, lake trout and, in the deeper waters of Lake Ontario, lake, brown, and rainbow trout and salmon. A boat ramp and charter guide services are available on the island. Fishing licenses are available in Marysville at Mosier's Groceries as well as other establishments.

Golf—The Wolfe Island Riverfront Golf Course is a par-35, nine-hole course overlooking the St. Lawrence Seaway. Alston Moor Golf Links is a par-35, nine-hole course that advertises "Golf among the windmills."

DOWNSTREAM TO THE THIRD FRONTENAC ISLAND: HOWE ISLAND

Howe Island is accessed by a cable ferry—the Howe Island Ferry—across a narrow channel to the island's eastern tip from Gananoque, Ontario. This ferry is known as the "Foot Ferry," leaving as it does from the "foot" of the island, its farthest point downstream. A county-operated ferry lands at the west end of the island, leaving from Pitts Ferry on the mainland, a part of Kingston. Besides the farms and cottages that dot the island, you'll want to look for St. Philomena's, a very photogenic Roman Catholic limestone church with barn-red doors and white-trimmed windowpanes.

This quiet rural island (12 square miles/31 square kilometers) also has one winery and one bed-and-breakfast, paired together in Wendy and David Jones's Howe Island Winery B&B, known for it hospitality. (On my overnight there, according to Trip Advisor, I had the distinction of staying in the number one room in the number one B&B in the Thousand Islands!)

From the rooftop deck of the property's dock, jutting out into the mighty St. Lawrence (often the site of wedding ceremonies), we watched several loons on the water approach while minks played below on the bank, both species closer than I have ever witnessed before. Howe Island is truly an island where less is more.

Visit Simcoe Island—Take the *Simcoe Islander,* the smallest ferry in Ontario, an on-demand *cable* ferry from the northwestern corner (known as "the Head") of Wolfe Island (at the time of my trip, the cost was $1 per person round-trip) to bike the four-mile (6.5-kilometer) length of Simcoe Island, past the cows—who outnumber the 20 year-round residents. (Since its years of being known as Isle de Foret, "Forest Island," Simcoe has been used as farmland and in particular for grazing.) The island is the site of the Nine Mile Point Lighthouse, the 40-foot "Imperial Tower"–style lighthouse built in 1833, now automated, and recognized as a Federal Heritage Building in 1989. The west point of Simcoe Island, where the lighthouse is located, is all either Coast Guard or private land, but you can view the lighthouse from the gate to the property or by private boat.

SPECIAL ISLAND EVENTS

Wolfe Island's Classic 5k–10k Annual Races (July).
Wolfe Island Musical Festival (August).
Wolfe Island Corn Maze (August 1–mid-November).
Frontenac Stewardship Foundation Seminar Series (as announced).

For More Island Information

www.wolfeisland.com.
Wolfe Island Historical Society—http://wolfeislandhistoricalsociety.org/.
Big Sandy Bay Conservation Area—http://municipality.frontenacislands.on.ca/?q=big_sandy_bay.
Windword: The Annual Journal of the Wolfe Island Historical Society (Wolfe Island Historical Society).
Growing Up on Wolfe Island: An Island History, edited by Brian Johnson and Sarah Sorenson (Wolfe Island, ON: Wolfe Island Heritage Committee, 2008).
Wolfe Island: A Legacy in Stone, by Barbara Wall La Rocque (Toronto: Dundurn, 2009).

Wolfe Island Past & Present, by Winston M. Cosgrove (1973), which can be found on Our
    Roots: Canada's Local Histories Online at www.ourroots.ca/e/toc.aspx?id=4424.
"Ganounkouesnot": The Long Island Standing Up! by Renie Marshall (Wolfe Island, ON: np,
    2000).
Simcoe Island, an Eves Perspective: A Chronicle of the Island and It's [sic] *People,* by Sanford
    Sydney Eves (Cobourg, ON: self-published, 1994).

How You Can Support the Island

Wolfe Island Historical Society
PO Box 31
Wolfe Island, ON K0H 2Y0
www. wolfeislandhistoricalsociety.org

Friends of Big Sandy Bay
Box 99
Wolfe Island
ON K0H 2Y0
www.bigsandybay.ca

The Frontenac Stewardship Foundation
PO Box 394
Verona, ON K0H 2W0
www.frontenacstewardship.ca

Parting Thoughts

June 20, 2014

Lucinda and I were (spontaneously, over the phone) invited to have dinner on this Summer
Solstice at Margaret and Grant Pyke's Victorian-style farmhouse, the Blue Horizon B & B on the
south side of the island. Their house sits at the river's edge, their windows looking out to the
shipping channel. The Pykes are farmers and remind me of grown-up versions of my cousins on
Aunt Maggie's Ontario farm.

We have a comfortable conversation at the dinner table, looking out through the picture
window at the lake. After a casserole of canned tomatoes, ground meat from their own organ-
ically raised bison, elbow macaroni, and melted cheese; a relish tray; tossed iceberg salad;
and pie, Margaret and Grant show us around the house and the huge old green and white
barn complex.

As the sun is setting, we go with Grant to see a wind turbine planted on his land. We find
ourselves on a rise of land, rolling fields falling away on all sides. The horizon is contracting to
a thin line of red. Across the road, the windbreak of trees at the field's edge and the blades of
the turbines towering over them are becoming silhouettes. I stand at the base of the windmill
and try to connect what I am seeing and feeling move above me with the statistics Grant had

spun out about the marine cable, the million tons of stone, of sand, the pads, the rebar. I can't. The numbers do not translate to the sheer height of the tower, the length of the blades. Someday, will our descendants connect these structures fallen back to earth to sarsen stone, their nacelles to the lintels of Stonehenge?

Driving back in Grant's truck, as Lucinda and Grant talk and the evening river chill begins to settle around us, I am slowly transported to a childhood memory of returning home late at night from somewhere: lying on my back in the back seat of my parents' car, the straps of my patent leather shoes pinching the tops of my feet as I pressed my heels into the car's armrest. In a tired daze, out the opposite window, I watched the telephone poles flash by, the pulse of red lights on the radio towers as we passed them in the dark fields.

The world seems very big. I am on the largest of 1,864 islands, at the entrance of the mighty St. Lawrence River—two Great Lakes and two rivers away from my home—and dark is falling through the blades of windmills. Yet I feel at home.

Wellesley Island, New York

A LIKELY INTERSECTION OF LEY LINES

June 12, 2013

Unwittingly, we have arrived at the Thousand Island Park on Wellesley Island a week before the season starts here; along the river, the weather doesn't warm up until spring is almost summer. But we do have reservations and eventually find someone to check us into our room at the Wellesley Hotel on the St. Lawrence, a Victorian hotel built in 1903, the only one of three large wooden hotels to have survived fires in 1892 and 1912.

Bronwen and I decide to take a bike ride around the empty Thousand Island Park, a national historic district of 294 buildings located on the southwestern tip of Wellesley Island. We pedal past the sweet little library on the square, surrounded by a freshly mowed lawn, to the Pavilion at the dock and then into a neighborhood of almost 300 wooden-frame Victorian "cottages." Back in 1890, before the fires and the Depression, there were double that number.

We admire all the beautifully restored and maintained (by Landmark Society standards) "painted ladies"[99] and sit a bit on the lattice-trimmed and sheltered bench with the instruction "Sit N Rest" painted on it. Thousand Island Park, New York, has its own stone post office (decorated with flower boxes) and its own zip code (13692). We locate the Tabernacle, which played an important role in the start of this Chautauqua-like community. It's currently advertising four weekly movie nights, and on Sundays one Catholic Mass and one Protestant service.

And then, as we we're riding back, away from the houses, I see the trailhead sign for "Rock Ridges Nature Trail"—the beginning of our real adventure.

GETTING THERE: Bridge; private boat

GETTING AROUND: Bring your car; bring your own bike; boat rentals

OVERNIGHT ACCOMMODATIONS: One historic hotel, one motel and efficiencies, cabins; vacation rentals; campgrounds

FOOD: Restaurants; groceries

DAY TRIP? Yes, but a longer stay is recommended if you are a camper and/or hiker

STATE / PROVINCIAL / NATIONAL PARK? Wellesley Island State Park, Waterson Point State Park, and DeWolf Point State Park; Thousand Island Park is a national historic district

---

What do Minna Anthony Common, Swami Vivekananda, and the Reverend J. F. Dayan have in common? They are all integral parts of the intriguing history of Wellesley Island, or at

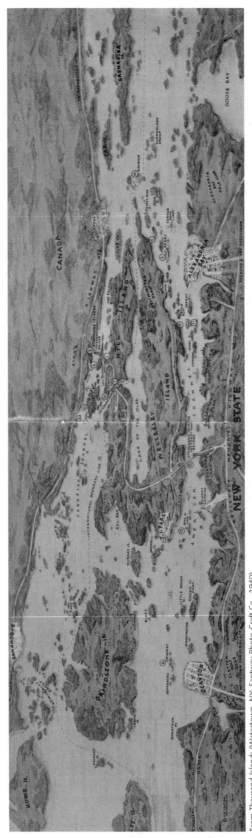

From *Thousand Islands* (Watertown, NY: Santway Photo–Craft Co., 1940)

least of one island village there. Wellesley Island has five residential communities: Grandview Park, Moore Landing, Fineview, Westminster Park, and Thousand Island Park. Thousand Island Park, at the southwestern tip of the island, is well over a century old and contains 294 historic buildings, primarily large Victorian cottages. Since 1982 the district has been listed on the National Register of Historic Places as "an outstanding concentration of substantially intact late 19th century and early 20th century resort architecture."[100] Perhaps of even greater interest is the history of Thousand Island Park, woven with several fascinating strands.

In 1875, the Reverend J. F. Dayan, a Methodist minister, created a "camp-meeting-style" summer village in New York on the St. Lawrence River, following the model of Chautauqua, New York, some 300 miles (500 kilometers) southwest, which had been founded the year before at Lake Chautauqua. The intent in both places was to create a place "where families could benefit from a change of scene and air and perhaps, in their manner of living."[101] To that end, outdoor public lectures, concerts, and dramatic performances of a religious nature were provided. The only way to the park was by boat, and as the park gained in popularity, steamships docked at the Pavilion on the St. Lawrence River to allow passengers to disembark at the resort.

The Thousand Island Park resort began as a tent city in which campers leased lots, with the prime spots being closest to the Tabernacle, the center of the park, the site where campers came to participate in social activities and attend the rectifying events. Initially an enormous tent, the Tabernacle was replaced in 1884 by a semicircular and tiered wooden building with open-air seating for 3,000. By 1900, 7,000 visitors were coming to the resort each summer, and the camping tents were eventually replaced by cottages. At the height of its popularity, the resort contained over 600 cottages. In 1912, a fire destroyed the island's second great hotel, the Columbian (the Thousand Island Park Hotel had burned in 1890), plus 100 cottages. This second fire and the Depression changed the size and nature of the park.

In the meantime, there had been an important—and, perhaps, given the time and place, a more exotic visitor to the park. In 1895, Swami Vivekananda, a Hindu monk who represented India at the 1893 Parliament of World Religions and is often credited with introducing Eastern philosophy and yoga to the West, was invited by American devotee Elizabeth Dutcher to visit her summer cottage in Thousand Island Park. During his seven-week visit, he reported, he obtained *nirvikalpa samadhi,* the highest form of enlightenment, while meditating in the woods behind the cottage. The Ramakrishna-Vivekananda Center purchased the cottage in 1947 to use as a spiritual retreat. Today, its grounds are open to visitors and meditators; the cottage itself is open as a place of pilgrimage for several hours a day over a six-week summer period.

Swami Vivekananda was not the only person to be influenced by the beauty of the woods surrounding Thousand Island Park. In the summer of 1935, Minna Anthony Common, a trained naturalist and a summer cottager from Watertown, New York, following trails originally used by Native Americans, created the 1.5-mile (2.4-kilometer) Rock Ridges Nature Trail on a densely wooded hill behind her cottage. The trail opened in August. Common had first become interested in nature study in summer courses conducted at Thousand Island Park. Later, Common's nature articles and sketches were published twice weekly for 25 years in the *Watertown Daily Times.* After her death in 1951, the trail became overgrown. In 1985, one of Common's daughters, Catherine Common Johnson, organized a group of people to clear the old trail. On July 3, 1985, the restored trail became accessible to hikers again.

Obviously, what these three historical figures have in common is their significant relationship to the Wellesley Island village of Thousand Island Park: Dayan as founder of this over 135-year-old community on the St. Lawrence River on 176 acres of former pastureland;

Vivekananda as a visitor who retreated during two years of lecturing in the United States to achieve enlightenment here; Common as a summer resident who, with the eye of a naturalist, created the opportunity for many to walk the trails used by Native Americans. Why were these three people drawn to the Thousand Island Park area of Wellesley Island? The power of the river here, perhaps? It may seem enough of a coincidence for the more fanciful to wonder if this southwestern peninsula of Wellesley Island might be situated on what has been called in Britain a ley line, or perhaps an intersection of ley lines, a place imbued with a mystical energy radiating from a spiritual alignment of landforms. Perhaps such fanciful theorists might want to take another look at those rock ridges in the woods behind the Thousand Island Park. Is it just coincidence or an instance of some sort of synchronicity of place?

How to Get There

In Ontario, take Highway 401 or the 1,000 Island Parkway to Highway 137, which crosses the international Thousand Islands Bridge. Cross to Hill Island, Ontario—stopping at the skydeck if you'd like to see an aerial view of the islands—and on to Wellesley Island, New York.

In New York, take I-81 to the Thousand Islands Bridge and onto Wellesley Island.

What to Expect

Wellesley is a sprawling island located in the upper end of the St. Lawrence River, in the first third of the river as Lake Ontario drains into it. The interior of the island is the large Lake of the Isles, which almost splits the island into two, providing for much more island waterfront, secluded camping, and opportunities to kayak or canoe.

The Thousand Islands Bridge crosses over and across this island, which contains five communities, three state parks, two golf courses, one cemetery, and one nature center.

Paths to Adventure

NATURAL SITES

Rock Ridges Nature Trail—Common's trail is located in the community of Thousand Island Park (not within the Wellesley Island State Park).

The Minna Anthony Common Nature Center—In 1969, the nature center building, located northeast of the Thousand Island Park on the southern shore of Eel Bay and within Wellesley Island State Park, was dedicated as the Minna Anthony Common Nature Center in honor of the woman who had inspired so much interest in the area through her observations, sketches, and writings and helped to initiate the founding principles of environmental conservation and education. The nature center includes a "Children's Discovery" room of hands-on displays, a classroom for programs, a fireplace for winter activities, a gift shop, and the Butterfly House. In addition to the building, 10 miles (16 kilometers) of hiking/skiing trails wind through the wildlife sanctuary also considered a part of the center. During July and August, voyageur canoe tours in a 16-passenger, 36-foot-long canoe are offered along the water's edge, which involve a three-mile (five-kilometer)

In 1935, Minna Anthony Commons, a naturalist and artist, created the 1.5-mile Rock Ridges Nature Trail following earlier Native American trails on Wellesley Island. In 1895, Swami Vivekananda meditated here, achieving, some say, *nirvikalpa samadhi,* the highest state of consciousness. If you can take just one hike in the Thousand Islands region, this very beautiful, very special trail in Thousand Island Park may be the one to choose.

paddle in Eel Bay with a naturalist who explains some of the geological features that make up the Thousand Islands.

Wellesley Island State Park in Fineview, New York—The 600-acre park located on the western end of Wellesley Island, which includes the Minna Anthony Common Nature Center and a wildlife sanctuary, was purchased by the Thousand Island Park and Historic Preservation Commission, led by one of Common's daughters, Catherine Common Johnson, in 1962. The park is divided into sections that are on different parts of the island and has a full-service marina and three boat launches, a sandy beach, a recreation barn, and a golf course as well as the nature center. In addition to tent/trailer sites and group camping areas, there is a cabin colony and 12 vacation cottage rentals.

DeWolfe Point State Park—This small, intimate state park is located on Lake of the Isles and has cabins and campsites available.

Waterson Point State Park—This small park is ideal for fishing and boating. It offers two docks for overnight or day dockage, picnic facilities (including a century-old gazebo), public restrooms, and access to shoreline fishing.

Mary Island State Park—Accessible only by water, this park is separated by a small channel from the easternmost tip of Wellesley Island.

HISTORY PRESERVED

Thousand Island Park Historic District (known as TI Park)—Listed on the National Register of Historic Places in 1982, this district contains almost 300 Victorian wooden summer

The Minna Anthony Common Nature Center, in Wellesley Island State Park,
600 acres on two pristine island peninsulas in the St. Lawrence River.

"cottages," the TI Park main dock pavilion, the library, the Tabernacle, and the Wellesley
Hotel and Restaurant.

Thousand Island State Park Museum—Two TI Park residents created this museum on the
porch of the historic Wellesley Hotel.

Westminster Park Chapel—This chapel is located in a wooded area of Westminster Park,
a community at the other end of Wellesley Island from TI Park. A Presbyterian colony
(established in 1875), Westminster Park was planned to be similar to Thousand Island
Park (a Methodist Episcopal colony). The chapel, dedicated in 2003, is tiny, with two
chairs and four benches for seating. Where you might expect a crucifix is a sculpture of a
Native American created by Carmen D'Avino, a New York artist who works in animated
short film and oil painting as well as sculpture. Westminster Park residents Randy and
Mary Hannah Arnot donated the chapel to the community to be used for reflection
and meditation.

Boldt Castle Yacht House—Located off County Route 100 on Boathouse Road, this is also
accessible by boat tour from Boldt Castle on Heart Island.

Fineview Methodist Church—This Colonial Revival–style church, built in 1908 for a congregation organized in 1891, is now known as Wellesley Island United Methodist Church.

Riverside Cemetery—Also known as Wellesley Island Cemetery.

Densmore Methodist Episcopal Church—Established in 1902 on Densmore Bay on the St. Lawrence River.

Rock Island Lighthouse—Can be seen from Fineview and Thousand Island Park (accessible only by private boat or Clayton Island Boat Tours).

CULTURAL ATTRACTIONS

Westminster Park—This year-round community features several facilities open to the public. George Boldt purchased part of Westminster Park and created one of the area's two golf courses, complete with a maze of historic canals, a polo field, Tennis Island, and other facilities related to his estate on Heart Island such as the Wellesley Farm.

Riverview Cottage and Park Antiques—A knock or call may get you inside this charming cottage to look at the antiques.

OTHER ISLAND THINGS TO DO

Camp—Wellesley Island State Park has the largest campground in the Thousand Islands area.

Hike—You can access a Wellesley Island State Park trail map at http://parks.ny.gov/parks/attachments/WellesleyIslandTrailMap.pdf

Bird-watch—Bald eagles can be spotted in the state park.

The Wellesley Hotel in the Thousand Island Park, a summer community and a historic district on Wellesley Island. One can seek accommodations here, enjoy fine dining, and visit the Thousand Island Park Museum, accessed from the porch of the hotel. More important, one can practice the relaxation inspired by such a very fine porch.

Fish—Here you'll find smallmouth bass, pike, and muskie. Take advantage of Wellesley Island State Park's full-service marina or one of the three boat launches there.

Golf—At Wellesley Island State Park Golf Course (nine holes) or Thousand Islands Country Club (18 holes).

SPECIAL ISLAND EVENTS

Thousand Island Park Cottage and Garden Tour (July)

Annual Densmore Concert Series (Sunday evenings, end of June through August)

Summer activities at the Minna Anthony Commons Nature Center

For More Island Information

Wellesley Island—www.wellesleyisland.net.

www.tiparkcorp.com—This Thousand Island Park Corporation website includes the history of the park as well as news pertaining to the community and the hotel.

www.jubileeinitiative.org/sacredvivekananda.html—This website includes history and guidelines on how to experience Swami Vivekananda's cottage in Thousand Island Park on Wellesley Island.

You can read more about Minna Anthony Common and her daughter here: http://aauw jeffco.wordpress.com/women-in-history/minna-anthony-common-catherine-common -johnson/.

Wellesley Island in the 1000 Islands: A Great Getaway, by Sandra Scott (self-published, 2014)—11 pages of things to do on Wellesley Island.

Thousand Island Park: One Hundred Years, and Then Some, by Helen P. Jacox and Eugene B. Kleinhans Jr. (Thousand Island Park, NY: Centennial Book Project, 1975).

The Thousand Island Park at Wellesley Island: Its Origin and Progress as an International Center of Moral, Religious, and Scientific Thought and a Health-Giving Summer Resort, by Arthur W. Moore (Montreal: John Dougall and Son, 1881), https://archive.org/details/ cihm_11148.

"The Thousand Island Park," from "The Growth of a Century," in *History of Jefferson County, New York from 1793 to 1894,* by John A. Haddock (Albany: Weed-Parsons, 1895).

TI Park Gazette—A source of news since 1875, this is available online at www.tiparkcorp/ pdf/tip.gazette.

River Views: A History of the 1000 Islands in 3-D, by Tom French (Machias: University of Maine Stone Island Press, 2011)—Silver medal winner in 2012 for the Best Regional Non-fiction Book in the Northeast, this is a collection of over 100 historic stereoviews of the Thousand Islands taken during the 1870s and 1880s. A large section of the book is of TI Park. A stereoviewer is included with the book.

How You Can Support the Island

Friends of the Nature Center, Inc.
Minna Anthony Common Nature Center
Wellesley Island State Park
44927 Cross Island Rd.
Fineview, NY 13640

315-482-247
http://macnaturecenter.webs.com/

Thousand Island Park Landmark Society
PO Box 712
Thousand Island Park, NY 13692
315-482-5150
Shop and office located on St. Lawrence Ave.

Library, exhibits, and shop open house: Tuesday–Sunday, 11:00–2:00 from the end of June through the end of August.

According to its website, Thousand Island Park Landmark Society is a tax-exempt, charitable organization "dedicated to preserving the historical and architectural resources of Thousand Island Park, New York for [the TI Park] community, visitors and future generations."

Parting Thoughts

The Rock Ridges Nature Trail that Minna Anthony Common reimagined over the footprints of the Native Americans who once walked these ridges is the loveliest nature trail I have ever hiked, and I have hiked hundreds—no, more likely thousands—of miles on such trails in my lifetime. I wager that if "ley lines" do exist, there would surely be an intersection in the vicinity of this trail. The quality of the light here, the small brook, and yes, the rock ridges leave a spiritual impression on the hiker. A walk on this trail is more than the sum of its parts.

Iroquois Island, Ontario

CANALS AND DAMS AND LOCKS . . . OH, MY!

June 22, 2013, 6:00 p.m.
Parking lot

On Iroquois Island, at Seaway Heritage Park, I discover my chair in a bag is not in my trunk. Unable to join any of the clusters of folding chairs and their occupants who, I presume, are waiting for the next ship to come through the lock, I prowl around the small island instead. Within view of the Iroquois Lock is the one business on the island: a gift shop and snack bar that has a green chalkboard out front with information on what ships are expected to come through the Iroquois Lock at what time. One is overdue.

I buy a sugar cone with strawberry ice cream and wander around the cemeteries on the island while I wait for the ship. An evergreen tree has been planted "in memory of Mr. William George Palmer who died accidentally in 1958 during construction of the St. Lawrence Seaway and power projects."

I come back and lean my elbows on the chain-link fence. A middle-aged daughter and her elderly frail father arrive by car and make a slow trip to one of the benches. She tells me they learned of the approaching ship—they keep tabs on the lock activity via the Internet—and packed up to come. "It's Sunday, after all," she says. Her dad starts to tell me about the ospreys, but we're interrupted by the arrival of the *Torrent* bearing down on us, a ship appearing far too wide to squeeze through the lock. But squeeze it does.

GETTING THERE: Bridge

GETTING AROUND: Bring your car to get you onto the island; the entire island can be easily walked

OVERNIGHT ACCOMMODATIONS: None

FOOD: Snack bar

DAY TRIP? Yes, only option

STATE / PROVINCIAL / NATIONAL PARK? No

Today, the Iroquois Lock allows ships to bypass the Iroquois Dam, which controls the level of Lake Ontario, but in history, Iroquois Point was a headland famous in legend and history as a camping ground of the Iroquois. The United Empire Loyalists—subjects who had been living in the original 13 colonies when the American Revolution took place and who supported the king—settled the place in 1776. The original location of the town of Iroquois was across the Galop Canal from Iroquois Point. The post office, established in 1789 in what was then New France, was called Matilda after the township. In 1812, when the War of 1812 broke out, the first British fort on the site had not been completed or named. A second fort was built on the riverbank in 1814, but U.S. troops did not attack, so the fort was nicknamed Fort Needless. In 1856, the post office name was changed from Matilda (the town had also been unofficially known as Cathcart) to Iroquois, which was incorporated as a village of 750 residents in 1857.

One hundred years later, in 1954, the point's proximity to the Canadian-U.S. midriver boundary line caused it to be selected as the Canadian terminus of the international dam built to control water levels for the waterway. The village was the largest residential and business community along the St. Lawrence River to be entirely relocated during construction of the St. Lawrence Seaway in the mid-1950s. A new canal, cut through the headland to avoid the dam, turned Iroquois Point into a small island. The relocated town of Iroquois is north of the original site.[102]

The original village stretched along the riverfront and was reportedly "bustling" and "picturesque" until the construction of the St. Lawrence Seaway in 1954. "Old Iroquois is one of the lost villages, demolished, burned and buried under acres of grassland and water. The grassland park now separates the inhabitants of the new village of Iroquois from the river. This was not intended originally. Published plans and illustrations in the *Iroquois Post* in 1954 distinctly showed that the waterfront aspect of the village would be recreated."[103]

Instead, the town center became a shopping plaza on Highway 2, and the town's new and moved homes were organized on a suburban street grid away from the river and the dam. Where the old town stood is a large green space including a golf course (1959) and airfield (1967). There is parkland between the river and Elizabeth Drive and from Carman Road to the golf course; the area includes a small beach area and a beach house with facilities. The old Main Street is now a pathway for pedestrians and bicyclers, and the old Galop Canal and locks have become the Iroquois Marina for pleasure boaters.

How to Get There

Iroquois is located just minutes south of Highway 401 and Highway 2 via the Carman Road exit, between an hour and two hours from Ottawa, Montreal, and Kingston.

What to Expect

Once you cross the bridge and turn right toward the lock, you can expect the road to end in a parking lot between the lock on the river and Seaway Heritage Park.

If you're fortunate, as I was, Halee's will be open for ice cream or snacks as well as lock information and mementos. The green blackboard in front of Halee's will list the shop's hours, the names of all the ships expected through the lock in the near future and what their status currently is, and a list of special area events for the season (for example, Canada Day, a Fly-in Breakfast, the Galop Marina Poker Fun Run, and a performance by Eddy and the Sting Rays).

Folks set up their own folding lawn chairs to await the ships coming through; some picnic at the tables provided under shelters while they wait. Walkers out for exercise head down

Halee's Lockview Gift Shop, the only business on Iroquois Island, keeps a chalkboard listing of when ships are expected to come through the locks. For example, according to this list, the *Torrent*, a ship from Cyprus, was expected to be downbound through the lock at 13:25 (1:25 p.m.).

to the island's south end to check on the osprey nest, and locals and visitors alike wander through the cemetery grounds, gleaning what they can of people from another time.

Paths to Adventure

NATURAL SITES

Given the history of this island in the last 60 years or so, since the construction of the St. Lawrence Seaway, nothing on this original headland of Iroquois Point could be considered "natural."

HISTORY PRESERVED

Seaway Heritage Park—The park has posted informational plaques about the area's involvement in the War of 1812, including facts regarding the First Regiment of the Dundas Militia, the Toussaint Island Ambush, the Battle of Crysler's Farm, and "Fort Needless." Other plaques detail the construction of the St. Lawrence Seaway. Note the memorial plaque, mounted on a stone under a tree planted in his memory, dedicated to William George Palmer—one of 22,000 workers who were employed on the project—who died in the construction of the seaway.

Iroquois Point Cemetery (aka Iroquois United Cemetery) and Iroquois Presbyterian Cemetery—The former, established in 1825, occupies the western two-thirds of the graveyard, and the latter, circa 1874, comprises the eastern one-third. One simple marble slab within reads: "John De Groat, a soldier of the Revolution. Died June 23, 1852, age 87 years." The oldest stone is that of Henry Brown, who "died 1829—Age 20 years."

Galop Canal—The historic canal is now used for pleasure boats at the Carman-Galop Park off Carman Road on the riverside. Facilities include a boat launch, picnic tables, and parking.

CULTURAL ATTRACTIONS

Iroquois Lock—Read the informational signs on the chain-link fence about the features and operation of the lock.

Watch for a ship to come through the lock.

Halee's Lockview Gift Shop and Outback Chips ("Information, Gift Shop, Snack Bar")—Get an ice cream cone and browse the information about the lock at 6020 Carman Road.

Other Nearby Things to Do

Look for the tangible traces of the past still present in the neighboring landscape today:

- Forward House (lawn bowling clubhouse)
- Grand Trunk Railway line
- Old Iroquois' Main Street
- Old Locks
- County Road
- Iroquois Point
- Tindall House (the Lockmaster's House)
- Old Locks shed at the swing bridge

The *Torrent* arrived at the Iroquois Lock at 17:46 (5:46 p.m.), several hours late.

Visitors have been coming to the locks to watch more than ships in the last several years. A pair of ospreys that nested atop a crane next to the Iroquois Lock in 2009 were relocated, along with their eggs—which successfully hatched—to this specially built platform atop an 36-foot (11-meter) pole in 2010. The ospreys have returned to the site every year since to raise their young.

Carman House Museum—This United Empire Loyalist heritage home built in 1815 has been restored as a living history museum set in 1835. Open in July and August, 10:00–5:00, it is located off the Carmen Road exit on Highway 401, south on Carman Road, next to the campground. For more information, call 613-652-4422.

Lost Villages Museum—This museum provides an understanding of what existed here before the construction of the St. Lawrence Seaway. For more information, visit www.lost villages.ca/.

St. Lawrence Power Development Visitor Centre—Displays many interactive electricity exhibits related to the St. Lawrence Seaway and presents the history of the seaway. The visitor center is located on the banks of the St. Lawrence River east of the Robert H. Saunders Generating Station, at 2500 Second St. W, Cornwall, ON. For more information on the center, see www.opg.com/communities-and-partners/host-communities/Ottawa-St. Lawrence/Pages/St--Lawrence-Power-Development-Visitor-Centre.aspx.

Upper Canada Village (www.uppercanadavillage.com) at 13740 County Rd. 2, Morrisburg, ON.

Canada's Waterfront Trail (www.waterfronttrail.org/).

Golf—There are three golf courses in the area: Iroquois Golf Club, Morrisburg Golf Club, and Upper Canada Golf Course.

SPECIAL ISLAND EVENTS

The freighters going through the Iroquois Lock daily and the ospreys nesting seasonally above the lock are what are special on this island.

For More Island Information

The Seaway System—www.greatlakes-seaway.com/en/seaway/locks.

Tommy Trent's ABC's of the Seaway, by the St. Lawrence Seaway Management Corporation, www.greatlakes-seaway.com/en/pdf/tommy_trent_abc.pdf.

Iroquois Waterfront Conservation, Protection and Enhancement Plan, by Iroquois Waterfront Advisory Committee, April 2013.

St. Lawrence Seaway: Let the Flooding Begin, a 16.5-minute video from the CBC Digital Archives, www.cbc.ca/player/Digital+Archives/Science+and+Technology/Engineering/ID/1832281864/. The video includes an interview with the Iroquois mayor.

How You Can Support the Island

The business Halee's was for sale last time I was there; this throwback to another era could be yours!

Parting Thoughts

Besides the entertainment of watching oceangoing ships move through the lock from the edge of Iroquois Island, you may also have the opportunity to observe the activity at and around an osprey nest. This opportunity began when an osprey family set up housekeeping in a nest they had built on a boom pendant of a crane next to the lock in 2009. Supplied with a nesting platform by St. Lawrence Seaway officials in 2010, osprey families have become tourist attractions—as well as Internet social media stars[104]—in their own right, along with the ships traversing the locks.

The osprey (*Pandion haliaetus*) is also sometimes called the "fish eagle," "sea hawk," or "fish hawk." It is a large fish-eating bird of prey that hunts during the day. Around two feet in length, the raptor has an almost six-foot wingspan.

Bring along your binoculars, not necessarily for the ships, which are close enough that you won't need them, but for the island's feathered stars, who were still enjoying their own perfect view of the lock in 2014.

Long Sault Parkway Islands, Ontario

THE LOST VILLAGES

September 16, 2013

Although I have an entire other notebook full of notes, the only journal entry I have written on this trip consists of seven lines of observation, the beginnings of the first draft of a poem, perhaps. Most of the few notes I took were on our visit to the Lost Villages Museum. The reason why this is all I wrote, I think, is because this island story is a sad one, a piece of history that happened in my lifetime and is not easily absorbed.

July 1, 1958: the flooding began. Flooding of American, Canadian, and Mohawk territory. They called it—and still do, here—Inundation Day.

GETTING THERE: Bridges and causeways; private boats (boat launches available)

GETTING AROUND: Bring your own car and/or bike and/or kayak; boat and watersport rentals at Mille Roches Beach

OVERNIGHT ACCOMMODATIONS: Camping only

FOOD: Mille Roches Beach offers a snack bar; bring your own

DAY TRIP? Yes, or a camping destination

STATE / PROVINCIAL / NATIONAL PARK? No, but the eleven islands strung together by the Long Sault Parkway are managed by the St. Lawrence Parks Commission

What is important here is what you *don't* see. At one time the two biggest barriers to navigating through the Great Lakes Basin in its entirety were the Niagara Falls and the Long Sault Rapids. The writer Charles Dickens wrote of his 1842 experience of going partway through the Long Sault Rapids in his travel journal *American Notes*: "In the afternoon we shot down some rapids where the river boiled and bubbled strangely, and where the force and headlong violence were tremendous."

If you're wondering why you've never heard of these rapids, it's because they no longer exist. The Long Sault Rapids disappeared on Inundation Day, July 1, 1958, when 10 Canadian communities along the St. Lawrence River were flooded as a result of the Moses-Saunders Power Dam construction project and to make way for the St. Lawrence Seaway. The flooded communities became known as "The Lost Villages." This loss involved 6,500 displaced people, many of them members of the Mohawk Nation at Akewsasne ("Land Where the Ruffed Grouse Drums"); 530 moved buildings; and 30 tons of dynamite. About 34 square miles (88

A modern-day vehicle parked on the submerged provincial Highway 2, which was flooded along with everything else on Inundation Day, July 1, 1958.

square kilometers) were flooded on that day. "On the Canadian side of the International Rapids section, 225 farms, seven villages and three hamlets (often referred to as 'The Lost Villages'), part of an eighth village, 18 cemeteries, around 1,000 cottages, and over 100 kilometers of the main east-west highway and main line railway were relocated."[105]

How to Get There

The Long Sault Parkway islands in the St. Lawrence River are accessible by causeway from County Road 2, between Morrisburg and Cornwall, Ontario, at either Ingleside in the southwest, or Long Sault in the northeast. The closest exits on Highway 401 are 770 and 778.

What to Expect

The highest points of "The Lost Villages" have been incorporated into the Long Sault Parkway, which traverses 11 islands, most of which are named after the settlements or farms that were situated on each:

- McLaren Island (also written as "Mclaren" and on some maps shown as West Woodlands Island)
- Woodlands Island (on some maps shown as two islands: Centre Woodlands Island, East Woodlands Island)
- Fraser Island

- Hoople Island
- Dickinson Island
- Heriot Island
- VanKoughnet Island (also written as "Vankoughnet")
- Phillpotts Island (also written "Philpotts")
- Macdonell Island (also written "MacDonell")
- Mille Roches Island
- Snetsinger Island

A twelfth island, Moulinette, not a part of the parkway, is accessible—by bridge from Mille Roches—as well. Moulinette is "the northernmost island of the Parkway and the first island from the mainland at Long Sault. A few small vestiges of Moulinette . . . remain. The Magnificent Christ Church was relocated to Upper Canada Village. . . . Zina Hill's Barbershop and the small Grand Trunk railway station have both been restored and now [are] part of the Lost Villages Historical Society grounds at Ault Park. The name 'Moulinette' has been commemorated both as a street name and as one of the islands that is [connected to] the Long Sault Parkway."[106]

Paths to Adventure

NATURAL SITES

Long Sault Parkway—The parkway is just that, a park, with plenty of recreational opportunities (see below).

Canadian Waterfront Trail (www.waterfronttrail.org)—Cycle this portion of the trail, which runs from the Lost Villages Museum to the Long Sault Parkway.

Upper Canada Migratory Bird Sanctuary—Established in 1961 after the construction of the St. Lawrence Seaway as a part of the St. Lawrence Parks, the sanctuary has more than eight kilometers of self-guided nature trails (and five kilometers of cross-country ski trails) traversing several wildlife habitats: mature upland forest, early successional woods, old fields, wetland, and open water. Up to 200 species of waterfowl, raptors, and passerines live in or migrate through the sanctuary. Biking is allowed, and camping is also available. Look for outdoor educational programs and special events at www.stlawrenceparks.com/index .cfm/en/bird-sanctuary/.

HISTORY PRESERVED

Lost Villages Museum
16361 Fran Laflamme Dr.
Long Sault, ON K0C 1P0
www.lostvillages.ca

Located in Ault Park, two miles (three kilometers) east of the eastern end of the Long Sault Parkway, the museum features self-guided tours through a reconstructed "village" of buildings saved from the flooding of 20,000 acres on the Canadian shore of the St. Lawrence River, from Iroquois to Cornwall, for the construction of the St. Lawrence Seaway. The buildings include a general store, barbershop, train station, blacksmith shop, corncrib, log house (where photographs and memorabilia of the flooded villages are displayed), a stone home, a church, a drive shed, and a reading room. Picnic areas are available.

The Moulinette railway station was relocated to the Lost Villages Museum grounds after the area was flooded in 1958 for the St. Lawrence Seaway.

Open: Summer to September 1, 10:00 a.m. to 5:00 p.m. daily; September 1–30, Tuesday to Sunday, 11:00 a.m. to 4:00 p.m.

Upper Canada Village

13740 County Rd. 2

Morrisburg, ON K0C 1X0

800-437-2233/613-543-4328

www.uppercanadavillage.com

The year is 1866 in a rural English Canadian setting. Founded in 1961, Upper Canada Village is one of the largest living-history sites in Canada. Featured in the village are over 40 historical buildings, many moved here prior to the flooding of the Lost Villages during the construction of the St. Lawrence Seaway.

CULTURAL ATTRACTIONS

Nightingale House—Built in 1880 in the village of Wales, Ontario, this was the largest wooden structure to be moved before the flooding of the St. Lawrence Seaway. Now a bed-and-breakfast located in Ingleside, Ontario, it provides convenient, charming accommodations in the Lost Village area. For more information, see www.nightingale-house .on.ca/.

OTHER ISLAND THINGS TO DO

Hike—Walk a piece of Canada's Waterfront Trail.

Bike—Go the length of the six-mile (10-kilometer) Long Sault Parkway.

Picnic—There are any number of lovely spots on all 11 islands.

Kayak/canoe—Paddle around the islands in the St. Lawrence River and/or in Lake St. Francis (between the islands and the mainland).

Camp—There are three campgrounds to choose from: McLaren (206 campsites, RV sites, five cabins), Woodlands (wooded campground facing Lake St. Francis, two sandy beaches, RV sites, and mini-cabins), Mille Roches (214 sites, 63 waterfront sites, spread over two islands, Mille Roches and Snetsinger, under forest canopy), plus four exclusive waterfront sites on Hoople Island (no services).

Swim—There is a sandy beach on the river in the western part of Woodlands Island.

Dive—Scuba dive at Lock 21 at Macdonell Island to explore the 200-foot lock at the western entrance to the Cornwall Canal, which ran for 11.5 miles (18.5 kilometers) along the Canadian shore of the St. Lawrence River to bypass the Long Sault Rapids. Building began in 1834, but the canal was not opened until 1842, and it went through several reconstructions before being flooded. An information kiosk, sponsored by the S.O.S. Diving Club, is on the island. For more history of Lock 21, visit www.stlawrencepiks.com/seawayhistory/beforeseaway/cornwall/.

SPECIAL ISLAND EVENTS

Long Sault Farmers Market (first Friday in June until Canadian Thanksgiving weekend)—Located in front of the Long Sault Plaza at the entrance to the Long Sault Parkway, featuring (in season) apples, asparagus, baked goods, blueberries, carrots, cauliflower, cucumber, jams and jellies, strawberries, and zucchini.

Thunder on the River Hydroplane Regatta (mid-June weekend)—More than 70 hydroplanes compete at Mille Roches Beach.

The Long Sault Parkway intersects 11 hilltops, several of which once belonged to the lost villages of Aultsville, Dickinson's Landing, Farran's Point, Maple Grove, Mille Roches, Moulinette, Santa Cruz, Sheek's Island, Wales, and Woodlands.

KAWEHNO:KË (CORNWALL ISLAND): WHERE THE RUFFED GROUSE NO LONGER DRUMS

The island in the St. Lawrence River shown on many maps as Cornwall Island is known as Kawehno:kë to the Mohawk Nation at Akwesasne (population 12,000), the territory in which it is located.

Today, Akwesasne land straddles both the U.S.-Canada border (north to south) and also the Ontario-Quebec border (in the northern portion, east to west). Akwesasne means "Land Where the Ruffed Grouse Drums," referring to the rapids that at one time stretched nearly 10 miles west of the island and were known in English as the Long Sault Rapids.

The Long Sault created quite a navigational challenge, which was solved first with canal locks and then, as ship traffic increased, by the construction of the Moses-Saunders Power Dam, a very significant part of the St. Lawrence Seaway. In addition to flooding the six villages and three hamlets now known as the "Lost Villages," the construction of this dam resulted in changing the water levels of the river by creating Lake St. Lawrence behind the dam; the relocation of 6,500 people, the majority of whom were members of the Mohawk Nation at Akwesasne; and significant harm to the river environment on which the nation depended for its way of life.

Mohawk Council of Akwesasne Chief Tim Thompson itemized the damage: "[T]he OPG [Ontario Power Generation] (then known as Ontario Hydro) projects of the 1950s 'silenced' the rapids of the river, killed off many of the harvesting and hunting opportunities created by it and damaged Akwesasne's general health, community and [traditional culture]."[*] In 2008, the OPG made an official apology to Akwesasne as part of an almost $46 million settlement agreement.

Cornwall Island is a part of the Three Nations Crossing border crossing and is accessed by the Seaway International Bridge, which is made up of two bridges. The North Channel Bridge (1962) crosses the North Channel of the St. Lawrence River, connecting the city of Cornwall, Ontario, to the island, and the South Channel Bridge (1958) crosses the St. Lawrence Seaway, connecting the island to Massena, New York.

In addition to the Kawehno:kë Community Centre, the Akwesasne Child Care Centre, and the beautiful Ahkwesâhsne Mohawk School, Kawehno:kë is home to the Native North American Travelling College, celebrating almost 50 years of cultural education and revitalization of Mohawk and Native American culture. The college includes a Cultural Centre, art gallery, and the Travel Troupe, a group of traveling presenters, providing outreach and bringing Native culture to people worldwide.

Another island institution is Kawehno:kë's fire department, Hogansburg Akwesasne Volunteer Fire Department (HAVFD) Station 2, possibly the only fire station in the world whose motto is "Serving two countries." In effect, it serves *three* nations.

[*] Michael Peeling, *Cornwall Standard-Freeholder*, October 3, 2008, http://www.standard-freeholder.com/2008/10/03/opg-offers-apology-to-akwesasne.

The winter parkway—In the winter, the parkway road is closed and not maintained (generally beginning December 1). Hikers, snowshoers, cross-country skiers, and snowmobilers have the Long Sault Parkway to themselves.

For More Island Information

Lost Villages Historical Society
PO Box 306
Ingleside, ON K0C 1M0
612-534-2197
www.lostvillages.ca

The St. Lawrence Parks—www.stlawrenceparks.com.

St. Lawrence Seaway History website—www.stlawrencepiks.com/seawayhistory/before seaway.

Jeri Danyleyko's Lost Villages website—www.ghosttownpic.com.

Voices from the Lost Villages, by Rosemary Rutley (Ingleside, ON: Old Crone, 1998).

St. Lawrence Seaway: Let the Flooding Begin, a 16.5-minute video from the CBC Digital Archives, www.cbc.ca/player/Digital+Archives/Science+and+Technology/Engineering/ID/1832281864/.

How You Can Support the Island

Lost Villages Historical Society
PO Box 306
Ingleside, ON K0C 1M0
www.lostvillages.ca/about-the-society/

The society's mission is to collect, preserve, and display the heritage of the lost villages of Mille Roches, Moulinette, Wales, Dickinson's Landing, Farran's Point, and Aultsville; the hamlets of Maple Grove, Santa Cruz, and Woodlands; and the farming community of Sheik's/Sheek's Island.

Friends of the Sanctuary
PO Box 156
Ingleside, ON K0C 1M0
www.friendsofthesanctuary.org

Parting Thoughts

A September blue:
flocks divide before,
above my car, divide.
Out on the city highway,
a line of deer stare
into mist over the fields.
Do they still see
what is long gone?
Whom do they watch over?

Epilogue

FERRYING TO ISLAND TIME

You come to an edge of your world, or the end of your rope. Something you imagine to be Providence leads you to water. But instead of drinking, you consult a ferry schedule. And then wait. There are gusty winds. Or there is engine trouble. Or there are 10-foot waves. Or the captain, on docking, has nudged the ferry into a yacht, and there is a two-and-a-half-hour delay and then an hour more wait for the Coast Guard to arrive and conduct an investigation.

This is a good introduction to island time. It does not matter how late you stayed up finishing work, doing laundry, packing. It does not matter how early you rose to load the car, capture your cat who escaped out the back door, enter the ferry ticket office address into your GPS navigational device. It does not matter how many rest areas you stopped at to check the bike's position on the carrier in under two minutes flat because, after the summer road construction you encountered, you are running late for check-in time, and a ferry waits for no one. It does not matter how much you yearn to be on your way, to set foot on the freedom of an island. Island time applies now.

The *Emerald Isle* about to ferry into "island time" on Beaver Island.

Spiderweb on *Voyageur II*, captured during a slowing down to "island time" en route to Isle Royale.

You gain freedom only by giving up control and riding the wave of what happens next. The several groups of musicians who, with the delay, are probably going to miss their performance times at the island music festival, shrug, grin, and then stake out territory, open their cases, and pull out their instruments. Scattered around the ferry deck, they draw in and blow out, bending the notes on their harmonicas, saw on their fiddles, strum their guitars. Other passengers join in with stomping feet, clapping hands in time. Musicians may well understand the time signature of islands better than many of us.

Whether you understand it yet or not, you will have two waterborne hours to get over the delayed departure. Meanwhile, you will listen to the music, doze to the thrum of the engines, get into the book you've been wanting to read, perhaps drink a beer, have that talk with your friend or lover, meet a new acquaintance. The first European explorers might have called these lakes *Les Mers Douces*—Sweet Seas—for reasons other than their lack of salinity.

But eventually, four hours later than you expected, the ferry sounds its horn, the heavy loops of mooring line are lifted from the bollards, and the ferry pulls away from the wharf.

The two Coast Guard officers wave at you from under the drawbridge as you head out onto the Great Lake.

You are on your way, and the island awaits you. Regardless of what you will undoubtedly have forgotten to bring. You may have remembered to bring a camera, a notebook, a pen. But then you forget about the camera, the notebook, the pen, and simply watch the sun set over the water. You are here. Now. On island time.

It is windy or rainy, cold or hot. The ferry is rolling on dark waves or heat shimmers above the glass of the lake's surface. Your bones adjust because adjusting is the only choice you are given. You packed your intentions and arrived clad in your control. And then you gave it all up when you bought your ferry ticket. You give over to island time.

You have to cross the water, you need to pay more attention to the weather, and your choices are, at once, both more limited and more rich, like tea steeped one cup at a time. Once there, you may find you have fewer choices in food, clothing, hardware, plans. A welcome paring down. And with this comes the possibility for adventure in every meeting, at each intersection, with any shift in the weather. The basics of food and sleep take on more significance: sleeping in a breeze—even when the mainland is hitting record three-digit temperatures with humidity—cooking meals on a campfire or a cottage stove or going out to a place where the island locals go to eat fresh fish just caught offshore and to drink wine made from island grapes. On an island, you will often have the opportunity to walk back from your dinner to the place you will sleep that night, and you will take it. You may just find yourself singing aloud as you walk that gravel island road in the evening, whether you're alone, with traveling companions, or accompanied by new island friends.

As the engines cycle down and the ferry heads into the harbor, you find yourself anticipating the island you now will explore—note by note—while composing your own tune, in island time.

You've arrived. According to the sign at Papin's Resort: "You're on Drummond Island Time."

Notes

1. After I had begun visiting some islands as a preface to the project that became this book, I found *Islands: Great Lakes Stories,* by Gerry Volgenau, a retired *Detroit Free Press* travel writer and editor, which presented 21 islands/archipelagos in the Great Lakes proper (Ann Arbor, MI: Ann Arbor Media Group, 2005).
2. Rachel Lyman Field, "If Once You Have Slept on an Island," in Hugh L. Dwelley, *An Islesford Jabberwocky & Other Stories of the Cranberry Isles* (Islesford, ME: Islesford Historical Society, 1992).
3. Holling Clancy Holling, *Paddle-to-the-Sea* (New York: Houghton Mifflin, 1941).
4. John Muir, quoted in S. Hall Young, *Alaska Days with John Muir* (New York: Fleming H. Revel, 1915).
5. Mary Oliver, "The Summer Day," in *New and Selected Poems* (Boston: Beacon, 1992), 94.
6. The Red School House is an example of "Indian alternative education" that supports the cultural and language background of Native students.
7. A grandson of the Cadottes, William Whipple Warren (1825–53) was born in La Pointe and was elected as a legislator from Minnesota Territory in 1851. A native speaker of Ojibwe, he wrote the first history of the Ojibwe people, *History of the Ojibway People, Based upon Traditions and Oral Statements* (1885; repr., St. Paul: Minnesota Historical Society, 2009).
8. "The Annotated Ramsar List: United States of America," Ramsar Convention on Wetlands. January 30, 2013, http://archive.ramsar.org/cda/en/ramsar-documents-list -anno-list-usa/main/ramsar/1-31-218%5E15774_4000_0__.
9. "Kakagon and Bad River Sloughs," http://www.ramsar.org/kakagon-and-bad-river -sloughs.
10. Ibid.
11. John Johnston and Lousi François Rodrique Masson, *An Account of Lake Superior, 1792–1807* (New York: Antiquarian, 1960).
12. Phillip C. Bellfy, *Three Fires Unity: The Anishnaabeg of the Lake Huron Borderlands* (Lincoln: University of Nebraska Press, 2011).
13. Aquatic Research Lab, www.lssu.edu/arl/about.php.
14. Tim Sweet, "Chester Thordarson's Rock Island," http://washingtonisland-wi.com/ wp-content/uploads/2010/01/archive_22_1_rockisland.pdf.
15. Ibid.
16. www.chicagobusiness.com/article/20130420/ISSUE03/304209991?template= printart.
17. www.hydepark.org/parks/jpac/woodedanderson.htm.

18. Frederick Law Olmsted, "Address to [the] Prospect Park Scientific Association, May 1868," in *The Papers of Frederick Law Olmsted,* Supplementary Series, vol. 1, ed. C. E. Beveridge and C. Hoffman (Baltimore: Johns Hopkins University Press, 1997).

19. www.michigan.gov/mshda/0,4641,7-141-54317_19320_61909_61927-54605--,00 .html.

20. http://beaverisland.net/beaver-island-history/A_Rich_History/A_Brief_History_of_ Beaver_Isla/index.htm.

21. Ibid.

22. www.beaverislandrealty.com/Ireland/.

23. Beaver Island Head Light, Beaver Island, MI, www.lighthousefriends.com/light.asp? ID=205.

24. Beaver Island Harbor Light, Beaver Island Harbor (St. James), MI, www.lighthouse friends.com/light.asp?ID=206.

25. Elizabeth Whitney Williams, "Find a Grave," www.findagrave.com/cgi-bin/fg.cgi? page=gr&GRid=67671308.

26. "Stone Circle," *Beaver Beacon,* www.beaverisland.net/Projects/The_Stone_Circle/ the_stone_circle.htm.

27. Brandie Dunn Glass/Studio Dunn Designs, "Seek and Ye Shall Find: Part II," https:// studiodunndesigns.wordpress.com/2011/12/16/seek-and-ye-shall-find-part-ii/.

28. "The History of the Episcopal Church of the Transfiguration, 1905," www.bbicf.com/ documents/Churchhistory.pdf (researched and prepared for the centennial celebration in 2005).

29. Philip McM. Pittman, *The Les Cheneaux Chronicles: Anatomy of a Community* (Cedarville, MI: Les Cheneaux Venture, 1985).

30. Paul Gingras, "DNR: Lake Huron Near Shore Fishing Prospect Excellent," *St. Ignace News and Les Cheneaux Islands Weekly Wave,* May 16, 2013.

31. PBS, "Prisoners of War in 1812," in *The War of 1812* (www.pbs.org/wned/war-of-1812/ essays/prisoners-war).

32. James McCommons, "Weekend Wilderness: Ontario's Bruce Peninsula," *Backpacker,* February 1992, 62.

33. William Anthony Monague, "The Story of Fairy Lake," www.williammonaguenativeart. com.

34. Parks Canada, "Georgian Bay Island National Park of Canada: Cultural Heritage; History," www.pc.gc.ca/eng/pn-np/on-goerg/natcul/natcl3.aspx.

35. Parks Canada interpretive sign at cemetery on Beausoleil Island in Georgian Bay Island National Park.

36. Parks Canada, "Georgian Bay Island National Park of Canada: Cultural Heritage; Ojibwa Reserve (1836–1856)," www.pc.gc.ca/eng/pn-np/on-goerg/natcul/natcl3.aspx.

37. "Beausoleil Island," in *A Taste of Honey Harbour: The Area and Its People,* ed. Su Murdoch (Honey Harbour, ON: Harbour Historical Committee, 1999), 38.

38. www.ontarioarchaeology.on.ca/publications/pdf/oa_73_part_08.pdf.

39. Marie Eidt, "The Windows of St. Mark Church," *Delta News,* reprint available at www .stmarkonline.net/history.php.

40. Arthur M. Woodford, *Tashmoo Park and the Steamer* Tashmoo (Charleston, SC: Arcadia, 2012), 7, 21–30.

41. Rachel Lyman Field, "If Once You Have Slept on an Island" (1926), in *An Islesford Jabberwock and Other Stories of the Cranberry Isles* (Islesford, ME: Islesford Historical Society, 1992).

42. *We the Peoples: 50 Communities,* www.iisd.org/50comm/.

43. Peter Douglas Elias, *Development of Aboriginal People's Communities* (North York, ON: Captus, 1991).

44. "Walpole Island First Nation and the Rt. Hon. Herb Gray Parkway: A Case Study in Relationship and Capacity Building," September 2014, www. hgparkway.ca/sites/default/files/11%20WIFN-HGP%20Report%20final.pdf.

45. "Candian Indian Residential School System," *Wikipedia,* www. en.wikipedia.org/wiki/Canadian_Indian_residential_school_system.

46. Mary Annette Pember, "When Will U.S. Apologize for Boarding School Genocide?" *The Huffington Post,* www.huffingtonpost.com, June 24, 2015.

47. Silas Farmer, *All about Detroit: An Illustrated Guide, Map and Historical Souvenir with Local Stories* (Detroit: Silas Farmer, 1899), 12.

48. Belle Isle Conservancy, "History of the Park,"http://belleisleconservancy.org/learn-more/history-of-the-park/.

49. "Historic American Buildings Survey, Engineering Record, Landscapes Survey," Prints & Photograph Online Catalog, Library of Congress.

50. Dan Austin, "James Scott Memorial Fountain," *Historic Detroit.Org,* www.historicdetroit.org/building/james-scott-memorial-fountain.

51. http://belleisleconservancy.org/annual-events/polish-the-jewel/.

52. Gertrude Rogers O'Brien, "Unveiling Ceremonies of the Treaty Tablet of Grosse Ile, Michigan on July 6, 1906," in *The Treaty Tree and Memorial Tablet* (Lansing, MI: Women's Improvement Association, 1907), 7–8.

53. *Ile Camera* (weekly Grosse Ile newspaper), April 21, 2012.

54. www.fws.gov/refuge/Detroit_River/about.html.

55. "Relative to the Subject of Slavery: Opinion, Supreme Court, 23d Oct. 1807," in *Collections and Researches made by the Pioneer and Historical Society of the State of Michigan,* vol. 12 (Lansing, MI: Thorp & Godfrey, State Printers and Binders, 1888), 521.

56. "Elizabeth Denison Forth," Michigan Historic Marker, dedicated November 1992, www.michmarkers.com/startup.asp?startpage=L1860.htm.

57. "Elizabeth Denison Forth Biography," *Encyclopedia of World Biography,* www.notablebiographies.com/supp/Supplement-Fl-Ka/Forth-Elizabeth-Denison.html.

58. "Pilot House History," Grosse Ile Pilot House, www.gipilothouse.com/pilot-house-history.

59. Dan Boileau, "Fishing the Detroit River," *Angler's Digest* (2015), www.tightlinecom.com/Anglers_Digest/fishing_river.htm.

60. Annessa Carlisle, *Bob-Lo: An Island in Troubled Waters* (Royal Oak, MI: Momentum Books, 2005).

61. Named after the steamship the SS *Ste. Claire*, which for 81 years carried passengers from Detroit to Bob-Lo Island, a record of service on a single run in U.S. maritime history surpassed only by her sister ship, the SS *Columbia*, which served the same run for a slightly longer time.

62. Carlisle, *Bob-Lo.*

63. In the fall of 2015, after seeing the development's current map of Bob-Lo with over 200 lots marked off—the entire remaining two-thirds of the island for sale—I realize that this may have been my last opportunity to see this structure as well as much else of what remains from before Windsor developer Dominic Amicone claimed the island for upscale development.

64. The location of *Le Griffon,* wrecked on the return trip of its voyage—a voyage from where it was built, above the Falls in the Niagara River, across Lakes Erie, Huron, and

Michigan to Green Bay—was discovered in Lake Michigan in 2011 and revealed in December 2014 by two treasure-hunting divers searching for Confederate gold.

65. "Fish Point Provincial Nature Reserve—Birding Primary Site," Ontario's Southwest, www.ontariossouthwest.com.

66. Ronald Tiessen, *A Bicycle Guide to Pelee Island,* 2nd ed. (Pelee Island, ON: Pelee Island Heritage Centre, 1992), 68.

67. http://pelee.org/i?page=brownsalvar&sid=A514330364456B.

68. Tiessen, *A Bicycle Guide to Pelee Island,* 69.

69. Ibid., 42.

70. David T. McNab, *Circles of Time: Aboriginal Land Rights and Resistance* (Waterloo, ON: Wilfrid Laurier University Press, 1999).

71. Tiessen, *A Bicycle Guide to Pelee Island,* 37.

72. Ibid., 36.

73. Ibid., 34.

74. Ibid., 72.

75. Ibid., 73.

76. Ted Ligibel and Richard Wright, *Island Heritage: A Guided Tour to Lake Erie's Bass Islands* (Columbus: Ohio State University Press, 1987), 5.

77. Ibid., 18.

78. Sarah Mervosh, "Scars Remain from Tragedy at Lonz Winery," *Blade,* July 1, 2010.

79. Jessica Denton, "What's Next for Lonz Winery?" *Port Clinton News-Herald,* April 3, 2015.

80. Rebecca Williams, "Sure, There Were Pirates in the Caribbean, but the Great Lakes Had Them Too," *Michigan Radio,* October 14, 2014, based on an interview with Chris Gillcrist.

81. *Leonard B. Johnson v. The United States,* in *Cases Decided in the Court of Claims of the United States, with Abstracts of Decisions of the Supreme Court in Appealed Cases, from December 6, 1895 to May 18, 1896,* reported by Charles C. Nott and Archibald Hopkins, vol. 31 (Washington, DC: Government Printing Office, 1896).

82. Sarah Weber, "Civil War Monument Marks 100th Anniversary," *Sandusky Register,* June 8, 2010.

83. "Lakeside Daisy," *Michigan Natural Features Inventory* at mnfi.anr.msu.edu/abstracts/botany/hymenoxys_herbacea.pdf.

84. Presque Isle State Park, "Mysteries of Presque Isle: Facts, Legends and Historical Tidbits You Might Not Have Known," *Presque Isle Erie, PA,* July 19, 2014, www.presque isle.org/blogs/presqueisle/2014/07/mysteries-of-presque-isle-facts-legends-and -historical-tidbits-you-might-not-have-known/.

85. Dana Massing, "Paradise on a Pond: Presque Isle Houseboat Owners Enjoy Life on the Water," GoErie.com, August 1, 2014, www.goerie.com/paradise-on-a-pond-presque-isle -houseboat-owners-enjoy-life-on-the-water#.

86. Kevin Woyce, *Niagara, the Falls and the River: An Illustrated History* (Raleigh, NC: Lulu, 2015).

87. *Niagara Wine Trail, USA,* 2013, www.niagarawinetrail.org.

88. Edward T. Williams, *Official Record of the Niagara Falls Memorial Commission, in Succession to the William B. Rankine Memorial Commission: Together with Biographical Sketches of . . . Distinguished Citizens of Niagara Falls, the Memory of Whose Outstanding Accomplishments Is Being Perpetuated by Monuments Erected in Front of the City Hall* (Niagara Falls, NY: Niagara Falls Memorial Commission, n.d.),18, http://archive.org/ stream/officialrecordofoowilluoft/officialrecordofoowilluoft_djvu.txt.

89. The Blue Flag, awarded at deserving sites internationally, indicates that a beach/marina has met detailed criteria in the areas of environmental education and information, water quality, environmental management, and safety and services.

90. A baymouth bar results in a spit that closes access to a bay, sealing it off from the main body of water.

91. Dictionary.com Unabridged, http://dictionary.reference.com/browse/terroir.

92. International Joint Commision, "History of Water Regulation in the LOSLR Basin," http://www.ijc.org/loslr/en/background/.

93. Ontario Environmental Review Tribunal, Case Nos. 10-121/10-122, July 18, 2011, 6, www.ert.gov.on.ca/files/201108/00000300-AKT5757C7CO026-BHH51C7A7SO 026.pdf.

94. CANWEA (Canadian Wind Energy Association) municipality brochure, http://canwea.ca/pdf/canwea-municipality-brochure-web-v1.pdf, 3.

95. Ibid.

96. Roy D. Jeffery, MD FCFP, Carmen Krogh, and Brett Horner, "Adverse Health Effects of Industrial Wind Turbines," *Canadian Family Physician: Official Publication of the College of Family Physicians of Canada*, (Mississauga, ON: CFP-MFC, 2013), 1.

97. Ontario Environmental Review Tribunal, Case Nos. 10-121/10-122.

98. Mary Alice Snetsinger, "Wolfe Island's Lighthouses," *Thousand Islands life.com*, November 12, 2009, www.thousandislandslife.com/BackIssues/Archive/tabid/393/articleType/ArticleView/articleId/358/Wolfe-Islandrsquos-Lighthouses.aspx.

99. "Painted ladies" refers to Victorian houses painted in three or more colors to accentuate their architectural details. The term was first used by writers Elizabeth Pomada and Michael Larsen in their *Painted Ladies—San Francisco's Resplendent Victorians* (New York: E. P. Dutton, 1978). See paintedladies.com for some examples.

100. John Harwood, *National Register of Historic Places Registration: Thousand Island Park Historic District* (New York State Office of Parks, Recreation and Historic Preservation, September, 1982).

101. John A. Haddock, *A Souvenir: The Thousand Islands of the St. Lawrence River from Kingston and Cape Vincent to Morristown and Brockville* (Alexandria Bay, NY: Thousand Island Club of Alexandria Bay, 1895).

102. David E. Scott, *Ontario Place Name: The Historical, Offbeat or Humourous Origins of Close to 1,000 Communities* (Vancouver: Whitecap Books, 1993).

103. Iroquois Waterfront Advisory Committee, *Iroquois Waterfront Conservation, Protection and Enhancement Plan,* April 2013, Iroquois%20Waterfront%20Advisory%20Committee%20-%20revised%20April%202013(part%201)%20(1).pdf.

104. If you'd like to see more of the ospreys, search for images online using "Ospreys, Iroquois Lock."

105. Daniel Macfarlane, "Rapid Changes: Canada and the St. Lawrence Seaway and Power Project," in "To the Heart of the Continent: Canada and the Negotiation of the St. Lawrence Seaway and Power Project, 1921–1954" (PhD diss., University of Ottawa, 2010).

106. Jeri Danyleyko, "Moulinette: The Twentieth Century," *Ghosttownpix.com*, www.ghosttownpix.com/lostvillages/moulinet3.html.

Other Books about the Great Lakes

OTHER BOOKS ABOUT THE GREAT LAKES

The Living Great Lakes: Searching for the Heart of the Inland Seas, by Jerry Dennis (New York: St. Martin's, 2003).

Great Lakes Journey: A New Look at America's Freshwater Coast, by William Ashworth (Detroit: Wayne State University Press, 2000).

The Great Lakes Reader, edited by Walter Havighurst (New York: Collier Books, 1966).

The Women's Great Lakes Reader, 2nd ed., edited by Victoria Brehm (Tustin, MI: Lady-slipper, 2000).

The Great Lakes: The Natural History of a Changing Region, by Wayne Grady (Vancouver: Greystone Books and the David Suzuki Foundation, 2007).

A Pictorial History of the Great Lakes, by Harlan Hatcher and Erich A. Walter (New York: Bonanza Books, 1963).

The Great Lakes, by Pierre Berton (Toronto: Stoddart Publishing Co., Ltd., 1996).

Fresh Water: Women Writing on the Great Lakes, edited by Alison Swan (East Lansing: Michigan State University Press, 2006).

Islands: Great Lakes Stories, by Gerry Volgenau (Ann Arbor, MI: Ann Arbor Media Group, 2005).

AND FOR YOUNGER READERS

Paddle-to-the-Sea, by Holling Clancy Holling (New York: Houghton Mifflin, 1941).

The Story of the Great Lakes, by Marie E. Gilchrist (New York: Harper & Brothers, 1942).

Stories from Where We Live: The Great Lakes, edited by Sara St. Antoine (Minneapolis: Milkweed, 2003).

Index

Italicized page numbers indicate maps, photographs, and their captions.

General recreational activities (hiking, biking, boating, etc.) have not been indexed as many islands featured in this book offer some variation of these. Please see "What to Expect" snapshots at the start of each chapter and the body of the chapters for listings about activities available on specific islands.